explorations in
nonverbal and
vocal behavior

RAYMOND HERBERT STETSON
(1872–1950)

george f. mahl
yale university

explorations in
nonverbal and
vocal behavior

LEA LAWRENCE ERLBAUM ASSOCIATES, PUBLISHERS
1987   Hillsdale, New Jersey   London

Lawrence Erlbaum Associates, Inc., Publishers
365 Broadway
Hillsdale, New Jersey 07642

Library of Congress Cataloging in Publication Data

Mahl, George F., 1917–
    Explorations in nonverbal and vocal behavior.

    Bibliogrphy: p.
    Includes indexes.
    1. Interviewing in psychiatry. 2. Nonverbal
communication. 3. Oral communication. I. Title.
[DNLM: 1. Interview, Psychological. 2. Nonverbal
Communication. 3. Verbal Behavior. WM 141 M214e]
RC480.7.M34 1987   616.89'0751   87-6827
ISBN 0-89859-757-9

Printed in the United States of America
10 9 8 7 6 5 4 3 2 1

This book is dedicated to
Raymond Herbert Stetson
Professor and Chairman of Psychology, Oberlin College, 1909–1937

*". . . scientist par excellence, analyst of the motion
that is life, Leonardo turned at last psychologist . . ."**

**(From the citation of Ernest Hatch Wilkins, President of Oberlin College [1942], upon
the awarding of the Honorary Doctor of Science degree to Professor Stetson.)

Contents

Preface

This book is a collection of selected papers about nonverbal and vocal behavior during clinical and investigative, psychological interviews. They are some of the studies conducted by students, colleagues, and myself over the past 35 years. More than half of the papers have never been published, although most of them were presented at scientific meetings. The previously published papers have appeared in widely scattered places, often as chapters in books. This volume makes available for the first time a fairly complete presentation of a coherent body of work.

The psychotherapeutic interview is the point of departure and the arena of investigation for most of these studies. We did, however, turn to experimental, investigative interviews when we wished to test certain hypotheses that had arisen in the course of the research. In general, we have tried to deal with basic issues, rather than with matters pertaining to psychotherapeutic technique. Thus, our studies of nonverbal behavior are concerned with general processes of such behavior as it occurs in therapeutic interviews, rather than with ways in which the therapist might put such knowledge to use in facilitating the therapy. I very rarely commented to my patients on their nonverbal behavior; never about matters under investigation. Likewise, much of our work with vocal behavior has been concerned with the development of a method for measuring the patients concurrent anxiety in interviews that might be put to many investigative uses, rather than with how a therapist might put such a method to use in his daily, clinical practice.

This volume, therefore, is addressed primarily to those behavioral scientists concerned with basic questions about nonverbal and vocal behavior— questions about their nature and about how their study can facilitate research using the interview situation. Such behavioral scientists might comprise members of various disciplines, such as psychologists, psychiatrists, psychoanalysts, linguists, and anthropologists. We do believe, nevertheless, that practicing clinicians will also find material here that they will be able to use in their own way in their daily work.

ACKNOWLEDGMENTS

Whatever I have been able to achieve in the research reported here is due to a significant degree to the influence of various people. Professor Raymond H. Stetson, to whose memory I dedicate this book, was my mentor when I was an undergraduate psychology major and then a master's degree aspirant at Oberlin College from 1937 to 1941. He entered my life during a "sensitive period." His major research areas were the experimental analysis of skilled movements, and, especially, the motoric basis of phonetics. His research in the latter area, culminating in his *Motor Phonetics* (Stetson, 1928), achieved international recognition. From Professor Stetson, I acquired abiding interests in the role of the body in psychic life and in the speech processes. These interests lay dormant for some time only to surface at an appropriate juncture in my research career. Professor Stetson would probably disapprove of the final forms in which those interests appeared, but he would tolerate them with skeptical interest. I appreciate and acknowledge their origin in my relationship with him. His legacy also includes great respect for empirical data and regard for disciplined workmanship in obtaining them. The latter stood me in good stead over the years, especially in the detailed work with speech. My debt to the thought and spirit of Sigmund Freud will be apparent to all who know his works. Professor Frederick C. Redlich, my chairman in Yale's Department of Psychiatry for some 25 years, when I did most ot the research reported here, provided its members with a fertile intellectual climate and allowed my own research inclinations to thrive in it. I have always been grateful for that.

I have been very fortunate in being able to associate and work with such bright and diligent former students as Jack Austin, Arthur Bender, Burton Danet, Stanislav Kasl, Carol Lassen, Gene Schulze, and Lonn Wolf (to mention only those who contributed significantly to the particular research presented here). In every case, I enjoyed, learned and profited from our work together.

Thrice Lady Luck has been at my side for extended periods of time in the form of exceptional secretaries: Genoveva Palmieri, Maureen Bosquet, and Carmel Lepore. Life would have been very different, and much harder, without them, for they cared about their work and mine. Carmel Lepore worked with her usual companionable dedication on the preparation of this volume.

A number of other colleagues have contributed to this research, and I appreciatively acknowledge that at various places in the volume. In some cases that acknowledgement is indicated by the stated authorship of some of the chapters.

I wish to acknowledge the financial support of large segments of this research by The Foundations' Fund for Research in Psychiatry and by NIMH, USPH Grants M-1052 and M-07317-01. A fellowship at The Center for Advanced Study in the Behavioral Sciences, 1963–1964, also facilitated this work. In certain chapters I have acknowledged other sources that supported the specific research reported in them. I wish to express my appreciation to those publishers and editors who have granted permission to excerpt at length from the previously published works.

The woman behind me has been my wife, Martha. And standing beside her much of the time was our daughter, Barbara. I thank them both for their forbearance, as I diverted attention and energy to things that did not involve them.

George F. Mahl

I EXPLORATIONS IN NONVERBAL BEHAVIOR

1 Introduction

This chapter contains some general considerations about nonverbal behavior that orient the reader in this field of research and thereby provide a background for the reports of specific studies that follow. Our general considerations concern varieties of nonverbal behavior and a distinction often made between social and personal behavior.

THE MANY VARIETIES OF NONVERBAL BEHAVIOR

People display a wide range of nonverbal behaviors and signs of them. To illustrate this diversity, we cite the following:

1. Familiar *gestures*, such as winking, finger pointing, nodding or shaking of the head, etc.
2. *Idiosyncratic acts*, some familiar, others not, such as scratching, licking one's lips, touching various parts of the body, handling nearby objects, etc.
3. *Postures*, such as sitting expansively with legs outstretched and arms spread, or sitting compactedly with legs and arms drawn close to the trunk.
4. *Spatial behavior* (the proxemics of Hall, 1955, 1966), such as choosing to sit in the farthest or the closest chair.
5. Choice of *clothing*, such as between formal or informal attire, between unisex clothing and that which clearly marks one's gender, even at a distance. (See, for example, Bouska & Beatty, 1978; Fortenberry, MacLean, Morris, & O'Connell, 1978; Harris, James, Chavez, Fuller, Kent, Massanari,

Moore, & Walsh, 1983; Lurie, 1981; Mathes & Kempher, 1976; Rosenfeld & Plax, 1977; Solomon & Schopler, 1982.)

6. *Visible signs of normally covert activity.* These may include evidence of tension in *skeletal muscles*, such as a furrowed or bulging brow. They might include visible signs of *autonomic activity*, such as tearing, foot throbs caused by intense pulse strokes, changes in skin color, the appearance of sweat beads on the forehead or sweat marks in the armpits.

7. *Other sensory signs of covert, usually autonomic, activity.* These might be various *body scents*. (See Doty's 1981 review of relevant research.) Or these might be *audible signs* such as various breathing noises, the various sounds of intestinal action, the smacking of lips. Under certain conditions these might include *tactile cues*. A greeting or parting handshake may reveal moisture, body temperature, muscular tone, and aspects of handling body contact.

Mindful of this range of behaviors and their signs, I realize that our research involves only a few categories of behavior, and mainly those visible to the therapist or observer, or—in a few instances—those felt by the client and reported to the therapist.

SOCIAL AND PERSONAL BEHAVIOR

Most investigators find it useful to distinguish between actions with primarily a communicative, social function and actions with primarily a personal, "expressive" function. Nodding and shaking of the head to indicate "Yes" and "No" are examples of primarily communicative actions. The person here intends to communicate a message, "Yes" or "No" and uses actions that have a meaning shared by sender and receiver of the message. This meaning is culturally determined. In another culture, nodding the head may signify "No," rather than "Yes." Intentionality and culturally patterned, shared meanings are characteristic of communicative actions. Such actions are often called *emblems*. Further discussions of them and their cultural variations and distributions are presented in Ekman, Friesen, and Bear (1984), LaBarre (1964), and Morris, Collett, Marsh, and O'Shaughnessy (1979). Scratching or stroking oneself in a manner unrelated to the concurrent verbalization are examples of primarily personal, expressive actions. The person here does not intend to communicate a message, and the acts do not have culturally patterned, shared meanings.

Although not communicative, personal-expressive actions are not exempt from, or devoid of, social influence. In the first place, they may be culturally patterned, albeit not part of a culturally patterned code. A given society, for example, might prohibit public self-scratching as ours taboos public nose picking. In the second place, these actions might be informative to the other person, although not communicative. They might suggest, for example, that something—one can't be sure what—was operative in the speaker that he was not talking about and did not intend to talk about. Or they might inform a very knowledgeable individual of the nature of that unspoken matter: that the speaker who scratched himself was harboring some inhibited annoyance somehow related to the verbal interaction, or that the person stroked herself because of some unspoken, to-be-secret sensuous current aroused in the interaction. Such knowledge would not be based on a shared code, but on such things as intimate knowledge of the regularities of the nonverbal behavior of the individual concerned or of regularities in the nonverbal behavior of most people in a given culture.

In the third place, personal-expressive actions may have unacknowledged social consequences. The self-scratching and stroking might arouse the same affects in the other as we have attributed to the speaker. And the other might engage in the same or contrary action. Thus, the self-stroking by one person, might arouse a sensuous current in the other, who then unintentionally starts to stroke him or herself. Or the other might become privately annoyed and unintentionally scratch himself. Thus, a "conversation of gestures" might accompany an unrelated verbal "conversation of symbols" (to use phrases of George Herbert Mead, 1934). Two people talking about the weather, might end up stroking themselves.

Just as personal-expressive actions are not exempt from social influence, so communicative actions are subject to personal influence, at least in our culture. This is because our rules of communication allow great latitude to the use of symbolic acts. It is not obligatory to use them at all. And, if used, considerable stylistic variation is permissible. Thus, we may or may not signal "Yes" or "No" with our head. And if we do so, we may nod or shake our heads with varying speeds, amplitudes, etc. One of the observations in the next chapter provides a very clear example of the personal determination of the use of a communicative gesture, *the finger*. In chapter 7, we illustrate how the type of clothing may reflect psychic states as well as signal the gender of the wearer.

Many clinicians, including myself, tend to concentrate on personal-expressive actions, rather than permissible variations in communicative acts, when we focus on the nonverbal manifestations of personal psychodynamics. This is more habitual, than logically necessary. I believe this emphasis is due to a combination of factors: (a) the greater degree to which such actions capture our attention (e.g., self-scratching is more noticeable than a slight change in the vigor of a communicative gesture), (b) the frequency with which they are *un*related to the concurrent *manifest* verbalizations, and (c) the degree to which we are interested in what is *not* being said, especially in what is unconscious.

The distinction between personal-expressive and communicative actions and the role of personal determinants in the latter are very important issues, in my opinion.[1] Thus, they are discussed further in later parts of this book, especially in the latter parts of the next chapter. (There we use Krout's (1935) term *autistic* instead of *personal-expressive*.) Related discussions appear in Part II of this book, for analogous issues arise in the area of vocal behavior. (See chapter 19, for example.)

---

[1]Our classification of nonverbal behavior into personal-expressive and communicative actions has had heuristic value for us, as well as highlighting what we believe is a very important distinction for investigators in this field to keep in mind. But we do not claim it to be the only useful classification. Others have found different classifications useful or significant. Thus Freedman (1972); and Freedman and Hoffman, (1967) have found the distinction between body and object focused movements to be useful. The most widely cited classification is the five-fold one of Ekman and Friesen (1969): *emblems*, communicative substitutes for words; *illustrators*, accompaniments of speech that variously illustrate it; *affect displays*, primarily facial expressions of emotions; *regulators*, actions regulating the reciprocal interaction between speaker and listener; and *adaptors*, largely unintended manifestations of needs and emotions. Ekman and Friesen present their categories in the context of the most thorough and penetrating discussion known to us of issues of usage, origin, and coding processes of nonverbal behavior. Our personal-expressive category includes their adaptors and overlaps with unintended affect displays. Our communicative actions include their emblems, illustrators, regulators, and intended affect displays. We would still use our categories for the type of research of interest to us, adding theirs, when indicated, as subcategories of ours. Researchers with different interests might well find theirs more useful. Readers interested in a variety of ways to categorize and study nonverbal behavior will find the handbook edited by Scherer and Ekman (1982) very informative.

Gestures and Body Movements in Interviews[1]

2

> *He that has eyes to see and ears to hear may convince himself that no mortal can keep a secret. If his lips are silent, he chatters with his finger-tips; betrayal oozes out of him at every pore.*
> —S. Freud (1905/1953b, pp. 77–78)

Psychotherapy research [largely] neglects the study of gestures and body movements during interviews. . .

This situation is indeed remarkable when viewed from the standpoint of clinical experience and lore, and in historical context. Clinical lore has it that some of the most significant interaction between patients and therapists transpires by means of a nonverbal channel, and that experienced, skillful clinicians are preconsciously, if not consciously, guided by the bodily behavior of their patient. They have a sensitive "third eye," as it were. Such clinical precepts rest on a very respectable historical foundation. From Darwin's *The Expression of Emotions in Man and Animals* (1872/1955) down to the present, keen observers and investigators of human behavior have contrib-

---

[1]Adapted from J. M. Shlien (Ed.). (1968). *Research in Psychotherapy*, Volume 3. Washington, DC: American Psychological Association, pp. 295–346. Copyright 1968 by the American Psychological Association. Adapted by permission of the editor and publisher, with slight editorial and stylistic revisions. This chapter was prepared for the Third Research in Psychotherapy Conference, Chicago, May 31–June 4, 1966. The aforementioned volume contains the proceedings of the conference.

My sincere appreciation goes to Genoveva Palmieri for all her assistance in the preparation of the original manuscript.

7

uted to the laying of that foundation. Their work has provided very suggestive evidence that the gestures and body activity of interview participants are functionally related to variables of central concern to both psychotherapists and investigators of psychotherapy.

Very brief mention of some of the highlights of this historical background is worthwhile in itself and useful as part of the introduction to my own work in this area. Darwin's work remains the most monumental one, in my opinion. The scope of his data was extremely broad. It included observations of animals as well as man, cross-cultural material, developmental data, and observations of human behavior in various clinical conditions—for example, in health, in psychosis, and in blindness and deafness. The breadth of his thinking matched that of his data. Although he presented his work in a broad biological context, he introduced concepts (or emphasized those of others) that anticipated the ideas of disciplines as widely divergent as psychoanalysis and modern structural linguistics. The ideas of Darwin that are most relevant for our purposes can be summarized as follows:

1. He concluded that distinctive nonverbal behavior patterns are characteristic of many distinct emotional states. He thought these patterns often consisted of very slight movements that have developed from larger movements and more extensive patterns present in childhood. (He suggested the clenched fist of an angry man, for example, is a remnant of a more extensive attack pattern. The downturned mouth of sadness and the frown of displeasure, he proposed, were remnants of screaming in childhood.) [See chapter 7 for further discussion of these ideas of Darwin.]

2. He emphasized that these remnants of emotional patterns become involuntary.

3. They may occur transiently or chronically.

4. When an individual attempts to repress overt emotional expression, movements of some kind are very likely to occur. These might be expressive remnants that have become involuntary, or they might be random, "purposeless" acts—like the tail switching of an annoyed cat. The latter are a result of the sheer quantity of excitation of the nervous system.

5. Many expressive movements may also have a signaling or communicative function. He articulated the principle of contrasting pairs in this connection, which has become a fundamental concept of modern linguistics. Darwin noted, for example, that an angry cat crouches with a depressed back whereas a friendly cat arches his back and that these contrasting patterns might very well have a signaling function. The same might be true, he speculated, of the depressed mouth of the sad person and the upturned mouth of the happy one.

6. Although Darwin emphasized the universality of expressive behavior patterns among the cultures of man, he also noted that cultural patterning might occur. [Modern research has confirmed the pan-cultural existence of

facial expressions of some basic emotions in literate and preliterate cultures (Eibl-Eibesfeldt, 1970, pp. 408–431; *especially* Ekman, Sorenson, & Friesen, 1969; Ekman & Friesen, 1971; Izard, 1969).]

Freud's main contribution to our topic was his proposal that conflicted, repressed-unconscious impulses, wishful thoughts, emotions, and memories were often manifested in action instead of in thought. The action might consist of innate responses or of responses that had occurred on some earlier occasion in the person's life when these inner states had existed. This proposal was an extension of Darwin's ideas, as Freud occasionally indicated (e.g., Breuer & Freud, 1893–1895/1955, pp. 91, 181). Freud extended the inner states to include more than emotions and left the way open for idiosyncratic movements on the response side.

He found his formulation to be a very useful working assumption in attempting to understand the patient's stream of behavior in analytic hours. How useful it was, and how seriously he applied the formulation, are indicated by the fact that each of his four major clinical reports based on actual analytic treatment included citations of significant instances of such expressive action in the treatment situation. *Dora's* "chance" fingering of a reticule worn at her waist, for example, appeared to occur when repressed memories of childhood masturbation were stimulated (by Freud's remarks) but not recalled (Freud, 1905/1953b). When *Little Hans* was defending against admitting his hostility towards his father, the boy "accidentally" dropped a toy horse he was playing with at the time. Because there was abundant evidence that Hans had displaced his Oedipal conflict from his parents to horses, this appeared to be a symptomatic act prompted by his inhibited Oedipal hostility (Freud, 1909/1955a). The *Rat Man* went through a phase in his analysis in which he would get up from the couch, look at Freud with a terrified expression, and pace about the room staying as far away from Freud as possible. He seemed to be expressing in action an unconscious memory (that he later verbalized) of a severe beating he had experienced as a child at the hands of his father (Freud, 1909/1955b). When the *Wolf Man* (Freud, 1918/1955c) first started analysis, he used to repeatedly turn on the couch and look at Freud "in a very friendly way as though to propitiate" him (p. 40) and then look away at a grandfather clock in the room. The total analytic material suggested this nonverbal behavior had two interrelated determinants. One was a childhood memory of a disturbing fairy tale about little goats being eaten up by a wolf. One goat had saved himself by hiding in a grandfather clock. The other determinant was an early transference relationship in which the Wolf Man unconsciously feared that Freud would eat him up, as the wolf had eaten up the little goats in the fairy tale.

The preceding examples illustrate the aspect of expressive actions most frequently noted by Freud—their apparent relationship to repressed unconscious variables of a transitory nature. Although he certainly didn't ignore them, he never emphasized the direct manifestation of defenses or of stable personality traits in expressive actions. The fact that his explicit discussions of expressive action all came in the early phases of his life work undoubtedly accounts for his emphasis. Had he been as interested in expressive action after he turned from a primary concern with unconscious drives to a primary concern with ego psychology, it is very likely that he would have also emphasized the effect of defenses and stable personality characteristics. The early Wilhelm Reich (1928/1948. . .) was the psychoanalyst who did just this. In his classic writings on character analysis, he advanced the thesis that an individual's stable defenses were manifested in the "how" of his skeletal behavior, and of his speech. Deutsch (1947, 1949, 1952) integrated both approaches in his work. (We cite on page 43 an instance where Freud did refer early on to the bodily enactment of defenses.)

General psychology has also made its contribution, independent of psychoanalysis. The work of Allport (1961; Allport & Vernon, 1933) is illustrative. Careful observation of motor behavior in a variety of task situations revealed consistent individual differences in stylistic dimensions—for example, rhythm, tempo, amplitude. Presumably, these individual differences are consistent or congruent with personality traits and structure. This general viewpoint is similar to Reich's, but it differs in that it does not single out defenses for special emphasis.

Gestures and body movements have aroused the interest of some anthropologists. It is no surprise that they have emphasized the cultural and interactional dimensions. The work of Efron (1941, 1972) and Birdwhistell (1952, 1970) illustrates the main relevant contributions and viewpoints of anthropology. Efron demonstrated the extent to which culture may pattern gestural activity in his descriptive study of nonverbal communication in Southern Italians and Eastern European Jews. He also documented the changes in gestural behavior of these groups occurring with American acculturation. (Shuter, 1979, has published a recent study comparing the gestural behavior of assimilated American Jews and Protestant Americans of Anglo-Saxon descent.)

Birdwhistell's contribution has gone far beyond the traditional culture-behavior relationship. He has insisted that nonverbal behavior is organized according to the same structural principles found operative in oral languages—that there are, for example, basic movement elements, *kines*, analagous to phonemes; substitutable forms, allokines, analogous to allophones; larger units of organization corresponding roughly to sentences, etc. Birdwhistell holds that a continual stream of linguistically structured movements occurs in human interaction, and that there are two communicative attributes of this kinesic channel: (a) The nonverbal behavior may be an essential aspect of the verbal communication. For example, slight raising of the eyes and head at the end of a utterance may be part of the "markers" signifying the end of a question; lowering of the eyes and head may "mark" the end of a declarative sentence. Or some movement or other (e.g., a head nod or a foot tap), may contribute, along with the voice, to encoding the stresses that differentiate *six pack* from *six pácks*. (b) But beyond such a function, the kinesic channel may constitute a relatively independent channel of communication, as it clearly does in the language of signs and finger spelling used by the deaf, or in the less conventionalized, but no less real, communication between intimates by facial signaling with certain degrees of frowns, varying degrees of arching eyebrows, etc. An important feature of Birdwhistell's work is its insistence that the kines typically consist of movements occurring outside of awareness—on the part of the performer, the other participant, and other members of their culture. And, he argues, whole kinesic "conversations" may occur outside of awareness or conscious intention. Regardless, the kines and their systems of organization are culturally patterned.

On a historical basis, then, there is some reason to believe, or at least to assume as a working hypothesis, that nonverbal behavior is significantly related to many variables germane to the process and outcome of psychotherapy: variables such as emotions, inhibited emotions, unconscious wishes and memories, defenses, personality traits, degree of acculturation, and communication or regulation of interaction outside of awareness.

Why, then, has research in psychotherapy so badly neglected the area of nonverbal behavior? Partly, I think, because psychology in general has neglected it. Allport's revised personality text (1961), for example, is one of the few in the field today giving more than lip service to the topic of expressive behavior. For a long time now, psychology has been concerned with theoretical issues, not with behavioral description. It is concerned with techniques of description, but only if they can be used to measure variables relevant to the investigation of theoretical issues. Further, no great principles have emerged from past studies of nonverbal, skeletal behavior comparable to those arising from Cannon's work on autonomic behavior. These may be important reasons why psychology in general has neglected the topic.

The specific neglect by psychotherapy research has been due to additional factors. The traditional, nearly exclusive, preoccupation of therapists with verbal content has certainly been one decisive factor. Investigators of psychotherapy have been subject to the same bias. Methodological shortcomings have also played their part. There is no cheap and easy way to record interview nonverbal behavior comparable to the use of tape recordings and transcriptions. Filming is inconvenient and expensive. But beyond that, the film cannot be transformed into a useful record, as the tape recording can be transcribed into typescript form. One wonders if the post-World War II technical advances in sound recording would have had the impact they did on psychotherapy research if a written language did not exist in our culture. Would that research have followed the same paths it did?

One of the primary reasons, of course, why films cannot be transformed into another record is the absence of articulated, conventionally defined basic units of nonverbal behavior. The word is an agreed on equivalent of audible actions of speech, but this situation does not exist in the domain of nonverbal behavior. Birdwhistell, and others with the same orientation, have only begun to isolate the basic units that might be culturally determined and operative; they are just beginning to see if there really are communicative units to be annotated and to make a dictionary and grammar for them. Many years from now interested scientists, at least, might have a written code, or its equivalent, for transcribing much of the nonverbal behavioral stream. . . .

A lack of conviction in the claims that gestural and body movements have psychological significance may be another reason for their neglect, in both general psychology and psychotherapy research. The toughminded scientist certainly can provide arguments for a position of skepticism.

1. He can argue that systematic studies of the facial expressions of emotions cast serious doubt on Darwin's claim there were characteristic expressions for various emotions. It *appeared* from that research that one cannot tell from facial expressions alone what the accompanying emotional state is. It seemed one needs to know the situation in which the person is behaving. Perhaps it is that knowledge alone which serves as the basis for inferring the emotional state of our fellow man in everyday life. (But see the work of Ekman and colleagues, and of Izard, previously cited.)

2. He can argue that the conclusions suggested by personality studies such as Allport and Vernon's (1933) must be regarded as very tentative hypotheses because no substantial further research has been attempted to confirm them. Furthermore, one must distinguish between the demonstration of individual consistency in expressive behavioral style and the demonstration that such individual styles are a function of personality variables. The skeptic can reinforce these warnings by pointing out that so far the more energetic attempts to demonstrate a comparable relation between speech style and personality characteristics have been inconclusive.

3. He can argue that naturalistic, clinical observations, such as those of Freud and Reich, are subject to many possible errors. One of them, for example, is the possibility that clinicians only remember positive instances. Maybe Dora and Little Hans engaged in the same acts or similar ones (fingering the reticule and knocking over the toy horse) when there was no independent evidence that unconscious masturbatory memories or repressed hostility were activated. If they did, and if these instances were selectively forgotten by the clinical observer, then one could hardly conclude that these were the expressive actions they are claimed to be.

4. And he can argue that so far the claims of Birdwhistell and of those influenced by him in the study of therapy interviews (e.g., Scheflen, 1963,

1964, 1965) have been largely asserted, and only anecdotally illustrated. This orientation sounds extremely interesting and exciting, because it opens up an entirely new approach to the study of nonverbal interaction, but we expect more evidence to be reported. And besides, he can argue, this "communicative" approach minimizes the significance of the "discharge" or the "expressive" functions that psychology has traditionally claimed for nonverbal behavior. Thus Birdwhistell (1956) writes that his approach, "places the emphasis on the *interpersonal* rather than the *expressional* aspects of kinesic activity" (p. 143, italics in original). And Scheflen (1963) asserts the following about recurrent postural shifts that appear to play an important part in the regulation of interview interaction: "Any intuitive speculation about unique motivation or psychopathology in performing them may be correct, but misses the point. What a postural shift signifies is *not a personal quality but a communicative structural event*" (p. 325). It seems that people operating from different orientations see different meanings in nonverbal behavior, with neither group yet being able to convincingly support their orientations.

The preceding discussion points up today's dilemma of the person interested in studying gestures and body movements during interviews. His situation is that of a man climbing on sand or trying to pick up quicksilver. There is no secure footing, nor anything firm to take hold of. If his clinical experience and the clinical literature tell him the study of nonverbal behavior is an important area of psychotherapy research, he finds little sound research upon which to base his plans for further research. Essentially he must begin by convincing himself of the soundness of his belief in the fruitfulness of such research and by mapping out for himself potentially useful leads for future work. And he must evaluate the expressive and communicative orientations. In effect, he must do his own exploratory research in order to evaluate the arguments of our imaginary tough-minded psychologist.

At least this was my estimate of the situation several years ago when I decided to extend my research of extralinguistic interview behavior from the nonlexical dimensions of speech to gestures and body movements. Because of the paucity of previous research, it seemed necessary to do the following:

1. Obtain a clearer idea than I had of individual differences in nonverbal interview behavior.
2. Explore the phenomenon of intraindividual variability in nonverbal behavior.
3. Explore the relationships between both individual differences and intraindividual variations in nonverbal behavior, on the one hand, and personality variables or other aspects of the individual's behavior during interviews, on the other hand.

4. Begin to evaluate the traditional expressive and the relatively new communicative approaches to the study of nonverbal behavior.

We have done three things toward these ends: (a) conducted a structured clinical study of the gestures and body movements of psychiatric patients in their initial interviews at an outpatient clinic; (b) conducted an experimental study of changes in certain aspects of nonverbal behavior when the usual face-face interview condition is changed to one in which the participants sit back-back, that is, to a situation in which they neither see, nor can be seen by, the other person; and (c) gathered a body of observations of nonverbal activity manifested by people during psychoanalysis.

The next portion of this chapter deals with these three studies. We first present the initial interview study and supplement its results with some of the psychoanalytic observations. Then we report on the experimental study in which the visual conditions of the interview were manipulated. This experiment deals with the expressive and communicative orientations. We draw upon our psychoanalytic observations again in a further discussion of the expressive and the communicative viewpoints. Finally, we conclude with some further comments about certain points considered in this introduction.

GESTURES AND BODY MOVEMENTS IN INITIAL INTERVIEWS[2]

The purposes of this study were to accomplish the first three aforementioned goals: (a) to obtain a clearer idea of individual differences in nonverbal interview behavior than is provided by everyday clinical experience; (b) to explore intraindividual variability in nonverbal behavior during the interview; and (c) to explore the relationships between individual differences and intraindividual variations in nonverbal behavior, on the one hand, and personality variables or other aspects of the individual's behavior during interviews, on the other hand.

---

[2]A preliminary report of this study was presented at the Annual Meeting, American Psychological Association, 1959 (Mahl, Danet, & Norton, 1959).

I want to express my appreciation to Nea Norton, [then] Chief Psychiatric Social Worker, Department of Psychiatry, Yale University, for her willingness to conduct the interviews under the conditions of tape-recording and observation entailed by the study and to Burton Danet for his assistance in processing the gesture records, and in their quantitative analysis.

[Ruesch and Prestwood's study (1949) of assessing patient anxiety from different channels of spoken communication suggested our procedure of splitting-up the speech and nonverbal channels while making our inferences about the patients' psychic states from their initial interview behavior. Other researchers elaborated on such a methodology, but K. Scherer, U. Scherer, Hall, and Rosenthal (1977) developed it to the utmost.]

Method

The initial interviews of patients applying for treatment at a psychiatric outpatient clinic in a metropolitan, university-community hospital provided the materials for this study.

An experienced female psychiatric social worker conducted all the interviews in a room especially designed for the sound recording and observation of psychiatric interviews (Mahl, Dollard, & Redlich, 1954). The patient was told that the interview was being recorded. The interview was recorded on one tape. An observer (the author) also *watched* the interviews through a one-way mirror, *but did not hear* any of the verbal exchange. He dictated a running account of the patient's behavior onto a second tape. Occasionally, he also noted "on-the-spot" impressions about the psychopathology and general traits of the patient. The same person was the observer throughout the interview series. A common signal was recorded on both tapes for use in later synchronizations. All the tapes were transcribed and eventually the two records for each interview were collated.

The gesture record was processed as follows. First, it was timed in successive 1-minute intervals. Then we tabulated for successive 1- or 2-minute intervals, all the actions noted in the gesture record. This tabulation was done by the following broad categories of behavior:

1. *General postural changes*—recrossing legs, or changing trunk position.

2. *Communicative gestures*—those actions judged to be common substitutions for verbal utterances; that is, actions with a meaning shared by sender and receiver. Examples: shaking head "yes" or "no," pointing, pounding with fist, shrugging shoulders, illustrative motions.

3. *Autistic actions*—those actions judged *not* to be common substitutions for verbal utterances. (The paradigm of this class is a conversion symptom.) Examples: playing with jewelry, clothing; scratching, rubbing, random touching of various parts of body.

The preceding steps produced a sequential picture of categorized patient behavior. Also, counts of the more specific gestures and actions were made for the interview as a whole so that overall frequency comparisons could be made.

The dictated "running account" of the nonverbal behavior is obviously no substitute for a permanent photographic record of the interview. The record is incomplete. For one thing, it is almost completely limited to the patient's behavior, at the expense of largely ignoring the interviewer's behavior. For another, the record does not cover facial expressions. This limitation restricted the data, but it enabled the observer to follow the remaining activity of the patient more accurately than would have been possible if he had been attempting to follow precisely facial expressions also. Finally, it is certain that not every act was always recorded. The frequency measures derived from the gesture record can only be regarded as indices of relative frequency, not absolute measures. In spite of all these limitations of the gesture record, it was judged adequate for our exploratory aims and more appropriate for our purpose at the time of the study than films.

The person who had served as the original observer studied the ordered activity material thus obtained and also listened further to the gesture tape. This last step provided some cues about the rhythm of the patient's behavior, which were lost in the sequential tabulation. After absorbing and digesting as much of the behavioral data as he could, this person then wrote down whatever inferences he felt he could make about each patient's diagnosis, leading conflicts, character structure, and other personality traits. He also recorded the behavioral bases for these inferences. For 14 of the 18 patients these inferences were completely uncontaminated by other information. The inferences and the occasional on-the-spot impressions recorded on the original gesture tape were then compared with independent "criterion" materials. The latter consisted of the verbal content of the intake interview, and, most importantly, entries in the complete clinic case records—the clinical diagnosis, descriptive symptomatology, and the discharge summary. The entries in the clinical records were made by the intake interviewer and by a therapist, if the patient subsequently entered therapy. Neither the intake interviewer, nor the therapists, knew of our inferences at the time of writing the clinic records. The original observer, who had also made the inferences, was the person who subsequently studied the criterion material and selected whatever criterion information seemed relevant to the inferences. The danger of subjective bias in this procedure is obvious. However, this was exploratory work and only uninterpreted, obviously relevant, verbatim statements in the case records or the initial interview were used in testing the inferences. Because we had future work in mind, we wanted to be cautious.

We also compared selected actions of interest to us with the details of the verbal behavior in the initial interviews in order to obtain further understanding of the "meaning" of gestures and movements and to explore the various relationships between verbal and nonverbal activity.

There were 18 patients, 9 women and 9 men. The median age was 31 years, range 18–64, with 13 falling between the ages of 26 and 38. All were white and born in this country. Their ancestral backgrounds were as follows: 11 were of Anglo-Saxon origins; 3 middle-European; 1 was of Greek stock; the ancestry of 3 was unknown. There were 9 Catholics, 5 Protestants, 2 Jews, and 2 religion unknown. Judging from the occupational status of the patients, or the heads of their households, there were 4 patients from the lower middle class, 12 from the middle class, 1 from the upper middle class,

and 1 whose socioeconomic level was unknown. Twelve patients were diagnosed as psychoneurotics and 6 as character disorders. All in all, there is
nothing remarkable about the sample. It does not seem to be skewed in any
way that would limit the usefulness of the data obtained from it.

Results

Subjective Experience of the Observer

When the observer watched the initial interview *without hearing* it, he had
an experience altogether comparable to that of listening to tape recordings of
therapy interviews for the first time. His awareness of how people act was
markedly heightened, far beyond anything he had experienced before—
either in regular clinical interaction or even when observing and hearing
interviews behind one-way mirrors. In the latter situation one perceives
more of the patient's nonverbal behavior than in the former, probably because he is free of the immediate involvement with the patient. But removal
of the verbal behavior leads to a geometrically increased awareness of the
nonverbal behavior.

We note later that on a few occasions very definite, precise impressions of
patients "came to" the observer in this situation.

Individual Differences

The patients differed strikingly from one another in their basic postures
and in their characteristic communicative gestures and autistic actions. The
reader can form an impression of the extent of these individual differences
by examining the ranges in frequencies of selected actions presented in
Table 2.1, by reading down the first column of Table 2.2, and by looking at
the drawings in Fig. 2.1 through Fig. 2.5.

1. First consider the frequency data for the 15 categories of behavior
listed in the first column of Table 2.1. Group the men and women together
in doing this. The ranges in the frequency are considerable.

2. As you scan down the first column of Table 2.2, the phenomenon of
individual differences becomes more concrete. Mrs. A very frequently pats
and strokes her hair and fingers her mouth, but this is not at all characteristic
of Mrs. B. Her most characteristic actions are to slide her wedding ring back
and forth on her finger and then to play with a ring on her right hand.
Although Mrs. A and Mrs. B do not sit in their chair exactly the same way,
there is nothing unusual or striking to the observer about their basic posture.
Mrs. C, however, makes a "nest" out of her chair by slipping out of her coat
after being seated, keeping it loosely about her and nestling back into it. In
addition she crosses her legs in an exhibitionistic manner and slowly rotates

TABLE 2.1

Sex Differences in Frequency of Selected Gestures and Body Movements
of Psychiatric Patients during Intake Interview with Female Interviewer[a]

Gesture or movement	Male (n = 8)		Female (n = 7)		p (one-tailed) by Mann-Whitney U
	Median	Range	Median	Range	
Communicative gestures					
Pointing (out)	14	(4–∞)		(7–∞)	.04
Making fist		(6–∞)		(10–∞)	—
Shrugs shoulders	69	(20–∞)	30	(3–∞)	.09
Shakes head "no"		(20–∞)	10	(3–∞)	.06
Shakes head "yes"		(4–∞)	25	(8–∞)	.03
Turns palms out-up	46	(1–∞)	6	(1–36)	.12
Autistic gestures					
Rubs, touches nose	34	(11–∞)	62	(13–∞)	—
Scratches self	11	(4–∞)	10	(4–42)	—
Finger-mouth	10	(3–∞)	8	(1–∞)	—
Rubs self	5	(1–∞)	6	(1–40)	—
Picking, smoothing, cleaning, arranging	8	(3–∞)	15	(5–40)	—
Pats hair		(∞–∞)	15	(2–∞)	.005
Hand-arm positions					
Folds arms across waist		(46–∞)	30	(4–∞)	.03
Hands held or clasped together	2	(0.4–∞)	15	(3–∞)	.004
General postural changes	6	(2–20)	7	(4–30)	—

[a] $X = n$ minutes per gesture or movement, smaller number = higher frequency.

∞ = the gesture or movement never occurred.

Three patients were omitted because their gesture records were judged too incomplete for quantitative analysis.

her foot and ankle throughout the interview. (When I asked a woman to assume the leg cross of Mrs. C and repeatedly rotate her foot as Mrs. C had done, that woman said it produced erotic sensations in her genitals.) Further reading of the first column continues to reveal ways in which the patients differed from one another.

3. The drawings of Fig. 2.1 through Fig. 2.5 provide even clearer impressions of the different basic positions and characteristic gestures and acts for 5 of the 18 patients.

Sex Differences Contribute to the Individual Differences

Leg crossing is different in men than in women. Six out of eight women (inadequate data for one of the women) kept their legs crossed at their knees throughout the interview. Only two women deviated from this pattern and they kept both feet on the floor: one of these was 64 years old—the only

TABLE 2.2
Summary of Characteristic Gestures, Acts, and Body Positions, Inferred
Personality Characteristics, and Relevant Clinical Data

Patient	Characteristic Acts and Body Postures in Initial Interview	Related Inferences about Traits, Conflicts, Symptoms	Relevant Data from Initial Interview or Clinic Record
Mrs. A	a. Complete absence of "turning palms up and out" (See Fig. 2.1) or motor evidence of helplessness.	a. Surprisingly, will not feel helpless.	a. Patient is here for follow-up interview after discharge from private psychiatric hospital. She only comes upon advice of therapist at hospital. She feels good, capable at time of interview. Doesn't want treatment.
	b. Very frequent patting and stroking of hair. Even gets up and preens hair in front of mirror on wall at one point.	b. Very narcissistic, vain.	b. A major complaint in initial interview is that people don't pay attention to her, don't like her.
	c. Very frequent hand-mouth contacts; fingering around mouth highest rate of entire sample.	c. Orality themes prominent.	c. Returns for treatment 6 months after initial interview. One of chief complaints is anorexia and weight loss.
	d. Moderate amount of scratching self and rubbing nose.	d. Considerable aggression, which she is prone to turn against self.	d. Diagnosed upon return for treatment as depressive reaction. Ventilation of considerabel hostility towards husband during 4 therapy interviews with relief of symptoms.

(Continued)

19

TABLE 2.2
(Continued)

Patient	Characteristic Acts and Body Postures in Initial Interview	Related Inferences about Traits, Conflicts, Symptoms	Relevant Data from Initial Interview or Clinic Record
Mrs. B	a. Great deal of "ring play" (See Fig. 2.1)	a. Marital conflict.	a. Clinic summary: Major concerns are that too many demands are placed on her by marriage and children, and that she must "bottle-up" her anger and retaliatory impulses felt towards her husband. Complains that husband doesn't help with care of house and children, and never takes her out.
	b. Frequent inspection of finger nails and self-scratching.	b. Conflict over expression of hostility, with turning of aggression onto self.	b. Symptomatology includes depression, feelings of inferiority, and "bottling up" of aggression.
Mrs. C	a. "Nestles" into chair and coat; crosses legs in exhibitionistic manner; slow sensuous foot-ankle rotations throughout interview; pats hair frequently. Gives general impression of languid, erotic woman.	a. An erotic, sensuous woman whose psychopathology should be of hysterical nature. Genital urges strong; coupled with repression and denial resulting in low anxiety, but dammed-up libido pressing for discharge.	a. Diagnosis: Hysterical character. From Clinic Summary: "patient has been very flirtatious and has found herself provoking many men, and also being stimulated by them.—has many strong moral feelings about—certainly adultery. Able to express some of her sexual impulses in treatment, with relief of somatic symptoms."
	b. Appears very relaxed throughout interview.	b. Low anxiety.	b. Initial interviewer remarks about patient's "la belle indifference"

Mrs. D	a. General constraint of gestural activity except for "nervous fingering" of clothing & appointment slip and tense, "nervous" foot movements. b. Spasmodic clutching of bodice of dress during one phase of interview (see Fig. 2.2) reminding observer of terrified heroine menaced by the villain in horror movies. c. Scratching, rubbing nose, "mild pounding" with appointment slip, negativistic head shaking occasionally interrupt her inhibited state. d. Holds appointment slip prominently in interview, like child with ticket at baseball game.	a. Anxiety level will be quite high, will experience conscious anxiety symptoms. b. Fears of body damage or mutilation. c. Major conflict will be over expression of hostility, not sexuality. d. She perceives treatment as valued sanctuary.	a. Diagnosis: Passive-aggressive disorder with symptomatic anxiety state and phobic features. Descriptive symptomatology: anxiety, social inhibitions, and b. Fear of death, illness, hospitals, and medical procedures, (e.g., D & C). c. Passive-aggressive disorder was main diagnosis. Symptomatology also included depression. Treatment summary emphasized "ventilation of hostility." d. Treatment summary emphasizes that patient was "thrilled at being in miraculous treatment."
Mrs. E	a. Very high frequency of helpless "palms-up" gesture, shrugging of shoulders. b. Considerable fist-clenching, and a variety of	a. Traits of negativistic-helplessness and traces of stubbornness. b. A great deal of hostility which will be both directed outward and	a. and b. Diagnosis: Depressive reaction: obsessive-compulsive personality. Clinic summary: "As therapy progressed, she attempted to get the therapist to make minor and major decisions for her. When this

(*Continued*)

21

TABLE 2.2
(Continued)

Patient	Characteristic Acts and Body Postures in Initial Interview	Related Inferences about Traits, Conflicts, Symptoms	Relevant Data from Initial Interview or Clinic Record
	other "hostile" acts: pressing and squeezing arm of chair, wiping under nose with finger, scratching self.	turned against herself.	was refused . . . she began to express much anger and irritation . . . she continued to remain depressed. She expressed feelings of worthlessness, inadequacy, guilt throughout the course of treatment and spoke several times of doing away with herself." These suicidal threats finally led to hospitalization.
	c. Exhibitionistic leg cross; great deal of pulling-down on hemline, slides fingers inside bodice and rubs; "picks and cleans" dress in abdominal area several times.	c. A personality-character disorder with traces of obsessive-compulsive features in a predominantly hysterical character. Should be evidence of erotic genital life present, but feelings of guilt and shame over it, rather than fear.	c. Diagnosis included "obsessive-compulsive personality." Symptoms included "obsessive doubting." A positive erotic transference with a private therapist caused patient to abruptly break-off of that treatment-relationship and now brings the patient to this clinic. N.B. Inferences re hysterical character apparently not substantiated.
Mrs. F	a. Upper half of body is relatively quiet throughout interview. Sits primly in center of chair, purse on lap, hands	a. The pattern described in a and b (first column) leads to inference that her character will be one featuring gener-	a. Diagnosis: Obsessive-compulsive neurosis. Clinic summary: "Many of her communications were very ambiguous as far as their feeling content went. They were most fre-

	clasped over purse, little fingers making a "church steeple." b. In marked contrast to the relative motionlessness of the upper half of the body, her feet and legs are in continual "jumpy," agitated activity. c. The controlled state is periodically disrupted by a variety of "hostile" acts: scratching, biting nails and fingers, clenching fist, shaking head "no." d. General spinsterish quality.	al repressive control and inhibition of affects and impulses. b. Extremely high level of tension and anxiety, uncontrollable. This will come out in ego-alien manner not in ego-symptonic passive-helplessness. c. Very strong conflict over expression of aggression. d. Strong sexual conflict.	quently indecisive, obsessional . . . ruminating, obsessive, and challenging approach." b. Anxiety attacks upon leaving house. c. Obsessional fears she will harm her child. Once shot her brother "half accidentally." d. Clinic summary: Had illegitimate child. "Erotic phantasies showed through . . . early experience with her father frightened her about libidinal feelings which have incestuous tinge. Denial of any affectionate feelings."
Mr. G	a. Basic position is very expansive, sprawl: arm thrown over back of chair, one leg extended straight out, with other leg curled back against front of chair. All hand	a. Assertive, masculine intrusive behavior as defensive facade in	a. and b. Diagnosis: Passive-aggressive personality disorder. Only thing mentioned about wife in initial interview was that he has arguments with her about her cooking. Clinic Summary: "Most of the time his voice was loud and

(Continued)

TABLE 2.2
(Continued)

Patient	Characteristic Acts and Body Postures in Initial Interview	Related Inferences about Traits, Conflicts, Symptoms	Relevant Data from Initial Interview or Clinic Record
	gesturing expansive and emphatic		assertive and his manner poised and self-confident. The main conclusion from the interview is that the patient feels deeply insecure and inadequate.
	b. Very frequent rubbing of lips and mouth area; and frequent "palms-up," helpless gesture.	b. an oral-dependency conflict.	
	c. Frequently takes off glasses.	c. Use of denial as a defense.	c. Clinic summary: "His defenses mainly were obsessional intellectualization, especially about his struggle for a higher status; and denial of his intense feelings of insecurity and worthlessness."
	d. Absence of motoric inhibition and of "hostile" acts like clenching fist.	d. Expect to find no conflict over expression of aggression.	d. *N.B.* His diagnosis alone is not compatible with this inference.
Mr. H	a. Is a general tenor of control and composure in both basic position (see Fig. 2.5) and in fact that keeps hands locked together good deal of time and gestures with interlocked hands (see Fig. 2.5) in slow movements of limited aptitude. *But* this general	a. Problem is one of control over hostility, with emphasis on control.	a. Diagnosis: Compulsive personality. Symptomatology: indecisiveness in business decisions, ruminative. Clinic Summary: Great use of intellectualization and ventilation of hostility in treatment.

	tenor *is* interrupted by "aggressive" acts: pressing thumbs together, making fist, and pounding. b. Rubs nose when female interviewer moves in her chair.	b. Did not want treatment with female therapist.
Mr. I	a. Expanded basic position. And all gestures are expansive, often done quite suddenly and vigorously. Frequent pounding with fist, and intrusive finger pointing at interviewer.	a. Violent temper outbursts. Diagnosis: Anxiety reaction.
	b. Will show a distaste for women, for "femininity."	
		a. and b. Patient is "acter-outer." Has problem of hostile impulse control: too much impulse, too little control, giving rise to feelings of helplessness in this respect. Definitely should not be obsessive-compulsive character.
	b. The preceding gestural activity often gives way to turning "palms up."	b. Problem with passive-dependency.
	c. General vividness of his actions and total presentation of self.	c. Exhibitionistic and adolescent flavor to his character.
		b. Fear of failure on new job and feelings of inadequacy as a man. *N.B.* Not clearly supportive.
		c. *N.B.* No supportive evidence. (Inference of this quality may have been in error because it ignored his ethnic background: Greek-American. Possible confusion of "culture" with "personality.")
Mr. J	a. Symmetrical, highly controlled basic position. Emphasis on symmetry	a. There should be an intense conflict over expression of hostile
		a. Diagnosis: Hysterical personality, with depressive and compulsive features. Clinic Summary: "consid-

(Continued)

25

TABLE 2.2
(*Continued*)

Patient	Characteristic Acts and Body Postures in Initial Interview	Related Inferences about Traits, Conflicts, Symptoms	Relevant Data from Initial Interview or Clinic Record
	in hands and glasses activity (see Fig. 2.3). Keeps hands locked together good deal of time and works them and thumb tips against each other. Frequent "picking and cleaning" of eyes, head, teeth.	impulses, with emphasis on the control rather than on impulse expression. Would expect to find compulsive features but also anxiety and tension, which he attempts to control by pontifical and stilted behavior.	erable evidence came up to indicate that this is a man with violent aggressive feelings towards competitors - - - which he ordinarily deals with by very rigid control, passivity, and compliance - - - on the few occasions when he has lost control of this rage it has expressed itself in dissociated states."
	b. Removes glasses for extended periods.	b. Will use denial and withdrawal from social situations that arouse his anxiety.	b. "He also makes strong use of denial and displacement." Difficulty in getting out of bed in morning.
	c. General effeminate quality to movements.	c. Effeminate quality in make-up.	c. *N.B.* No clear supportive evidence.
Mr. K	a. Keeps face almost completely hidden from interviewer behind left hand throughout interview.	a. Central problem pivots on *shame* and *great* dissatisfaction with himself.	a. and b. Diagnosis: Schizoid personality. Descriptive symptomatology: Withdrawal anxiety, inability to concentrate, ruminations about homosexual episode. Clinic Summary: "He has been obsessed with his unworthiness to a degree that he has cut himself off from social activities."
	b. Effeminate, high-tight leg cross and loose-graceful quality to arm-hand movements.	b. Has a homosexual problem and is very embarrassed about it.	

c. Excessive picking at his skin in interview, frequent "drumming" with fingers, and rubbing top of head in fashion of exasperated adolescent.	c. Feelings and expression of irritability and hostility. Also turning of this hostility against self.	c. In treatment expressed irritability and anger towards priest who made him feel so ashamed at confessional. *N.B.* No clear supportive evidence.
Mr. L a. Being methodical and putting things in order; methodical handling of cigarette, setting tie in place, brushing clothing. b. In addition to above, varies between restricted posture and expansiveness of gestures and, the unrestricted end. Often scratches self, clenches hand into fist, frequent clasping hands. c. Exceedingly frequent "palms-up" helpless gesture and excessive, continual foot jiggling.	a. Predominantly obsessive-compulsive character (or possibly passive-aggressive character). b. Strong conflict over the expression of hostile impulses. Subject to fits of temper which he struggles to control and probably does 'control' much of the time by turning it onto himself & feeling guilt. c. High level of anxious helplessness in initial interview.	a. Diagnosis: Obsessive-compulsive neurosis. b. In addition to diagnosis, Symptomatology: fears of harming some one, resultant anxiety, depression, agoraphobia. c. Summary of intake interview made by initial interviewer: "good manners, none of the tension and anxiety he describes is easily discernible in his posture or delivery. His smiles and blandness are inappropriate to degree of discomfort and anxiety he is experiencing." (Inference clearly supported; interviewer unaware of degree of motor expression of anxious helplessness.)

(Continued)

TABLE 2.2
(Continued)

Patient	Characteristic Acts and Body Postures in Initial Interview	Related Inferences about Traits, Conflicts, Symptoms	Relevant Data from Initial Interview or Clinic Record
	d. High tight leg cross; and often puts hand between these tightly crossed legs.	d. Heterosexual fears.	d. Cinic Summary: Was always shy with girls. Wife trapped him into marriage by making him believe he was father of her child.
	e. Great deal of "preening" activity.	e. Strong element of narcissism.	e. N.B. No clear supportive evidence.
	f. During course of interview, is a general progression towards less restriction in movements. Many postural shifts in tune with interviewer's. Offers interviewer cigarette, a match, slides ash tray to her—at various times in interview. Interviewer gives many behavioral cues that interview is at end, but he shows no behavioral recognition of this.	f. Predict high degree of involvement in treatment if he enters therapy.	f. Patient comes for 34 therapy interviews; only a few patients stay in therapy that long in our clinic.

28

| Mr. M | a. Throughout interview sits tensely upright, on edge of chair. Never assumes relaxed basic position. Very little gestural activity in interview. All visible action limited to hands and forearms. During most of interview hands are tightly clasped together, thumbs pressing against each other. Toward end of interview starts to part hands ever so slightly, separating them at most 2 inches (see Fig. 2.4). | a-1 Fearful of authority figures.
a-2 Anticipate restricted interaction with people.
a-3 A strong conflict over aggression with the accent on tightly superimposed controls. Will be a fear of aggression, not frequent temper outbursts of Mr. I. | a-1 Cannot hold a job; becomes frightened when production inspector appears and quits work to avoid these meetings. Then stays in house all by himself.
a-2 Clinic Summary: "Sits by self all time. When people visit he either goes out for a while or turns white and starts shaking . . . some dearth of spontaneous production . . . innate rigidity in conversational manner."
a-3 Diagnosis: Sociopath-alcoholism. Clinic Summary: "He attempts to maintain rigid control of his hostile and aggressive impulses which seem to be occasionally expressed in ill-considered manner . . . depression . . . with irritability . . . directed irritability onto wife, saving "good" side for physician." Some time abusive child-beater. |

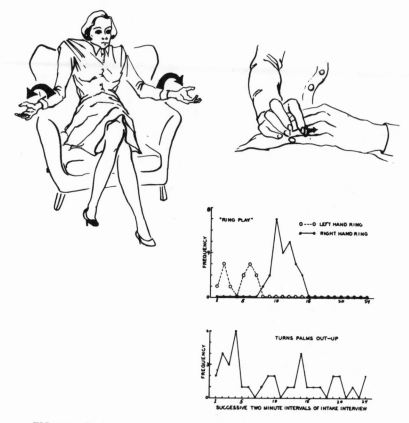

FIG. 2.1. Demonstrates Mrs. B performing the communicative gesture of turning her palms out-up and ring play, first with her wedding ring on her left hand than a ring on her right hand, and the frequency of these acts.

woman over 40—and the other was an awkward 18-year-old girl—the only female under 26 in the sample. Women prefer a "high-closed-leg cross." Only four of the nine men, however, kept their legs crossed at the knee throughout the interview. Of the five who did not, two placed one lower leg or ankle on the knee of the other leg in an "open-leg cross," two kept both feet on the floor, and one varied between a "high-closed cross," the "open-leg cross," and crossing his outstretched legs below the knee. It is not surprising that women do not use the "open-leg cross," but it is notable how rarely the women deviated from the "high-closed cross."

We compared the *frequency of other actions in men and women*, with the results presented in Table 2.1. The entries in this table express the frequencies of various acts in terms of the number of minutes of the interview elapsing per act; so the smaller the number entered in the table, the more

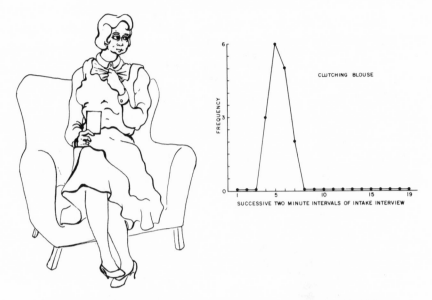

FIG. 2.2.   Demonstrates the frequency of Mrs. D's "blouse clutching" during the intake interview.

frequent the act. The gesture records of three patients were not detailed enough to be included in this analysis. Sex differences were most common in the case of *communicative gestures*. The men pointed more frequently than the women. On the other hand, the women shrugged their shoulders, shook their heads, and turned their palms-up-and-out more frequently than did the men. There seemed to be much less of a trend for sex differences in *autistic gestures*. The only instance here is the not surprising, more frequent patting of the hair by the women. Moving down the table there is next the striking difference in the frequency of the two hand–arm positions noted. The women folded their arms across their waist more frequently but held or clasped their hands together less frequently than the men did. There was no difference in the frequency of general postural changes.

We regard these data pertaining to sex differences as being valuable primarily as clues for further research. They raise questions and prompt speculations that may be useful to follow up.

1. The findings about *male pointing* and *female folding the arms across the waist* suggest the possibility that very basic, culturally reinforced, biological factors may be operating. There is an *intrusive* quality to pointing, and an *inclusive* quality to folding one's arms in this manner, which *may* be instances of the male-intrusive and feminine-inclusive modes conceptualized by Erik-

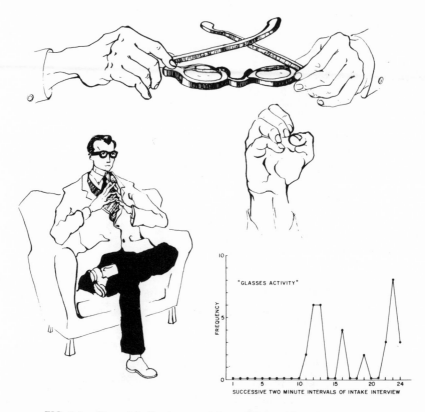

FIG. 2.3.   Shows Mr. J's glasses activity and the position taken during the intake interview.

son (1950). Perhaps the feminine high-closed-leg cross reflects this inclusive mode, as well as condensing the functions of "being lady-like" and sexually attractive. One wonders if the folded arm position is not also dependent in some way upon the presence of the female breasts and the possessor's feelings about them. Breasts may be made less conspicuous, may be supported, or may be protected—in fancy, if not in fact—by this arm position.

2. The data on communicative gestures of Table 2.1 raise several questions. If one could measure all communicative gestures in a variety of situations would it be discovered that women consistently use them more frequently than men? Or is this difference unique to this sample and a function of the fact that the interviewer was a woman? Does the more frequent use of communicative gestures indicate freer, less inhibited interactions, and is this more likely between woman and woman, or is it more likely when the participants are of the same sex, either male or female?

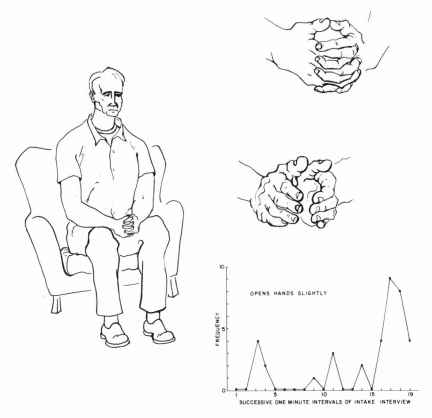

FIG. 2.4. Demonstrates Mr. M's frequency of open-hand gesture and the
tense, erect position assumed during the intake interview.

3. Except for the culturally permitted, or defined, hair patting of the
women, the data on autistic gestures suggest that the frequency of these is
not sex related. As is indicated later, the autistic gestures seem only to be
manifestations of general personality traits and of momentary emotional–
ideational states; they do not seem to have a communicative function. For
example, in making inferences we often interpreted the autistic gestures of
Table 2.1 as follows:

   a. Rubs-touches nose—attitude of contempt, disgust, negative feelings.
   b. Scratching self—inhibition of aggression.
   c. Finger-mouth contact—oral-erotic needs and gratifications.
   d. Rubs self—general erotic stimulation, or tension reduction.
   e. Picking, smoothing, cleaning, etc.—obsessive-compulsive traits.

I do not know of any evidence that the traits just listed are sex related. The
absence of a sex difference in the corresponding gestures is compatible with

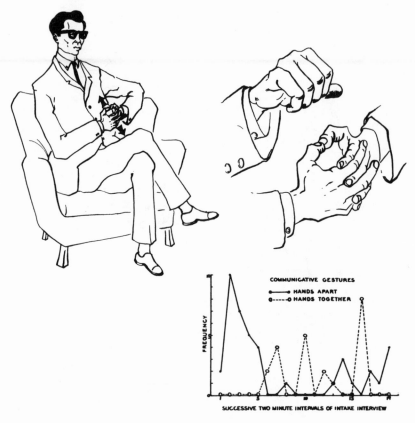

FIG. 2.5.   Demonstrates the frequency of Mr. H's communicative gestures
with his hands.

this understanding. A similar supposition is used to explain the almost identical frequency of general postural changes in both sexes. Such acts seem to
us to be clearly a function of shifts in the general level of tension occurring
right during the interview itself. We presume that changes in tension are
equally likely for male and female patients.

Personality Characteristics and Gestures and Body Movements

We conducted our "inference" or "prediction" substudy to trace possible
associations between personality characteristics and nonverbal behavior.
Table 2.2 presents the results of this substudy. The first column of this table
lists those acts and body postures revealed to be characteristic of a given
patient on the basis of which we felt able to make personality inferences. It is
important to remember that these acts and body positions were *not* "re-

called" or determined to be characteristic of an individual *after the fact*. The gesture record and the analysis of it were completed before the personality inferences were made and before the verbal content of the initial interview and the clinic records were known. Thus the entries in the first column of Table 2.2 are free of any selective tendency biased by knowledge of personality variables. The second column of Table 2.2 lists the personality inferences. These inferences are listed opposite the nonverbal behaviors on which they were ostensibly, manifestly based in the conscious thinking of the judge. The third column of the table presents data deemed relevant to the personality inferences. The entries in this column are listed opposite the inferences to which they pertain.

Those who prefer not to regard this as a "prediction study," because of the unsystematic and possibly biased selection of criterion observations, may read Table 2.2 in another way. They may simply ignore the second column containing the inferences and regard the matching entries in the first and third columns as potential, or hypothesized, associations between nonverbal behavior and personality characteristics that should be properly evaluated by future, systematic correlational research.

Only a close, leisurely reading of Table 2.2 conveys the apparently intimate relationship between personality characteristics and nonverbal behavior, and the degree to which an observer *might* be able to infer personality characteristics from gestures and body movements. *I urge the reader to mimic the acts and postures listed in the first column as he reads the inferences in the second column*. But, some points concerning Table 2.2 deserve mention.

First, there are 43 personality inferences listed in the second column; 36 of these seem to be amply confirmed, with an additional one largely, but not completely, confirmed (see Mrs. E, Inference c).

Secondly, we feel that we avoided the "Barnum effect" of making very general predictions for each patient that would be true for all patients. Notice, for example, that in the case of the first patient in the table, Mrs. A, the inference was made that she would *not* feel helpless, which was indeed the case at the time of the interview. We also made a specific inference that she would have an orality problem, which was confirmed by the fact that she returned 6 months later with a complaint of anorexia and weight loss. You find such specific inferences for nearly every patient. A marital conflict, fears of body damage, the defenses of denial and of assertiveness, an aversion to women, shame over homosexuality, readiness for a high degree of involvement in treatment, fear of authority figures are examples. Other inferences were often quite general ones, such as inferred conflicts over aggression or over sexuality. But these were not made indiscriminantly about all patients, and we attempted to be as precise as possible in specifying which side of the conflict would be most pronounced.

In the third place, it should be pointed out that the observer's on-the-spot impressions of major concerns and personality characteristics of the patients were often fairly accurate. While watching the initial interviews, he recorded such impressions for 8 . . . patients, and was correct in 7 of these 8. These seven impressions and the time recorded on the gesture tape were as follows:

1. The marital conflict of Mrs. B—eighth minute.
2. The sensuousness of Mrs. C—fourteenth minute.
3. The immediate concern of Mrs. E over her genital urges—eighth minute.
4. The inhibited hostility of Mrs. F—eighteenth minute.
5. The obsessional thinking and character of Mrs. H—twenty-third minute.
6. The shame over homosexuality of Mr. K—second minute.
7. The fear of authority figures of Mr. M—second minute.

In the negative instance, a sexual conflict and an effeminate quality was recorded during the twenty-third minute for Mr. J. The clinic records did not provide clear supportive evidence for these impressions.

Finally, we must acknowledge that an undetermined number of traits, conflicts, prominent ideational themes, etc., were not inferred from the nonverbal behavior. This is not surprising, nor does it in any way diminish the significance of gestures and body movements. Rather, this observation merely highlights a problem for the future—the establishment of the limits to the inferential powers of observers and to the psychological significance of nonverbal behavior during interviews.

We now attempt to illustrate the inference process we followed. Our starting point was the general assumption that any discrete gesture or action that a patient repeated *relatively* frequently, or that was unusual no matter what its frequency, or any characteristic posture, were indications of basic attitudes, drives, conflicts, prominent ideational themes, etc. We assumed that actions of both an instrumental-interpersonal and a symbolic nature occur. We further assumed that we could infer the psychological determinants of actions and postures by drawing on our shared, but rarely verbalized, cultural patterning of behavior, on our previous clinical experience, and on our ordinary capacity for empathy. These statements become more meaningful if they are applied to specific patients.

Mrs. B, as shown in Fig. 2.1, performed the communicative gesture of turning her palms out-up once every minute on the average and shrugged her shoulders about every 3 minutes of the interview. She achieved the highest rates in the sample for these acts. Often she did both at the same time. These acts were regarded as manifestations of a deeply ingrained attitude of passive helplessness, tainted with a negativistic, complaining flavor. We also assume this behavior functions as an appeal to the interviewer. The autistic ring play, first with her wedding ring on her left hand and then with an unknown ring on her right hand, was regarded as a symbolic representation of conflicting feelings over her marriage. Occasional scratching and inspection of her fingernails, which we considered as weapons for attack, suggested a rather strong undercurrent of hostility no doubt related to the negativism suggested by her shrugging shoulders. The fact that she *scratched herself*[3] produced the inference that she predominantly turned this aggression onto herself. All of these characteristics appear in the criteria data. Her diagnosis was "anxiety reaction in passive-dependent personality." Her descriptive symptomatology listed: somatic symptoms, weepy spells, depression, feelings of inferiority and inadequacy. The discharge summary said: Major concerns are that too many demands are placed on her by her marriage and children, and that she must "bottle up" her anger and retaliatory impulses felt towards her husband; complains that husband does not help with care of house and children and never takes her out. It should be noted that we did not predict the anxiety nor the somatic symptoms of this patient.

The "blouse clutching" of Mrs. D, Fig. 2.2, provides another illustration of the application of our inference procedure. While watching the interview and studying the behavioral records, the observer was impressed with this highly idiosyncratic autistic behavior. But any possible meaning of it, other than general discomfort, eluded him until nearing the end of the inference process. After writing down all the available inferences, he "took a 10-minute break" from the work. Thinking about this behavior and mimicking it, he was reminded of scenes from horror movies in which the heroine leans away in terror from the menacing monster, frantically clutching her garments around her throat as she does so. Such a sense of certainty accompanied this association of the observer that he immediately wrote down the inference, "She has fears of body damage or mutilation." It was striking to then dis-

---

[3]Since completing this study, further observations have convinced us of the validity of the assumption that when "scratching" occurs it is a manifestation of aggression, usually of inhibited aggression. (a) It commonly occurs in this context in everyday interaction. (b) The act of scratching the body wall signifies "anger" in the sign language of the deaf (Long, 1944). (c) An occasional instruction in the pantomime literature uses *scratching* to represent the state of inhibited anger (e.g., Pardoe, 1931, Pantomime No. 79). (d) We find that Shakespeare used the word "scratch" and hence allied imagery 26 times in his plays. In 16 instances the meaning is "aggression." In one instance (Julius Caesar, II, i. 237–47), he even has Brutus scratching himself when in a state of inhibited anger. (I wish to thank Steve Ford for his assistance in reviewing Shakespeare's use of scratch.) (e) Laura Nader, the anthropologist at the University of California, Berkeley, showed me a film of a young Zapotec-Mexican man standing trial in a village near Oaxaca. At the outset he engaged in prolonged agitated self-scratching. Soon he was leaning across the magistrate's desk, jabbing a pencil at the table-top. Prof. Nader was present at the trial and confirmed my inference that he had changed from a state of inhibited to freely expressed anger. (f) A patient scratched herself as she dreamt of murder (see page 52).

cover that this generally phobic woman was afraid of hospitals, either to visit or to be a patient herself, was afraid that if she became pregnant again her pelvis would be too small, was afraid of D and C procedures, and was preoccupied with thoughts and dreams of dead people and cemeteries. (The blouse-clutching phase of activity portrayed in the graph followed immediately the description by her of being told at the age of 8 that she and her twin sister had "killed her mother" during their birth and introduced and accompanied the description of the symptoms I have just described.) The way in which this patient intruded the appointment slip into the interview reminded the judge of a child's coveting a ticket to some cherished event—a ride at an amusement park, or a world-series game or a boxing match. In the context already implied by the blouse clutching, it was accordingly inferred that "she perceives treatment as a sanctuary." This attitude was corroborated even during the interview, for the interviewer was prompted to comment on and question with the patient the way in which she placed herself with complete trust in the hands of the clinic staff.

Mr. J, Fig. 2.3, sat centered in the chair and leaned against the back; he placed his legs in an open cross, one ankle resting on the knee of the other leg. Each elbow rested on its chair arm and his hands were either held in the pontifical gesture shown with all fingers accurately opposed, or he neatly opposed thumb and finger. Or he held his glasses in the balanced composition illustrated—they were centered between his hands and the stems were crossed precisely. The patient was an engraving of symmetry, precise balance, and delicacy. This behavioral picture was part of the basis for inferring significant compulsive features in his makeup, as well as an emphasis on control over the expression of hostility. In the case record, his diagnosis included "compulsive features" and his therapist observed in his summary that the patient ordinarily dealt with his violent aggressive feeling "by very rigid control, passivity and compliance." The judge equated the removal of the glasses with a tendency . . . to use *denial* as a defense. When the therapist later closed this man's series of interviews, he commented specifically on "strong use of denial" by this patient. The latter part of the intake interview itself, when the patient was removing his glasses, dealt actively with the problem the patient has in "facing certain things" (i.e., problems). . . .

Some more specific assumptions evolved and were followed in making predictions about aggression, its control, and its direction. Because some of these have been alluded to previously, there is some repetition in what follows. First of all, certain specific acts seemed to have common determinants in the various patients. Thus, shrugging the shoulders, making a fist, rubbing or wiping one's nose, interest in teeth and fingernails were regarded as indices of a generally hostile attitude. Self-scratching, as already mentioned, was interpreted as evidence for a tendency to turn hostility around on the self. But equally as useful for predicting conflicts over aggression was the dimension of freedom–restraint in use of the hands and arms. One of the male patients, Mr. I, was distinguished by the fact that in gesturing his hands would suddenly fly out to the full extent of his arms, and just as suddenly drop back to his body. Violent outbursts of aggression were suggested by this characteristic, in the total context of his behavior. This patient described a "violent temper" as a central problem. At the other extreme there was the highly inhibited behavior of Mr. M, Fig. 2.4. This patient was truly remarkable for the great restraint he exercised during the interview. He achieved this partly in maintaining for the entire interview the tense, erect position shown in the sketch, but it was even more obvious in an extreme limitation of variety and amplitude of hand gestures. He did virtually only two things with his hands: he either kneaded, squeezed, or rubbed them heavily together, or he parted them ever so slightly, 2 inches at most, and usually less than an inch. This behavior was regarded as the literal manifestation of tightly superimposed controls over aggressive impulses. His case record states that this man was a sociopath, that "he attempts to maintain rigid control of his hostile and aggressive impulses which seem to be occasionally expressed in ill-considered manner."

Mr. H, Fig. 2.5, falls in between the two cases just discussed. He showed some freedom in hand activity, including loose fist making, but he shifted in reciprocal fashion from moderately free-hand activity to that in which his hands were moved together. As indicated by the arrows in the whole figure, he would raise and lower his interlaced hands in forceful movement. Often he pressed and worked his thumb tips energetically against each other. Following the rationale already indicated one inference about him was that there would be "a problem of control over his aggression with emphasis on the control." His diagnosis of compulsive personality is in keeping with these observations and predictions, as were two of the features of his therapy—"great use of intellectualization, ventilation of hostility."

Another principle, not especially novel, seemed to be useful enough in making inferences to be mentioned specifically. The frequency of rapid foot movements,[4] and the frequency of general postural shifts, both appeared to provide estimates of the overall level of anxiety, there being a positive relationship between anxiety and these actions.

Intraindividual Variation in Actions and Postures

For many of the patients, one could detect "activity phases" in which the frequencies of one or more of their characteristic gestures systematically increased and decreased as the interview progressed. The graphs contained

---

[4]It is my impression that a "sudden foot twitch" by a patient in psychotherapy or on the analytic couch is invariably caused by a thought coming into consciousness with a "jolt," or by a remark by the therapist that touches a sensitive conflict area. (But such events may not always be accompanied by a foot twitch.) Is this impression a valid one that would be substantiated by experimentation? Is the "sudden foot twitch" a remnant of the startle reflex?

in Fig. 2.1 through Fig. 2.5 have illustrated this point. From a purely quantitative, objective viewpoint, it is obvious that nonverbal behavior during interviews is a lawful phenomenon.

How were variations in nonverbal behavior related to the verbal utterances and interchange of the initial interviews? We detected four principal relationships.

1. *Some actions "expressed" the same meaning as the concomitant manifest verbal content.* Mrs. B (Fig. 2.1), for example, described in words the feelings of helplessness expressed in her gesture of turning the palms-out-up. The man who removed his glasses did so as he and the interviewer actively explored his difficulty in "facing certain things."

It is notable that, as in these examples, either communicative gestures having a culturally shared meaning (palms-out-up) or autistic actions having idiosyncratic determinants (removing glasses) may be congruent and redundant with the manifest verbal content.

2. *Some gestures do not appear on the surface to be related to the manifest verbal content but anticipate later amplifications of the current content.* Mrs. B illustrates this point clearly. All the time this patient was playing with her wedding ring, she was describing her symptoms, with practically no mention of her husband. Then she verbalized overtly and extensively her complaints that her husband did not help her and that he contributed to her feelings of inadequacy. As she did this, she ceased completely playing with her wedding ring. Mrs. B provided another example of this type of relationship. At one point she was discussing her feelings of inferiority towards her husband. As she did so, she momentarily placed her *fingers to her mouth*. Three minutes later she stated that her feelings of inferiority actually date from feelings she had as a child—namely, that she was homely and not as pretty as her sisters because she then had two *front teeth that protruded badly*. We presume she used to cover those "buck teeth" with her hand, as she appeared to do in the initial interview when the latent memories of those early days were activated by her thoughts of her present feelings of inferiority.

Here is another example of the same type of relation. Mrs. E was in private treatment with a male therapist before applying for treatment at our clinic. About the eighth minute of the interview she flicked off a speck from the abdominal area of her dress. At this time she was explaining that she broke with the private therapist because she "wasn't getting anywhere," her family did not support it, and because she was running out of money. Approximately 40 minutes later she confessed to having developed a strong erotic transerence to this therapist, with so much attendant guilt and shame that she had to interrupt treatment with him. At first this sexual conflict had only been "alluded to" by the seemingly casual gesture directed towards her abdominal area.

3. *Some gestures betray meaning contrary to concurrent verbal content.* The clearest example of this was afforded by a male patient, a bench hand and

machinist's helper by trade, who deftly manipulated a pencil through a motley of maneuvers extended over most of his interview. His skill failed him at only one point. When he was defensively claiming that his work efficiency was 100%, he lost control of the pencil and dropped it to the floor (cf. with the parapraxis of Little Hans cited earlier.)

4. *Some gestural activity and body movements seem directly related to interaction with the interviewer,* with the patient's manifest verbal content playing a secondary role. This was almost always found to be the critical factor in determining the general postural changes of the patient. These shifts only made sense when regarded as changes in the tension due to the immediate interaction in the interview.[5] Occasionally it appeared that specific gestures, with or without a content connection, were also influenced directly by the interview interaction. This point can be illustrated by turning again to the sketches and the accompanying graphs. Look first at the graph in Fig. 2.1, for Mrs. B's gesture of turning her palms out-up, an act regarded as an expression of helplessness. We see a sudden and relatively sustained drop in the frequency of this gesture after the eighth minute of the interview. Toward the end of this initial phase the interviewer manifested considerable empathic understanding and sympathy for the patient, events that could be token gratifications for the need for help sustaining these gestures. Consider next the activity of Mr. M in Fig. 2.5. Near the end of the interview there was a relatively sustained period of 4 minutes in which this man felt free to part his hands slightly. This change is understood as follows. According to the patient's statements in the interview, he came to our clinic at the urging of a Veterans Administration psychiatrist and his family. He did not want to enter treatment now, though he stated he wanted to be sure it would be available on a stand-by basis if he needed it in the future. Just before the 4 minutes of sustained free-hand activity, the interviewer openly agreed with and supported his desire not to enter treatment but to postpone any further evaluation until he had tried life further on his own. Thus it was apparent that when he felt reassured and unthreatened by the interviewer he manifested greater freedom in bodily activity.

Summary of Initial Interview Study

The *goals* of this study were the exploration of: (a) individual differences in the nonverbal behavior of psychiatric patients during their initial interviews; (b) intraindividual variations in nonverbal behavior during the initial interviews; and (c) the relationships between these individual differences, and within-interview variations and personality variables or other aspects of the individual's behavior during the interview.

---

[5]These words were written in 1959. Essentially the same evaluation of postural changes was reached independently, and greatly extended in theory and detail, by Scheflen (1963).

The method and materials were as follows: The intake interviews of 18 people seeking psychiatric outpatient treatment were tape-recorded. An observer also *watched* the interviews through a one-way mirror, *but did not hear* any of the interview. He dictated a running account of the patient's behavior onto a second tape. All tapes were transcribed and the two records for each interview were subsequently collated.

Upon completing a qualitative and quantitative analysis of the gesture record, uncontaminated inferences of leading conflicts, character structure, traits, and concerns were made for 14 of the patients. Independent criterion materials included the verbal content of the initial interviews and, most importantly, entries in the clinic records.

The *results* were as follows: (a) There were marked individual differences in nonverbal behavior. (b) Some of these differences appear to be sex related. (c) Many of these differences appear to be a function of personality variables. Based only on the nonverbal behavior 36 out of 43 personality inferences appeared to be confirmed. The behavioral bases for these inferences were specified and the inference procedure was illustrated. In some cases, very precise impressions of patient's conflicts were formed while watching the initial interviews. (d) Gestures and body movements may be patterned in time within individual interviews. (e) We observed four kinds of relationships between the nonverbal behavior and the verbal transactions within interviews:

- Some gestures and acts have the same meaning as the concurrent manifest verbal content.
- Some betray contrary meanings.
- Some anticipate later verbal statements.
- Some seem to be a direct function of interaction with the interviewer.

We *conclude* that psychotherapy research could profitably enlarge its scope and pay more attention to gestures and body movements.

EXPRESSION OF THE UNVERBALIZED IN AUTISTIC ACTIONS: PSYCHOANALYTIC OBSERVATIONS

Now we are going to focus upon one particular aspect of nonverbal behavior: the expression of unverbalized, often unconscious, behavioral processes in transitory, autistic actions. Nearly all of the empirical observations to be presented are psychoanalytic ones.

Shortly after Freud discovered that many hysterical symptoms were expressions of unconscious memories, phantasies, and wishes, he demonstrated that many "chance actions" of everyday life also had unconscious determinants (Freud, 1901/1960). He also observed that actions occurring during psychoanalysis often arose from the same origins. This was the case with those observations of his mentioned earlier: Dora's fingering of her reticule, Hans' dropping of his toy horse, the Rat Man's frightened pacing, and the Wolf Man's placating glance at Freud followed by turning to look at the grandfather clock. Freud later reported (1913/1958a) that "chance actions" committed by the analysand upon lying on the couch for the first time often indicated the nature of the unconscious wishes and conflicts, which subsequently became conscious as a result of the process and work of analysis. One of his examples is of a young woman who quickly pulls down the hem of her skirt to cover her ankles when first lying down and who proves later in analysis to be proud of her beauty and exhibitionistic. In his theoretical writings, Freud had a place for these discoveries. Many of the actions occurring in the psychoanalytic situation were subsumed under his clinical concept of "repetition-instead-of-recollection" (Freud, 1914/1958b). The general phenomenon of the motoric expression of unconscious thoughts and action tendencies is subsumed under his concept of there being alternative "discharge" pathways: the affective, the ideational, and the motor (see, e.g., Freud, 1915/1957c, p. 179).

These brief historical remarks indicate that the expression of the unverbalized in transitory actions is an old, familiar phenomenon. They also indicate the chief aspects of the phenomenon that were discovered by Freud. In this section we present some clinical observations and comments pertaining to this phenomenon. The first portion of these remarks deals with an aspect not previously considered in any detail in the literature, as far as we are aware. The other two portions are merely small addenda to Freud's discussions of the phenomenon.

Nonverbal Anticipation of Spontaneous Verbalization[6]

When you are talking with someone and are in a position to listen carefully to what they say and also to watch closely what they do—as in the clinical interview—you can frequently observe the following pattern of events:

While the person is talking about *one thing*, he may perform a certain action, which is seemingly unrelated to what he is saying.

Then, later, the person may *spontaneously* mention *something else*, which is associatively linked to the first topic and also quite clearly related to the former action.

---

[6]An abbreviated report of the following material was presented at the symposium on, "New Approaches to the Study of Facial Expression and Body Movement," Annual Meeting, American Psychological Association, 1966, September.

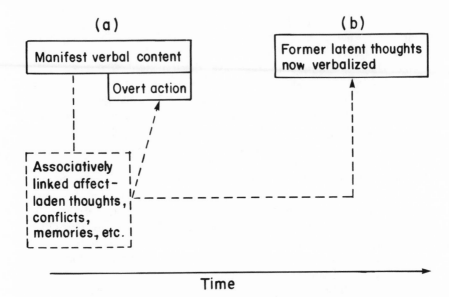

FIG. 2.6. Theoretical paradigm for the nonverbal anticipation of spontaneous verbalization.

The pattern of events is such that the *action has anticipated the subsequent verbalization.*

The initial interview study provided a particularly clear example of this pattern. When Mrs. B was speaking of her symptoms she slid her wedding ring back and forth on her finger; soon she started to talk about her marital problems, which were associatively linked to her symptoms. *Her wedding-ring play anticipated verbalization.*

What appears to happen in such episodes may be schematized as shown in Fig. 2.6. The solid boxes and lines pertain to observable or manifest behavior; the dotted, to inferred latent responses and relationships. We assume the thoughts, affects, etc., which are subsequently verbalized are preconsciously or unconsciously activated when the person talks about the first topic and cause the action to occur at that time. Subsequently, we infer, the latent thoughts become conscious and are verbalized.

The first observation is an obvious one. Part *a* where the individual verbalizes one thing as he simultaneously betrays another preoccupation in incongruent nonverbal behavior is familiar to every experienced interviewer. The subsequent emergence of this latent concern after therapeutic intervention is also familiar. The novelty here, for us, is the *spontaneous* occurrence of the total pattern, the transition from *a* to *b,* which yields the spontaneous nonverbal anticipation of verbalization.

Now, it has been our experience that this phenomenon can be observed almost daily in a moderate schedule of 2 or 3 clinical interviews a day, especially psychoanalytic ones, without making any special effort to do so. Usually the acts are more subtle and transitory than in the first example. But once the general pattern is comprehended, the relevance of the actions to the verbalizations they anticipate is apparent. Thus, we believe that many of the seemingly random acts accompanying verbal interaction conform to the a → b pattern. Here are several examples involving subtle and transitory actions.

1. Mrs. B of the initial interview study also provided the first of these. There we noted that as she continued to speak about her marital life, she discussed feelings of inferiority toward her husband, and while doing this she momentarily placed her fingers to her mouth. Three minutes later she was stating that her sense of inferiority dated from childhood when she felt she was not as pretty as her sister because she had two buck teeth. Applying our paradigm to this episode, we have the [schematization of Fig. 2.7]. . . . We assume the childhood memories of feeling uglier than her sister and of the tendency to hide them behind her hand were activated at Point *a* and produced the hand-mouth action, even though they emerged into conscious recollection and verbalization at Point *b*.

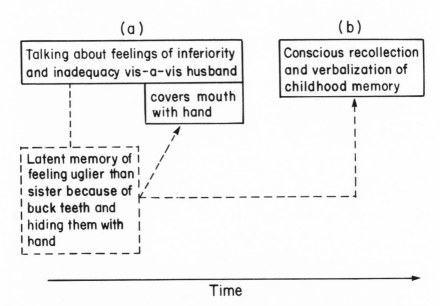

FIG. 2.7. Theoretical schematization of how Mrs. B's covering-of-her-mouth anticipated recollection of childhood feelings about her "ugly" teeth.

2. The following instance occurred one day in the third year of Mrs. C's analysis. She was verbalizing her affection for her analyst. Meanwhile, she touched the wall next to the couch with her left hand and briefly rubbed the back of her hand on the slightly rough, "scratch-plaster" surface of the wall. A moment later she looked at the back of her hand, said it was tingling—perhaps from having rubbed it on the wall. The analyst said nothing. Over the next 10 minutes her associations drifted to her childhood love for her father. Embedded among these associations was a recollection of pleasant "bear hugs" he would give her in the evening. She would climb onto his lap, they would embrace and rub cheeks. *Her* cheeks would get all tingly from this because of the scratching of his day's growth of whiskers.

We infer the a → b pattern: that when she verbalized her transference affection, the memories of the exciting, tingling bear hugs and the desire to repeat them had been latently activated; that they caused the wall rubbing; and that conscious, verbal recollection of the memories occurred spontaneously in a few minutes.

3. The next observation comes from a session in the fifth year of a woman's analysis. The nonverbal action was a momentary, barely perceptible, incipient turning onto her side accompanied by a very slight curling of her legs. This movement was very unusual for this woman. And, of course, this is true of all the examples we are presenting; otherwise we would merely be speaking of chance phenomena, selectively and spuriously noted post hoc.

When this slight rolling and leg-curling occurred, she was in the midst of a reverie-like imagining of how she had felt when still sleeping in her own bed in her parent's bedroom, at the age of 4 or 5. The reverie included the sensation of her bones "rattling inside," the thought of her bed shaking, and the wondering if she had ever heard her parents having intercourse. Then she fell silent. Next she said that an odd sensation had come over her: it was as though she were a child in her bed and was lying on her side with her legs curled, masturbating. She can picture herself doing this while she heard her parents in their bed; she knows she did, but she has no concrete memory of doing so.

Again the a → b pattern of behavior, although the two components appear to be nearly simultaneous, possibly even fused. Presumably the masturbatory memories had been activated by the parts of the reverie we mentioned; and presumably the motor components of these memories were manifested first and the ideational components assimilated and verbalized spontaneously in a few minutes.

4. A young man in analysis tucked in his slightly bulging and gaping shirt front, an action never performed before in over a year and a half of analysis. He did this as he told of a hot mountain hike he had recently taken. His associations drifted briefly to other things. Then he spontaneously told that he capped the hot hike by stripping completely and bathing in a cool moun-

tain stream. Then he spontaneously spoke of the erotic bathing he enjoyed in childhood from the hand of his mother. Again the a → b pattern seems to be operative. And, as in the other examples, the content of the subtle, transitory action has a precise relevance to the subsequent verbalization.

In all of the preceding observations, spontaneous verbalization followed the nonverbal behavior within minutes. The time interval may be greater. In some of our observations the action occurs one day and the spontaneous verbalization follows 1 or 2 days later. Two brief examples:

1. A young man spoke of his current unsatisfactory heterosexual escapades and as he did so he played with a small glass tube about an inch long and the diameter of a pencil. It is part of a visual *inspection system designed for determining small quantities of things*. The next day he told of his fear that his penis was too small to satisfy women, of how he repeatedly lost erections during one of the escapades described in the previous hour, and he said that for years he *wanted to look at his sperm under a microscope* to see if they are viable. He hadn't, though, for fear he would discover they weren't. Later analytic material showed that these doubts and fears were phantasies he had about the effects of masturbation.

The only other occasion in nearly 2 years of analysis when this man played with this glass object occurred several months later under the following circumstances. As he was talking about his masturbatory conflicts, he heard a zipping noise behind him: the analyst had zipped open his tobacco pouch, filled his pipe, and then zipped the pouch closed. The analysand said, in a bit of aggressive humor, that he just pictured the analyst zipping open his trousers and masturbating behind him. The analyst rose to the challenge and remarked: "You could be attributing to me your own wish to masturbate—a wish you feel very conflicted about." A brief silence ensued. During it the analysand slipped his fingers into his shirt pocket and out came the small glass object. He played with it as he changed the subject.

Everything points to the conclusion that the object-play of the first hour was an anticipatory sign of his spontaneous verbalizations of the next hour.

2. One day on the fifth year of her analysis a woman spent most of the hour in a conflicted description of something new in her recent lovemaking with her husband. A central event in it was that she had danced nude before him in a very erotic manner. Both had become exceptionally excited. As she told about these things she did something she had never done before in the analyst's presence. Throughout the hour she kept rotating her right foot. Near the end of the hour she had slipped her foot part way out of her shoe so that it was merely hanging on her toes. She continued to move her foot, so naturally her shoe fell off onto the floor. She seemed completely oblivious to this very obvious behavior. The analyst said nothing about this minor "dancing" and "undressing"; he waited for her spontaneous verbalizations. In the

next few hours she gave them, referring several times to the recent lovemaking and now "confessing" that she had phantasied dancing the same way before her analyst. Her earlier foot activity must have derived from these wishful thoughts, activated as she told of her lovemaking with her husband. It clearly anticipated verbalization.

The following observation suggests that the a → b pattern may also apply to mere muscular contractions. The incident occurred one day in the third year of a woman's analysis. At the time, she was in her fifth month of pregnancy and was preoccupied with rivalry with men.

It was in this context that she suddenly had an image of an erect penis. She had also wondered, but had not said so immediately, if her analyst's penis was erect. At this moment she felt her abdominal muscles suddenly contract. She thought about this and said that recently she has been contracting these muscles quite frequently. She has been trying to make her "belly into a hard, protruding ball . . . to make the baby stick out hard."

Two sessions later she reported the following dream:

> She was lying down and was looking down her body. She saw her pregnant abdomen sticking up. The baby inside was moving rapidly and extensively, causing the wall of her abdomen to be pushed way out in places, as though the baby was pushing out with a leg here, a leg there, an arm here and then there. Then a place on her abdomen was pushed out, making a protruberance a few inches long, about the size of a thumb. This was either sticking out her navel or near it.

Her associations to the dream included the following. The baby might have had an erection (in the dream), which was causing the protrusion near her navel. *Then she recalled that as a little girl she pretended her protruding belly button was a penis.* Next she recalled that we had spoken recently of her competitiveness with men.

Just as visible actions do, these contractions of the abdominal muscles anticipated verbalization. Presumably, her tendency to make her belly stick out, her unconscious wishful phantasies of her baby as a penis substitute, and her childhood phantasies that she actually had a penis had all been activated when she thought about the analyst's penis and were expressed at that moment in the contractions. Then she verbalized or experienced each of these—first her belly behavior, in her immediate associations; then the slightly disguised wish that her baby supply her with a penis in the dream; and then her childhood phantasy that she had a penis in her dream associations. (The similarity of the muscular contractions and their meaning for her to the dream content is notable. We discuss it later.)

Spontaneous transition from nonverbal to verbal expression does not always occur, at least within a reasonable time. In such instances a comment by the analyst about the action and the analysand's resulting associations may still bring forth evidence that the action was functionally related to unverbalized processes. Here we have the typical eruption of the repressed-unconscious into motor activity—acting instead of verbalizing, repetition in action instead of verbal recollection—emphasized by Freud and familiar to all clinicians. Here is an example.

The analyst's office is separated from the waiting room by double doors. These are left open when his secretary is absent so that he can hear analysands enter the waiting room. The location of his desk precludes direct vision to and from the waiting room.

One female analysand discovered that when the doors were open at certain angles, she could use their polished surfaces like mirrors and from the waiting room could see the reflection of the analyst seated at his desk. Many months went by before she told him that she had been taking every opportunity to watch him in this way. Once she let out this secret, she would occasionally tell him at the start of an hour that she had been looking again. Eventually she acknowledged she felt secretive, devlish, and like giggling about it. Some time went by with further repetition of this behavior but with no spontaneous transition to the verbal expression of the affect-laden thoughts or gratifications, which were presumably involved. So one day, when she repeated it, the analyst said this behavior must have some special meaning for her, which she was reluctant to think and talk about. Thereupon, memories of repetitive childhood behavior popped into her head, but she communicated them very hesitantly. These were recollections of how, as a little girl, she used to sneak into the upstairs hall when some adult had gone to the bathroom. And if they had left the door ajar she would enjoy mischeviously watching through it. It was especially pleasing to watch her father, and she later described hilariously how she once surprised him on the toilet by "accidentally" walking in on him.

Because it horrified this woman to have any thoughts in the analyst's presence about excretion, especially when sexualized, let alone to talk about them, we assume that strong conflict and defense prevented the spontaneous transition from the nonverbal behavior in the waiting room to conscious recall and verbalization.

Comments

It seems quite possible that conflict also plays a role in the production of the a → b pattern. Table 2.3 pulls together the observations we presented and presents the *a* and *b* matters side by side. Generally speaking, the *b* items seem more conflictful—both communicatively and intrapsychically—than the *a* items. Possibly conflict involving the *b* items leads to the cleavage between the nonverbal and verbal manifestations of them and the temporal displacement.

TABLE 2.3
Comparison of the Content of *a* and *b* Items

a	*b*
1. Current symptoms (ring play)	Marital tension.
2. Feelings of inferiority towards husband (hand to mouth)	Childhood ugliness vis-a-vis sister because of buck teeth.
3. Transference affection (rubbing hand on "scratch-plaster" wall)	Bear hugs with father, rubbing her cheek on his scratchy cheek stubble.
4. Reverie concerning possibility of witnessing primal scene (incipient turning onto side and curling legs)	Childhood masturbation.
5. Unsatisfactory current heterosexual escapades (playing with small glass tube used in visual inspection system)	Long standing concern that penis is small and sperm not viable. Desire to examine sperm under microscope.
6. Love making and dancing nude before husband (foot wiggling and wriggling until shoe falls off)	Phantasy of dancing nude before analyst.
7. Hot mountain hike (closes and tucks-in slightly gaping shirt front)	Swimming in nude; erotic childhood bathing by mother.
8. Rivalry with men; erect penises (tensing of abdominal muscles)	Desire to have protruding hard-ball abdomen; dream of foetus' erection; childhood belief that navel was a penis.

It is also our clinical impression, which we cannot yet document, that the degree of temporal displacement is proportional to the strength of defenses and resistances. When the individual seems only minimally anxious and there is otherwise a relatively free progression to his associative drift, the transition from the nonverbal to the verbal seems to occur in minutes, as in some of the examples. With greater anxiety and conflict, the transition may extend over several hours, as in other of the examples. With still greater conflict, the *spontaneous* transition may not occur at all, as in the last observation. Anxiety reduction may be a crucial process in bringing about the transition.

Yet we cannot avoid mentioning another hypothesis too: perhaps the motoric–verbal transition is the normal sequence in remembering, verbalizing, in cognizing in general; perhaps this motoric stage is greatly abbreviated in the adult, reduced from visible action to covert muscular tensions (a la J. B. Watson and others); perhaps the motoric provides feedback recruitment or facilitation that raises the excitatory potential of the unverbalized to the threshold for awareness and verbalization. Maybe conflict and defense simply exaggerate and slow down this entire process. Our observations lead to such a hypothesis, but they cannot prove it. (In the following chapter, I examine in further detail the a → b phenomenon and the hypotheses just raised.)

The a → b phenomenon justifies a broadening of the concept of congruency between the verbal and nonverbal channels. This concept presently refers to *simultaneous congruence*. It may be useful to also think of *sequential congruency*, the degree of which might be measured by the time elapsing between the anticipatory-motor expression and the later verbalization. One could then set about to investigate the controlling variables or the correlates of this dimension of behavior.

Transitory Actions and Dreams

Occasionally we have observed that dreams (a) will be related to or represent transitory actions of waking life and at the same time (b) will be concerned with the unverbalized wishes, thoughts, memories, etc., which those actions seemed to express.

One of the observations already described included a particularly clear instance of this phenomenon. We summarize it in a form that highlights the points with which we are now concerned.

1. The transitory action was a tensing of her abdominal muscles by a pregnant woman.
2. The context in which this action occurred included:
    a. General preoccupation with rivalry with men;
    b. The image of an erect penis; thoughts about her analyst's penis being erect;
    c. and thoughts about her attempt to make her baby-filled belly stick out in a hard protruding ball.
3. From this context, we can infer that her tensing of her abdominal muscles was the expression of her unconscious penis-envy and of the equation of her baby with a penis in her unconscious phantasies.
4. Then she has the dream presented earlier. The dream depicts her abdomen in the state she hoped to achieve by contracting her abdominal muscles: it looms up prominently in her field of vision and it contains protruberances. The manifest and latent dream content are obviously concerned with her wish to have a penis and her phantasy that she has one, i.e., with those things we inferred had been unconscious and expressed when the transitory action occurred.

In waking life an action occurred and we inferred unconscious determinants from the context; in the dream, *both* the action and these unconscious determinants are represented in her body-state percept.

In the following example, the action actually occurs sometime during the night in which the person dreams about the things inferred to be among the unconscious determinants of the action in waking life.

1. In the first few months of her analysis, a woman frequently scratched her arms and scalp during the analytic sessions.

2. From the context, the analyst inferred that this activity was the expression of inhibited, unconscious aggression. A typical pattern would include scratching herself as she mentioned someone's name and subsequent emergence of anger towards this person.

3. One night in her fifth month of analysis she had nightmares off and on all night long. She couldn't remember their details—only the idea in them— there were groups of people and somebody was trying to kill . . . [someone].

She went on to say she discovered scratches on her arm today and she showed them to the analyst. Because she found blood on her pillow or arm in the morning, she thought she scratched herself during these nightmares.

(During a protracted phase of repressed hostility 3 years later, exacerbated by a lengthy interruption in her analysis instigated by her analyst, this woman scratched herself into a state of badly infected forearms requiring medical management.)

The following example is similar to the first of these in that the transitory action of waking life is represented pictorally in the dream. It differs from both the preceding examples, however, in two respects: there is a much longer time interval between the action and the dream [and] in the dream the action and the latent dream content are more disguised. The analysand is the same as in the last example cited.

1. In the second week of her analysis, she started to play with a loose end of thread on a pillow on the couch.

2. She noticed this act and said it made her feel comfortable to do that because it made her feel "anchored to the couch" . . . . The positive tone of this remark was in keeping with another event. The preceding hour was marked by her first reported dream since starting her analysis. And in it she was on the couch and the analyst was present in a protective role. This context of the thread-playing activity suggested that it was a manifestation of an unverbalized, embryonic, developing positive transference.

3. Some 9 months later she had a dream: She is on a boat. First it is threatened by a huge tidal wave, but then it is "tied to a dock" . . . in a beautiful, calm bay.

4. To understand the relationship of this dream to the early episode in her analysis, we begin with the nature of the unconscious wishful-thoughts underlying the manifest dream, including the experience of being "tied to a dock." The nature of these unconscious wishes became clear if we place the dream in its context.

    a. She had the dream just as an erotic transference erupted with an intensity that took her completely by surprise.

    b. She repeatedly spoke of *waves of feeling* when referring to her transference turmoil.

    c. *Tidal wave* was a recurrent dream element for this woman; one of its meanings was orgastic excitation.

    d. Coincident with the transference outbreak, was a striking intensification of frequency of intercourse with her husband. Furthermore, for the first time reported in her analysis they tried to have intercourse in the *shower* and completed it on the bed while their bodies were deliberately left *wet*.

    e. In another dream, her father appeared in a *bathing suit* with a piece of *rope* serving as a phallic symbol.

One plausible conclusion is that the dream was a representation of having intercourse with the analyst, with the tidal wave representing sensual, orgastic excitation and the being "tied to a doc(k)" in a calm bay representing sexual union, probably continued as a peaceful aftermath.

In other words, the unconscious wishes represented by the dream were positive transference wishes. Although intensified and sexualized by nearly a year of the analytic process, they are in the same category as the inferred unconscious determinants of the thread play occurring months before.

What about the thread play? Where was it represented in the dream? In the experience of being "tied to a dock" we concluded—after noting the resemblance of "thread" and "rope," as well as the similarity of the analysand's nautical description of the thread play ("anchored to the couch") and the nautical scene of the dream and after undoing the dream work that translated being "tied to Doc" into "tied to a dock."

Comments

We have several reasons for presenting these observations about transitory actions of waking life and dreams.

The first has to do with evidence that there are unconscious determinants for the transitory actions. The assumption that this is in fact the case underlies the whole argument that transitory actions may anticipate verbalization and, in part, the attempt in the initial interview study to infer personality variables from nonverbal behavior. Finding that dreams dealing with inferred unconscious determinants of transitory actions also include representations of these very same actions provides us with independent evidence compatible with the basic assumption.

The second reason for doing so is methodological. We need to develop methods for determining the idiosyncratic significance of transitory activity. These observations suggest that we should explore the use of dreams for this purpose. The key to this method seems to be the realization that the tendency to perform transitory actions of waking life may be transformed into the sensory images of dreams, just as the latent dream throughts are. In principle there is nothing new here. The same general process occurs in "dreams of convenience," as for example, when an urge to urinate is represented in a dream by the image of one doing so or of a mountain stream. The only novel notion is the suggestion that this process operates specifically in the domain of transitory autistic actions. These observations also suggest that other techniques using other forms of phantasy should be explored. Perhaps the "TAT approach" utilizing simple pictures of people performing actions of interest to the investigator would help in getting at the idiosyncratic significance of body movements. Possibly "tailor-made" sketches, appropriate for unique actions of specific individuals, could be used.

The final reason for presenting these dream observations is the number of questions they raise for further research. Is the phenomenon we have reported a frequent one that has escaped attention because of the kind of disguised representation contained in the third example? Apparently transitory actions can be represented in dreams in different ways: in an appropriate image of the dreamer's body as in the first observation; or in an image pertaining to "external" setting of the dream scene, as in the third. Also, transitory actions may actually occur sometime during the night's sleep, as in the other observation. How general are these alternatives? What actually are all the various ways in which transitory actions may be represented in, or related to, dreams? Is the *instigation* to perform transitory actions a regular part of the state of [the dreamer]. . . ? Are such instigations an important source of the content of the dream? Is the peripheral motor inhibition of the REM state a crucial determinant of the transformation of such motoric instigations into sensory images?

"Ego Processes" in Transitory Actions

The assertion that *unconscious* processes may be manifested in transitory actions does not mean that all such revealed processes are "Id processes," nor that transitory actions are simple manifestations of the repressed unconscious. Some actions *are* simple bodily expressions of unconscious drives; for example, the mouth-fingering of the anorexia patient in the initial interview study. Other actions reflect unconscious defenses, as well, in a direct manner; as, for example, in scratching oneself when turning aggression against the self. But many actions are influenced even more drastically by the process of unconscious defense. And transitory actions may also be primarily reflections of unconscious aspects of "the Super-Ego." The following remarks amplify and illustrate the last two points.

Defense

We have inferred that the process of defense played a significant role in the production of all the transitory actions in the preceding observations by repressing response tendencies or affect-laden thoughts and thereby creating the dynamic conditions conducive to their bodily expression. In some instances, defense also inhibited the actions most relevant for bodily expression. This role of defense created the dynamic conditions conducive to expression in displaced activity. The observation of the analysand who played with the small glass tube illustrates this double role of defense. Repression of his thoughts about the size of his penis, the viability of his sperm, and masturbation created in that man the dynamic conditions favorable for bodily expression. If the effect of defense had ceased at that point, he might have touched his genitals off-and-on instead of playing with the small glass object. He might have done so without realizing it, or under some pretext—such as that he was making himself more comfortable by readjusting things. But he didn't, for the process of defense continued to be active and took his bodily behavior as a target too. The outcome was displaced bodily activity. He played with the glass object instead of touching his penis.

Now, the process of defense might have been extended to even the tendency towards the displaced bodily action. He might have clasped his hands together, for example, or sat on them. That is, the observable action would have been the expression of the defense against the tendency for displaced bodily expression. All of these variations are clear in this case, but this is not always so.

The following observation concerns a brief episode of behavior influenced by all three effects of defense. It occurred one day when a woman started an analytic hour near the end of her fourth year of analysis. She was not conscious of the nature of the defenses. And they were so intricate and decisive to the final outcome that no observer who relied solely on the premise that such actions are simple, direct "Id" expressions could infer the complex set of determinants of the activity.

1. After the analysand entered the room, the analyst turned to close the doors. The analysand followed her customary practice of going directly to the couch and lying down. When the analyst turned from the door and walked by the couch to his chair he sensed that the woman was holding her entire body in a rigid position and was staring straight ahead, fixedly, at a blank wall. When he sat down, the woman unstiffened from toe to head. Her legs,

crossed at the ankle, relaxed. She rearranged her buttocks, trunk, head, and arms into more relaxed positions. The original "stiffening" is the transitory behavior with which we are concerned.

2. Several minutes went by of freely flowing associations that contained no apparent reference to what had just happened. Because her behavior had been unusual, the analyst interrupted; he described what he had observed and noted that she had said nothing about it. She replied that it was true she had felt tense until he was in his chair, but she hadn't realized it was "all that obvious." The rest of her associations that day, and other material from her analysis, made clear why she had made her body rigid for that initial moment in the hour.

She first told of how "direct eye contact is too intimate." She must avoid it. But then she imagined their looking at each other and got a "feeling of painful tenderness" as she did so. Now her eyelid twitched and this reminded her of times past when she had caught a glimpse of the toe of the analyst's shoe out of the corner of her eye. A moment ago, she said, she had in fact just turned her head slightly and done that. The analyst remarked that the twitching in her eyelid was a manifestation of her wish to look at him and the inhibition of the looking. Thereupon she said that several times recently she had thought of suddenly flipping over onto her stomach, propping her head up on her arms-on-elbows, and just facing him in that position. Analyst and analysand would be gazing silently at each other. In fact, she said, she had been thinking of this as she came today. But, she went on, the mere thought of doing this horrified her so much she had put it out of her mind immediately. She hoped she would not think of it here and that she would not do it here. The analyst noted to himself that the urge must be an almost overpowering one. But he only asked [the] . . . patient what occurred to her about flipping over that way. Her first thoughts were of how exposed she feels on the couch. "That reminds me," she went on, "I didn't tell you anything about my D and C." (This had occurred a week earlier.) She related that she has thought of her D and C several times, and always she thought of the doctor *looking at her labia.* At this point she dropped further reference to her subjective experience of the D and C, but the theme of *"female genitals being observable"* ran through her associations: her husband noticed hers as she stepped from the bathtub, a little girl she knows toilets standing up with legs spread apart.

Several months later, the analysand had the *sensation of slightly parting her legs and raising her knees while on the couch.* She did not do it, but felt as if she were. With this came a sense of relaxation and relief from conflict and self-hatred. Then the scene of the D and C recurred to her. She said now that *she had enjoyed that situation,* but had felt very guilty and surprised at that reaction. One other fact about the analysand fills in the picture: throughout her analysis her lips, nose, and eyes were genital substitutes—zones for displaced genital sensations, phantasies, and masturbation. Often her entire face was.

The material points to one conclusion: as the patient lay down on the couch that day and stiffened her body and arms, and kept her eyes averted, she was not only literally inhibiting the repressed, horrifying urge to raise and open her legs, but especially the urge to flip over and prop her head up, for the analyst to gaze at her. It was this thought and urge to action that she had just "put out of her mind" before arriving at the analyst's office. But this action was a displacement for the more strongly inhibited urge to live out the repressed memories of the D and C experience, and the repressed phantasy that the analyst, not the gynecologist, was looking at her labia.

Now this conclusion will sound absurd to many. The key to it is the inference that there is displacement between the two action tendencies (flipping over and lying with legs raised) and also between the two corresponding systems of thoughts and memories. This inference seems inescapable if one considers the following.

1. Associations pertaining to one were followed immediately by associations pertaining to the other.

2. The sense of horror at the thought of flipping-over etc., is only appropriate for the urge to raise her legs and exhibit her genitals. Affect has clearly been displaced.

3. There was a great deal of independent evidence that her face was a genital substitute.

4. If one visualizes her face propped up on her bent arms, then inverts the image and remembers the genital significance of her face, the precision of the bodily displacement and the similarity to the gynecological position become apparent.

5. She mentioned the themes of *intimacy* and *painful tenderness* in connection with her body stiffening in the analyst's presence; they are equally appropriate to the experience on the operating table.

6. A nascent performance of leg raising and parting on the couch is accompanied by full verbalization of the conflicted pleasure she associated with the D and C situation.

Other Ego Reactions

Transitory actions may also reflect other aspects of the Ego besides defense. Affects motivating the defenses may be manifested directly in this way; either in such "mechanical" reactions as the trembling of fear or in more "expressive" reactions as in the face covering of the very ashamed young man of the initial interview study. These ego aspects of nonverbal behavior are so familiar they are not particularly interesting. It is more interesting that "Super-Ego" processes and the Ego-Ideal may be manifested in transitory actions just as in chronic postures and expressions.

A female analysand intermittently "created a commotion" on the couch. Eventually I realized she did this whenever "Id-type" thoughts and sensations became conscious. As time went by the patient began to say it "exasperated" her to have such things occur to her. Then I perceived that "the commotion" consisted of specifiable components: a slight "kick" of a leg, a forceful but slight throwing aside of the hands, accompanied by an audible expiration gasp, and at times a sideward turning of the head. In my imagination I stood the patient up and pictured her doing all this on her feet instead of on her back on the couch. I concluded she was pantomiming a state of *exasperation*. Now, this was one of her typical "Super-ego reactions," taken over from her parents. In *self-exasperation* she was stamping her foot, throwing her arms apart, and exhaling noisily. She reacted to her Id-intrusions as to a mischievious child.

A young business trainee, who usually hung his coat on a rack and always placed anything he was carrying on the floor at the foot of the couch, caught the analyst's attention one day by placing *his briefcase on a chair and laying his coat on top of the case*. In subsequent hours he resumed his former behavior. Neither analysand nor analyst said anything about this unusual bit of behavior.

Within a few minutes he was speaking about his ambivalent relation with a particular supervisor, Mr. K, to whom he had been assigned for several weeks. Some of his remarks described an episode of the night before. He had gone to the office the night before to do some extra work. When he entered he saw his *supervisor's briefcase and raincoat on top of a table in one of the offices*, but Mr. K himself was not in sight. The young man got little work done, for he was continually distracted by thoughts about Mr. K. He wondered where K was in the building and hoped that K would see him there working. And due to a strange, compelling urge the young man moved his work from one office to another in the hope that K would come upon him. After describing this episode, the analysand went on to say that another group of employees, with slightly more seniority, had arranged the day before to have Mr. K supervise them too and thus spend less time with the analysand and his peers. Now he feels jealous, to his surprise.

In the succeeding days, the analysand spoke of Mr. K in terms of the greatest respect and admiration. And he also demanded that clerks treat him with the same respect in front of customers as they accorded to Mr. K.

This observation presents in miniature the process of unconscious identification with an idealized object upon the loss of the object. The transitory act of placing his briefcase and coat on the chair appeared to be one manifestation of this process.

General Comments

We have been impressed with the extent to which interest in the intrapsychic aspect of transitory actions has decreased in the literature. On the one
hand, psychoanalytic discussions of nonverbal behavior have emphasized
increasingly chronic nonverbal behaviors (see e.g., Braatoy, 1954; Reich,
1958) and their relation to personality characteristics. Allport's (1961) most
recent discussion of expressive behavior has the same accent. Our observations suggest that the study of nonverbal behavior in the therapeutic interview can still profitably include the study of transitory actions as well as
chronic behavior. Such study will not only result in a more complete understanding of the individual involved; it may also lead to new discoveries, as is
suggested by the novel findings that some transitory actions anticipate verbalization and that dreams may contain representations of transitory actions
of waking life.

Those investigators who have shown the most interest in transitory actions have approached this area primarily from the standpoint of interpersonal regulation and communication (see e.g., Birdwhistell 1952, 1956,
1970; Scheflen 1963, 1964, 1965). Consequently, most of the recent discussions of such nonverbal behavior have been concerned with these interpersonal aspects. There is a danger in the emphasis of psychoanalysis on the
chronic and the emphasis of these workers on interpersonal regulation and
communication: the intrapsychic aspects of transitory actions may be ignored, if not actually forgotten. Observations such as those presented earlier
strongly suggest that transitory actions cannot be adequately accounted for
only in terms of interpersonal communication, signaling, or regulation.
There must be a significant place for internal variables of the types discussed. In the next two sections, we consider this point further.

THE VISUAL SITUATION OF THE INTERVIEW: ITS
EFFECT ON GESTURES AND BODY MOVEMENTS[7]

In this section of the chapter, we report briefly an experimental study of the
changes in the *frequency* of communicative gestures and autistic actions when
one moves from the usual face-to-face interview situation to a back-to-back
situation. In the latter condition, one can neither see the other participant,
nor be seen by that person.

---

[7]I am very grateful to several people for their assistance in executing this study: especially to
Burton Danet, but also to Susan Cohen, Betty Jo McGrade, and to Gene Schulze. Some of the
following material was part of a paper presented at the 16th International Congress of Psychology, Bonn, 1960 (Mahl, 1961b).

Background. Freud's early observations, the initial interview study, and clinical observations of the type just presented left us convinced that a very large number of transitory, idiosyncratic actions occurring in interviews were expressions of internal states. If one wanted to assign them a primary function, we have assumed it would have to be a "discharge" or "expressive" function, in contrast to a "communicative" or "interpersonal-regulative" function.

Birdwhistell's approach (1952, 1956, 1963, e.g.,) cast considerable doubt upon such a conclusion. The purely interpersonal orientation to psychotherapy did too. One often hears, even from [one's] . . . own careless lips, such statements as the following. "When the patient played with her wedding ring, she was trying to communicate her conflicting attitudes about her marriage." "When the patient rubbed his nose as he told you he had benefited greatly from his therapy with you, he really wanted to communicate his contempt for you." And so forth.

The combined impact of the purely interpersonal orientation to therapy and of Birdwhistell's very compatible, linguistic-communicative kinesic approach is made even stronger by the discovery that some of the actions we have regarded as purely "expressive," or "discharges," are used intentionally, and as symbols (i.e., as institutionalized, arbitrary signs assumed to have a shared meaning for sender and receiver), in the arts and in the language of signs used by the deaf. Shakespeare used the work and the image of "scratching" in referring to "aggression;" so does the pantomime literature (see Footnote 3). We find in the deaf sign language (Long, 1944) several instances in which "autistic actions" are actual communicative symbols, referring to the same affects that we have assumed they "expressed." In the sign language, for example, covering the side of the face with the hand signifies "shame," scratching the body wall, "anger," grasping the end of the nose indicates "snubbing" or "turning up one's nose at something," and flicking one's finger signifies "dislike" or "despise." In the initial interview study, we had ascribed identical expressive meanings to these same actions—unwittingly, we should add. It is apparent that hearing-people also use such actions for intentional communication under various conditions. Thus, one could argue that the patients we have observed were doing preconsciously what others often do consciously—communicating, not expressing or discharging, via these actions.

Furthermore, our observations focused only on the patients, not on their interaction with the interviewer or therapist. This methodological deficit could very well result in a distorted conclusion about the determinants of autistic actions, because the latter were studied out of interpersonal context. Their role in interpersonal regulation, (Scheflen, 1963, 1964, 1965), for example, could have been completely overlooked.

All of these are powerful arguments that autistic actions are communicative and regulatory, more relevant to interpersonal interaction than to intrapersonal processes. But they are not final and conclusive arguments. The purely communicative, interpersonal orientation to psychotherapy is obviously one sided, in our opinion. And, when carried to extreme, it uses the concept of communication in such a broad sense that it loses its customary and useful meaning. At least it places one in the danger of viewing everything the patient does that is *informative* to the therapist, or observer, as though it were also *communicative* in motivation. If one speaks of a patient communicating via a parapraxis, one might as well speak of a thermometer communicating a change in temperature to an observer by a change in the height of the mercury column. Such a practice would obviously contribute nothing to our understanding of the conditions controlling the behavior of thermometers. Nor does it help us to understand nonverbal behavior.

The fact that actions can be intentionally performed for communicative purposes does not mean they are never expressive. A startled look can be used for communication, but this does not mean that every startled look is determined by a communicative intention, nor by any interpersonal variables. One can be startled directly and automatically by external or internal stimuli, when alone or when in a group.

The methodology used by those of the interpersonal and communicative approach has its weakness too: the ignoring of the internal, intrapersonal variables. Consequently, the interpersonal view of autistic actions may be just as one-sided as the intrapersonal view.

There is something else, however, that is even more suggestive that autistic action is not intended to be communicative. This is the observation that autistic actions are inhibited when the performer realizes that the other participant is aware of them. Anyone can satisfy himself on this score by letting his gaze settle on someone's jiggling foot, scratching or tapping finger, or mouth stimulation. These actions will then stop, usually with behavioral signs that the performer has suddenly become uneasy—such as momentary tension and postural shift. A related phenomenon can frequently be observed when people are seated at tables: a great deal of autistic action may occur below the tabletop, with minimal action in the directly visible portions of the body above the tabletop.

These observations are consistent with the emphasis on intrapersonal variables. For if such actions are caused by repressed, unverbalized affect-laden processes, one would expect that the actions themselves would frequently be the targets of defense. Some of our clinical observations were consistent with this expectation.

In short, it is possible to support (at least) two views of transitory autistic actions. One emphasizes their interpersonal-regulatory, communicative function, and often their communicative motivation. In a sense, this view maintains such actions occur *because* of the interpersonal-communicative situation. The other view emphasizes their intrapersonal, expressive function, and denies they have any communicative motivation. The spirit of this view is that these actions occur *in spite of* the interpersonal-communicative situation. The present experiment was done to *explore* the validity of these two views.[8]

An increase in the frequency of autistic actions upon changing from the face-to-face to a back-to-back interview situation would be consistent with the "expressive view." In the latter condition the subject would not be influenced by any negatively toned visual feedback from the interviewer and, because he knew *he* was not seen, he would be relieved of the inhibitory effect we have assumed is exerted by the face-to-face condition. The expressive view says nothing about the kind of change that might occur in the frequency of communicative gestures. (See chapter 1 and the report of the initial interview study for the distinction between communicative gestures and autistic actions, and for illustrations.)

The kinds of changes one would predict on the basis of the interpersonal, communicative view are difficult to specify; it has not been addressed to behavior in a situation comparable to the back-to-back condition. Perhaps the most reasonable expectation to attribute to this view is that the frequency of communicative gestures and that of autistic actions should change in the same direction with the manipulation of the visual situation.

Procedure

The following procedure was developed in a pilot study involving 12 young adults.

Subjects

Sixteen college students, 8 male and 8 female, were interviewed according to the schedule to be described. All were attending summer school and were recruited through the student employment office. They were paid at a nominal rate. Their ages ranged from 19 to 29 years; the mean age was 21.

The Interviews

Instructions

Each subject was told at the outset about the procedures he would directly experience: that he would be interviewed about his personal life, on

---

[8*1986*. The reader will find in Dittmann (1971) and Kendon (1972) the views of two other psychologists concerning Birdwhistell's (1970) work. Both writers have been seriously involved in studies of nonverbal behavior. Dittman's review is largely skeptical; Kendon's is largely a very clear, and laudatory, explication of Birdwhistell's approach.]

two different occasions, once by a male interviewer and once by a female interviewer; that one-half of each interview would be conducted in the face-to-face situation, and the other half in the back-to-back situation; that the interviews would be tape-recorded for later study; that his palmar perspiration would be measured before and after each condition; that he would be asked about his reactions to the face-to-face and back-back conditions, and that he would also take a personality test (MMPI).

The purpose of the experiment was explained as the exploration of people's reactions to, and "inner experiences" in, the face-face and back-back conditions. The elements of how they felt and internally experienced these conditions were emphasized. The other procedures were explained as additional sources of information that would enable the investigators to determine how different kinds of people reacted to the two conditions. The subjects were not told until the end of the second interview that we had been interested in the effect of the manipulation on their nonverbal behavior, nor that they had been observed through a one-way mirror during the interviews.

The Interviews

Each subject was interviewed on two different days. Each interview lasted for 50 minutes, 25 minutes in each of the two conditions. One entire interview was conducted by a male interviewer, the other by a female, each a few years older than the subject. The sequence of the sex of the interviewer over the two interviews was varied systematically in a counterbalanced design. The sequence of the face-face and the back-back conditions was the same in both interviews for a given subject, but this sequence was varied systematically from subject to subject in counterbalanced fashion.

The content of the interviews was standardized to the following extent. In the first condition of both interviews the areas of school, hobbies and recreation, and dating were explored for about 12 minutes and then his vocational interests were discussed for the other 12 minutes, approximately. The discussion during the second condition of both interviews concerned the subject's family life, with roughly the first 12 minutes being devoted to his current family life and the remaining 12 minutes to his early life. Within the restrictions of topical areas and time detailed previously, the interviews were open-ended. Two male and two female interviewers participated in the study.

Dependent Measures: Frequency Ratings of Communicative Gestures and Autistic Actions

Two, and sometimes three, independent raters observed the subjects through a one-way mirror. They did not hear the interviews. At the end of each condition, each judge rated the frequency of the two classes of activity on 5-point scales. In addition, they checked on a list, designed for this

TABLE 2.4
Reliability Coefficients of Mean Ratings for the Three Pairs of Observers

Ratings	Observer pairs[a]		
	1	2	3
Freqeuncy of communicative gestures	.75***	.64***	.78***
Frequency of autistic gestures	.52*	.58***	.87***
Expansiveness of basic position	.85***	.82***	.75*
Frequency of shifts in basic position	.93***	.92***	.81***

[a]All p values are one tailed.
*$p < .09$.
**$p < .003$.
***$p < .001$.

purpose, the most characteristic communicative gestures and autistic actions manifested by the subject in that condition. The relevance of this device for the present report is that it served to specify a broad range of activities for the raters to observe. The data analysis to be reported was based on the mean ratings of the independent observers. The reliability coefficients of the mean ratings for the three possible pairs of observers are presented in Table 2.4.

Ratings of Expansiveness of the Basic Postural Positions and of the Frequency of Shifts in the Basic Position

Independent ratings of these variables were also made by the observers at the end of each interview condition, on 5-point scales. The reliability coefficients of the mean ratings on these scales are also presented in Table 2.4. These ratings are relevant for this report as possible indices of the degree of discomfort or anxiety induced by the experimental manipulation.

Palmar Perspiration

This was measured by the technique described by Mowrer, Light, Luria, and Zeleny (1953). The fingerprints were taken at the beginning and end of each condition in each interview. These measures were also to be used as indices of the degree of discomfort induced by the experimental manipulation.

Non-Ah Speech Disturbance Ratios

The interviews were transcribed and this measure of speech disruption (see chapter 9) . . . obtained for each condition. It too was to be used as an index of the difference in anxiety in the two visual situations (see chapter 10–15) . . . The scoring reliability of the person determining these ratios was consistently above .85 in other studies; no separate interscorer reliability was determined for this particular scoring.

Evaluation of the Inquiries

At the end of each interview, the interviewer inquired about the subjects' inner reactions to the two conditions. Usually 5 minutes was spent in this exploration. Two of the people who had been interviewers subsequently listened to the tape recordings of the inquiries and independently judged whether the subject felt "more comfortable" in one condition or the other, or the same in both conditions. They made these judgments for each interview and for both interviews combined. In making this latter "overall judgment," which is the one to be used later in the report, the two judges agreed exactly in their evaluations for 15 of the 16 subjects.

Results and Comments

When the subjects moved from the face-to-face situation to the back-to-back situation were was a significant increase in the frequency of autistic actions and a significant decrease in the frequency of communicative gestures. Inspection of the details of the data, and appropriate tests of significance where suggested, revealed this effect was the same in both male and female subjects, in both interviews, and with both male and female interviewers. The mean ratings in the two conditions, in both interviews, for all subjects are shown in Table 2.5. The p values are for t tests for correlated measures.

The differences found cannot be attributed to the general topics discussed, nor to the sequence of the two conditions, for the design controlled for such spurious effects. There must be some other explanation.

One possibility deserving serious consideration is that the subjects were made anxious and uncomfortable by the back-to-back condition. Because "autistic actions" include such responses as rapid foot movements, picking at the chair arms, self-scratching, touching parts of the body, etc., one could argue that these are "nervous actions" and that they increased in the back-to-back condition because that situation made the subjects anxious and tense. Furthermore, the decrease in the frequency of communicative gestur-

TABLE 2.5
Mean Frequency Ratings for all Subjects in Both Interviews

Type of movement	Visual condition of interview		
	Face-face	*Back-back*	p^1
Communicative gestures	3.06	2.36	< .001
Autistic acts	3.05	3.73	<.001

ing may simply be an indirect result of that effect. Maybe that decrease was due to the fact that less time was available for such gesturing because the subjects were performing more nervous acts.

None of the measures obtained as indices of anxiety or discomfort, however, support that explanation. (a) The inquiry evaluations reveal that only four subjects reported feeling more uncomfortable in the back-to-back condition. Seven reported experiencing greater comfort in that condition! Five said they were equally comfortable in both conditions. So the group trend of reported comfort–discomfort is not consistent with the explanation based on "nervousness" or discomfort.[9] Moreover, the four subjects reporting greater discomfort in the back-to-back situation actually showed a smaller effect of that condition on autistic activity than the other subjects. This effect was only significant, however, when these four were compared with the five subjects reporting no difference in comfort in the two conditions ($p^1 = .05$; t test). (b) The ratings of expansiveness of basic postural positions and of the frequency of changes in basic positions were the same for the two conditions. In other words, the subjects did not assume more cramped, constricted positions, nor shift about more frequently, in the back-to-back condition than in the face-to-face condition. (c) Finally, the frequency of speech disruptions and the amount of palmar perspiration were no greater in the back-to-back than in the face-to-face situation.

We believe the results might be due to two different consequences of the removal of the *seen and seeing* participant in the interview. The decrement of the communicative gesturing seems to be best explained as a direct reflection of the fact that the stimulus conditions under which we usually engage in such activity were removed with the shift to the back-to-back conditions. Although people occasionally engage in communicative gesturing when there is no visible and seeing audience present, they usually don't. Entering into a face-to-face situation provides the adequate and appropriate stimulus situation for communicative gesturing, posturing, facial expressions, and the like. Quite the contrary for autistic action manifesting unverbalized, repressed processes. Defense sustained on purely intrapersonal grounds is directed towards the motoric expression of the unverbalized, as well as towards the process of conscious ideation and verbalization. To this internal

---

[9]*1986*. Siegman and Reynolds (1983) also studied the behavior of college student interviewees in the face-face and back-back conditions. They used a between-subjects design and one interview that was apparently shorter than ours. They did not study nonverbal behavior but they did obtain self-ratings by the subjects of their discomfort, anxiety, and ease of communication during the interviews. The results of these self-ratings were generally similar to our comfort–discomfort data. Their female subjects reported no difference in discomfort, anxiety, and ease of communication in the two conditions with either male or female interviewers, nor did the male subjects with female interviewers. The males did report greater discomfort, anxiety, and less ease of communication in the back-back condition with male interviewers.]

inhibitory pressure, the presence of a "seen and seeing audience" adds another. Entering into a face-to-face situation creates a condition for further inhibition of autistic action. (People get on their "good behavior" in the presence of others.) The assumption that moving from a face-to-face condition provides a "disinhibition" of autistic actions seems to provide the best explanation for the greater frequency of autistic actions in the back-to-back condition.

Two suggestive observations obtained in the course of the study are compatible with this explanation. The first is the description of the back-back condition by seven subjects as being the more comfortable, relaxing one. These reports are only suggestive, for they may simply reflect deliberate or unconscious compliance by the subjects with what they perceived as our wishes. But the reports are consistent with our general impression of the subjects' "being freed motorically" in the back-to-back condition. In this regard, we were particularly struck by two subjects. One was an exploratory subject who displayed transitory flashes of vivacious behavior in the face-to-face condition. When she moved into the back-to-back condition, it was as though a heavy mail garment which previously allowed for only slight bursts of vivaciousness had suddenly been cast-off. For now she literally vibrated and bounced in her chair for most of the back-to-back condition. The other was a male subject who rubbed his genitals in the back-to-back conditions of both interviews, but never in the face-to-face conditions.

If the increase in the frequency of autistic actions in the back-back condition is due to "disinhibition," why then were not the speech disturbance and the palmar perspiration measures decreased in that condition, and the ratings dealing with the basic posture appropriately affected? One can only speculate about these questions. One possibility is that the disinhibition may not have been strong enough to affect all these response systems. But our experience with the speech disruption measure is that it is an extremely sensitive index of anxiety and conflict. The fact that it did not reflect the inferred disinhibition, but that the autistic actions did, suggests an interesting *hypothesis:* that *the disinhibition was "channel specific," in keeping with the fact that the visual situation was altered.* Because the interviewer could not see the subject, the subject's visible motoric behavior could be disinhibited; but because the interviewer could still hear the subject talk, no channel specific disinhibition of speech could occur.

What seems to us to be the most plausible explanation of the results concerning autistic actions, rests squarely on the assumption that most such actions in the interview situation have an expressive or discharge function, not a communicative function. This conclusion is not only compatible with that reached from our psychoanalytic observations, but also with the finding in the present study that *the changes in the frequencies of communicative gestures and autistic actions diverged.* If our ratings are valid, this finding alone suggests that the functions of the two classes of actions are distinct. Replication of this finding should be attempted. If that is accomplished, theory dealing with nonverbal behavior could take a step forward, for it would be apparent that the treatment of *all* activity as communicative would be questionable. . . .

(In chapter 6, Wolf reports a further study of the visual situation of the interview, as well as the effect of gender in interview interaction.)

PSYCHOANALYTIC OBSERVATIONS ON A COMMUNICATIVE GESTURE

By now the reader has no doubts of my conviction that no adequate account of nonverbal behavior can ignore the extent to which it is controlled by the subject's internal, personal world. So far, the role of internal processes in the determination of transitory autistic actions has been especially emphasized. But we believe the influence of repressed internal processes extends further than that. We have noted several times that previous research has shown it also extends to chronic, characteristic postures and motor attitudes.

We assume this intrapersonal control also extends to characteristic *communicative* gestures. Some of the results of the initial interview study were compatible with that assumption. Now we are going to present some psychoanalytic observations concerning a specific communicative gesture. These observations do not tell the whole story about either the interpersonal nor the intrapersonal determination of the gesture. But they do tell enough to clearly demonstrate the importance of internal, personal events in the performance of a single communicative gesture by one individual. They point to a barely explored area of research.

The gesture, *the finger*, appears in Fig. 2.8. The subject was a very intelligent, upwardly mobile, businessman who entered analysis because of work inhibitions and repeated conflicts with authority figures.

One of his earliest communications when he started analysis concerned a recent episode of rebellious behavior towards his superior, who was a respected person in the concern. One day his superior had called a meeting of his lieutenants, including the analysand. At one point in the discussion, the superior said something that made him appear in our man's eyes as unfair and inconsiderate in the treatment of subordinates. Before he realized what he was doing, the analysand had given his superior *the finger* in front of the entire group.

Several months of analysis went by in which the analysand referred several times to having given *the finger* to someone or other. Now it was done in open anger and defiance, now in joking, bantering competitiveness with peers, never without any affect. A prominent concern of being "one-up" in

FIG. 2.8.   "The finger" gesture.

personal relations permeated this phase of his analysis and was always associated with *the finger*. When he had committed this gesture in the staff meeting, part of his message had been the angry accusation that his superior was playing a cruel one-upmanship with his subordinates. Most of the other gestural instances he referred to in the early analytic months were times when he consciously felt either that the other person had somehow "one-upped" him and he was evening the score by giving that person *the finger*, or that he was simply one-upping the other for the sheer pleasure involved. During these early months, the analysand had not committed *the finger* spontaneously in the analytic situation.

Then one day his associations included the following childhood memories. When he was 7 years old, he and a little girl had played "doctor." She was the sick patient and he, the doctor. His ministrations included pulling down her panties and giving her an enema by holding the tip of his loosened belt to her buttocks. Later that day the two children told the two mothers of their game. The talion principle governed his mother's reaction. "Oh, so you want to play enema? OK I'll give you one so you'll never forget. I'll give you one so you can see what it can be like." And she did. Using lots of water. He still remembered the rage he felt at his helplessness as she forcibly carried out the punishment.

The analysand fairly bustled into the next analytic session. He felt great when he left yesterday, he said, and still felt that way. He described how he had returned to his working establishment after yesterday's session. Upon passing by a room he saw a friend sitting with others about a table. He was feeling so good, he went on, that he paused at the door to the room and, thrusting his arm in the air, gave the friend *the finger*. His friend nearly collapsed with laughter. The analysand repeated the whole story again, this time with a vigorous demonstration of how he had made *the finger*.

Then his thoughts drifted to a wide variety of other things. He would touch on something only to drop it when the analyst responded in any way whatever. But then the analysand paused and said, "I'm jousting, wrestling with you. I want to be one-up on you." The analyst commented: "You may be reacting to recalling the things you remembered yesterday."

The analysand thought of *the finger* episode that occurred after he left yesterday. And he described it again, adding that he felt one-up on his friend by giving him *the finger* in front of the others, where there was nothing the friend could do in return. Again, the analysand spontaneously and vigorously made *the finger* from the couch, spiraling his hand upward from the surface of the couch to a point in the air limited only by the length of his fully extended arm. And all of this was now with sound effects, similar to those made by the turning of the screw. He was thoroughly enjoying himself.

He suddenly quieted down as he talked again about how he felt one-up on the analyst today and how he felt like wrestling. The analyst now noticed that the man had slid his hand under his buttock. This prompted him to comment on the conflict over, and inhibition of, his wish to be one-up on the analyst, his need to inhibit making *the finger* at the analyst, the similarity between the gesture and the enema, and that between "wrestling with the analyst" and "being forcefully given an enema by his mother." (Many aspects of the theme of being one-up, etc., with his mother and the analyst were subsequently worked through including the hidden erotic gratifications involved in it.)

A year went by, after this hour, before there was any further reference to *the finger*. One day the analyst inadvertently got one-up by discovering a minor instance of unconsciously motivated forgetting by the analysand and communicating that to him. The man acknowledged tha analyst's "victory" with a grin and a half-hearted, curled, barely perceptible *finger*.

The finger is a communicative gesture; it is provided by culture; it is interpersonal; it occurred in this man's behavior under the pressure of current motivations. All this fits the paradigm for linguistic behavior so clearly stated by Bloomfield (1933). But an explanation limited to this frame of reference does not adequately account for this man's use of the gesture. In fact, such an explanation seems to be one that stops after barely beginning.

This man used the gesture *to be* one-up. But being one-up meant a particular thing to him: that he was the active administerer of enemas instead of the passive receiver. That is why this was his favorite communicative gesture. There are many other verbal and nonverbal devices for being one-up. But none of them so aptly expressed his internal phantasied version of being one-up.

These remarks assume that the repressed memories and phantasies of his childhood enema experience, and the anxiety and rage associated with them, were among the critical sources of his need to be one-up, of the phantasies of being one-up, *and the expression of that need and those phantasies in the finger.* This assumption seems inescapable in view of the analytic data: the flare-up of this gestural activity with the recall of the memories, the subsequent subsidence of the activity, and the similarity between current life situations that evoked the gesture and the "unfair" enema administered by his mother who thereby was literally one-up, and the transformation of the exuberant *finger* in the analytic hour to *the finger*-placed-under-his buttock.

One would feel more confident that reactions stemming from the enema experience were important determinants of this gesture, if there were "independent" evidence of such reactions in other areas of his life. There is such evidence. He had a repetitive conscious phantasy of sewing shut the apertures of a woman's body and having it filled with fluid by various ingenous means until it burst. In the phantasy, this man is actively doing to the woman what he "experienced" passively at the hands of his mother. In performing *the finger*, he is doing the same thing essentially. Only the means and the object have been modified.

Comment

One cannot help wondering if many communicative actions, and those many subtle actions that regulate interpersonal relations in the fashion described by Scheflen (1963, 1964, 1965), might not be under the same kind of *ultimate* control by internal, intrapersonal processes as seemed to be the case for *the finger*. And we cannot help wondering if an explanation of nonverbal behavior in terms of social system concepts will not be significantly altered as it incorporates intrapersonal determinants.

CONCLUDING COMMENTS

Each section of this chapter included specific comments about the observations reported in it and about the questions raised at the end of the introduction. Therefore, our concluding comments are more general and consider further the general issues with which we opened this chapter.

The two previous conferences on Research in Psychotherapy did not include papers on nonverbal behavior simply because there aren't many people investigating gestures and body movements during interviews. Very few relevant papers appeared in the past 10 years. There is only an occasional paper in the psychoanalytic literature reporting detailed, concrete observations (e.g., Zeligs, 1957). And only Scheflen's recent papers (1963, 1964, 1965) have presented any substantial, systematic material cast in the framework of Birdwhistell's "linguistic" approach (1952, 1956, 1963). Boomer and Dittmann and their colleagues, have steadily pursued their rigorous studies of movement frequency and emotional states (Boomer, 1963; Boomer & Dittmann, 1964; Dittmann, 1963) and of the affect cues provided by movements in the head and body (Dittmann, Parloff, & Boomer, 1965). They have also been studying the temporal distribution of hand, head, and foot movements during the phonemic clause (Dittmann, 1966). Ekman, of course, will be describing his own work in his conference paper (Ekman & Friesen, 1968).

Even though the amount of work being done is small, it is helping to undo a gross generalization and self-deception committed by American psychology following the failure of earlier studies using posed photographs to support the commonly held belief that one could identify emotional states from facial expression. American psychology seems to have tacitly concluded that not only were those particular posed facial expressions devoid of cues of emotional states, but also that no expressive behavior really reflected anything of psychodynamic significance. This conclusion produced a malaise. The aforementioned work, as well as Ekman's and ours, should be the antidote. Contemporary research provides ample ground for believing that many aspects of nonverbal behavior are for many reasons relevant variables for psychotherapy research and for more general personality research as well. This is one reason it should stimulate future work on nonverbal behavior in psychotherapy research. There is another reason too: contemporary work is developing research tools. *Research tools include conceptual frameworks and researchable questions, as well as methodological techniques.* The investigators previously mentioned, and Ekman, of course, are developing all three kinds of tools. Whatever value our own work has, consists, we believe, of its contribution to these research tools.

Methodological tools. (a) *The technique of experimentally manipulating the visual conditions of interaction* appears to be a promising one for investigating some of the controlling effects of the interpersonal situation on nonverbal behavior. It might be useful, for example, in differentiating between the inhibitory and the instigating or shaping effects of the seeing and seen presence of various kinds of participants, on various kinds of behavior, performed by various kinds of people. (b) We hope we have demonstrated how valuable the *psychoanalytic technique* is for obtaining information about the determinants of expressive and communicative actions and also for the making of observations that may turn out upon further clinical and experimental work to be new discoveries. The observations concerning the nonverbal anticipation of verbalization and the possible representation of autistic actions in dreams are examples of what we mean by the latter. No other technique we know of provides the opportunity for making such observations.

Researchable questions have been raised at various points in the . . . [chapter], either in the explicit form of questions or in the form of hypotheses, and are not repeated here. Every conclusion we have asserted we actually regard as a researchable question, in view of the exploratory nature of our work.

Conceptual tools. (a) We hope we have shown how useful *psychoanalytic conceptions* are for research on nonverbal behavior, a point that we would take for granted and not mention if it weren't for the present-day renewed skepticism and even antagonism towards psychoanalytic thinking and for the ignoring of these conceptions in recent discussions of nonverbal behavior. (b) Our observations at least give cause for hesitation to anyone who regards the *"expressive model"* as irrelevant to all nonverbal behavior—whether it is communicative gesturing or idiosyncratic and autistic actions. We ourselves have concluded that the expressive model cannot be dispensed with in understanding any kind of nonverbal behavior. But we do not want to leave the impression that we regard the communicative or the interpersonal-regulatory orientations as erroneous or irrelevant in regard to any kind of nonverbal behavior. That stance would not only be unjustified, but absurd. Our research has not focused on the interpersonal matrix. We take it for granted that the two approaches must be integrated. That is one of the major tasks ahead.

Some people wonder what concern with such general issues has to do with psychotherapy research. . . . Our response is that one must be concerned with such issues, for the type of research one does with the nonverbal behavior in psychotherapy will be influenced by his position on them. We also believe, however, that an important reason for investigating nonverbal behavior in psychotherapy is because the general psychology of this behavior stands to gain from it.

Of course psychotherapy as a discipline stands to gain too. Exactly what potential gains one foresees is an individual matter, and the actual ones are hardly predictable. So whatever reasons one gives for including the study of nonverbal behavior in psychotherapy research reflect personal interests and curiosities. At the moment we are curious about the following things. Let us suppose that astute observers only *watched* psychotherapies from beginning to end. Would they be able to describe meaningful changes in the patient's nonverbal behavior over the course of therapy? If so, would they then be able to relate these changes to identifiable *verbal*, intentional therapeutic interventions by the therapist? To other qualities of the therapist's behavior, including his nonverbal behavior, not intended by him? Would the pattern of changes be the same in therapies guided by different theoretical precepts?

How would the nonverbal picture of the natural history of a psychotherapy compare with pictures based on verbal content analyses? The observations of the initial interview study suggest that the patient's nonverbal behavior reflects significant aspects of his current conflicts and defenses. Would changes in nonverbal interview behavior be valuable additions to outcome criteria? These would be interesting experiments. (See chapter 7 for a further discussion of this matter.)

Many people, including nonverbal behavior researchers themselves, keep raising one particular question: does nonverbal behavior really provide the therapist or researcher with any additional information about the patient beyond that supplied by his verbal behavior. If it does not, then the costly study of nonverbal behavior during psychotherapy will be unjustified, they feel. Now, this question is not only imprecise (it does not specify, for example, the point in time in psychotherapy to which it applies, nor what kinds of information are being referred to), it misses the point. Nonverbal behavior occurs during psychotherapy and is apparently relevant to factors and processes of concern to psychotherapists. The point is to study it and determine its principles of operation. Whether, when, and how it serves as an independent source of information about what relevant variables are important but subsidiary issues. And they can only be judged after a great deal of research. Worrying about such reasons for studying nonverbal behavior is like ruminating over whether one should climb Mt. Everest simply because it is there or whether one should have a baby because its future is unknown.

Body Movement, Ideation and Verbalization During Psychoanalysis[1]

This chapter presents a detailed study of the A → B phenomenon that was discussed briefly in the preceding chapter, pages 43–51.

INTRODUCTION

I focus on *one* role of actions in the process of verbalization in psychoanalysis. The actions I discuss are familiar to every analyst, who usually regards them as expressions of the repressed. In his case reports and technique papers, Freud cited such actions and saw them in that light (Breuer & Freud, 1893–95/1955; Freud, 1905/1953b, 1909/1955a, 1909/1955b, 1913/1958a, 1914/1958b, 1918/1955c). To mention but one example, he noticed that Dora repeatedly opened her handbag and put her finger in it during one of her analytic hours. Only a few days earlier, she had claimed she had no memories of masturbating in childhood. Freud concluded that Dora betrayed her secret in these actions (Freud, 1905/1953b).

In *Remembering, Repeating, and Working Through*, Freud (1914/1958b) proposed that such actions were instances in which the analysand "does not *remember* anything of what he has forgotten and repressed, but *acts* it out. He

[1]Reprinted with the permission of the editors and publisher (with slight editorial and stylistic revisions) from N. Freedman and S. Grand (Eds.), *Communicative Structures and Psychic Structures*. New York: Plenum, 1977, pp. 291–310. Proceedings of a symposium held at the Downstate Medical Center, Brooklyn, January 15–17, 1976. A version of this chapter was presented to the Western New England Psychoanalytic Society, June 20, 1970.

reproduces it not as a memory but as an action; he *repeats* it, without, of course, knowing that he is repeating it" (p. 150). And he said, "in the end we understand that this is his way of remembering" (p. 150). Freud added that this repetition was a function of the resistance.

Our findings suggest that many such actions are not simply alternative ways of remembering. Instead many of them appear to be integral to recollection and verbalization. The following observation, made over 15 years ago during a study of initial interviews at an outpatient clinic (Mahl, 1968; Mahl, Danet, & Norton, 1959) suggested this alternative view. [See chapter 2, pp. 43ff.].

When Mrs. B was discussing her inferiority feelings as a wife and homemaker, she *once placed her fingers over her mouth for a moment.* Three minutes later she was saying, *spontaneously,* that her feelings of inferiority dated from her childhood. Then she had felt she was homely and not as pretty as her sister, because she then had *two ugly protruding front teeth.* We inferred that the slight action of putting her fingers to her mouth anticipated, and perhaps facilitated, this recollection and verbalization about her childhood buckteeth.

The remainder of this chapter is concerned with the phenomenon illustrated by this observation. For convenience, I call it the A → B phenomenon. The initial interview study provided several other instances of it. Then I began to notice it occurring during the analytic hours of three analysands. Eventually I started to keep daily records of portions of two additional analyses, so as to establish a systematic body of clinical data pertaining to the phenomenon.

These records consist of process notes [written after each hour], supplemented by detailed records of the analysand's nonverbal behavior. I recorded the behavioral observations immediately following the hour, annotating them with mnemonic keys to the verbal content of the hour. The more complete reconstruction of the hour was nearly always completed later the same day, and always before the analysand's next analytic hour. The global postures were recorded in stick figure drawings comparable to Felix Deutsch's posturograms (F. Deutsch, 1952). Smaller unusual, or repetitive, idiosyncratic actions, as with the hands, for example, were indicated in improvised sketches, or with appropriate labels. Such systematic, daily records are the raw data for nearly all that follows in this chapter.

At no time did I comment to my analysands about their A → B phenomena. I tried not to vary my interaction with them because of this research. I continued to mostly listen—and watch.

The presentation is organized as follows: First, I summarize and sometimes illustrate what I believe to be certain attributes of the A → B phenomenon. Then I present excerpts from the first few weeks of a single analysis. Finally, I discuss theoretical ideas prompted by all the clinical observations.

SOME ATTRIBUTES OF THE A → B PHENOMENON

1. *The empirical paradigm* covering most of the clinically observed A → B's is shown in Fig. 3.1. While the person is talking about one thing at Point A, he performs a certain action, which is usually not obviously related to what he is saying. Then later, at Point B, the person *spontaneously* mentions something else, which is thematically linked to the first topic and very clearly related to the former action. The pattern of events is such that the action has anticipated the subsequent verbalization. This paradigm schematizes what is observed in most clinical instances. It becomes apparent in this chapter, however, as it did in my research, that this is an incomplete paradigm.

2. *The frequency of A → B's.* It is my impression that for most patients a minimum of one clear-cut A → B occurs every 3 or 4 analytic hours, but I have not rigorously documented the frequency. The important point is that they are not rare events.

3. *The A → B time interval.* This may range from seconds to several weeks. Impressionistically, most clear-cut sequences seem to be completed within 1 to 3 analytic hours. Long term A → B's may span several weeks, during the course of which many relevant short-term A → B's may occur as though in the service of the long-term process. *Resistance* does seem to prolong the time interval.

4. *Specific muscular tensions and preparations for actions may substitute for overt acts in the A → B sequence.*

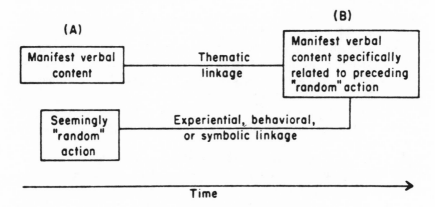

FIG. 3.1.   First empirical paradigm.

5. *All components of the personality may be expressed in the A-actions:* Id-impulses, Ego-defenses, and central *Super-ego* attitudes or developmental experiences.

The preceding five points about the A → B phenomenon have been stated in summary fashion. I illustrate the next three points, using material that also illustrates some of the preceding points.

6. *A → B phenomena stem from most important aspects of the person's life. And they may occur during very significant phases of the analytic process.* One day, near the end of his third year of analysis, Alec, a young, recently married man, was discussing a prospective visit he and his wife might make to his parents. It would be the first real visit they would have had since his marriage. While he was saying that he didn't want to go because he knew his mother would be full of critical comments about how he and his wife were leading their lives, he *removed the pillow* from under his head and placed it against the wall beside the couch. He lay his head back, flat down on the couch, and continued speaking dysphorically about the visit. In about a minute, he replaced the pillow under his head and, without making reference to this singular action, he continued along the path of his conscious thinking. This was the only occasion in his nearly 4 years of analysis that he did this with his pillow. I have never seen another patient do this.

Two hours later Alec recalled something new concerning his mother and his adolescent masturbation. (a) His mother and father went out one evening, saying they would return about 11 o'clock. About 9, he was in bed masturbating against his pillow. Suddenly his mother's voice filled the room. They had returned early and she was standing in the dorrway to his bedroom. (b) *His mother punished him by taking away his pillow for 4 years.* As he said now, although he used to tell his curious adolescent friends that there was never a pillow on his bed because he preferred to sleep without one, the absence of his pillow was always a private symbol of his guilt over masturbating. Here is a clear-cut A → B phenomenon. While speaking dysphorically about what he anticipated would be his mother's disapproval of his current marital (sexual) life, he removed his pillow on the couch. A short time later, crucial, relevant memories emerge for the first time. This example also illustrates how the Superego, and passivity–activity shifts, may contribute to the actions in the A → B sequences. He felt guilty about his marriage, and he now punished himself as his mother had punished him; *he took his pillow away from himself.*

This A → B was one step in an extended phase of his analysis dealing with his masturbatory complex, and during which he and his wife were attempting to achieve conception. There were visits to the fertility clinic, and then his adolescent phantasies that he was using up his sperm each time he masturbated emerged. Soon after, his wife was pregnant. Thus, this man's pillow A → B involved a very significant dimension of his life. It was also an important feature in an ongoing phase of his analysis.

7. *The sensory feedback from the transitory actions may be consciously perceived and become part of the associative drift leading to the verbalizations.* (a) *This feedback may be kinaesthetic.* A pregnant woman, Mrs. C, felt the tensing of her abdominal muscles while she imagined her analyst's penis was erect. This awareness of the tension led to her telling that recently she had been contracting her abdominal muscles to make her baby-filled belly "stick out in a hard protruding ball." We follow this episode further. (b) *The feedback may be an indirect consequence of the action rather than kinaesthetic.* Another time, Mrs. C noticed the tingling she had produced in the back of her hand by rubbing it against the roughly plastered wall by the couch as she spoke of her affectionate transference feelings. She then recalled "bear hugs" with her father in her childhood. When he came home in the evening he would hold her in his lap and they would hug and rub cheeks vigorously. The stubble of his 5-o'clock shadow would leave her cheeks tingling. Most A → B sequences include no report about such sensory feedback.

8. *Dreams containing imagery highly relevant to the A action may occur in the midst of an A → B sequence that extends over 2 or more days.* The pregnant woman just mentioned had a dream the night after her abdominal muscles contracted in the analytic hour. In the dream, she is lying down, and can see her large abdomen looming up. The baby inside is moving about, causing the wall of her abdomen to be pushed out in places as though the baby is pushing out with a leg here, a leg there, an arm here, and then there. Then, either her navel or a spot near is pushed out, making a protuberance about the size of a thumb. Her associations to the dream included the thought that the baby might have had an erection, which caused this protrusion near her navel. Then she recalled that as a little girl she had thought her [protruding] navel was her penis.

This woman's unconscious, childhood wish to have a penis was first expressed in the abdominal tensing, then in the abdominal imagery of her dream, and then it was recalled and verbalized.

I have completed listing attributes of the A → B phenomenon and I turn now to some excerpts from the first 35 hours of the analysis of Edward.

THE INTRICATE INVOLVEMENT OF A → B
PHENOMENA IN THE ANALYTIC PROCESS

Edward is a youngish married man who sought analytic therapy because he was experiencing certain heterosexual inhibitions and he feared his reaction to the possibly pending death of his mother. She had undergone surgery for a serious illness a few months earlier. The material I present is one sided, coming primarily from the more ego-alien trends in his personality. In contrast to the impression one might form solely on the basis of what follows,

TABLE 3.1
Summary of Edward's A → B Sequences

Time Span of Sequence	A Bodily Action (Theme of Verbal Content)	Primitive Ideation	B Subsequent Verbalization
Within 2nd hour	Places wallet on table.		Hopes analyst will be tough but kind: honest and warm. "No bullshit." "Ass on table."
4th–5th hours	Wiggles and settles buttocks onto couch. Slams calendar on table (Analyst's absence.)		Father's wiping him after bowel movement, and shaming him, age 7–8 Mother's delay causes him to soil pants, age 6–7–8.
Within 5th hour	Two-handed bosom. (Mother doesn't take care of his needs.)		Mother's mastectomy. Anger at her indifference to loss of femininity.
6th–18th hours	Left-hand breast, 6th–11th hours. (Women, needs for nurturance.) Buttock wiggling onto couch, chest expansion, pelvic thrust; two-handed bosom, 12th hour. (My evaluation of his work competence.) Urge to sit up and look at me, to walk about room, 12th hour.	*Image* of self as naked woman on couch, facing me, 12th hour.	Wish to be woman on couch, 13th hour. Adolescent fixation on girl's breasts, loss of love objects, identification with them. Mother's illness—feminine identification. Father substitute mother. (14th–18th hours)
Within 33rd hour	2-hand bosom. (Phantasy that analyst more interested in women, than him.)		Wish he were female. Father's desire for little girl. Playing "girl" with brother as child. Envy of woman's passive role in intercourse.

TABLE 3.1
(*Continued*)

Time Span of Sequence	A Bodily Action (Theme of Verbal Content)	Primitive Ideation	B Subsequent Verbalization
33rd–35th hours	"Finger-inside," 33rd hour (his phallic penetration in intercourse). Sensation of having to move bowels, 33rd hour. (Forgotten dream of woman.)	*Image:* Woman lying on floor, exposed thighs and buttocks, ready for intercourse. (33rd hour)	
	Breasts and bosoms; pectoral spasms, 34th hour. (Anger at analyst's absence, making up.)	*Dream:* Anal intercourse between man and woman. (after 34th hour)	Discovery of anal-erotism; passive homosexual phantasies in reaction to mother's serious illness; wish for analyst's penis in rectum. 35th hour "Loss" of wallet, after 35th hour.

Edward was quite effective in his occupation and showed much "masculine" strength. Table 3.1 summarizes the events I describe more fully; reference to it may make it easier to follow the narrative description.

Edward removed *his wallet from his hip pocket and placed it on the side table* as he got onto the couch at the outset of the second hour. He *moved his buttocks about slightly on the couch* as he settled into it. Later in the hour, he said he wanted me to be tough, kind, honest, and warm. He thinks I will be. In the screening period, I had seemed tough, like I would stand for no "bullshit." The expression, *"Ass on the table"* came to mind when he thought of the impression I made on him. Placing his wallet on the table preceded these spontaneous verbalizations. It is also the beginning of other A → B sequences in which the less prominent buttock wiggling-in is important.

At the beginning of the fourth hour, Edward *checked his trouser pockets* carefully and spent what seemed to be quite a *long time wiggling and settling his buttocks into the couch.* Then he started to talk.

At the beginning of the next hour (the fifth), only a trace of this buttock wiggling was apparent, but he *slammed his calendar onto the table.* He used the calendar partly to verify the dates of three sessions I would be missing the following week. Towards the end of the hour, two significant childhood anal memories emerged. Until he was 7 or 8, he would always call for his *mother or father to wipe him after a bowel movement.* One time, his father asked, "Am I going to have to wipe you until you are 10?" Edward felt shamed. He then recalled another experience from about the same period of time. Suffer-

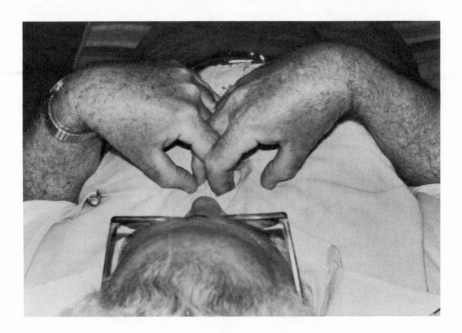

FIG. 3.2.   Two-handed bosom. (As seen from analyst's position.)

ing from diarrhea, he had rushed straight home from school to go to the toilet. But when he arrived, the door was locked. While his mother took her time unlocking the door, he lost control and *soiled his pants*. He was *furious* at her for keeping him waiting so long. His excessive buttock wriggling on the couch and his slamming his calendar onto the table preceded the emergence of these two memories. The wiggling onto the couch seems most relevant to being wiped by his father; the slamming of his calendar, to his infuriating, maybe infuriated, loss of control because of his mother's momentary absence.

His thoughts drifted on to his mother's current health. He worried that she will die. He also complained about the lack of affection by his parents. His mother, particularly, didn't take care of his needs, like in the episode just described. As he was voicing these complaints, his *two hands appeared* over his pectorals in the position shown in Fig. 3.2. He had made on himself, for the first time, what I will be calling a *two-handed bosom*. He then spoke bitterly about her "sick" joking about her left *mastectomy*. She had recently said the left side of her chest was like a boy's now; and, her remaining breast was like a penis. He cursed in the hour at her lack of concern for her femininity. Here, Edward had first made breasts nonverbally, and had then immediately spontaneously verbalized highly relevant thoughts and feelings.

Had he also made himself into a woman? A woman on the couch? And if so, would he be speaking of this?

From the sixth through the eleventh hours he made a left-hand breast for brief periods of time. Typically he did this when his thoughts touched on women and on his needs for nurturance. His buttock-wiggling onto the couch became unnoticeable in these hours.

When he was settling himself on the couch at the outset of the twelfth hour, however, his *buttock-wiggling* was again noticeable, and was followed by several deep sighs or *chest expansions* and *thrusting of his pelvis*. In a few minutes he was making a *very prominent two-handed bosom*, while speaking, incidentally, of how I might respond to any inquiries about him from his employer. Soon he reported an *urge to sit up and look at me, to walk about the room*. Later he was telling of an article he had once read about Susan Strassberg's experience in Reichian therapy. She had sat naked, facing the therapist. Then an *image* formed in his mind's eye—he was a woman on the couch and was facing me. In the next hour his associations drifted to his explicitly saying that he wishes he were a female here; if he were, I would be warmer to him.

He *had* made himself into a woman with his two-handed bosoms and breasts. In this hour, this act was joined by other consonant ones, including a motor urge. There followed an image containing a pictorial rendition of his motoric state earlier in the hour. The next hour he verbalized the wish.

In the next 4 hours, material emerged that began to fill-out the background of his feminine actions. Object-loss, grieving, and identification formed the nexus of this material. He told of how, in adolescence, the girl he first loved suddenly broke-off with him. He had worshipped her. He never had enough of "suckling" her breasts. He mourned losing her for over a year. He also recounted his grieving the assassination of one of the Kennedys. While listening to the news reports, with his family, he went alone into another room, closed the door, and fell to the floor where he lay weeping and sobbing. Thus he identified with his adored hero who was now mortally wounded. He mourned Kennedy's death for a long time. Once, telling me of a television documentary about the life of Kennedy, moved him to uncontrollable, convulsive crying.

His thoughts also touched upon the loss of his mother's breast, and the anticipated loss of her whole self. Associations to a dream, in which he succeeded in sucking on his own penis, led him to recall that he became troubled by thoughts about fellatio and of semen resembling milk after he had heard of the necessity for his mother's operation. At the same time, he had started to feminize his appearance. His thoughts drifted on to memories of some prepubertal homosexual play involving the boys' buttocks. Then he fell silent and covered his brow. Struggling against a sense of shame, he said, "I may want something from you . . . *a bill* . . . a rich analysis . . . maybe

something homosexual." I replied, "If you do, it would seem to be substitute mothering, a replacement for your mother." He answered, "My father replaced my mother for me in many ways. He was more generous, and
more giving, and more emotional." When I handed him the bill at the end of
the next hour, incidentally, he stuck it in his mouth, between his teeth,
while he put on his coat.

A picture of Edward emerges: object loss grieves and angers him deeply.
He copes with it by powerful identification. The immediate basis for his
current feminine transformation—which was first and so clearly manifested
in his nonverbal behavior—was the loss of his mother's breast, the real or
phantasied loss of her motherliness, and the threatened loss of her totally.
Thus identified with her, he has turned to his father for the masculine
versions or equivalents of mothering. His A → B's, starting from his first
hours, and the material of the last 4 hours, bring us to this point, (and the
end of his 18th hour).

The theme of femininity now largely disappeared from his verbalizations
for approximately 2 weeks. But in nearly every hour of the dormant phase,
breasts and bosoms appeared briefly, and on occasion were followed by relevant brief verbal references—to embraces, soft-breasts, and cravings for oral
stimulants. Thus, nonverbally, he was continuing to partly make himself
into a woman in the analytic situation. But consciously he was attempting to
strengthen his sense of masculine strength—to build his "ego muscles," he
said.

In the 33rd hour, he spent a great deal of time talking about a woman
acquaintance who was in psychotherapy. Finally, he said that he felt like his
hour was being devoted to her, not to him; that he was a messenger between
her and me. I replied that he seemed concerned that I would be more
interested in her than in him. Thereupon, he *made a two-handed bosom*,
which he held as he told the following. What I had said was true. And he has
often had the phantasy of being a girl on the couch. He has wished he were a
girl. If he were a female patient, I would be more interested. "I really
believe that I believe this about myself," he said. He then made brief, but
new, references to his childhood. His father [futilely] wanted a girl after he
was born. His brother used to dress him up in girls' clothes when he was a
youngster. His mother let his hair grow long when he was little. Finally, his
father became enraged and had it cut.

He also spoke of his envy of the woman's passive role in intercourse: they
don't have to work, and they don't have to get an erection. His hands were
still in the two-handed bosom position. He went on to say that usually his
penis only became fully erect when he had "penetrated" and was "inside."
In the course of this associative drift to "penetration" and being "inside,"
the bosom was transformed into the form shown in Fig. 3.3. This *"finger
inside" position* had never appeared before. He held the "finger inside" and

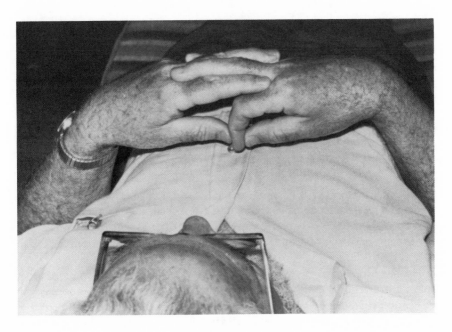

FIG. 3.3.   "Finger-inside" hand position. (As seen from analyst's position.)

went on to think about the way his penis recently emerged from his wife covered with blood. He also became aware that he had dreamt about women last night. While he tried unsuccessfully to recall the dream, he *felt as though he had to move his bowels.* He then thought about a woman co-worker. His hands now separated. An *image* formed in his mind: she was lying on the floor of his office ready for intercourse, with her skirt pulled up exposing her large thighs and buttocks. This sight was unattractive to him, and her genitals would be unattractive looking. I only want to point out about this material that the sensations in his bowels joined the "finger inside," and that a highly relevant *image* followed. We saw this kind of sequence in an earlier episode. But one cannot help but also hypothesize that in this hour he had bodily made himself into a girl with an erection inside her, all done on the couch— i.e., on me?

A 4-day separation now occurred, occasioned by one of the long weekend holidays. He had forgotten my having told him earlier of this break. When we resumed work in the 34th hour, he spent a great deal of time being angry about my taking a holiday and then making-up with me. While doing these things, he also made *breasts and bosoms* with his hands *almost continually throughout the hour.* He was apparently also doing so within his body, for he felt *spasms in his left pectoral muscle group and massaged it.*

We hypothesized that before the break, Edward had pantomimed a girl with a penis inside her and had felt bowel activity. After the break, he was making breasts strenuously. In the next hour, he reported a dream that had occurred during the break. Thus, it had actually followed the complex of "finger-inside," bowel activity, and image of the large thighs and buttocks of his woman colleague. The dream report was as follows: A man and a woman are naked. Their faces aren't in focus. The man is sitting down in a chair and the woman is straddling him, but with her back to him (cf. analytic situation). They are having intercourse. His penis is very large, and she is going way up, down, way up. The man is white, but his penis is a brownish-red color, as though the skin had been pulled off. He then said the color of the man's penis reminded him of a "piece of shit." I commented, "and the scene is as though his penis were in her rectum." He then made the "finger-inside" gesture, and except for one brief right-[hand] breast, he held the "finger-inside" position as he spoke about the following anal-erotic material for the first time.

He has often thought of having anal intercourse with his wife. Shortly before his mother's operation, but after he had heard it might be necessary, he learned about his own rectum. He felt it, put his finger in it, and then did this while masturbating. His wife occasionally does it to him during intercourse. After discovering his rectum, he started having passive homosexual phantasies, both of fellatio and of anal intercourse. His thoughts drifted to his relationship to me. He mentioned, again, seeing me as tough and successful. His wanting to have my penis in him is a wish to absorb my power, [he said].

The emergence of these anal trends completes the immediate short-term sequence that started 3 hours earlier with the "finger-inside" and the bowel urge, progressed to the image of the anal woman, then to the dream, and finally to explicit verbalization. This emergence was also part of a long-term sequence that started with that little A → B in the second hour when he placed his wallet on the table and later said I reminded him of the expression "Ass on the table." In a phone call following this 35th hour, Edward furnished evidence that this might be so. He called to ask if he had left his wallet in my office that morning. "It's gone. It's probably stolen," he said, "but I wanted to check with you before reporting it."

DISCUSSION

Freud repeatedly raised the questions: What is the difference between something that is unconscious and that which is conscious? How does the unconscious become conscious? Perhaps the data about the A → B phenomenon can make a contribution to the solution of these questions, for the

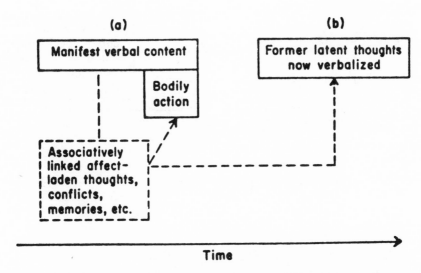

FIG. 3.4.   First theoretical paradigm (From Mahl, 1968).

sequences we have described included events that we refer to as the "emergence of the repressed," or as "the unconscious becoming conscious."

Repetition Instead of Recollection; or Motoric Expression of the Repressed

If we treat the first empirical paradigm with the concepts Freud presented in his paper on *repetition and recollection,* we have the *theoretical paradigm* presented in Fig. 3.4. This contains the usual psychoanalytic explanation of what is observed. It assumes that the later conscious content was unconscious at Point A, that it was dynamically operative then, that it either produced the A-content or was, in some way, associatively connected with it, that it found side-wise expression in the action, and that it later became conscious when the defenses were mitigated. Thus, there is first *repetition instead of recollection. Later there is recollection.*

The Intervening Occurrence of Body Perceptions, Images, and Dreams

Our investigation showed that such primitive cognitions often followed relevant motor acts and that, in turn, relevant verbalization occurred. This calls for a modification of the first observational paradigm, which will recognize the intervening occurrence of body perceptions and primitive ideation. Fig. 3.5 contains this *second empirical paradigm.*

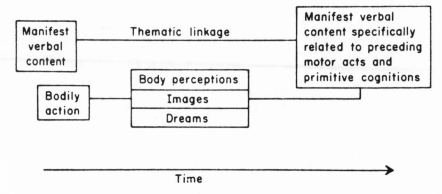

FIG. 3.5.   Second empirical paradigm.

The comparable *theoretical paradigm* is presented below in Fig. 3.6. It is essentially the same as the one presented in Fig. 3.4, the only difference being that the primitive cognitions, as well as the motor acts, are viewed as being produced by the unconscious processes. This is the usual view of the primitive cognitions and, of course, of dreams. According to this paradigm, the new elements in it are simply *alternative side-effects* of the unconscious.

But are the motor acts merely alternative side effects to the process of something becoming conscious and verbalized, or are they integral to that very process? We turn to this question now, considering two alternatives to the theoretical formulation we have followed so far.

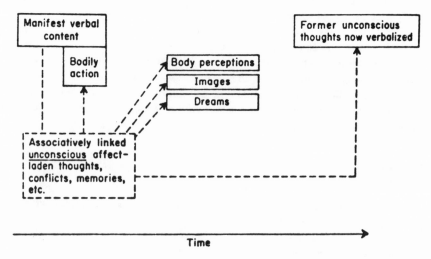

FIG. 3.6.   Second theoretical paradigm.

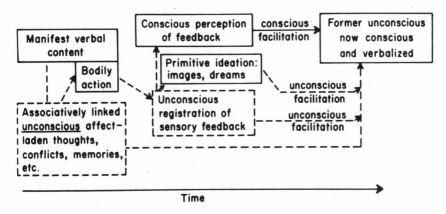

FIG. 3.7.   Third theoretical paradigm. The facilitation hypothesis.

Facilitation of the Unconscious Becoming Conscious

The first alternative, schematized in Fig. 3.7, is the proposition that in some instances nonverbal expression *facilitates* the spontaneous process of something becoming conscious. This hypothesis speaks of repetition in the service of recollection, in addition to repetition instead of recollection. This is a modest proposal for it only suggests that *some, not all*, nonverbal expression may have this facilitative effect. It does not propose any other changes in the customary view of unconsciousness or the process of becoming conscious. Some of the observations suggest one possible way in which facilitation might come about—namely, by way of sensory feedback that becomes part of the *conscious associative process*.

There is good reason to suppose that essentially the same facilitative process may occur spontaneously without *consciousness* of the sensory feedback from the body action. As with stimuli in experiments on subliminal perception, it is possible that the feedback may be registered though not consciously perceived. One effect of such registration might be the direct emergence of the repressed into consciousness and verbalization. Another effect of such an unconscious registration might be the instigation of primary process ideation such as images or dreams, and then the emergence and verbalization of the repressed.

Neither we, nor the speaker, may have direct evidence that the feedback entered into the flow of events. But both psychoanalysis and cybernetic studies have shown that feedback is an integral factor in behavior. We know now that feedback operates silently and ubiquitously in such complex behavior as language and secondary process functioning just as in simple motor skills (Klein, 1965; Lee, 1950a, 1950b; Mahl, 1961b, 1972, [See chapter 21]).

The role of "unconscious perception" of body feedback and the hypothesized progression from it to primitive imagery and to eventual consciousness that we are suggesting here is envisaged as analogous to the common nighttime experience in which a bodily need arises in the middle of our sleep, is first manifested in our consciousness by a "dream of convenience"—after having been necessarily registered mentally but unconsciously—and is eventually consciously appreciated when we wake up to satisfy the need.

Transitional Stages in Becoming Conscious

The second alternative to the usual theoretical formulation is more speculative and differs more radically from it than does the facilitation hypothesis. In the earlier paradigms we assumed that the thoughts, memories, etc. verbalized at Point B were present but repressed at Point A, and were being expressed in the actions and associated verbalizations at that time. Just as Freud did in his *repetition and recollection paper*, we were explaining the observable events by means of the early paradigms he developed to account for hysterical symptoms and later extended to dreams. In both cases, Freud assumed that the unconscious memories and wishes existed in cathected *ideational form*. Hysterical symptoms were the result of the "discharge" of the charge of affect on the *memory trace* (Freud, 1894/1962; [of the fulfillment of wishes and phantasies in his later formulation, Freud, 1905/1953b]); dreams were *thoughts* (wishes, purposive ideas) transformed into sensory images by regression and the dream work (Freud, 1900/1953a). In *Repression* (1915a/1957b), Freud wrote in the same vein. What was repressed was "an instinctual representative, and by the latter we have understood an idea, or group of ideas which is cathected with a definite quota of psychical energy (libido or interest) coming from an instinct" (p. 152).

The idea or derivatives of it could become conscious, and the quota of energy could be discharged over body pathways, resulting in affect. In the paper *The Unconscious* (1915c/1957d) when discussing the same theoretical idea, he spoke of "the development of affect and the setting-off of muscular activity" (p. 179). These statements comprise the theoretical framework for *Remembering, Repeating, and Working Through* (1914/1958b), which was published a year earlier.

At the same time, however, Freud began to discard this theoretical framework. In the paper, *The Unconscious*, he also spoke of the theoretically "enigmatic Ucs" (p. 196), and of many transitional stages in the process of something becoming conscious. In hypothesizing the unconscious "thing-cathexes" and the preconscious "word-cathexes," and translation of the former into the latter as the essence of something becoming conscious, Freud was clearly introducing a new theoretical paradigm. He no longer believed that the dynamic unconscious contents were of the same form or substance as when they were conscious.

But what were "thing-cathexes"? In the case of objects, he said only, "[thing cathexis] consists in the cathexis, if not of the direct memory-images of the thing, at least of remoter memory-traces derived from these" (p. 201). In the case of thoughts and wishes, his discussion of "organ-speech" in the schizophrenic and of hysterical symptoms seems to clearly imply that he considered the thing-cathexis to consist of bodily innervation. Beginning with a reference to Tausk's patient, who experienced a jerk in her body and a sense of having her body position being forcibly changed by somebody, Freud wrote as follows:

> The physical movement of 'changing her position', Tausk remarks, depicted the words 'putting her in a false position' and her identification with her lover. I would call attention once more to the fact that the whole train of thought is dominated by the element which has for its content a bodily innervation (or, rather, the sensation of it). Furthermore, a hysterical woman would, in the first example, have *in fact* convulsively twisted here eyes, and, in the second, have given actual jerks, instead of having the *impulse* to do so or the *sensation* of doing so: and in neither example would she have any accompanying conscious thoughts, nor would she have been able to express any such thoughts afterwards. (pp. 198–199)

These remarks imply that Freud would include bodily innervation as part of the thing-cathexis, but he never came out and explicitly said that a potential for bodily innervation was part of the thing-cathexis, a step he never hesitated to take in discussing the nature of an unconscious emotion.

I believe Freud's indefiniteness about the nature of the thing-cathexis was scientific uncertainty, not stylistic vagueness. He made this scientific uncertainty quite explicit when he again discussed these issues in *The Ego and the Id* (1923/1961). There he wrote, "an idea that is conscious now is no longer so a moment later, although it can become so again. . . . In the interval the idea was—we do not know what" (p. 14) and "I have already, in another place, suggested that the real difference between a Ucs. and a Pcs. idea (thought) consists in this: that the former is carried out on some material which remains unknown, whereas the latter (the Pcs.) is in addition brought into connection with word-presentations" (p. 20).

It is at this point that the observations we have made might make a contribution. (a) The frequency with which one can observe that relevant bodily events precede conscious experiences suggests that at bottom *the essence of an unconscious wish or memory, of a thing-cathexis, may be a potential for bodily innervation, or perhaps covert innervations and their sensory feedback;* (b) The frequency with which, one can observe *the regular progression from a bodily expression, to primitive ideation, to eventual verbalization* suggests that these *are some of the usual transitional stages in the process of something becoming conscious;* (c) The considerations we presented in discussing the facilitation

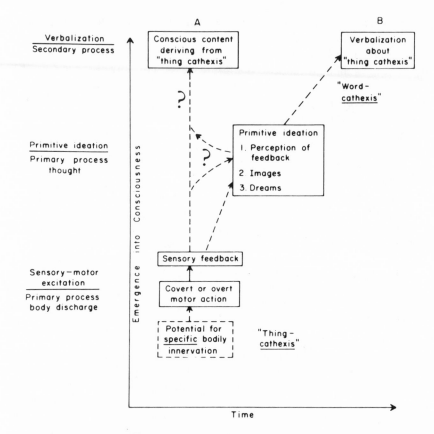

FIG. 3.8.   Fourth theoretical paradigm. Transitional stages in something becoming conscious.

hypothesis suggest that *sensory-feedback plays an important role in the progression from one stage to the other.*

If we combine these three assumptions we arrive at the theoretical paradigm contained in Fig. 3.8. This paradigm comes from our observations taken together with Freud's distinction between thing-cathexes and word-cathexes and his remarks linking bodily innervations to thing-cathexes.

The hypothesis outlined in Fig. 3.8 assumes that the nucleus of the unconscious content at Point A is a potential for body innervation. The core of the "thing-cathexis" becomes, for us, nearly identical with Freud's idea of the essence of an unconscious affect: a potential for bodily innervation. What we have in mind here is the assumption that the nucleus of unconscious wishes and memories consists of excitatory potentials for very *concrete bodily excitations,* which are *specific instances* of the *abstract categories termed "wish,"* or *memory.* The core of the unconscious wish of the woman who rubbed her hand on the rough wall until it tingled, for example, is assumed to be the excitatory potential tending to reproduce the actual experiences of the bear hugs with her father. Similarly, the core of Edward's unconscious wishes to be a woman is assumed to consist of the corresponding concrete bodily strivings for excitation of his anus and for female breasts on his chest.

The scheme of Fig. 3.8 raises the possibility that the verbal content at Point A derives from the unconscious potential assumed to be operative then. Perhaps the A → B sequence operates at every moment—nearly simultaneously, as well as being perceptibly spread out over longer time intervals. But this is so speculative as to deserve the question marks shown.

ADDENDA (1986)
(1)

I have recently discovered that by 1924 Freud had modified the views about *action* (reproduction, repeating), which he presented in *Remembering, Repeating, and Working Through* (1914/1958b), those views that I used as a point of departure in the preceding report. My discovery resulted from a rereading of a portion of Jones' (1957) biography, which discussed the early stages of the ultimate breaks of Rank and Ferenczi with Freud, and from a study of material referred to by Jones. Here is what happened that led to Freud's revelation of the revision in his thinking.

Ferenczi and Rank coauthored a book late in 1923, *The Development of Psycho-Analysis* (Ferenczi & Rank, 1924/1925). In general, this was a book about psychoanalytic technique, including innovative developments. One of the major themes of the book was the tendency of patients to repeat in action, instead of remembering, crucial experiences. Recall that in his 1914 paper, Freud attributed this tendency to resistance to the analytic process and looked askance upon it. In contrast, Ferenczi and Rank (1925) wrote as follows:

> we must connect directly with Freud's last technical work ("Remembering, Repeating and Working through," . . .) in which a different degree of importance is attached to the three factors mentioned in the title, inasmuch as remembering is treated as the actual aim of psycho-analytic work, whereas the desire to repeat instead of remembering, is regarded as a symptom of resistance and is therefore recommended to be avoided. From the standpoint of the compulsion to repeat, it is, however, not only absolutely unavoidable, that the patient should, during the cure, repeat a large part of his process of development, but also as experience has shown, it is a matter of just those portions which cannot be really experienced from memory, so that there is no other way open to the patient than that of repeating, as well as no other means for the

analyst to seize the essential unconscious material. It is now a question of understanding also this form of communication, the so-called language of gesture, as Ferenczi has called it, and of explaining it to the patient. . . .

The first practical necessity resulting from this insight was not only *not to suppress* the tendency to repetition in the analysis *but even to require it* [emphasis added], provided, of course, that one knows how to master it, for otherwise the most important material cannot be expressed and dealt with. On the other hand, certain resistances—perhaps even biologically founded ones—oppose themselves to the repetition compulsion, particularly the feeling of anxiety and of guilt which we can only overcome by active intervention, that is by requiring the repetition. Thus we finally come to the point of attributing *the chief role in analytic technique to repetition instead of to remembering.* This however, must not be understood as simply permitting effects to vanish away into "events," but consists rather, as is described in detail further on, in a gradual *transformation of the reproduced material into actual remembering* (first permitting the reproduction and then explaining it). (pp. 3–4)

The authors believed that this view of action would shorten analyses.

These ideas, as well as others in the book, and Rank's simultaneous (1924/1952) *The Trauma of Birth*, caused considerable consternation among the analysts close to Freud, i.e., the Committee. In an attempt to calm these troubled waters, Freud dictated on February 15, 1924 a lengthy circular letter sent to all members of the Committee. In it he included the following remarks about Ferenczi's and Rank's view about the role of action in psychoanalysis.

The joint work I value as a correction of my conception of the part played by repetition or acting out in the analysis. I used to be apprehensive of them, and used to regard these happenings—'experiences' you call them nowadays—as undesired mishaps. Rank and Ferenczi have called attention to the fact that these 'experiences' cannot be avoided and can be made good use of. In my opinion their description has the shortcoming of not being complete; i.e., they give no account of the changes in technique with which they are so concerned, but only hint at them. There are certainly many dangers attaching to this departure from our 'classical technique,' as Ferenczi called it in Vienna, but that doesn't mean that they cannot be avoided. Insofar as it is a question of technique, of whether for practical purposes we could carry out our work in another way, I find the experiment of the two authors entirely justified. We shall see what comes of it. In any event we must guard against condemning at the outset such an undertaking as heretical. All the same, we need not suppress certain misgivings. Ferenczi's 'active therapy' is a risky temptation for ambitious beginners, and there is hardly any way of preventing them from making such experiments. Nor will I conceal another impression or prejudice I have. In my recent illness I learned that a shaved beard takes six weeks to grow again.

Three months have passed since my last operation, and I am still suffering from the changes in the scar tissue. So I find it hard to believe that in only a slightly longer time, four to five months, one can penetrate to the deepest layers of the unconscious and bring about lasting changes in the mind. Naturally, however, I shall bow to experience. Personally I shall continue to make 'classical' analyses, since in the first place, I scarcely take any patients, only pupils for whom it is important that they live through as many as possible of their inner processes—one cannot deal with training analyses in quite the same way as therapeutic analyses—and, in the second place, I am of the opinion that we still have very much to investigate and cannot yet, as is necessary with shortened analyses, rely solely on our premises. (Jones, 1957, pp. 60–61)

A year later, Freud wrote in a similar vein in the following interchange by mail with Ferenczi. They are discussing a recent review of Ferenczi's and Rank's book by Franz Alexander. In a letter of Easter-Monday, 1925, Ferenczi said:

In his review of *Entwicklungsziele* [Development], Alexander makes a remark that in your technical papers you did *not* favor a technique that works *against* the patient's tendencies toward reproduction. But then I have often heard you say this; moreover, somewhere you wrote that you regard it as the triumph of analysis when we succeed in obtaining memories rather than reproductions.

Freud's letter on April 14, 1925, contained the following reply: I liked Alexander's review very much. He may have been slightly off key in regard to my attitude toward reproduction. I did, after all, change it somewhat—influenced by experience and your remarks.[2] Freud had, by 1924, obviously changed his attitude about *action* in the positive direction of the conclusions of this chapter. Ferenczi believed one gained the positive results as a result of *interpretation* of the actions. We cannot tell with certainty whether Freud also believed only that, or if he had also observed our *spontaneous* A → B phenomena.

This bit of historical research led me to a careful rereading and renewed appreciation of Ferenczi's early papers (1919/1952a, 1921/1952b, 1925/1952c) on *action* during psychoanalysis. His work, as well as Freud's and F. Deutsch's, is clearly a forerunner of my own.

---

[2] I am grateful to Ilse Grubrich-Simitis and the committee sponsoring the publication of the Freud-Ferenczi-correspondence for providing me with the excerpt from Ferenczi's letter and with Freud's letter, and Sigmund Freud Copyrights Ltd., Colchester, S. Fischer Verlag, Frankfurt a.M., and Judith Dupont, Paris, for permission to quote them here. Also, I am grateful to Lottie Newman for her authoritative translation of the excerpts. Ms. Grubrich-Simitis discovered that Jones' volume had misprinted the date of April 4, 1925 instead of the correct date of April 14, 1925. (Jones, 1957, p. 501).

(2)

I do not claim originality for such phrases as "the action anticipated the verbalization," for both Freud and Felix Deutsch used similar expressions for observations related to ours. Thus, as we noted in chapter 2, Freud (1913/1958a) wrote that patients' actions in the first interview often anticipate the emergence of important psychodynamic themes later in analysis. And Deutsch (1952) described how general postures or classes of activity often precede classes of psychodynamic themes during the course of analytic hours. What seems novel in our own research is the observation of very discrete actions anticipating the verbalization of very discrete memories and wishes, the frequent intervening images and dreams, and the spontaneous, facilitative progression.

(3)

Several colleagues have commented to me that the observations I have reported in this chapter and the final hypothesis about the transitional-stages-in-becoming-conscious or in verbalization are "Piagetian," in that the hypothesis traces emergent thought to a sensorimotor basis. I am not enough of a scholar of Piaget's work on cognition to adequately evaluate the bearing of my work on his theory. But it would indeed be a bonus if my work did relate significantly to that theory, as well as Freud's work, and the motor theory of thinking, as mentioned in the preceding chapter. In that event, our observations might be a bridge between these various lines of thought and might contribute to their eventual synthesis.

The Embodiment of Interpersonal Relationships[1]

4

PRELIMINARY CONSIDERATIONS

When we are concerned with the function of personal, symptomatic actions in contrast to communicative gestures, we tend strongly to conceive of the acts as *individualistic*, rather than as *interpersonal*. For example, we tend to follow Freud in emphasizing the individualistic, masturbatory reference of Dora's finger activity (Freud 1905/1953b; Chapter 2, p. 9) and not to consider the possibility that she was also enacting an unconscious wish for intercourse with Freud, or other unconscious phantasies involving other people as well as herself. (Other events did lead Freud to infer that she wished for them to kiss.)

Very often the context seems to only refer to individualistic factors—to the expression of an impulse or affect of the subject himself and not to be directly concerned with the other person involved. Yet our observations of nonverbal behavior during analysis, beginning with those of A → B's and subsequently, have suggested that very often nonverbal behavior is the enactment or reenactment of an interpersonal relationship and that the subject is doing so within his own body, or indirectly through the use of inanimate nearby objects; that is, the nonverbal behavior often seems to be *the embodiment of an interpersonal relationship*.

My analysand, Mrs. C, provided a very clear example of this phenomenon that day she briefly rubbed the back of her hand on the rough, "scratch-

---

[1]This chapter is a revision of a paper presented at the 31st International Psycho-Analytic Congress (Mahl, 1979).

plastered" wall next to the couch as she was speaking of her affection for me. She felt the tingling in the back of her hand, and her associations drifted spontaneously to her "bear hugs" with her father. After he came home in the evening, she would climb into his waiting lap. They would embrace and rub cheeks. The scratching of his "5 o'clock shadow" made her cheeks tingle. Apparently, her transference desires were related to her wish to recreate within her own body those exciting, tingling bear hugs with her father that used to occur some 25 years earlier. (See Chapter 2, p. 46, and Chapter 3, p. 79.)

Our study of A → B's reported in the preceding chapter yielded other similar examples which I include in the clinical material that I now present. That the same behavior can both anticipate recollection or verbalization and embody an interpersonal relationship does not imply a contradiction. Such an event is simply a manifestation of one ubiquitous aspect of human activity familiar to every psychoanalyst: *multiple function*, and its obverse *overdetermination*.

I do not elaborate on the frequent transference significances of my observations. Transference is not a necessary condition. I focus here on the phenomenon of immediate interest—the embodiment of interpersonal relationships.

One of Freud's early discoveries was that the sensory-motor symptoms of conversion hysteria were often the disguised enactments of unconscious memories or phantasies of interpersonal experiences (Breuer & Freud, 1893–95/1955, Freud, 1905/1953b.)[2] Thus, Dora's nervous cough was in

---

[2]One of the earliest and most explicit statements by Freud concerning the role of the embodiment of interpersonal relations in hysterical symptoms that I know of is included in his letter of December 22, 1897 to his intimate friend Wilhelm Fliess. In the following excerpt from that letter, Freud is discussing an hysterical seizure of the mother of one of his patients.

The father belongs to the category of *men who stab women* [italics original], for whom bloody injuries are an erotic need. . . . The mother *now* [italics original] stands in the room and shouts: "Rotten criminal, what do you want from me? I will have no part of that. Just whom do you think you have in front of you?" Then she tears the clothes from her body with one hand, while with the other hand she presses them against it, which creates a very peculiar impression. Then she stares at a certain spot in the room, her face contorted by rage, covers her genitals with one hand and pushes something away with the other. Then she raises both hands, claws at the air and bites it. Shouting and cursing, she bends over far backward, again covers her genitals with her hand, whereupon she falls over forward, so that her head almost touches the floor; finally she quietly falls over backward onto the floor. Afterward she wrings her hands, sits down in a corner, and with her features distorted with pain she weeps.

. . .

Can one doubt that the father forces the mother to submit to anal intercourse? Can one not recognize in the mother's attack the separate phases of this assault: first the attempt

part an expression of unconscious fellatio phantasies. Freud (1914/1958b) realized that transitory bodily actions might also be expressions of such memories or phantasies.

Felix Deutsch (1924, 1959) argued that conversion was a universal process, not limited to hysterics. He cited clinical data suggesting that parts of the body may personify members of one's family, and that sensations and activity in these body parts may express feelings, conflicts, and memories about these people. Deutsch (1952) hypothesized that "all automatic . . . movements represent in some way the search for a desired . . . [person] . . . from the past" (p. 210). He speculated, further, that such a function of movements originated in the earliest months of life.

This chapter is an extension of the work of Freud and Deutsch.

First I present observations of the phenomenon. Then I enumerate some characteristics of the phenomenon illustrated by those observations. Finally, I discuss implications of the phenomenon for the theory of identification and of the internalization of interpersonal relationships.

OBSERVATIONS

An Observation From Comparative Psychology

The following reminded me of my patient's wall rubbing. Nightly in her second year of life, our cat Puff would pounce onto my abdomen as I lay reading in bed and start to rub her head vigorously against the edges of the book. If I ignored her, she would rub harder, turning upside down in her fervor. Eventually she reminded me what this driven behavior was all about. When she was a very young kitten, being separated from her mother, I used to soothe her at night by lifting her onto my chest and stroking her head and body as I read in bed. Apparently, Puff was now actively recreating in her bedtime convolutions those pleasant interactions with me of a year before.

This surmise seemed to be proven when I then experimented by intermittently stroking her face and body. When I stroked, her antics ceased. When I stopped, she again went into her rubbing antics. She did seem to be striving to recreate those pleasant stroking experiences. She had found a way to stroke herself.

---

to get at her from the front; then pressing her down from the back and penetrating between her legs, which forced her to turn her feet inward. *Finally, how does the patient know that in attacks one usually enacts both persons (self-injury, self-murder), as occurred here in that the woman tears off her clothes with one hand, like the assailant, and with the other holds onto them, as she herself did at the time* [italics added]? (Masson, 1985, pp. 288–289)

An Observation from Child Psychology

The study by the Gaddinis of *rumination* in infants provides this observation (Gaddini & Gaddini, 1959).

They describe *rumination* as "the *active* bringing up into the mouth of swallowed food which has already reached the stomach, and which may have started to undergo the process of digestion . . . in rumination there are *complex and purposeful preparatory movements* [italics added], particularly of the tongue and of the abdominal muscles. . . . When the [infant's] efforts become successful and the milk appears . . . [in the back of the mouth], the child's face is pervaded by an ecstatic expression" (p. 166). "one part of the milk, usually the larger amount, is again swallowed, [and] a lesser amount dribbles from the corners of his partly opened mouth. The expression of the baby at this point is quite similar to that of the sucking infant who, completely gratified, spontaneously gives up the breast" (p. 168).

The Gaddinis studied the psychosocial context of the appearance of rumination. Its onset ranged from the 3rd to 8th month of life. It always started after a brief period of intestinal upset characterized by involuntary vomiting. Traumatic weaning had usually preceded that intestinal upset. The mothers were generally ambivalent, but not totally rejecting. Warm mothering by maternal surrogates cured the infants of their rumination. Despite an 8-year search, the Gaddinis failed to locate one case of rumination among children in foundling homes, who had never had a consistent mother figure.

The phenomenology of the ruminative pattern, and the psychosocial context of its appearance, led the Gaddinis to suggest that in it these infants might be striving to reexperience being nursed by their mothers. Thus the purposeful regurgitation of milk they had already swallowed might be the attempt to recreate by their own body actions the experience of getting milk by sucking at their mother's breast. The illness-produced vomiting might have enabled the infants to learn the ruminative motor pattern.

The Gaddinis' study offers some support for Deutsch's speculation that the conversion process originates very early in infancy when the infant–mother unity begins to resolve.

Clinical Observations From Psychoanalytic Interviews

1. Using Objects

First, I present observations in which the person creates or recreates an interpersonal experience by interacting with nearby objects. The object may be an inanimate or an animate one—in this case the analyst. In this category of examples, the person casts the object in the role of someone else, although he remains himself. Often the subject's associations strongly suggest that an inanimate object is cast in the role of both a significant person in the past and the analyst as a real and/or transference figure.

(a) The observation concerning Mrs. C is an example of this category. She had cast the roughly surfaced wall in the role of her father's stubbly cheek, and perhaps of mine as well. She had also modified what had been her childish behavior, for now she rubbed her hand—not her cheek—on the wall. In her active recreation she replaced one part of her body with another part. Perhaps the capacity to still reexperience very similar, tingling skin sensations made this replacement possible.

(b) In his first analytic hour, Edward, our bosom maker (See chapter 3, pp. 79ff.), grasped and held onto a wooden railing running along one side of the couch. He did this as he spoke of his dread of the regression he would experience in his analysis, and of his fear of becoming dependent on me. He held onto the rail again briefly in his second hour. His subsequent free associations that day spontaneously drifted to his childhood, when he was about 4 years old. At that time a college student, Joe, was a live-in baby sitter. He described Joe as a tall, powerful, protective, and admired figure. He recalled how Joe would grasp his hand when they would cross busy intersections on the way to the afternoon movies. He was frightened but also excited as he hung onto Joe's hand when Joe half led, half lifted him off the ground and rushed him across the street filled with whisking cars and noises.

In the next hour, Edward again touched the railing with his hand. In a few moments he was spontaneously recalling my firm handshake at the outset of our first consultation interview. He also said he was looking for a father in his analyst. Two interviews later Edward mentioned his father's strong protective hands.

When Edward grasped the rail, then, he appeared to be wishfully recreating past experiences involving the strong protective hands of Joe and his father, and my firm handshake. He had cast the railing of the couch in the role of the hands of the others.

(c) When Edward wriggled his buttocks onto my couch early in his analysis (see p. 81), he seemed to be not only anticipating the recall of his being wiped in childhood by his father but also to be actively recreating that experience with me. He seemed to have cast my *couch* in the role of *my hand*, as well as *that of his father.*

It is a small step from interacting with the inanimate objects in my office as if they were other people or parts of other people, to interacting directly with me as if I were someone else. The latter is, of course, the "typical" transference.

(d) Mrs. C did just this that day when she imagined I had an erection and felt her abdominal muscles contract. (See chapter 2, p. 48, 51ff., and chapter

3, p. 79.) Remember that her associations to that contracting included mention of her attempt to make her "[pregnant] belly into a hard, protruding ball . . . to make the baby stick out hard." And recall how her dream that night and her associations to it brought forth her wish for a penis. Among other things, she recalled that as a little girl she had phantasied her protruding belly button was a penis. In her analysis, Mrs. C often recalled another bit of her childhood. Her father usually worked in the evening at his desk in his upstairs study, leaving the door open. She delighted in parading back and forth before his open door, dressed only in her panties. She would slip the top down a bit and stick out her tummy as she did so.

It seems quite likely that when Mrs. C invisibly contracted her abdominal muscles before me, she was recreating with me those happy childhood evening experiences with her father, as well as fulfilling her competitive phallic phantasy. Notice that here again sensory experience (kinesthetic) played a role. And, incidentally, invisible, covert action accomplished here what overt, visible action did in our other examples.

2. Self-Contained Embodiment

In this category, the subject does not cast objects in the role of others. Rather, the subject is *simultaneously* him or herself and the other person—the quintessence of the embodiment process.

(a) One day, Dee reported she had had nightmares all night in which somebody was trying to kill her. She said she had discovered scratches on her arm today and that she had found blood on her pillow in the morning. She surmised she scratched herself during those nightmares. This surmise was consistent with my independent observations that she often scratched herself when she was inhibiting aggression towards others. Thus it appears quite likely that when Dee dreamt someone was trying to kill her she enacted that total interaction in scratching herself. (See also chapter 2, p. 52).

(b) Edward was being his mother to himself when he made breasts upon himself. Early, he seemed to be giving himself the breast that he felt she and others were keeping from him. But we also saw that this behavior was part of a trend towards feminizing his appearance that had started earlier when he first heard his mother had breast cancer, which he feared would lead to her death. All we know about identification and object loss and of Edward's proclivity to enact bodily such identifications very strongly suggests that in his bosoming he was keeping his mother with him, forestalling or coping with the anticipated loss of her breast and her herself.

(c) As we observed in the preceding chapter (p. 78), when he removed his pillow on the couch, Alec had punished himself as his mother had punished him.

(d) Fred, a young man about 30, frequently played out the roles of both himself and other people engaging in embracing. Sometimes he did this unconsciously, at other times consciously. One day, for example, he was expressing sympathetic concern about his weak, bedridden grandmother. He wished he were there to comfort her. Speaking thus, he wrapped his arms about his chest and held his sides with his hands. Soon he *felt* what he was doing and looked down at his body with surprise. Then he resumed his self-embracing and said he would tenderly hold her frail body in his arms, if he were with her. In other episodes of self-embracing, Fred held himself as he would hold and/or be held by a woman. On two occasions, he slightly modified this pattern while masturbating when he phantasied his hand was the hand of a woman fondling, moulding his penis.

(e) Gerald started to stroke and finger his hair in the early weeks of his analysis. Typically, he would show spurts of this activity for 5 to 10 minutes. Except on the rarest occasions, which I illustrate, his associations would have no ostensible relation to his hair play. I soon realized that Gerald's hair play was one of his characteristic, idiosyncratic nonverbal behaviors.

He eventually mentioned that when he left home to attend college he had stroked his hair and twisted the ends so persistently that his hairs became frayed. He had "cured" himself of this symptom by the transitional behavior of playing with and twisting the hairs of his pet dog instead of his own.

Occasionally, in the early months of his analysis, Gerald noticed his hair play and was reminded of pleasurable times he had in childhood: He loved to run his fingers through his mother's hair, often as she lay in bed with her hair down and spread on her pillow. He would while away the minutes this way. Sometimes he would stroke her hair as she sat in the living room when company visited. This activity became one of his identifying characteristics in both his nuclear and his extended family.

One day he was deeply involved in his associations when he started to play automatically with his hair. Eventually he commented on it, as though he had gradually become aware of what he was doing, of the immediate bodily sensations he was producing by it. The thought occurred to him: His mother used to do that to him. Then he thought I might reach out and do that to him. He continued to play with his hair. Now he suddenly felt as if his hand was a disembodied hand, belonging to someone else, doing that to his hair. He immediately elaborated the following phantasy:

> What would it be like if I were a beautiful female analyst? Sitting behind him, I would reach out and stroke his head. And I would tenderly touch his cheeks, even his chest. My breasts would touch the back of his head.
> And it would be wonderful if I had a sunken tub in my office: I would bathe him in it. This would be the most pleasant experience of all.

The preceding material suggests the following interpretation. Gerald's hair play was the embodiment of very pleasurable experiences he had in

childhood with his mother: of sensuously stroking her hair at every opportunity, and of her earlier smoothing and stroking his head as she held him in
her lap with his head against her breasts. He wished to repeat the latter in
the transference. He fulfilled this wish by substituting his stroking hand for
the hand of his real and transference mothers. At times his hair and head are
substitutes for his mother's. Thus, he recreated both the passive and active
versions of this memorable, repetitive interaction with his mother.[3]

Nonverbal Defense Against the Phenomenon

Such defense is not of major interest in this chapter, but I do want to note
that nonverbal behavior may occur, which defends against the phenomenon.
I have described one instance in detail elsewhere: A woman stiffened her
legs and trunk as she lay on the couch in order to ward off recreating the
exceedingly intimate situation of a recent gynecological examination (Chapter 2, pp. 55ff.).

SUMMARY OF CHARACTERISTICS OF THE
PHENOMENON

Our observations have illustrated the following characteristics of the embodiment phenomenon. I do not claim that this list is exhaustive.

   1. The phenomenon may be intentional or unintentional. All but one of
my observations were of unintentional action.
   2. Waking consciousness is not a necessary condition. The process may
occur while dreaming, and without awareness of what is taking place.
   3. The phenomenon may involve the recreation of past experiences, the
enactment of wishful phantasies, or both.
   4. Often transference seems to provide the relevant affects and wishes.
Yet transference does not seem to be a necessary condition, as is indicated by
the observations concerning my cat and Gaddinis' ruminating infants.

---

[3]I believe this clinical vignette illustrates what Ferenczi (1955) described without clinical
documentation.

   If, in the analytic situation, the patient feels hurt, disappointed, or left in the lurch, he
   sometimes begins to play by himself like a lonely child. One definitely gets the impression that to be left deserted results in a split of personality. Part of the person adopts the
   role of father or mother in relation to the rest, thereby undoing, as it were, the fact of
   being left deserted. In this play various parts of the body—hands, fingers, feet, genitals,
   head, nose, or eye—become representatives of the whole person, in relation to which all
   the vicissitudes of the subject's own tragedy are enacted and then worked out to a
   reconciliatory conclusion. (p. 135)

5. The process may be unlimited in the type of interpersonal relationships it may recreate or enact. We have observed it involving quite heterogenous interpersonal relationships, such as:
   a. Those of being nurtured and protected by parental figures.
   b. Generally sensuous ones.
   c. Specifically sexual ones, of various kinds.
   d. Hostile ones.
   e. Ones contributing to Superego development.
   f. Identificatory relationships, including those with lost objects.

6. We saw that the subject may cast objects in the role of the other person. Often the subjects treated objects in the consulting room as if they were extensions or parts of the therapist's body. (Freud once said [1913/1958a, p. 138] that if the patient began thinking about objects in the office he was displacing unconscious thoughts about the analyst. We can extend that notion to include the displacement of repressed wishes for bodily interaction with the therapist to interaction with objects in the office.)

7. The subject's body may be simultaneously his and that of the other person.

8. The nonverbal behavior may be overt and visible, or covert and invisible.

9. Sensory experiences created by the nonverbal behavior may be the immediate goal of the process. Sensations may be consciously perceived and reported, as Mrs. C did with her tingling hand and tense tummy, as Fred did with his self-embrace, or as Gerald did with his hair fondling. Or sensations may be unreported, when it would seem that they must be simply unnoticed or unreported as in Edward's "wiping" himself on my couch.

The literature of nonverbal behavior emphasizes the *action*, as far as the subject is concerned, and the effect of that action on the participant, as far as "the other" is concerned. But nonverbal behavior must always have sensory consequences for the subject—be it the kinesthetic feed-back alone, or also indirectly produced sensory experiences; be they consciously perceived, or only unconsciously registered. *Perhaps the production of sensory consequences is generally a significant aspect of all nonverbal behavior.* Taking this possibility seriously opens up new vistas in the realm of nonverbal behavior.

10. Displacement from one body part to another may occur in the embodiment process. Thus, with Mrs. C, there was displacement from her cheek to the back of her hand. *One* basis for the body-part displacement is similarity in the sensory experiences arising from the body parts involved. When one considers the general similarity of *kinesthetic feedback* the possibilities for body-part displacement on this basis alone seem very large in number. The body-part displacements contribute to the versatility of the embodiment process.

11. The individual often shifts from relative passivity to relative activity in embodiment. Thus, we saw that the subject may actively do to himself

what he passively experienced at the hands of the other person, and what he wishes the other would now do to him.

12. It seems probable that there is an important developmental dimension to embodiment. The process may evolve from a primitive, preverbal capacity, which can be observed in lower animals and in human infants. Perhaps the process has its roots in very early primary process hallucinatory experience, in autoerotic activity and phantasies, and in transitional-object phenomena (Winnicott, 1951; Wulff, 1946).

EMBODIMENT, IDENTIFICATION, AND INTERNALIZATION

The embodiment of interpersonal relationships is, among other things, an aspect of identification and the internalization of interpersonal relations. When Alec, for example, removed his pillow he was identifying with his mother. In thus identifying with her, and in doing that to himself, he was doing internally what had once occurred between himself and her.

One may regard the relation between the embodiment phenomenon and identification or internalization from different points of view. One could regard the phenomenon as simply a manifestation of an accomplished identification and internalization. This is probably how most analysts would regard Alec's behavior. Perhaps that is the most useful viewpoint, especially when the phenomenon occurs in a relatively mature individual.

It is also possible, however, to regard the phenomenon as an integral aspect of the very process of identification or internalization. Perhaps this nonverbal phenomenon reinforces or maintains identifications and internalizations. It might even be that this phenomenon is the basic aspect, the sine qua non of the process. Thus it might provide an ever-present, necessary substratum for the mental representations usually regarded as central to identification and internalization.

In making these suggestions, I am strongly influenced by the evidence that the sensory consequences of the nonverbal behavior is an important aspect of the embodiment phenomenon. I am also influenced by the study reported in chapter 20 that shows that the masking of auditory feedback of speech sometimes alters the *personas* of the speakers and their sense of self.

I agree with Schafer's (1968) emphasis on the subject's wish "to *experience* [italics added] being like, the same as, and merged with one or more representations of [the] object" (p. 140) in the process of identification. The *ultimate, basic* confirmation that one is "like, the same as, and merged" with an object is sensory experience coming from one's own body. I am here taking seriously Freud's (1923/1961) claim that the Ego "is first and foremost a body-ego" (p. 27).

In considering these suggestions, one should remember that the sensory experience may consist only of kinesthetic feedback from the nonverbal behavior. One should also remember the evidence that the phenomenon may be entirely covert. Thus the possibility of a sensory experience may be concealed from an observer. It may also be concealed from the subject, for the sensory output-input may operate entirely out of awareness. This is a ubiquitous feature of most sensory feedback from our behavior. That the sensory output-input of the embodiment might operate unconsciously in mediating identifications and internalizations is consistent with our theory that the most significant aspect of those processes is unconscious.

I am proposing that nonverbal behavior and its sensory feedback might operate in the identification process in a manner analogous to that in which the speech movements and their sensory consequences operate in the process of learning to speak in the style of one's parents. The child experiences himself speaking like his parents because he hears himself speaking and can match that sensory experience with that produced by hearing his parents' speech. These two sensory experiences are vital for this particular instance of identification. When they are not possible, as in congenital deafness, this identification does not occur.

Phantasies, largely unconscious, play an extremely significant role in the process of identification and internalization. Children act out their phantasies in verbal and nonverbal behavior. It seems possible that during the process of growing up the human being learns to miniaturize and make covert such nonverbal behavior, just as he learns to mute his speech. (Children learn to "be quiet!" by being silent *and* still.) If so, it is possible that such nonverbal behavior as the embodiment of interpersonal relations may covertly accompany all unconscious phantasies. This is another possible way in which the embodiment process might contribute to, or mediate, identifications and internalizations.

These are all hypotheses requiring investigation.

Effect of Proximity on Anxiety and Communication in the Initial Psychiatric Interview[1]

5

Carol L. Lassen
The University of Colorado Medical School

In the interaction between two conversing individuals, physical distance is usually considered to be simply background, and relatively unimportant. Recently, investigators have begun to reverse figure and ground to explore the dimension of interaction space as a variable in the relationship between persons. This . . . [chapter] reports the effect of physical distance, between psychiatrist and patient, upon the patient's ongoing anxiety as measured by speech disturbance and upon the patient's ability to communicate.

Anxiety and Proxemics

Edward Hall coined the word *proxemics*, "the interrelated observations and theories of man's use of space as a specialized elaboration of culture" (Hall, 1966, p. 1). Within the American culture, Hall has described eight categories of interpersonal proximity, from intimate–close to public–far, each with its own behavioral and interpersonal correlates (Hall, 1966). His cross-cultural

[1]This material was adapted from Carol L. Lassen (1973), "Effect of Proximity on Anxiety and Communication in the Initial Psychiatric Interview," *Journal of Abnormal Psychology, 81*, 226–232, Copyright 1973 by the American Psychological Association. Adapted by permission of the publisher and author. The author wishes to acknowledge the assistance and cooperation of the Connecticut Mental Health Center, where this research was carried out. In addition, the full cooperation of four anonymous but valiant second-year residents made this project possible.

This research is a portion of a PhD thesis submitted to Yale University in partial fulfillment of the PhD requirement. . . .

108

work suggests that interaction within the culture-defined spatial category appropriate to that behavior goes unnoticed, but if distance expectations are violated (too close or too far) anxiety may result (Hall, 1955).

Argyle and Dean (1965) have proposed an approach-avoidance theory of intimacy, in which physical distance is one variable. They suggested an equilibrium point, an optimum degree of intimacy, to which approach and avoidance forces contribute. Their model for intimacy is:

$$\text{Intimacy} = f \begin{cases} \text{eye contact,} \\ \text{physical proximity,} \\ \text{intimacy of topic,} \\ \text{amount of smiling,} \\ \text{etc.,} \end{cases}$$

in which an increase in any one component results in a decrease in one or more of the others. Utilizing the variable eye contact, they have partially confirmed this theoretical model: an increase in physical closeness results in a decrease in eye contact. They suggested that if affiliative or approach behaviors "go too far, anxiety is created" (p. 293).

Some empiricists have investigated the comfortable limits of physical approach (Argyle & Dean, 1965; Horowitz, Duff, & Stratton, 1964; Kinzel, 1970) and physiological response to approach (McBride, King, & James, 1965). Others have been concerned with avoidance responses to physical proximity, for example, decreased eye contact (Argyle & Dean, 1965; Goldberg, Kiesler, & Collins, 1969), leaving the field (Felipe & Sommer, 1966), and physical compacting (Storey & Mahl, 1967). All of these studies implicitly or explicitly cite anxiety as an intervening variable.

Considering distance as a *dependent* variable, a number of investigators have found that a social or friendly orientation results in a decrease in distance between persons (Little, 1965; Mehrabian, 1968; Rosenfeld, 1965; Willis, 1966). The question can be raised whether the *independent* manipulation of distance might affect perception, for example, warmth, indifference, friendliness, or hostility (Hall, 1955), which in turn might affect anxiety.

This experiment was designed to explore whether physical distance between therapist and patient during the initial interview might affect the interaction, the verbal content, the patient's level of affect, and his perception of the therapist. Only those data relevant to anxiety and communication are reported here. The distances utilized were determined by Hall's schema for distance and quality of relationship in the American culture (Hall, 1966). Thus categories personal distance–far phase (2½ to 4 feet), social distance–close phase (4 to 7 feet), and social distance–far phase (7 to 12 feet) provided the experimental distances 3, 6, and 9 feet.

METHOD

Sixty initial interviews, conducted by four psychiatric residents, were tape recorded for the purposes of this study. Patients were regular applicants to the Connecticut Mental Health Center outpatient service, who were routinely assigned to these four residents. Each resident interviewed five patients in each of three conditions: 3 feet, 6 feet, and 9 feet. (One interview was lost from one therapist.) Distance was measured face to face. The interviews were done in balanced order, and the experimenter was not aware of the distance conditions obtaining in any interview. After the interview, all patients returned to the information desk to fill out a 5-minute questionnaire administered by the experimenter.

Interviewers and Patients

For the purpose of this study only psychiatric residents who were white, male, and American born were used, since Hall's work is based on the assumption that these standards hold for the American middle-class culture. Residents were in their second year of training, primarily psychoanalytic in theoretical orientation. They knew that the experimenter was varying seating distance but were not aware of the dependent measures.

Procedure

Patients were processed through usual intake procedures. Then, on the way to the interviewing room the interviewer explained that the interview was to be taped for research purposes, and the patient was assured of confidentiality. No patient refused to be taped. Inside the room the patient was invited to sit in the chair closest to the door, though if he did take the other chair the distance was the same. At the end of the interview, the resident asked the patient to see this experimenter "for a couple of questions about the interview." The experimenter introduced herself as a psychologist and explained that the Center was interested in reactions to the first interview. Patients were told their doctors would not see their answers and they were encouraged to give their honest reactions.

The patient sample consisted of 31 males and 28 females, ranging in age from 16 to 61 years, the vast majority of whom would be categorized as middle class. No attempt was made to limit the type of patient included in the study, either by socioeconomic class or by diagnostic classification. Patients were routinely and presumably randomly assigned to therapists by the Supervisor of Admissions.

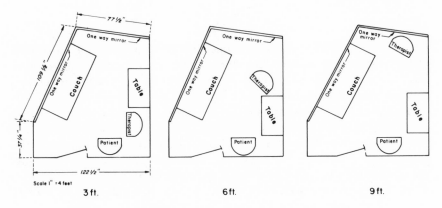

FIG. 5.1.   The interviewing room and the manipulation of distance.

Interviewing Room and the Manipulation of Distance

The interviewing room is a small room designed for observation and sound recording (See Fig. 5.1). The chairs are medium weight, and are difficult to move on a carpeted floor. The patient's chair was placed along the wall next to the door. In the 3-foot condition, the interviewer's chair was at immediate right angles to his, with the lamp table on the other side of the interviewer. At 6 feet, the lamp table could be reached by both interviewer and patient. The angle between them at 6 feet was about 135°. Nine feet was the absolute maximum distance attainable in this room, and the lamp table stayed within reach of the patient. At 9 feet, the angle between patient and therapist was about 150° (see Fig. 5.1).

Measures

Three measures were scored directly from the interview tapes: patient speech disturbances, rater-judged overt anxiety and rater-judged content anxiety. Other formal measures are all patient self-reports taken from the postinterview questionnaires. In addition, there was an informal attempt to evaluate therapist reactions through poststudy interviews.

The speech disturbance measures utilized were . . . [the Non-ah Ratios described in chapter 9.] They have been found to correlate with ongoing anxiety in a number of studies (Dibner, 1956; Kasl & Mahl, [chapter 12]; Mahl, . . . [chapter 10], 1959, 1963). Such disturbances can be shown to reflect moment-to-moment changes of anxiety in the individual subject (. . . [chapter 10, e.g.,]). Speech disturbances were tallied and a Speech Disturbance Ratio computed of disturbances/time spent speaking. In past research, the denominator used to compute the Speech Disturbance Ratio has been number of words, but ratios determined by the two methods are correlated .91 . . . [Mahl, chapter 9]. Time spent speaking was measured on a speech chronograph. Speech disturbances were scored separately for the main body of the interview and for the summing-up period, because the two periods differ in interaction and in content.

Two rater judgments are reported. The first judgment is of the patient's overt anxiety, or the anxiety demonstrated *during* the hour. This was a single judgment for the entire hour, on a 7-point scale. It was assumed that this scale would correlate with speech disturbances. There was also a rater judgment of anxiety content, this on a 5-point scale. Content anxiety was scored when the patient discussed situations in which he described himself as being fearful or anxious.

Twelve tapes were selected at random and scored independently by an experienced clinician in order to determine interrater reliabilities. These were: Speech Disturbance Ratio, .97; overt anxiety, −.02; and content anxiety, .82. Because of total lack of agreement on the scale of overt anxiety, the results for that measure will not be reported.

Patient questionnaire items were all rated on a 6-point scale. Questions included how anxious the patient felt during the interview, how clear he had been in expressing his problems, how open he had been in talking about himself, and whether he believed he had gotten his point across. Another questionnaire item is one concerning how sure the patient was about how his interviewer felt about him. This last item turns out to be related to some of the others of central interest.

Because most studies prior to this have reported distance as a dependent variable rather than an independent variable, and because there have been no experimental studies of distance in a psychotherapeutic setting (see review by Sommer, 1967), hypothesis testing was considered to be premature, and the data were analyzed a posteriori. All data were analyzed by analysis of variance for unequal n. Distance was analyzed as a fixed variable and therapists as a random variable. Results specify both F table values and Scheffé critical values of significance. The Scheffé test is considered an extremely conservative test of significance for a posteriori results (Winer, 1962).

RESULTS AND DISCUSSION

This . . . [chapter] concerns three sets of results related to distance: (a) speech disturbance effects, (b) communication effects, and (c) openness and the content of what is communicated. Therapist effects and the effect of distance on perception of therapists are discussed elsewhere (Lassen, 1969).

TABLE 5.1
Table of Means for Three Groups

Measure	Distance		
	3 ft.	*6 ft.*	*9 ft.*
Speech Disturbance Ratio—main body	.0801	.0911	.1134
Speech Disturbance Ratio—summing-up period	.0866	.0860	.1356
Patients said they got their point across	3.52	3.55	2.90
Patients reported themselves clear	3.2	3.2	2.3
Content anxiety	1.78	2.4	1.65
Patients sureness about therapist's reaction	3.41	3.85	3.05
Patients reported themselves open	3.75	4.32	3.35
Patients reported themselve anxious[a]	4.05	3.75	3.85

[a]Data on this measure are not significant.

The mean values obtained are reported in Table 5.1. The summary of the analysis of variance is shown in Table 5.2.

1. Speech Disturbance Ratio

The patient Speech Disturbance Ratio showed a consistent linear increase from 3 to 6 to 9 feet, in the main body of the interview, and a similar increase from 6 to 9 feet, in the summing-up period. These effects held for patients of all four therapists, though for two of the therapists the main difference was also between 6 and 9 feet in the main body of the interview.

TABLE 5.2
Analysis of Variance

Measure	Overall F	Comparison	Comparison F
Speech Disturbance Ratio—main body	14.00**	Linear	26.50[b]**
Speech Disturbance Ratio—summing-up period	9.24*	Linear	13.71[a]**
Patients said they got their point across	11.03**	3 & 6 ft. vs. 9 ft.	22.85[b]**
Patients reported themselves clear	4.25	3 & 6 ft. vs. 9 ft.	8.87*
Content anxiety	80.08**	Quadratic	156.82[b]**
Patient sureness about therapist's reaction	16.57**	Quadratic	27.21[b]**
Patients reported themselves open	4.51	Quadratic	7.25*
Patients reported themselves anxious	<1.00		

Note: For overall F, df = 2/6; for comparison F, df = 1/6.
*$p < .05$
**$p < .01$.
[a]$p < .05$ by Scheffé critical values.
[b]$p < .01$ by Scheffé critical values.

The findings were significant at the $p < .01$ level of significance ($p < .01$ by Scheffé test) in the main body and the $p < .02$ level ($p < .05$ by Scheffé test) in the summing-up period (see Tables 5.1 and 5.2).

Thus, patients displayed increased anxiety the farther they sat from the therapists. This is a somewhat surprising result, not easily predicted from a commonsense point of view. It is unfortunate that the one scale, rated overt anxiety, which would confirm this interpretation turned out to be an unreliable measure. . . . However, the relationship between the Speech Disturbance Ratio and overt anxiety has been demonstrated in so many other studies [see chapter 15] that it is assumed to be a valid one.

There are a number of possible reasons why increased distance might result in increased speech disturbance. A few of the more plausible ones are selected for discussion as follows. A major issue is that the angle of seating is more direct at 9 feet than at 6 feet, and slightly more direct at 6 feet than at 3 (see Fig. 5.1). It may be this more direct angle of confrontation which is anxiety producing. Individuals apparently have greater distance limits of approach (Horowitz et al., 1964) and show greater physiological response (McBride et al., 1965) when approached from the front than when approached from the side. In this experiment the two independent variables, distance and angle, are confounded. The two were varied together deliberately, according to natural and usual seating arrangements.

It is also possible that at greater distances "being observed" creates anxiety. Hall (1966) presented graphically the change in visual field and acuteness of vision which occurs with change in distance (1966, Plates 10, 11, 12). At 9 feet, one views the entire body of another individual, rather than just the upper trunk, as at 3 feet. Argyle, Lalljee, and Cook (1968) found the role of *being observed* rather than observing correlates with subjective discomfort and difficulty of communication. Haase and DiMattia (1970) found that clients expressed a verbal preference for an across the corner of the desk seating arrangement, which would create a barrier to visual observation as well as to physical contact. At 9 feet, distance and angle combine to expose a greater volume of the body to direct observation, and given a set for psychiatric evaluation, anxiety may well increase.

Speech disturbance is a component of communication, and there is a difference in communicating across 3 feet as opposed to 9 feet. The intensity of sound varies inversely with the square of the distance, so that at 9 feet one receives only one-ninth the volume that one does at 3 feet. Of course most people automatically raise their voices. But at 3 feet one can mumble, turn one's head away, and still be heard. At 9 feet one must focus and project one's voice to another part of the room. There is more work to communicating at 9 feet. Perhaps the task of focusing on another individual, in addition to communicating personal problems, contributes to increased speech disturbance.

RESULTS AND DISCUSSION   115

Certain defensive behaviors appear to increase with closeness. Eye contact decreases (Argyle & Dean, 1965; Goldberg et al., 1969), physical compacting increases (Storey & Mahl, 1967), mumbling probably increases, and in this study patients limited their discussion of fear at 3 and 9 feet (see below). If all these behaviors can be considered defensive maneuvers, it is conceivable that they permit more adequate defense against ongoing anxiety at 3 feet than at 9.

It is also possible that therapists conducted interviews differently at different distances, either by providing more structure at 3 feet (Dibner, 1958; Pope & Siegman, 1962) or by more probing into conflictful material at 9 feet . . . , either of which could modify the Speech Disturbance Ratio [chapters 10, 12, 14, 16].

Although the phenomenon of increased disturbance is highly significant, there is relatively little basis for choosing from among these alternative explanations without further investigation.

2. Communication Effects

Patients said they did not get their point across as well at 9 feet as at the other two distances ($p < .01$; Scheffé value $p < .01$). There was also a trend (nonsignificant) for them to feel they had been least clear at 9 feet (overall $F < .08$; comparison $F < .05$; Scheffé value $p < .07$) (see Tables 5.1 and 5.2). Both effects held for all four therapists' patients.

There appears to be a disruption in communications at 9 feet, one which patients are aware of. Feeling unclear and unable to make one's point, plus the observable increased Speech Disturbance Ratio, all would appear to reflect the disorganizing effect of anxiety. Patients did not, however, report themselves as more anxious (Tables 5.1 and 5.2), and anxiety that is reflected in speech disturbance is often not subject reported (Dibner, 1956; Kasl & Mahl, . . . [chapter 12]). In this instance, patients were aware only of the communication effect.

This finding, that the 9-foot condition makes it difficult for patients to express themselves, suggests that the 9-foot condition is considerably more threatening and/or disorganizing, or that it really is more taxing to communicate at that distance. Nor can this effect be explained by change in perception of the therapist. There is no evidence that at that distance patients see their therapists as uninterested, unresponsive, uncaring, rejecting, or cold (Lassen, 1969). If perception is not a viable explanation, one is thrown back on Hall's statement regarding *cultural expectations*. Apparently sitting at that distance, for the purpose of discussing one's own personal problems, is in violation of social expectations.

3. Curvilinear Effects for Distance

There was a cluster of three effects, all of which were highest at 6 feet. Judged content anxiety was highest at 6 feet (significant at $p < .01$; $p < .01$

by Scheffé test). Patients felt surer about the therapist's reactions to them at 6 feet ($p < .01$; $p < .01$ by Scheffé test). Those two effects held for patients of all four therapists. There was also a trend (nonsignificant) for patients to report themselves more open at 6 feet (overall $F < .07$; comparison $F < .05$; $p < .10$ by Scheffé test). That was true for three out of four therapists' patients (see Tables 5.1 and 5.2). Thus there does appear to be a constraining effect at 3 feet, as well as at 9, specifically of discussion of fear and anxiety as well as some evidence that patients are aware of being less open.

This set of findings permits some comparisons between Argyle and Dean's, and Hall's theories. In the close condition, there is support for Argyle and Dean's theory of optimum level of intimacy. If eye contact, openness, and discussion of fear (i.e., intimacy of topic) all decreased as a function of closeness, one can certainly argue that patients reduced the level of intimacy to one which they felt more comfortable. In terms of Hall's theory, 3 feet was not the culturally "expected" condition for a psychiatric interview and was therefore less productive of material. Similarly, the 9-foot condition was too distant in terms of appropriate expectations, and limited not only content anxiety but ease of communication. The results of the 9-foot condition are less easy to explain in the Argyle and Dean model. The theory predicts that with distance affiliative behaviors should increase. Eye contact probably did increase, but openness and anxiety content decreased.

Therapist Reactions

All the therapists preferred the 6-foot condition, but they were split evenly over their second preference, 3 feet or 9 feet. They seemed to adapt somewhat to the 3-foot condition, unless a patient was particularly flirtatious, hostile, odorous, or fat. They seemd to adapt less well to 9 feet, often feeling out of touch and having to prod themselves to listen. Generally they made more comments to the experimenter about the *distance* at 3 feet and more comments about the *person* at 6 and 9 feet. Except for their unanimous preference for the 6-foot interview, however, their reactions were relatively unsystematic and idiosyncratic.

Implications for Initial Interviewing

With the caution that this study was designed to be exploratory in nature and has not been replicated, one can consider some tentative implications for the initial psychiatric interview: (a) Despite overwhelming evidence that those with a positive attitude toward one another stand or sit closer to each other than those who do not, there is no evidence that one can create a more intimate relationship by sitting progressively closer for an initial interview. Sitting in the personal distance range is apparently too close for successful communication in an evaluation interview. There is also no evidence that distance affects perception of the interviewer. Porter, Argyle, and Salter (1970) obtained similar results concerning perception in the laboratory; (b) Six-foot distance may create optimum conditions for openness and discussion of fear, at least in a moderately small room; (c) Patients may have difficulty in communicating their problems when they get as far as 9 feet away, and they locate this difficulty in themselves, not in their response to the therapist (Lassen, 1969); (d) There is evidence to suggest that a patient becomes more anxious, the farther he is from his interviewer, and/or he is better able to defend against anxiety at 3 feet than at 9.

An important overall conclusion of this study is that Hall's categories gain additional empirical confirmation, not only for their descriptive validity but for their value as independent variables affecting behavior.

ADDENDA (1986, GFM)

Investigations of interpersonal distance and personal space have proliferated since the appearance of the most influential, basic works by Hall (1966) and Sommer (1969). Thus, Hayduk's (1983) review, intended to be as much critical as encyclopedic, listed 437 references. A computer search of *The Psychological Abstracts* (Psychinfo Data Base) for 1974–1985, the years following the publication of Lassen's paper excerpted in this chapter, yielded 629 references.

Our scrutiny of this material, and relevant original articles, leads to the remarkable conclusion that there is no study we know of which has replicated or extended Lassen's, in the instance of the psychiatric interview. Thus we found no other study of the *initial* psychiatric interview in which the distance between the interviewer and the patient was varied and the consequences examined. We did find seven relevent studies, however, six of which had results consistent with the curvilinear relationships found by Lassen. (The seventh study employed only two distances.) In our discussion of them, we have ordered the studies on a dimension of similarity of the participants to those in Lassen's study, rather than chronologically.

The research of Knight (1979; personal communication, March, 1986) is that which most resembles Lassen's. In that study female professional counselors conducted 15-minute intake interviews with (*paid*) female clients at distances ranging from 20 to 40 inches, measured from the front edges of the respective chairs. These are comparable to Lassen's face-face distances of 3 to 6 feet. The clients' self-reported anxiety was lowest at the intermediate distances, and higher at the closest and the furthest. In a similar study (Knight & Bair, 1976), male counseling students in graduate school conducted 15-minute, personal interviews with male undergraduates at distances of 18, 30, and 48 inches (front edge of chair seats). The interviewees reported, on posttest semantic differentials, levels of comfort that were highest for the middle distance, lowest for the close distance, and intermediate for the further distance.

Lecomte, Bernstein, and Dumont (1981) also had graduate school counseling students conduct 20-minute personal interviews with undergraduates at three distances comparable to those used by Lassen: 30, 50, and 80 inches, from the middle point of each chair. The clients' affective self-disclosure scores, based on tape recordings of the interviews, were highest at the intermediate distance in the second third of the interview. Stone and Morden (1976) trained a female, advanced undergraduate in psychology in nondirective interviewing who then conducted 15-minute personal interviews with volunteer female undergraduates at 2, 5, and 9 feet. These were presumably face-to-face distances, because the investigators attempted to replicate Lassen's distance manipulation. The dependent measures were the amounts of time spent talking about academic, social, and personal topics. The subjects talked longer about personal topics at the intermediate than at the close or far distance.

Rogers, Rearden, and Hillner (1981) replicated the seating arrangements of Lassen and the interview procedure of Stone and Morden, but with improved control over topic sequence in the interview. They too trained female undergraduate psychology majors in nondirective interviewing who then conducted 15-minute interviews with male and female undergraduate volunteer subjects. The interviews covered academic, social, and personal topics and were conducted at either 2, 5, or 9 foot distances, measured from the chair centers. In addition to measuring the time spent talking about the various topics in the interview, self-reported anxiety ratings were also obtained. Contrary to the findings of Stone and Morden, the results of this study showed no difference in the time spent talking about personal topics (or any of the topics, in fact) at the different distances. Rogers et al. suggest that Stone and Morden's results may have been due to the fact the procedure of the latter resulted in personal topics being discussed last in two-thirds of the interviews. Rogers et al. do acknowledge, however, that the reason for their failure to replicate the findings of Stone and Morden is uncertain and requires further research. (Because Stone and Morden randomly assigned their subjects to the various distances, it is unclear why their sequence procedure is implicated.) Of considerable interest is the finding by Rogers et al. that there was a significant curvilinear relationship between their subjects' reported anxiety and distance: it was lowest at the intermediate 5-foot distance. This is consistent with Lassen's (statistically insignificant) finding concerning reported anxiety and the other reported indices of comfort used by her and the three researchers cited above.

Fraum (1975; personal communication, March, 1986) used college students as both interviewers and interviewees in his attempt to extend Lassen's work. Using distances of 1.5, 3.5, and 8.5 feet between the participants and measuring the degree of self-disclosure in the interviews, he found a significant curvilinear relationship between the two variables: self-disclosure was greatest at the intermediate 3.5-foot distance.

Hansen and Schuldt (1982) investigated the degree of self-disclosure with male and female interviewers at *two* distances, 3 and 6 feet. The interviewers were graduate and undergraduate students, the subjects were undergraduate volunteers, and the interviews were a few minutes long (Schuldt, personal communication, March, 1986). The subjects talked more in response to self-disclosure questions at the 6 foot than at the 3 foot distances *only* when the interviewer was male.

Lassen cautioned us on the need for replication of her study. That bears repeating, because it still has not been replicated using the initial psychiatric interview. That lack seems all the more critical in view of Hayduk's (1983) conclusion that the presence of "psychological disorders" does seem to strongly influence personal space. Yet the analogue studies we have reviewed indicate that her findings of certain curvilinear relationships may have considerable generality. They suggest that efforts to replicate her study will be successful.

Might the distance between a therapist and patient play a significant role in individual psychotherapeutic interviews? In treatment outcome? Our literature search leaves these questions unanswered, for no one seems to have investigated them. However, Greene (1977, 1982) has taken a small, but significant, first step. He counseled clients at a weight reduction clinic, sitting at either the "close" 2-foot or "social" 5-foot distance from them (knee to knee) and providing them with either *accepting* or *neutral* verbal feedback to self-disclosure. The interviews themselves were 20 minutes long, although the length of the entire interaction with the clinic was greater. He found a significant interaction between those two variables and the degree to which the clients actually complied with his weight reduction recommendations. The latter was measured by actual weight loss 5 weeks later. *Accepting* feedback at the *"close"* personal distance, and neutral feedback at the "social" distance resulted in greater (and equal) compliance than either neutral feedback at the "close" distance or accepting feedback at the "social" distance. Greene suggests that *consistency* of type of feedback with interpersonal distance accounted for the greater effectiveness of his counseling recommendations at the relevant distances. This suggests that further studies of distance during individual psychotherapy should consider the consistency of the therapists' activities with the proxemics of his consulting room.

Effects of Visibility and Gender in Dyadic Interaction[1]

6

Lonn A. Wolf

College of Education, Governors State University

[In chapter 2, we reported a study in which we manipulated the visibility conditions of interviews so as to contrast the usual symmetrical face-to-face condition with the unusual symmetrical back-to-back condition. The latter produced a decrease in communicative gestures and an increase in autistic, noncommunicative gestures, although leaving unchanged the frequency of those speech disruptions indicative of anxiety. In chapter 12, we report a study in which we manipulated the visibility conditions so as to contrast the usual symmetrical face-to-face condition with a telephone-like situation. In the latter, some subjects believed (falsely) they were in an asymmetrical situation in which the interviewer was observing them, while they could not see the interviewer. Other subjects believed (rightly) they were in a symmetrical situation in which neither they nor the interviewer could see the other. As we show in chapter 12, we serendipitously found that in the telephone-type situation, whether of symmetrical or asymmetrical visibility, subjects said "ah" much more frequently than in the face-to-face situation.

In the present chapter, Wolf reports his study in which he extends the investigation of the effect of visibility in the interview beyond ours and that of others. He describes how gender and visibility affected certain aspects of both verbal and nonverbal behavior in his study—GFM.]

---

[1]Adapted from a PhD thesis submitted to Yale University in partial fulfillment of the PhD requirement (1975).

INTRODUCTION

The importance of visibility in social interaction has been clearly established in several interrelated research areas. *Eye contact*, for example, has been shown to regulate conversational flow, to indicate personality differences, and to provide interpersonal credibility (see review by Ellsworth & Ludwig, 1972). Research on *facial expressions* (Dittman, Parloff, & Boomer, 1965; Ekman, 1965; Ekman, Friesen, & Ellsworth, 1972; Tomkins, 1963), *body position* (Birdwhistell, 1963; Deutsch, 1949; Mehrabian, 1969; Scheflen, 1964) and *gestures* (Efron, 1941; Mahl, 1968, 1977 [chapters 2 and 3]) further demonstrates the wealth of information that is transmitted visually in social interaction.

Certainly we would expect that being able to see the other person in order to monitor this information would be useful. The question posed here is, are verbal, motoric, or psychological dimensions affected by changes in the relative visibility of the interactants?

In particular the two visual conditions examined in this research were chosen to coincide with symmetrical face-to-face psychotherapy (normal condition) and traditional asymmetrical psychoanalysis in which the analyst sits behind the patient who can be seen by, but not see the analyst (one-way-seen condition). The latter visual situation is somewhat atypical in our everyday experience as the interactants have asymmetrical visual access to each other. This asymmetry is very important in research, however, because the two factors of being-able-to-see and being-seen are separated so that they are no longer contingent upon each other. Comparisons of symmetrical and asymmetrical visual conditions must be interpreted cautiously, however, as effects might be caused by the asymmetry itself rather than the specific being-able-to-see or being-seen components being manipulated.

Theoretically the one-way visual condition used in psychoanalytic treatment helps to preserve the analyst's neutrality thereby facilitating the self-determination of the patient's free associations. Although this visibility arrangement is less "intrusive" for the patient, the analyst is deprived of the visual information provided by the eyes, very important organs of expression and communication of affect (Ekman, 1965; Tomkins, 1963). None the less, analytic patients still report that they feel seen or observed. What, then, is the effect of the visibility condition itself upon the patient's ability to talk about him/herself and his/her feelings?

Although the use of asymmetrical visual conditions involves the unequal loss of visual feedback (which might be interpreted by the subject in any number of ways), the use here of the "analytic" situation has several methodological advantages. Previous studies relied on one-way mirrors to create asymmetrical visibility conditions that separated interactants physically. It is not known if the use of the one-way mirror itself influenced those interactions as the mirror may have accentuated the unfamiliarity felt by the subject of both the situation and asymmetrical condition. Thus the manipulation of visibility conditions without one-way mirrors is seen as a methodological improvement reducing artifact as well as providing a parallel to the actual visibility conditions encountered in clinical situations.

Although a number of studies have manipulated total visibility conditions as independent variables (Exline, 1962; part of the study by Kasl & Mahl, 1958, 1965; Mahl, 1968, [also in chapters 2 and 12]), these studies have used symmetrical visibility conditions (normal-vision and no-vision) rather than asymmetrical visibility conditions such as the "analytic" situation. Four studies (Argyle, Lalljee, & Cook, 1968; part of the study by Kasl & Mahl, 1958, 1965 [chapter 12]; Rosenthal, 1974; Wolf, 1973) have used asymmetrical visibility conditions as independent variables. In comparing the results both Argyle et al. (1968) and Wolf (1973) found that verbal behavior was significantly affected by sex of subject *and* visibility conditions. That the results of these studies were complicated by sex differences was not surprising as they seem to be the rule rather than the exception in the visual channel of communication (Ellsworth & Ludwig, 1972). Specifically, however, the Argyle et al. (1968) results indicated that being-seen was the factor that predominately affected verbal behavior (speech rate), whereas Wolf (1973) concluded that being-able-to-see was the most salient factor affecting verbal behavior. In considering the "analytic" and face-to-face visual conditions (disregarding sex differences for the moment), one would expect from the Argyle et al. (1968) results that verbal behavior would not be affected by the former condition, whereas Wolf's (1973) results would predict that it would.

The choice of the present study to include all possible sex pairs was strongly indicated by the previous research. The Argyle et al. (1968) results (in which all possible sex pairs were used) would lead us to expect that verbal measures would be unaffected by the visibility manipulation that we have chosen here for male and female subjects. Wolf's (1973) results (in which only male experimenters were used) indicated that females had significantly more pauses (reciprocally related to speech rate) in the the one-way-seen condition than in the normal vision condition, although males were not significantly affected.

As Argyle et al. (1968) did report a sex-of-subject by sex-of-interactant by visibility-condition interaction, the possibility of differential effects due to sex of the experimenter requires further consideration. In trying to extrapolate Wolf's (1973) findings to female experimenters two possible outcomes seem likely. The first possibility is that the different verbal behaviors male and female subjects demonstrated in the different visibility conditions with male experimenters will simply be replicated for female experimenters. This would indicate that the responsivity to visual conditions that females demonstrated is a general trait of females and the stability of males across visibility conditions is a general trait of males. This possible outcome is supported by Exline's (1963) research that suggests that being able to see has a greater effect on females than on males. Exline (1963) found that in general females interacting with other females look more while listening, look more while talking, and have more eye contact than males interacting with males in normal visibility conditions. He also found that females sent and desired significantly more information when they could see the other person and sent and desired significantly more information than males. Exline, Gray, and Schuette (1964) further suggest that females' greater visual activity is related to sex differences in interpersonal orientation.

The second possible outcome would be that male and female subjects would reverse their roles with female experimenters: Male subjects would be affected by the visibility conditions, whereas females would remain stable across visibility conditions. This would imply that visibility conditions influence opposite-sex pairs but not same-sex pairs, rendering the being-able-to-see condition important only if the other person is of the opposite sex. The possibility that visibility conditions would interact with same-or opposite-sex pairs is supported by a number of studies. In general, opposite-sex pairs have been shown to have different levels of motivation or arousal than same-sex pairs (Kuhn, 1960; Stevenson & Allen, 1964). Argyle and Dean (1965) reported that conversation was more lively in opposite-sex pairs. Argyle, Lalljee, and Cook (1968) found that opposite-sex pairs were less comfortable than same-sex pairs. In reference to visual behavior, Aiello (1972) reported that opposite-sex pairs look at each other significantly less than same-sex pairs; and Argyle and Dean (1965) found that there was significantly less eye contact between opposite-sex pairs than same-sex pairs.

Having discussed the research and problems related to visual modes of interaction, let us now examine the verbal mode of communication. The previous studies have pointed to general speech production, either number of words spoken or number and length of pauses, as being sensitive to visibility conditions. The verbal productivity of an individual has been shown to be not only a consistent, but a very sensitive aspect of linguistic behavior. Although the rate of articulation remains remarkably constant, and highly characteristic for a given individual, there are large variations in overall verbal productivity and these are a function of the amount of hesitation or pause that occurs in the utterance (Goldman-Eisler, 1954). Wolf (1973) found that verbal productivity and pause time were highly negatively correlated. Mahl (1956a, 1961a) suggests that changes in amount of pause may be positively related to the degree of concurrent anxiety of the speaker. Pauses may be used as a defense in anxiety-provoking situations, as an individual can inhibit verbal output and better monitor and control verbal behavior.

Overall, pauses seem to clearly indicate inhibition on the part of the speaker. It is important to note that inhibition as used here and throughout this study is not meant in a neurotic or negative sense. Inhibition here refers to the way in which an individual regulates and controls his behavior relative to his immediate environment. It seems likely, however, that the amount of such regulation may directly relate to the amount of potential anxiety the situation presents for the speaker.

In addition to the visual and verbal dimensions, it is important to consider behavioral communication as well. Although gestures and gross body movements are clearly visual communications, they are qualitively different from facial expressions and eye contact, which can only be exchanged in a face-to-face situation. In the "analytic" situation, gross body movements and many gestures are observable from behind.

Changes in an individual's general level of physical activity during a dialogue may indicate the degree to which he can relax and express himself or feels restrained and inhibited in the situation. Ekman and Friesen (1967) suggest that when an individual's body is still, the observer of that person has a more restricted sensory input than he does when the person is moving. The observer does not have as much opportunity to infer specific emotion because such variables as speed of movement, area of excursion, emphasis qualities, and changing postures are eliminated. To the extent that the inhibition of motoric expression is successful, clues to the specific emotion will be absent. Ekman and Friesen (1967) also speculate that, apart from situations in which inhibitory effects are warranted due to situational or personality constraints on expression, a person who is emotionally aroused will tend to move rather than remain still. It might be expected however that this study, in which subjects were asked to talk about their personal feelings to a stranger for a limited time period, represents the former situation in which some inhibition or self-regulation was warranted.

The recording of body movement in this study is a significant addition to the range of dependent measures used in this area of research. The previous studies using asymmetrical visibility conditions measured only verbal behavior and self-report data. An important aspect of body movement is that it is not only a measure of motoric activity, but it is visually observable during an interaction as well. In his study of interview behavior in which symmetrical visibility conditions were manipulated, Mahl (1968, chapter 2, pp. 59–68) used self-report, physiological, verbal, and body movement measures. The only measures significantly affected by the visibility manipulation were motoric ones. There were more autistic gestures (scratching, fidgeting, preening, etc.) and fewer communicative gestures in the no-vision condition than in the normal-vision condition. General leg and trunk movement was not affected by the visibility conditions. Mahl suggests that some effects, specifically those of defensive inhibition, are likely to be channel specific.

Thus a visibility change may be more likely to engender a visible change (same communication channel) than a verbal or self-report response. Although Mahl was concerned with symmetrical visibility conditions, his theory of channel specific inhibition may be relevant to body movement in the one-way-seen condition used in this study. The use of body movement as a measure of visually observable behavior is further supported by Ekman and Friesen (1967) who suggest that the rules of conversation, which may inhibit extreme facial expressions, are not as stringently applied to body acts and positions, which may show the extremes and intensity not permitted in the face.

In order to implement and test these ideas in a laboratory setting, a number of methodological problems needed to be resolved. The use of pauses as a dependent measure presents several problems. Rosenthal (1974) suggested that a between-subjects design may greatly reduce the sensitivity of the verbal measures. This possibility is supported by the Goldman-Eisler (1954) results that indicated that the variance of verbal production between individuals is greater than variance for a specific individual across situations. The within-subject comparison that Argyle et al. (1968) used had its own problems in that the initial visibility conditions seemed to influence the later conditions. In light of the preceding research the present study manipulated visibility unobtrusively within subjects. As the possibility of order effects could not be ruled out, order of visibility conditions was included in the analysis as an independent variable.

Given the importance of verbal behavior, the actual conversation or interaction that subjects are to engage in is extremely important. To preserve the situational parallel with psychotherapy, it was decided to use feelings as topics of conversation in this study. It was thought that subjects would be personally involved talking about their feelings and would not have the sense of performing a task or filling up time.

An additional problem is the experimental format in which the interaction occurs. The choice of the structured dialogue used here involved a compromise between conflicting demands of spontaneity and control. In the Argyle et al. (1968) study, subjects interacted with other subjects for 3 minutes in each visibility condition. Because both subjects were allowed to interact with complete freedom during that time, there was no standardization of the interactions. Rosenthal (1974) and Wolf (1973) had subjects give a 5-minute monologue in which the experimenter or confederate did not interact at all. This provided excellent experimental control over the "interaction" but was very unnatural. There is the possibility that the monologue may not be representative of the more typical social and clinical interactions to which we would like to generalize the findings.

The use of a structured interaction in the present study enabled the experimenter to interact with the subject under strictly defined conditions that would appear plausible to the subject. To make the experimenter's interaction seem more natural than arbitrary, it was structured to respond to the subject's apparent need for interaction rather than to impose a standard, but possibly inappropriate, format on the subject. Although the structured interaction used here does not involve the level of interpersonal interchange found in everyday conversation, it does approximate a nondirective therapy style in which the therapist is more listener than active participant. Due to our expectation that the sex of the other participant (experimenter) might be a significant factor, the importance of experimental control cannot be over-emphasized. The structured interaction used here minimizes and regulates experimenter interaction as much as possible so that we can attribute effects to the experimenters' sex and not their dialogue behavior.

METHOD

Overview

Believing that they were participating in research designed to study the physiological correlates of conversation, subjects interacted with an experimenter in two different visibility conditions: normal face-to-face vision in which both participants could see one another, and one-way vision in which the subject could not see the experimenter but was seen from behind by the experimenter. In each visibility condition the experimenter initiated a 10-minute conversation with a question, listened attentively and positively until there was a 10-second pause in the subject's dialogue, and then asked another question.

The experimental design of the study was $2 \times 2 \times 2 \times 2 \times 2$, having two levels of visibility within each subject, two levels of visibility condition order, two levels of subject sex, two levels of experimenter sex, and two experimenters for each level of experimenter sex. The order of the visibility conditions given to each subject was counterbalanced across all factors.

The dialogues were tape-recorded. Body movement was monitored unobtrusively in each interaction. After both interactions were finished, subjects completed a questionnaire asking them to describe their perceptions of the situation as a whole and to compare the two interactions. This was followed by a free interview period with the experimenter in which additional open-ended questions were asked.

Subjects

The subject sample consisted of 36 male and 36 female undergraduates from the introductory psychology course subject pool at a large Eastern university.

Experimenters

The 2 male experimenters (ages 23 and 28) and the 2 female experimenters (ages 27 and 30) were selected by their actual appearance and maturity rather than chronological age. All experimenters were blind to the hypothesis of the study although they did know that visibility was being manipulated. They also knew that sex was balanced across subjects and experimenters, but not that it was an independent variable in the study.

Experimental Procedure

In preliminary procedures, the subject was seated and given a written description of the study indicating that the experiment was to record "what happens physiologically when one reflects on him/herself and gets involved in talking about feelings." Included was an informed consent form indicating that the content of the discussion would be confidential. Subjects indicated on a list two feelings that they would be willing to talk about. With the exception of seating the subject and later attaching dummy physiological sensors on the earlobe and wrist to a dummy electronic amplifier, the experimenter minimized initial interaction by leaving the room.

Upon the experimenter's final return, the actual experimental manipulation began, as the experimenter took a seat either in front of or behind the subject, according to a prearranged, randomized order counterbalanced across experimenters and subjects. A side chair held the dummy amplifier. In the front-first position, the experimenter moved the chair in front of the subject after closing the door. In the back-first position, the experimenter simply sat in the position behind the subject. Because it was the only empty seat in the room, subjects in the back-first position were probably not surprised when the experimenter sat behind them.

The experimenter then initiated the structured interaction with the question "What is it like when you feel X?," X being one of the two feelings the subject had checked (annoyed, affectionate, suspicious, etc.). These questions were asked in random order, as indicated by the subject's list. If a pause of 10 seconds occurred, the experimenter was then free to choose one of eight other predetermined questions about a feeling that seemed likely to facilitate further interaction with the subject. For example, "What do you think about when you feel that way?" "Do you have a specific instance in mind?," and so forth. In addition to the experimenter's questions, auditory presence was maintained by nondirective positive comments. The experimenter was instructed to intersperse 10 comments such as "uh-huh," "yes," "right," at appropriate points during each 10-minute interaction.

In addition to the structured verbal interaction, the experimenters were trained to present a consistent visual appearance to the subject, looking at the subject about 40% of the time. This is the approximate amount of time a listener looks at a speaker (Exline, 1963; Kendon, 1967). Experimenters were also instructed to maintain a casual, interested, and positive demeanor.

After 10 minutes the experimenter terminated the dialogue and indicated it was necessary to record the (presumed) physiological measures on a different electrical channel. In the process of changing and adjusting the electrical equipment, the experimenter also changed position, either removing the amplifier from the front chair and then sitting in front of the subject or placing the equipment on the previously occupied front chair (now moved to the side so the wires could reach) and then sitting behind the subject. The experimenter then asked the subject about the second feeling. Until this point, the subject had no idea that the experimenter's position would alter.

Following the structured interactions, the subject was given a questionnaire, assured confidentiality, and left alone to complete it. This was followed by the open interview and debriefing.

Measures

The dependent measures fall into three categories: behavioral, verbal, and subjective.

The behavioral measure was a physiograph record of the subject's gross body movement during the two interactions, effected by the use of a standard office tilting, swivel chair adapted to transmit to-and-fro and rotational movements to the physiograph. Body weight did not appear to affect the movement measure that was sensitive enough to register the major movements of a slender female and insensitive enough to not register the minor movements of an average male. Thus, not all visible behavior affected the movement record, but any movement recorded would have been visible. The movement score derived from the physiograph record was based on 5-second pauses in recorded movement.

Two verbal measures were reliably derived from the tape recordings by a judge blind as to content and visibility condition. Total pause time was scored by adding the number of pauses 2 seconds or more accumulated during each 10-minute period. This system distributed subjects evenly over the range of obtained scores, which extended from 0 to 118 2-second pauses for the 10-minute dialogue. The second measure was the number of long pauses that was scored by counting the number of questions that the experimenter asked during each of the interactions (each long pause was therefore 10-seconds long).

The self-report questionnaire consisted of 16 questions that were answered on 6-point scales with verbal anchors at each end. The first eight questions asked subjects to compare the 2 "halves" of the experiment. A factor analysis varimax rotation of these eight questions indicated 3 distinct factors accounting for 71% of the variance. Factor 1 related to the subject's depth of and involvement in feelings; factor 2, to ease and comfort speaking; and factor 3, to feelings about the experimenter.

The second eight questions asked for overall ratings of the procedure. A factor analysis varimax rotation of these questions indicated 2 distinct factors accounting for 62% of the variance. Factor 1 represents the subject's feelings about self; factor 2, overall feelings about the experimenter.

Two of the seven open interview questions were used as dependent measures. The questions were: Did one topic take longer than the other? and Which position did you prefer?

RESULTS

Final analyses of variance with 4 factors (visibility condition, order of visibility conditions, sex of subject, and sex of experimenter) were computed for each of the three dependent behavioral and verbal measures replicated across visibility conditions and are presented in Table 6.1. The final analyses of variance with 3 factors (order of visibility conditions, sex of subject, and sex of experimenter) were computed for the self-report and the free interview dependent measures and are presented in Table 6.2. The method of unweighted means was used in all analyses. The missing data on the verbal and behavioral measures were caused by mechanical failures of the recording instruments. In presenting the results of these analyses, we first consider the subjective measures and then continue with the behavioral and verbal measures.

Subjective Measures

The overall feelings-about-self measure was significantly affected by the sex of the experimenter. High feelings-about-self scores indicated that subjects felt more overall comfort, depth of feeling, and openness than subjects with low scores. Subjects with female experimenters reported themselves significantly lower than subjects with male experimenters. The mean scores were 8.09 and 9.78 for female and male experimenters, respectively ($F = 4.50$, $p < .05$).

A significant sex-of-subject by sex-of-experimenter interaction was found for the overall feelings-about-experimenter measure ($F = 4.24$, $p < .05$). This is illustrated in Fig. 6.1. High-feelings-about-experimenter scores indicated that subjects felt more overall liking for, involvement with, being liked by and being understood by the experimenter than subjects with low scores. Same-sex pairs had the highest scores and opposite-sex pairs had the lowest scores. There were no significant between-cell differences.

TABLE 6.1
Analyses of Variance for Behavioral and Verbal Measures

	Dependent measures								
	Body Movement Pauses			Number of Long Pauses in Speech			Total Pause Time in Speech		
Source	df	MS	F	df	MS	F	df	MS	F
Experimenter sex (E)	1	1748	.76	1	22.24	1.18	1	5700	.84
Subject sex (S)	1	18511	8.00**	1	10.76	.57	1	1102	.16
Order V condition (O)	1	334	.14	1	101.48	5.39*	1	15961	2.36
E X S	1	230	.10	1	16.28	.86	1	1841	.27
E X O	1	261	.11	1	19.42	1.03	1	574	.08
S X O	1	20	.01	1	12.02	.64	1	493	.07
E X S X O	1	3029	1.31	1	22.24	1.18	1	10313	1.52
Within	62	2313		63	18.84		63	6762	
Visibility (V)	1	3399	7.94**	1	.93	.50	1	15	.02
E X V	1	363	.85	1	2.76	1.47	1	150	.23
S X V	1	179	.42	1	.08	.04	1	45	.07
O X V	1	29	.07	1	32.40	17.31***	1	1277	2.00
E X S X V	1	421	.98	1	1.47	.78	1	338	.53
E X O X V	1	35	.08	1	1.13	.60	1	23	.04
S X O X V	1	24	.06	1	.45	.24	1	126	.20
E X S X O X V	1	1	.00	1	8.54	4.56*	1	2822	4.41*
V X Within	62	428		63	1.87		62	640	

$^*p < .05.$
$^{**}p < .01.$
$^{***}p < .001.$

A significant subject sex effect was found for the self-report ease and comfort speaking measure in which subjects were asked to compare the two dialogues conditions. The mean score for females was -1.22 and the mean score for males was .26 ($F = 6.88$, $p < .05$). Positive scores indicated more comfort speaking in the front condition and negative scores indicated more comfort speaking in the back condition. Thus, females reported comfort speaking in the back condition, whereas comfort speaking for males did not seem to be affected by the visibility conditions.

The order of visibility conditions was found to affect four of the self-report measures in which subjects were asked to compare the two dialogues. Significant order effects were found for comfort speaking, involvement in feelings, dialogue preferred, and longer dialogue. Positive scores indicate the front condition and negative scores indicate the back condition.

1. The mean score for comfort speaking in the back-first condition was .09 and the mean score for the front-first condition was -1.06 ($F = 4.15$,

TABLE 6.2
Analyses of Variance for Self-report Measures

Dependent measures

Source	df	Feelings-About Self		Feelings-About Experimenter		Ease and Comfort Speaking		Involvement in Feelings		Dialogue Preferred		Longer Dialogue	
		MS	F	MS	F	MS	F	MS	F	MS	F	MS	F
Experimenter sex (E)	1	51.15	4.50*	10.82	1.33	.07	.01	.19	.02	.06	.26	.00	.02
Subject sex (S)	1	10.92	.96	.17	.02	39.14	6.88*	.09	.01	.59	2.63	.07	.30
Order V condition (O)	1	13.89	1.22	27.33	3.36	23.60	4.15*	141.08	10.71**	2.65	11.78**	2.04	9.18**
E X S	1	5.37	.47	34.51	4.24*	8.39	1.48	12.55	.95	.11	.50	.17	.75
E X O	1	22.22	1.96	1.38	.17	5.12	.90	5.12	.39	.08	.37	.00	.00
S X O	1	.14	.01	.42	.05	3.64	.64	26.12	1.98	.02	.42	.37	1.67
E X S X O	1	2.15	.19	.22	.03	3.92	.69	12.71	.97	.04	.22	.42	1.87
Within	64	11.35		8.13		5.68		13.18		.22		.22	

*p < .05.
**p < .01.

131

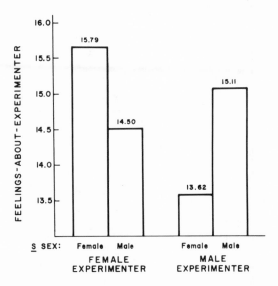

FIG. 6.1.   The effect of sex-of-experimenter by sex-of-subject interaction for feelings-about-experimenter.

$p < .05$). If the order of visibility conditions was back-first, the subjects reported equal comfort speaking in both conditions. If the order of conditions was front-first, then subjects reported more comfort speaking in the back condition.

2. The mean score for involvement in feelings in the back-first condition was 1.86 and the mean score in the front-first condition was $-.95$ ($F = 11.78$, $p < .01$). Subjects felt more involved in their second dialogue independent of the visibility conditions.

3. For longest dialogue the mean score for the back-first condition was .225 and the mean score for the front-first condition was .572 ($F = 9.18$, $p < .01$). Overall subjects felt the face-to-face condition took longer than the back condition, although this effect was significantly greater if the face-to-face condition was first.

In summary, if the order of visibility conditions was front-first, then subjects were more comfortable speaking and were more involved in feelings in the back condition and preferred the back condition dialogue. They also felt the front-first dialogue took longer. If the order of visibility conditions was back-first, then subjects preferred and were more involved in feelings in the front condition dialogue. They also felt that the front condition took longer but were equally comfortable speaking in both dialogues. In general subjects preferred and felt more involved in the second dialogue.

The feelings-about-experimenter measure (requiring a comparison of the first and second dialogues) and the free interview question about position preferred (not dialogue preference) showed no main effects or interactions for the experimental manipulations.

Behavioral Measure

A significant sex-of-subject main effect was found for pauses in movement across both visibility conditions. Here, movement scores represent the number of discrete 5-second pauses in movement that occurred for an average 10-minute period across both visibility conditions. Female subjects paused significantly more than male subjects. The mean score for females was 51.99 and the mean score for males was 28.89 ($F = 8.00, p < .01$). This indicates that females had less overall recorded body movement than males.

The visibility conditions also significantly affected subjects' movement. Here, movement scores represent the number of discrete 5-second pauses in movement that occurred during each of the 10-minute dialogues. Subjects paused significantly more in the back condition than in the front condition. The mean score for the back condition was 45.39 and the mean score for the front condition was 35.49 ($F = 7.94, p < .01$). Subjects' overall body movement was reduced when they could not see the other person.

Verbal Measures

Total Pause Time

A significant sex-of-subject by sex-of-experimenter by order-of-visibility conditions by visibility condition interaction was found for total pause time in speech ($F = 4.41, p < .05$). This four-way interaction is illustrated in Fig. 6.2. Scores indicate the total number of seconds of speech pause for each 10-minute dialogue. Small pause times indicate a spontaneous and free-flowing form of expression, whereas large pause times indicate a sporadic or cautious style of expression. There are two basic patterns that emerge from this interaction. In the first dialogue the difference between the front and the back condition means was significant for opposite-sex dyads ($p < .05$, Newman Keuls test). Opposite-sex dyads had significantly more pauses in the back condition than in the front condition. Visibility conditions did not significantly affect same-sex pairs in the first dialogue. This pattern was repeated in the second dialogue except that the visibility conditions were reversed. Again, the greatest between-cell differences for visibility conditions were for the opposite-sex dyads (although these differences in the second dialogue were not significant).

In assessing the overall pattern, visibility conditions significantly affected opposite-sex pairs in the first dialogue and subsequent visibility changes in

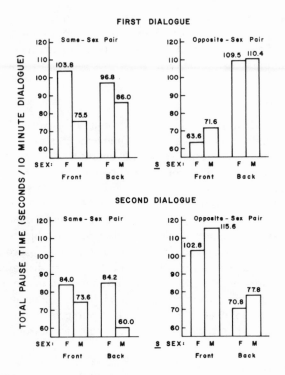

FIG. 6.2.   Four way interaction for total pause time in speech.

the second dialogue did not affect the already established verbal behavior. Opposite-sex pair subjects had less verbal production in the first dialogue when they could not see the other person than when they could see the other person.

Number of Long Pauses

A significant effect for the order of visibility conditions was found for the number of long pauses. Long pauses refer to discrete pauses of 10 seconds following which the experimenter was required to ask a question. The mean number of long pauses for subjects in the back-first condition was 4.23 and the mean number of long pauses for subjects in the front-first condition was 2.54 ($F = 5.29$, $p < .05$). These means refer to the number of long pauses that occurred for an average 10-minute period across both visibility conditions. Subjects in the back-first condition had more long pauses leading to experimenter "encouragement" to continue speaking than subjects in the front-first condition.

A significant order of visibility conditions by visibility condition interaction was also found for the number of long pauses that occurred ($F = 17.31$, p

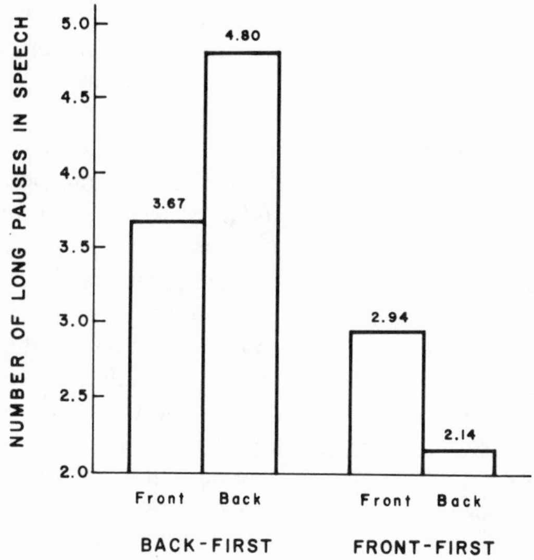

FIG. 6.3. The effect of order of visibility conditions by visibility condition interaction on the number of long pauses in speaking.

$< .001$). This is illustrated in Fig. 6.3. (It should be remembered that the difference between the front-first conditions and the back-first conditions is due to the significant main effect for the order of visibility conditions.) In general, the experimenter was required to ask more questions to facilitate speaking in the first dialogue than in the second dialogue independent of the visibility conditions.

In addition there was a significant sex-of-subject by sex-of-experimenter by order-of-visibility conditions by visibility condition interaction for the number of long pauses in speech ($F = 4.56$, $p < .05$). As total pause time was highly correlated with the number of long pauses ($r = .882$ in the front condition and $r = .814$ in the back condition) and the four-way interactions replicate each other, only the four-way interaction for total pause time, which is the more common measure, was presented here.

DISCUSSION

One of the most surprising results is the strong effect of the first interaction on the subsequent verbal interaction, which remained relatively unaffected by the fairly dramatic changes in visibility conditions. It appears that a basic verbal style of relating to the experimenter became established quickly in the initial dialogue and persisted in the second. That this occurred in spite of experimental efforts to find within-subject differences further suggests the strength of this "first impressions are lasting" phenomenon. Overall, it appears subjects were influenced by the initial conditions of the experimental situation, established a style of interacting and then maintained that style independent of subsequent changes in the situation. Perhaps subjects preferred and felt more involved in their second dialogue because they had already gone through the ambiguous (and possibly anxiety-provoking) task of establishing an appropriate role in their first dialogue. The experimenter's nondirective approach might make continuing that role the safest course, or it may have been construed as tacit approval of that style. The additional fact that the experimenter needed to ask more questions in the first dialogue (due to the subject's long pauses) further suggests that subjects were adapting their verbal behavior in the second dialogue to fit what they learned in the first (that they should keep talking).

Although the results here are severely limited to *verbal behaviors within a short initial interaction*, the implications of this "first impressions are lasting" phenomenon require further exploration. A consistent and resilient pattern of verbal interacting was established here in less than 10 minutes (cf. Hastorf, Schneider, & Polefka, 1970). How permanent is this style once established? Would it persist in another interaction a week later? Psychotherapists and psychoanalysts are both acutely aware of the importance of how sessions begin. As the client begins to deal with his feelings about the therapist, a great many hidden assumptions or expectations are found to be based on brief and fleeting initial impressions from either the beginning of the session or the beginning of the treatment. It is interesting to note that psychoanalysts interview the client face-to-face for one or more sessions before moving to the couch arrangement. This initial mode of interaction is used to establish the patient's suitability for treatment and to discuss business aspects of times and payment. These initial face-to-face interactions might create a pattern of relating influencing the subsequent on-the-couch verbal behavior. Perhaps, it is important for both therapists and analysts to recognize the potential magnitude of the style of the initial encounter in establishing the patient's subsequent verbal style of relating.

Focusing then on the initial dialogue as being the best unbiased indicator of the effects of the experimental manipulations on verbal behavior we find that both sex and visibility have a significant effect on the verbal behavior pattern established. Opposite-sex pairs talk more than same-sex pairs when they start the interaction face-to-face and less than same-sex pairs when they start back-to-front. If we interpret pauses of silence as verbal inhibition, it would seem that the back condition is more inhibiting than the front condition. Subjects in the back-first condition had significantly more long pauses requiring experimenter "encouragement questions" than subjects in the front-first condition.

Body movement was also significantly affected by visibility such that subjects moved less in the back condition than the front condition. An interpretation of lack of movement as motoric inhibition is consistent with the interpretation of the aforementioned findings. Subjects had a more difficult time talking freely or moving freely in the back condition. *Body movement did not seem to be affected by the "first impressions are lasting" phenomenon, however.* Although we can suggest that verbal norms become established, motoric behavior here seems to conform to the immediate situation. Overall, the findings indicate that the back visibility condition is potentially more inhibiting than the front condition under certain conditions (such as receiving it first or being with an opposite-sex partner) thus replicating Wolf's (1973) results, and, more generally, for the motoric mode.

The finding here that the verbal behavior of opposite-sex pairs was significantly affected by visibility conditions whereas that of same-sex pairs was not, clearly supports the opposite-sex pair hypothesis. This is true of both the first and the second dialogue subjects engaged in, even though the visibility conditions reversed between the dialogues. That opposite-sex pairs in this study were different from same-sex pairs was also reflected in the subjects' overall feelings about the experimenter. Same-sex-pair subjects felt more understood by, involved with, liking for and liked by the experimenter than opposite-sex-pair subjects. Perhaps opposite-sex pair subjects were in general more cautious and inhibited in this particular situation than same-sex pair subjects due to potential anxiety caused by an opposite-sex experimenter.

One possible reason why a same-sex experimenter would engender less potential anxiety than an opposite-sex experimenter might be that subjects could identify more with a same-sex experimenter. Subjects may have felt more confident that their dialogue was appropriate or interesting to someone they perceived as more similar to themselves. If subjects were initially unsure of themselves with an opposite-sex experimenter, the immediate feedback from the experimenter would be more important to those subjects for the regulation of their behavior.

A second reason might be underlying sexual feelings engendered by the opposite-sex experimenter. The potential for intimacy in terms of sharing private feelings was present as well as an accepting (albeit marginal) stance on the part of the experimenter. The ambiguity and lack of immediate feedback would again create an extremely difficult (and anxiety-provoking) situation for the appropriate regulation of behavior. Emerging sexual feelings would need to be carefully regulated and controlled or might be disturbing and disruptive to ongoing thought processes. As the experimenters were about 7 years older (on the average) than the majority of the subjects, this implies that the sex of interactant could have an effect beyond immediate peer relationships that has not been demonstrated in previous research.

The significant sex effect found for body movement shows that females were less active than males. There does not seem to be a single, good explanation for this sex of subject effect. Is it due to greater anxiety and inhibition in the females? Or is it due to a generally higher physical activity level for males? And might this latter difference be a result of cultural patterning? Part of this sex difference may also relate to the way in which subjects moved. Mahl (1968, chapter 2) reported that males engaged in more intrusive movements (such as pointing), whereas females had more inclusive movements (such as folding arms or crossing legs). The recording chair would be more sensitive to movements away from the body (intrusive) than movements close to the body (inclusive). These possibilities remain to be resolved by future research.

Several of the self-report results involving subjective ratings of comfort did not readily lend themselves to the interpretation of the findings advanced here. Subjects with female experimenters reported themselves as having significantly less overall comfort, depth of feelings, and openness (feelings-about-self measure) than subjects with male experimenters. Although this suggests that the experimenters' sex was a factor that was noticed and had an effect on subjects, the rationale for this single difference is not immediately apparent. The effect of visibility conditions on male and female subjects' experienced ease-and-comfort-speaking was also difficult to interpret. Females reported more comfort speaking for the back condition, whereas comfort for males did not seem to be affected by the visibility conditions. This finding did not relate to any of the other results in this study and contradicts the results Argyle et al. (1968) reported for comfort.

Self-reported comfort in speaking was also affected by the order of visibility conditions. If the order of visibility conditions was back-first, then subjects were about equally comfortable speaking in both conditions, whereas, if the order was front-first, then subjects were more comfortable speaking in the back condition. This effect is composed of two factors: that subjects were more comfortable in the back condition, and that subjects were more comfortable in the second condition. As these two factors are confounded, it cannot be determined what their relative contributions to the overall effect are. Considering the previously discussed order effects, it is most probable that the second factor is largely responsible for this effect, supporting the idea that subjects had already established their mode of verbal behavior by the second dialogue. Given the difficulty in interpreting the results found here for self-reported comfort in speaking and the inconsistencies found in the previous research, it seems that subjective ratings of comfort in speaking are very situation specific. Generalizations to other situations made on the basis of comfort ratings are probably not reliable.

Aside from research in clinical situations, these results are directly applicable to many other kinds of psychological research. Almost all studies involving human subjects require some form of social interaction between the subject and the experimenter and/or other subjects. Given the potential importance of initial norms of behavior established early in the experiment, more attention should be given to the effect this has on subsequent experimental manipulations. In addition, both the visibility condition and sex of the other person can be expected to interact relative to subjects' general inhibition in the experimental situation. Results commonly interpreted as sex differences may, in fact, be caused by the relative sex of the experimenter or confederate, the sex of seen or unseen observers, the visual condition in which the experimental task is performed, or by the visual situation and sex of interactants of the preliminary procedure. The one-way-seen visibility condition used here could be applicable to any situation in which the significant other cannot be seen. Situations in which the subject is forced to attend to a specific stimulus, such as slides, memory drums, or tachistiscopes, may induce various degrees of inhibition relative to the sex of the operator, experimenter, or observer. As the results here duplicated Wolf's (1973) study, which used a one-way mirror to create the one-way-seen effect, the possible effects of visibility and gender also need to be examined in any research using one-way mirrors.

SUMMARY AND CONCLUSIONS

This study demonstrates the importance of considering both gender and visibility as significant factors affecting behaviors in verbal, behavioral, and self-report modalities. Subjects had fewer body movements and more long pauses in speech when they could not see, but were seen by, the experimenter. Subjects quickly established a *verbal* mode of behavior influenced by the immediate interpersonal situation (sex of and visual status of the interactant) that, once established, was not influenced by subsequent changes in visibility conditions. The visibility condition affected speech only if the interactant was of the opposite sex. Subjects had more total pause time in speech when they could not see but were seen by an opposite-sex experimenter.

It is suggested that the results are a function of variations in anxiety and inhibition. And some of the findings are tentatively related to psychotherapeutic interactions. It is acknowledged that the findings may be limited to short-lived interactions. The interpretation of these results as reflecting variations in the general verbal and behavioral inhibition of subjects suggests further research in a variety of situations, including both clinical and research settings.

ADDENDA (GFM)

It is not easy to relate the results of Wolf's study to those we present in chapters 2 and 12 concerning variations in visibility conditions. This seems primarily due to the lack of comparability in the dependent measures in the three studies. Wolf's measure of the amount of body movement does not distinguish between various kinds of movements as did the frequency ratings for autistic (personal-expressive) and communicative gestures reported in chapter 2. Thus, we do not know if Wolf's finding of decreased body movement in his back-condition is comparable to our finding of decreased communicative gesturing in the back-to-back condition, or is inconsistent with our finding of increased autistic gesturing in that condition. Likewise, we cannot tell if the finding by Wolf of a tendency for greater pausing in his back-condition is consistent with our finding of greatly increased use of "ah" in our "telephone-type" situation. This uncertainty results from the fact that we do not know how the frequency of "ah" is related to the frequency of the pauses measured by Wolf.

Taken together, the three studies highlight for us the significance of at least four factors: (1) the need to thoroughly investigate the differences between the symmetrical face-to-face, the asymmetrical can't see-but-can-be-seen, and the symmetrical can neither see-nor be seen conditions. Such research will elucidate further the role of seeing the other, being seen by the other, and the presence or absence of symmetry of these factors; (2) the need to investigate the effects of the preceding variations on different modalities of behavior. Such research would not only investigate such general classes as verbal and nonverbal, but also significant categories of each of those. For example, both verbal content and "the hows" of speech need to be investigated in these regards. For example, the visible communicative gestures, autistic activity, postures, and the invisible autonomic activity and skeletal tensions also need to be studied in these regards; (3) Wolf's finding of a main effect of visibility on body movements but not on verbal behavior is consistent with our findings of a back-to-back effect on gesture type but not on speech disruptions. Together, these results underscore the need to investigate vigorously the channel-specific hypothesis advanced in chapter 2; (4) the need to investigate the interaction of the visibility conditions and all major, significant relationships between the interactants; such as: genders, age, social class, power status, affiliation (friend or stranger, e.g.,) etc.

7 Questions for the Future

Throughout the preceding chapters, I have mentioned numerous specific problems for future research. In this chapter, I wish to propose and discuss briefly four general areas of nonverbal behavior that I believe are important and would be very fruitful for the future researcher to investigate. These four areas are:

1. The use of nonverbal behavior to measure change in psychotherapy.
2. The contribution of nonverbal behavior to one's sensory experience.
3. Developmental changes in nonverbal behavior.
4. The embodiment of interpersonal relations.

THE USE OF NONVERBAL BEHAVIOR TO MEASURE CHANGE IN PSYCHOTHERAPY

This potential use of nonverbal behavior has always intrigued me. The objective nature of such an indicator is one of its chief attractions. Previous research has implied that change in nonverbal behavior might be useful as an outcome measure. Felix Deutsch's (1947, 1949, 1952) work on postures of psychoanalytic patients suggested this, as does the work of Ekman and Friesen (1968, 1974), Freedman (1972), Steingart and Freedman (1975), and Waxer (1976), which demonstrated nonverbal correlates of depression, and that of Freedman (1972) and Steingart and Freedman (1975), which suggests that there may also be nonverbal correlates of schizophrenia. The observations of Freud and of our own initial interview study, both of which were presented in the opening sections of chapter 2, also suggest such a use of nonverbal behavior because those observations indicate that specific conflicts may be manifested in body movements.

I know of only five systematic studies that have actually demonstrated that this potential is a very promising one. Ranelli and Miller (1981) found that pretreatment hand and head movements differentiated depressed patients who responded and those who did not respond to treatment with amitriptyline (Elavil). Four studies have demonstrated that the nonverbal behavior of severely depressed patients changes with remission (Ekman & Friesen, 1968, 1974; Fisch, Frey, & Hirsbrunner, 1983; and Kiritz, 1973 summarized in Ekman & Friesen, 1974). Such results are not unexpected because motor retardation and dejected behavior are among the outstanding symptoms of depression. But the preceding studies suggest that the changes in nonverbal behavior with remission from depression are not only increases in animation. Thus, Ekman and Friesen (1974) found that specific hand illustrator movements increased with remission, whereas hand touching of the body did not. And Fisch et al. found that complexity of body movements increased with remission, as well as general mobility and dynamic activation.

Here I present two observations from a psychoanalysis that suggest how changes in nonverbal behavior during the course of therapy might reflect psychological changes that are more specific than general diagnostic status.

Evangeline, a young married woman in her 20s, sought treatment to resolve her conflict over whether or not to continue her marriage. In the early months, her analysis was marked by the emergence and working through of a conflict over a wish to regress. Then, as her analysis progressed, a sexual-identity conflict emerged as a basic problem. Evangeline was in analysis for some 300 hours. Most of that time I kept the type of systematic records I described in chapter 3 (p. 76) when I discussed the A → B phenomenon.

A Change in Basic Position

The first observation I present concerns one of her basic positions on the couch in the first few months—her *curling up* on the couch. Figure 7.1 illustrates the vicissitudes and context of this posture during her analysis. She started to curl up in the third hour and repeated this in her fourth and fifth hours. In her sixth hour she reported the dream outlined in the illustration.

> First, she was in my office, with a "Do Not Disturb" sign on the door. Then, she was in an adobe room, where she covered with a blanket an American Indian maiden curled up on a bed.

In these early instances of curling up she was manifesting, first in her nonverbal behavior, her wish to regress. In the dream and in later telling of her urge to sleep on the couch she was *beginning* to think and talk about this wish.

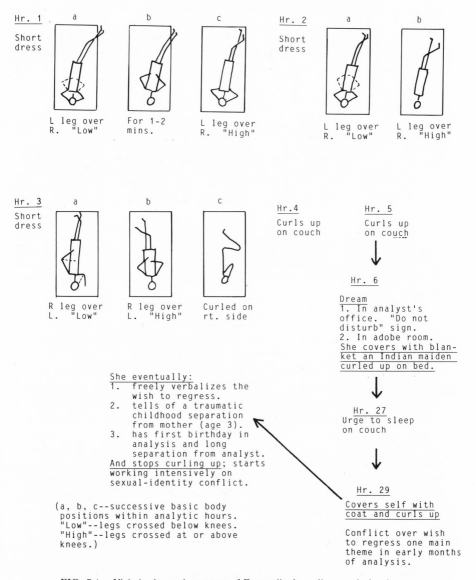

FIG. 7.1.   Vicissitudes and contexts of Evangeline's curling up during her psychoanalysis.

In covering herself with her coat as she curled up in the 29th hour, she was freer in fulfilling it. As the hours went by she freely, openly verbalized her regressive wish. (We have just seen, incidentally, the unfolding of a beautiful A → B.) In Fig. 7.2, we see the changing frequency of her curling up in her analysis. She curled up only in these early months.

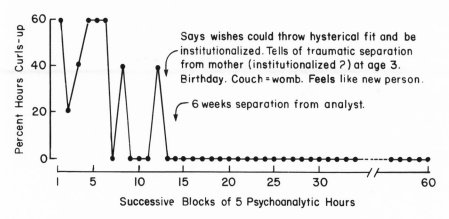

FIG. 7.2. The changing frequency of Evangeline's curling up over the course of 300 consecutive psychoanalytic hours.

Her verbalization of her wish to regress reached a crescendo in hours 60 through 64, shortly before our August interruption. Thus, she said:

> She wished to throw a hysterical fit and be institutionalized. She wished to sleep on the couch. Her birthday occurred. On it, she wished the couch were a hammock and she could feel like she was being rocked by her mother, felt like she could really return to her childhood and that she would like being back in the womb.

In the midst of all this she told of a traumatic separation from her mother that might very well have been an important cause of her current conflicted wish to regress. A long desired, only child, she was pampered and "spoiled rotten" by her mother in her early years. Then, at 3 or 4, her mother went away for a long time. Perhaps she had a nervous breakdown and was hospitalized; the patient isn't sure. Her life of indulgence now changed drastically. For example, her father refused to dress her in the morning as her mother had done. He just threw her clothes on the floor and said "Get dressed." She fussed and complained, but, she said "I learned to dress myself in one day."

Following these eventful hours, she said in hour 65; "I feel like a snail or a turtle. I'm changing. I'm not sure if I'm getting bigger or smaller. And my shell doesn't fit me anymore . . . I feel like I've shed the mothering bit." Two sessions later the summer break started.

As you can see, Evangeline never curled up again. And she progressed from being considerably involved with her conflict over regression to being greatly concerned with her sexual identity.

Just as the changing incidence of curling up reflected this change in her therapy, so another aspect of her nonverbal behavior reflected a general

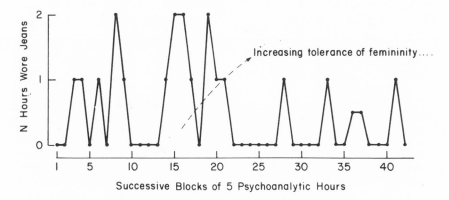

FIG. 7.3.   Changing frequency of Evangeline's wearing of jeans during 220 psychoanalytic hours.

movement from primarily a phallic-competitive position to primarily a feminine position.

A Change in Clothing

Her clothing reflected this therapeutic change, as Fig. 7.3 illustrates. You can see that there was overall a decrease in the frequency of her wearing jeans and a corresponding increase in her wearing skirts. (Twice in the course of all this she wore jeans under a skirt! I stopped recording her clothing after hour 220.)

The contrast between the following two dreams and their contexts reflects, I believe, the therapeutic change indicated by her changing clothes preference.

When she came to her 28th hour, Evangeline was wearing blue jeans and a white Mexican shirt. About her waist she wore a colorful woven belt, knotted with narrow, 12-inch tassled ends hanging down from her waist towards her groin. She looked decidedly "boyish."

The recounting of an argument with her husband in which he tried to lay down the law about her relations with other men and the aftermath to the argument were the focus of her associations. Well into the hour she suddenly spread her legs widely, the tassled ends of her belt fell between her thighs. She picked them up and toyed with them as she spoke of strong feelings of rebellion against her marriage and her husband. A phrase from the chorus of Marat de Sade kept running through her mind: She wasn't sure of the words, but it was the chorus of the song about the revolution.

In her next hour, she was dressed in a skirt. She continued to be preoccupied with her husband's anger at her. Finally, she reported having had a dream the night before. The following excerpt from the dream illuminates

the phallic substratum of her masculine attire and demeanor in the preceding
hour, as well as her marital rebellion.

She and group of cowboys were mounted on roundup type horses. They were
in a field alongside a cliff. Tigers kept coming over the cliff. She and the
cowboys were equipped with long poles. They used the poles to keep the
tigers at a safe distance and also to round them up and herd them into pens.
    Two of the tigers kept being run over and trampled on the ground. She felt
detached from, unsympathetic for, absolutely indifferent towards the tigers at
the end of her pole and even about those trampled and bleeding on the ground.
She knew there was nothing to fear about the tigers as long as she kept them at
a distance, at the end of the pole.

Some 8 months later, Evangeline's femininity was budding. One day
(122nd hr.) she came dressed in a yellow sweater-blouse and a beige suede
skirt, darkish hose, and beige knee boots. Her hair was long and loose.
About her mid-section was a most remarkable floral display: a belt and a
long-decorative bundle of grape-like flower beads made out of soft yarns of
reds, yellows, greens, and a touch of lavender. When walking upright this
decorative piece hung at her side. But when she lay on the couch she
unobtrusively placed it over the crevice between her thighs. It lay there,
colorful, varying from 2 to 4 or more inches in width and 6 to 8 inches in
length.
    A week later (126th hr.) Evangeline wore a muted lavender knit coat-
dress, lavender hose, and beige boots. Her hair was braided in two long
braids into which were braided rather wide colorful ribbons. My total impression of her the moment she entered my office was, *"Indian Maiden."* Some
20 minutes into the hour she said that as she entered my office today she
recalled a bit from a dream she had last night. She didn't want to tell it to me;
she wasn't sure why. She reported the dream fragment.

Her hands were submerged in something opaque and wet. She took them out
and *she was amazed at their whiteness, their pure whiteness, and they had perfectly
shaped fingernails.*

She went on to say that her hands were so feminine in the dream. She told
how in high school and college she had envied various girls for their feminine
hands and nails. By contrast, her hands were, and are, usually calloused and
her nails broken from her craft work. Then she told of a memory about her
10th year that had kept recurring to her the last few days.

As a 10-year-old, she discovered some clay in the hills back of her house. Day
after day, she carried buckets of the dirt down to the house. There she sifted it
repeatedly until she had fine clay powder. She mixed it with water and made

hundreds of small figures out of it. She had them all about the patio, baking in the sun.

She chuckled as she recalled how she sweated and toiled that summer. She felt this was how the Indians did it.

Referring to her dream of her hands being so white, and mindful of her reluctance to tell it to me, I asked: "Could it be that you are experiencing a birth of your femininity, and that you feel conflicted about this happening to you? Hence you *dream* of having such feminine hands?"

It could be, she said. And my remark "reminded" her that she had a *dream* this past weekend. (This was 2 or 3 days after she wore the display, which I had termed "floral" at the time in my process notes.)

> She was looking at the trunk of a young sapling tree. Its bark was smooth and gray. Then, as she watched, she saw that buds had formed and were blossoming into dogwood-like blossoms: pinks and whites. When she saw this, she said, "Damn, it is January. They will freeze."

I asked, "Are you afraid your femininity will blossom into a hostile environment?" She answered, "Rather, I myself am afraid of my femininity." Later she said she realized that she has always been in a struggle with it.

Two hours later, Evangeline told me that over the past 2 to 3 weeks she had been experiencing a new sense of her body. This was a sense of the bones in her body. For the first time in her life she had become aware of her joints: her shoulders, rib cage, and her pelvis. All her life her sense of her body had been of her muscles. Before she was a "muscle" person; now she was a "bone" person.

These last comments by Evangeline may cause the reader to wonder if she knew of my interest in nonverbal behavior and the body and was trying to please me with them. As far as I know, the answers are "No." I never told her of my interest and rarely commented on her nonverbal behavior.

I do not want to imply that I think basic postures and clothing are necessarily the very best potential nonverbal indicators of therapeutic change. My observations are only exemplary. As I discussed in chapter 1, the realm of nonverbal behavior is richly variegated. It is probably the source of numerous change indicators.

THE CONTRIBUTION OF NONVERBAL BEHAVIOR TO ONE'S SENSORY EXPERIENCE

Everyday life and experimental psychology convince us that sensory input from the external world and from our internal world of thought and bodily action play a crucial role in the maintenance of our usual modes of behavior.

"Experiments of nature," for example, make us aware of the significance for us of being surrounded by our *customary external environment.* Most of us work best when we have about us our preferred sounds and sights. Strange sounds and sights have various interfering effects on us: They can distract, excite, frighten, and so forth, as any traveler to strange cities and countries knows. Drastic changes in the external world lead to marked behavioral changes. The extreme environment of the Nazi concentration camps caused marked changes in the moral behavior of some inmates (Bettelheim, 1943). The social isolation and stimulus monotony of Polar explorers and prisoners in solitary confinement can seriously disturb psychological functioning, to the point of causing hallucinations.

Other, cruel experiments of nature demonstrate the vital role of *sensory feedback* for normal functioning. The congenital deaf do not learn normal speech; those deafened after learning to speak lose control over certain aspects of speech, such as loudness and intonation (see chapter 21). The loss of the usual kinesthetic sensory feedback leads to the characteristic, unusual gait of *tabes dorsalis.*

"Experiments of science" confirm and greatly extend what we learn from everyday life. Numerous laboratory experiments in *external sensory deprivation,* (e.g., Bexton, Heron, & Scott, 1954; Solomon, Kubzansky, Leiderman, Mendelson, Trumbull, & Wexler, 1961), stimulated largely by the thought of Hebb (1949), have shown that an influx of external stimuli is essential for ego functioning. Without it there may be loss of control of thinking, illusions and hallucinations, changes in fantasy life, and a shift in the drive-defense balance resulting in the emergence into consciousness of disturbing wishes. Such findings, and those from everyday life cited earlier, led Rapaport (1958) to the general formulation that a *continual influx of external stimulation is a prerequisite for maintaining the more mature secondary process mode of functioning and, indeed, for keeping all our behavior relatively free from domination by our basic drives.*

Many researchers have also studied the role of *internal sensory feedback* in the maintenance of normal functioning. Much of this work has involved *auditory feedback.* In chapter 21, we review this literature and report some of our own work. There you will see that interference with normal auditory feedback, either by such techniques as *delaying* it or by *masking* it, has marked effects on speech. Also, masking of auditory feedback results in more general changes as well, similar to those reported in the sensory deprivation literature.

Still another, quite different, source provides an impetus to attend to feedback from nonverbal behavior. This is a traditional line of thought in behavioristic psychology. J. B. Watson repeatedly emphasized the theoretical role of kinesthetic feedback in *"the stream of behavior"* (e.g., 1907, 1924). Clark Hull, one of his most illustrious descendants, made great theoretical use of the concept of response-produced cues, his symbolized r → s (Hull, 1943).

Missing from the literature is a body of data about the significance of sensory feedback from nonverbal behavior. We know, of course, that kinesthetic feedback is essential for motor skills. But what about the significance of the sensory feedback arising from the entire range of nonverbal behaviors sketched in chapter 1? *Everytime we act, in any way, we create sensory feedback.* This might be *kinesthetic* feedback from movements, tensions, postures; it might be *indirect tactile* consequences of our actions, such as the sensations of licking or touching our lips; it might be the *visual experience* provided by the sight of our body movements or bits of our clothing, and so forth. From all we know about the significance of external and feedback sensory input in other domains of behavior, briefly reviewed earlier, we should be prepared to find that feedback from our nonverbal behavior is of equal, but *largely unknown* significance.

We have discussed (chapter 4) why we know so little about this matter: the perspective of past researchers has been preempted by the paradigms of "expression" or "discharge" and of "communication" or "regulation" of interpersonal relations. Both paradigms emphasize the external *action* aspect of nonverbal behavior. Norbert Freedman and his colleagues are an exception: They have paid attention to the sensory consequences of nonverbal behavior (e.g., Freedman, 1977; Grand, 1977). Ekman and his colleagues are also exceptional: They have mentioned the possibility that noncommunicative gestures might function to provide the person with sensory experiences (Ekman & Friesen, 1969) and that the kinesthetic feedback from facial expressions might influence autonomic changes associated with emotions (Ekman, Levenson, & Friesen, 1983).

In chapters 2, 3, and 4 we reported various instances in which sensory feedback resulting from nonverbal behavior seemed to be significant in the subject's experience. And we discussed in chapter 3 how such sensory feedback might contribute to the emergence of unconscious material into dreams, conscious imagery, and recollection or verbalization. In chapter 4, we discussed how sensory feedback might be essential to the embodiment of interpersonal relationships and identification. We assume that with these observations and discussions we have barely scratched the surface.[1] In recent

---

[1]One of the results reported by some investigators in sensory deprivation illustrates the potential we have in mind. Subjects in those experiments frequently experienced marked changes in *body image*. I once summarized some of this data as follows (Mahl, 1971):

One subject said "My arms aren't here sometimes. . . . They feel to be in the back of my body . . . my head seems to be floating . . . parts of my body keep missing and coming back . . . [Azima, Vispo, & Azima, 1961]." Another subject felt herself getting "smaller and smaller [Zuckerman, Albright, Marks, & Miller, 1962];" another feared

years, we have become increasingly obsessed with the hunch that some of the future, great discoveries about nonverbal behavior will come from research in this area.[2]

Although our emphasis on the sensory consequences of nonverbal behavior arose directly from our research just mentioned, it is consistent with a growing interest in the sensory consequences of action in quite different domains of behavior. Increasing attention is being paid to the role of neuromuscular (Buck, 1980; Ekman, Levenson, & Friesen, 1983) and mechanical (Zajonc, 1985) feedback in emotional experience and expression. And the reinforcement of actions by their sensory consequences has been demonstrated in animals (Kish, 1966), in human neonates (Siqueland, 1968), in normal children (Rheingold, Stanley, & Doyle, 1964; Stevenson & Odom, 1961), in human adults (Benton & Mefferd, 1967), in autistic and retarded children (Aiken & Salzberg, 1984; Bailey & Meyerson, 1969; Fineman, 1968; Gunter, Brady, Shores, Fox, Owen, & Goldzweig, 1984; Rehagen & Thelen, 1972; Rincover, 1978; Rincover, Cook, Peoples, & Packard, 1979; Rincover, Newsom, Lovaas, & Koegel, 1977) and in Gilles de la Tourette Syndrome (Bliss, 1980). *Sensory reinforcement* appears to be a ubiquitous phenomenon, occurring in a wide range of subjects and with a wide range of sensory modalities.

Thus, we believe future investigators have the happy prospect of discovering a new world. An appreciation of three facts might be useful to the future worker. First, the feedback may be direct, kinesthetic, or indirect, movement-produced sensory experience. Second, the feedback may function unconsciously or consciously. Third, *some* of the effects of the feedback may be similar to those revealed by research in external sensory deprivation and to those exposed by the studies of auditory feedback.

---

that his body parts would disappear and disintegrate (Cohen, Silverman, Bressler, & Shmavonian, 1961); others felt that their bodies were floating or revolving in space, that their arms or legs were rising, or that one limb was much shorter than another (Zubek, Aftanas, Kovach, Wilgosh, & Winocur, 1963). Another felt that his arm was "like a ton-weight and feels fatter than my body [Smith & Lewty, 1959]." Some subjects feel they cannot control their muscles . . . (Cohen et al., 1961). (pp. 145–146)

In retrospect I would pay attention to the belief of some of these investigators that such perceptual distortions were the result of the marked alteration in kinesthetic and related feedback caused by the *immobilization* enforced in these experiments, rather than of deprivation of external sensory feedbacks.

[2]In writing this chapter, I recalled that my first publication, and one of my first original ideas as a young student of psychology concerned the feedback of motor behavior (Snodgrass & Mahl, 1941). Behind those events was the general influence of J. B. Watson and R. H. Stetson.

THE DEVELOPMENTAL HISTORY OF NONVERBAL BEHAVIOR

All adult behavior has evolved during the individual's life and knowledge of that developmental history deepens our understanding of the behavior. These are such important considerations that the *genetic* is one of the basic "points of view" of psychoanalytic theory (Rapaport & Gill, 1959).

We showed in chapter 2 (p. 8) that Darwin early on hypothesized that adult expressive behavior evolved from childhood reactions. Our own work reported in chapters 2, 3, and 4 supported Darwin's hypothesis and illustrated several processes of such evolution. We believe that these processes should become the focus of intensive future research. That research may show that these processes permeate a great deal of adult nonverbal behavior and it very probably will elucidate much about those processes. We are speaking about the processes of: a *passive-active shift, minimization, interiorization, and the development of displacement-substitutes.* In the following paragraphs, we briefly illustrate and discuss them hoping to provide a few starting points for future research. (Buck, 1980, Ekman and Friesen, 1969, and von Raffler-Engel, 1981 provide other discussions of developmental aspects of nonverbal behavior.)

The Passivity-Activity Shift

Our clearest example of this shift was provided by Alec when he removed his pillow on the analytic couch, actively repeating an experience suffered passively at the hands of his mother in his early adolescence (chapter 3, p. 78). In chapter 4, we reported numerous instances in which this shift was pivotal in the phenomenon of the embodiment of interpersonal relations.

The passivity-activity shift permeates human behavior and development, to such an extent that Freud once proclaimed it to be one of polarities that dominate psychic life (Freud 1915c/1957c). Thus we should not be surprised if future research showed that it is prevalent in nonverbal behavior. The full ramifications of this shift in this arena need to be discovered.

Minimization

Minimization, a "formular abbreviation" (Hartmann, 1939), is inherent in the development of all motor skills. Common examples are provided by the change from deliberate, gross movements to automatic, deft, and abbreviated actions in learning to drive a car or to hit a ball. Thus, it is to be expected that minimization might also take place in the evolution of adult nonverbal behavior.

Darwin (1872/1955) suggested instances of it when he proposed that the clenched first of an angry man was a remnant of a larger pattern of attack behavior and that the downturned mouth of sadness was a residual of childhood screaming. Ekman and Friesen (1969) endorse such views.

Communicative, symbolic gestures seem to be subject to mimimization. The modern "fingertips kiss" prevalent throughout Europe and the British Isles, for example, appears to have evolved from an elaborate pattern of symbolically throwing a kiss and bowing to idols of gods or royal figures (Morris, Collett, Marsh, & O'Shaughnessy, 1979). The appearance of minimization in the field of gestures may be an extension of its operation in the entire, broad domain of nonverbal behavior.

Our own observations have included numerous instances of minimization. Some of them cited in chapter 2 were: the brief hand-to-mouth touch of Mrs. B, which appeared to have evolved from covering her ugly teeth with her hand in her childhood (p. 45); Mrs. B "played" with her wedding ring instead of removing it (p. 44); a woman dangled her shoe from her foot instead of letting it drop and initiate undressing (pp. 47–48). Other observations illustrated how mere muscular tensions replaced more extensive overt actions. These behaviors, however, blended minimization and interiorization.

Interiorization

Mr. Z, my 40-year-old psychotherapy patient, confided to me that as a child he was an avid thumbsucker, and that now he secretly sucked his tongue. Some women secretly masturbate by pressing their thighs together beneath their skirts. People may merely tense muscles instead of acting overtly, as in the example of Mrs. C's tensing her abdomen instead of actually pushing out her belly before me (p. 48).

These examples illustrate three ways in which one may interiorize: acting beneath the shield of one's clothing, acting within body cavities, merely tensing muscles beneath the skin.

How prevalent is interiorization? In what ways may it be achieved? What brings it about? These are questions pressing for an answer.

"Be Still!" Decreasing the Visibility of Nonverbal Behavior

One factor conducive to interiorization might be training children to cease, or at least inhibit, their overt nonverbal behavior. This is a common feature of child rearing, caricaturized by commanding the restless, fidgety child to "Be still!" Children typically learn to mute their speech (Cameron & Magaret, 1951, pp. 107 ff.). Do they typically learn analogously to quiet their expressive actions? Do muting speech and quieting "aimless" acts procede apace? What aspects of general psychological development contribute to these processes? For example, does learning to control autoerotic activity contribute to them? Superego development?

In chapter 2 (pp. 59–68), we reported an experiment indicating that visibility plays an important role in determining the frequency of "aimless" actions. Wolf's study reported in chapter 5 revealed similar results. Does learning to "Be still" give rise to the inhibitory effect of visibility on the nonverbal behavior of the adult? Are the processes of minimization and interiorization both ways of decreasing the visibility of nonverbal actions?

Production of Displacement Substitutes

When Mrs. C rubbed the back of her hand against the rough, scratch-plaster wall alongside the couch (pp. 46, 79, 97), she substituted the skin of her hand for the skin of her cheek and thereby achieved sensations like those in her childhood "bear hugs" with her father. The action, body parts, and sensations were displacement-substitutes for cheek-to-cheek rubbing and tingling in her cheek. By means of displacement-substitutes she could do visibly what she could not do with her analyst, given the rules of analysis and her internal conflicts. Many of the other observations we presented in earlier chapters were displacement-substitutes.

A professional acquaintance reported the following to me after listening to one of my lectures about nonverbal behavior. Like Mr. Z, she was a passionate thumb-sucker in childhood. She broke that habit by substituting another action for it: rapidly rubbing together the tips of her thumb and forefingers. Now, when she is nervous, she automatically does that. Only she (and now I) know why.

The contrast between Mr. Z's hidden tongue sucking and her digit-tip rubbing illustrates the versatility of the displacement process, and the probable centrality in it of sensory experience.

The ubiquity of displacement-substitutes in nonverbal behavior is evidenced by the fact that it has clearly contributed to the evolution of many of the symbolic gestures studied by Morris et al. (1979). They make clear how the hand and its parts may substitute for many body parts: for the mouth, male genitals, female genitals, and the anus.

The Hand

My reading of Morris et al. (1979) and reflection about the frequent hand activity among my own observations raises the question: Is the hand, by virtue of its prominence in man's behavioral repertoire, a *preferred organ* for displacement from other body parts?

The production of displacement-substitutes during development clearly merits intensive study. It joins minimization and interiorization in adapting nonverbal behavior to the demands of the external world and in effecting defense against internal wishes. (The process of defense is not limited to these processes, however, as we have mentioned several times.) These three developmental processes also contribute to the embodiment of interpersonal experiences.

The Embodiment of Interpersonal Relationships

I feel in my bones that this is an extremely important phenomenon, about which very little is known. Our own observations constitute one tentative step along the way of exploring it. We raised numerous questions in chapter 4 that we believe require investigation. Here I want to underscore, by repeating them, two of those questions that seem to me to be of paramount significance.

First, what are the developmental roots of this process? Do they include primary process hallucinatory wish fulfillment? Hallucinating being nursed is after all an embodiment of an interpersonal experience. Do the childhood origins include transitional object relations (Winnicott, 1951), masturbatory phantasies, fantasy play with toys, enactment in play of fantasied roles? Positive answers to these questions would not merely elucidate the development of the embodiment process; they would indicate that it is one bolstered by the most potent influences and, hence, is one of the preemptive functions in adult nonverbal behavior.

Secondly, what part does the embodiment process play in the internalization of interpersonal relations? In psychoanalytic theory, internalization is conceptualized typically in terms of object-representations. And the latter are conceptualized typically as *cognitions*. What are such cognitions? Is there a persisting sensorimotor substrate to them? Does the embodiment process contribute significantly to this substrate? Answers to these questions would elucidate one of the most important psychological processes, according to psychoanalytic theory: the internalization of interpersonal relationships.

Sensory Experiences

It seems quite likely that sensory experience arising from nonverbal behavior is of basic significance in the processes of minimization, interiorization, the production of displacement-substitutes, and embodiment. Again, the sensory consequences of nonverbal behavior comprise a leading candidate for future research.

This concludes this first section of the book. We turn now from explorations in nonverbal behavior to explorations in vocal behavior.

II EXPLORATIONS IN VOCAL BEHAVIOR

8 Introduction

The focus of this second part of the book is research about a speech measure of a person's concurrent anxiety. I started this work over 30 years ago. In this chapter, I describe the initial context of this research, including the prospective purposes of the measure and my reasons for choosing the particular dimension of speech I selected. The initial context influenced the subsequent direction of our research. The next chapter describes the measure and its properties. Subsequent chapters present our investigations of its validity as an anxiety indicator.

THE INITIAL CONTEXT

Preceding the onset of this work, my research interests were mainly in psychophysiology. My concerns had evolved from the experimental production of increased gastric (HCl) acid secretion in dogs, monkeys, and humans via the instigation of chronic anxiety in the laboratory to a desire to study variations in HCl secretion in humans during spontaneously occurring, "real-life" fluctuations in anxiety (Mahl, 1949, 1950, 1952; Mahl & Brody, 1954; Mahl & Karpe, 1953). The intensive psychotherapeutic interview promised to be a fruitful situation for such research. Variations in the patient's anxiety regularly occur there, and that situation provides more information about the meaning of such variations than is usually the case for laboratory or life stress studies. To achieve my research goal I needed a measure that would be *unobtrusive* to make and that would portray the *immediate, fluctuating* intensities in the patient's anxiety as they occurred in the course of a therapeutic interview. Ideally, moreover, the measure should be a nonphysiological one: It should be a "psychic" one for the study of the psychosomatics of anxiety and HCl secretion, as well as for the future study of other somatic correlates of anxiety in this situation.

I had another nascent research interest when I started this work. I had become interested in the objective studies of the *process* of psychotherapy, which were flourishing at that time, due largely to the influence of Carl Rogers and his students (to cite only a few examples: Carnes & Robinson, 1948; Gillespie, 1952; Page, 1953; Porter, 1943; Raimy, 1948; Rogers, 1942, 1944; Snyder, 1945; Tindall & Robinson, 1947). Because the patient's anxiety is at the heart of the psychotherapeutic process, it was clear that significant research on the therapeutic process must include the study of the patient's anxiety. A review of the literature showed that only a few objective studies of therapy had tried to measure concurrent anxiety during interviews. Thus, the development of such a measure promised to be useful to psychotherapy research as well as in psychosomatic investigation.

The rapid development of high-fidelity sound-recording techniques following World War II made available a very convenient method for recording the ongoing vocal-verbal interchange of the patient and therapist. This constitutes a major, very important portion of the therapeutic interaction. Thus, I readily turned to the patient's recorded speech as a most promising medium for the desired measure.

The manifest verbal content, *what* is said, is an obvious part of the sound recording and is of special interest to most therapists. It was also of special interest to nearly all objective investigators of the therapeutic process: *Manifest verbal content measures were the order of the day* (e.g., Haigh, 1949; Hoffman, 1949; Seeman, 1949; Sheerer, 1949; Snyder, 1945; Stock, 1949; see review by Auld & Murray, 1955). Their primary method involved the development of numerous manifest verbal content measures. A measure of positive feelings about the self in interviews, for example, would be based on the number of patient utterances in separate interviews manifestly professing such feelings. Such a measure could be followed in the course of a therapy and might reflect the Rogerian goal of increasing as therapy proceeded.

I considered developing an analogous content measure of anxiety. To do so, in accordance with the typical procedures, I would prepare typescripts of recorded interviews, unitize the patient's talk into, say, sentences, and score these units for the presence of such manifest references as "fear," "nervousness," "scared," etc. A count of the number of such sentences would then be taken as an index of the level of the patient's concurrent anxiety. However, I rejected this approach because of what I regarded as two important flaws in the basic methodology: It ignored the complexity of function of manifest content and the significance of *how* the patient speaks, in contrast to *what* he or she says.

COMPLEXITY OF FUNCTION OF MANIFEST CONTENT

Sometimes, some people utter *anxious content* when they are in fact anxious. Thus, one frightened child might say "I'm scared." Another, not aware of his fear or not wanting to openly admit it, might make defensively distorted references such as "Are you scared?", or "He's scared."

But just as often frightened people may utter verbal content of quite a different kind. Another frightened child might speak with anger, another might, in effect, say "Help"; still another might simply say "Mom! Mom!". And sometimes people utter anxious content when they are not frightened, but are in fact feeling quite comfortable and are trying to maintain that state. Thus, a child might say "I'm scared, Mom" simply so that his mother will hold him or continue to do so. In all these examples, verbal content functions as *instrumental behavior*. Angry content may function to prevent awareness of one's anxiety and/or to ward off external sources of fear.[1] Pleading content may function to elicit comforting, protective behavior from another. Anxious content may function to elicit behavior from another that gratifies other needs. The situation is further complicated: Emotional states other than anxiety might prompt some of the same manifest content instigated by anxiety. An angry child may utter anger content; a dependent child wanting nurturance may call for his mother.

The following diagram illustrates the various relations between emotional states and the related verbal content just cited. By virtue of the instrumental function of verbal content, a given emotional state may prompt a person to utter diverse content, which may contain no reference to the emotional state. And diverse emotional states may cause the utterance of similar content. Such functional complexity makes manifest verbal content measures of anxiety, or other emotional states, very questionable. We have discussed this matter, especially the *instrumental viewpoint*, in detail elsewhere (Mahl, 1959, 1961a) and return to it again in chapters 16 and 17. Sullivan's (1954) explications of *security operations* were concerned with this issue and influenced our emphasis of it.

---

[1]Anna Freud's clinical illustrations of *identification with the aggressor* includes several instances in which anxiety clearly prompted angry verbalizations, as well as instances in which such verbal behavior had other sources (A. Freud, 1936/46, pp. 117–131).

There are still other problems with using manifest content. One is that *nonanxious content may arouse anxiety in the speaker* because of the psychodynamic significance of that content for the speaker. A child falsely telling his parent how "good" he has been, might become frightened that his lie will be detected. In chapter 10 (p. 195) we cite another concrete example when we describe an instance in which saying "I have a friend" apparently aroused anxiety and conflict in the speaker because of its psychodynamic ramifications.

Another, related problem is that *nonanxious content may be uttered by an anxious person because of the private meaning of the content for the speaker.* I have recently observed a very clear example of this phenomenon. In a hypnotherapy interview a woman relived being raped in her childhood by her uncle. As she did so she gave many vocal signs of reexperiencing the terror of the episode. And she made some manifest references to the terror. But the most frequent word in the account is *stairs.* That was because *stairs* had played a central role in the traumatic experience. In her reliving the experience, she said she was in her bed *upstairs,* she heard a noise *downstairs,* she went *downstairs,* someone who had been hiding in a closet behind the *stairs* grabbed her, he carried her down the cellar *stairs,* etc. Knowing the private meaning of the word *stairs* for this woman would enable one to include *it* in a content measure of fear in her case. But this type of interpretive content analysis plays no role in the usual methodology of content analysis.

HOW THE PATIENT SPEAKS

As usually practiced, manifest content analysis of psychotherapy interviews disregarded the patient's "tone of voice." This is a flagrant violation of clinical experience. *How* the patient talked seemed to me to be a more dependable indication of his emotional states than *what* he said (Reich, 1928/1948). Thus, I decided to develop a measure of anxiety and conflict based on *how* the patient talked.

The question was: Which of the many aspects of "tone of voice" would be appropriate ones? Pitch, volume, rate, etc.? Unfortunately there was no body of research on which to base a choice. I chose to use the phenomenon of "flustered," "disrupted" speech for two reasons. First, I believed that everyday clinical experience taught us that this aspect of the patient's speech was a very sensitive indicator of his anxiety and conflict. Second, I held the theoretical view that one effect of anxiety was to disrupt all complex ongoing behavior. Speech is an instance *par excellence* of complex, skilled behavior consisting of its peculiar blend of the execution of integrated, intricate motor and cognitive processes.

Over the years the *extralinguistic* status of this dimension of speech gained great appeal for me. By *extralinguistic* I mean that it is not part of the code, in contrast to certain other aspects of "tone of voice," such as some uses of pitch and volume. The contrast between an utterance with a rising versus a falling pitch, for example, distinguishes a question from a declarative statement. Similarly, the contrast between the different stresses in *síx-pácks* and *six pácks* is obviously of semantic significance (Birdwhistell in Sebeok, Hayes, & Bateson, 1964, p. 178). The phenomenon of "flustering" in speaking does not have any linguistic function. Because of its resulting freedom from restraint by the rules of language it is possible that this phenomenon is, along with other extralinguistic features, especially revealing of emotional status. It is also possible that its extralinguistic status renders "flustering" of speech less subject to voluntary (preconscious or conscious) control. Thus, in retrospect, I believe this extralinguistic status made the choice of this dimension of speech a fortunate one. (We have discussed extralinguistic phenomena in great detail elsewhere, see Mahl & Schulze, 1964. We consider this issue again at the close of the next chapter.)

I have not yet completed the account of the context for the origin of this work. So far, I have described all the *conscious, rational factors* that led me to choose *an aspect of speech* for intensive study. In retrospect, I have realized that an *unconscious, emotional factor* also contributed significantly to that particular choice. This purely personal factor was a complex one to which I alluded in the Preface. It arose from a strong intellectual-emotional attachment to my mentor, Professor R. H. Stetson, a world-renowned scholar of phonetics. My active mentorship, however, lacked any active interest on my part in phonetics. Over 10 years elapsed between the times of my active mentorship and my venturing into what was, heretofore, largely foreign territory for me. In the meantime, Stetson died a few years before this turn of events. Well after the fact, I realized that an unconscious, partial identification with him following the loss of him influenced my conscious, perfectly reasonable programmatic research decisions. Professor Stetson would turn over in his grave if he knew how I blended his indirect influence into my own evolving scientific career. What he cannot know will not disturb his peace, however, and I am able to give a more complete description of what would otherwise be understood as an episode in the supposedly impersonal, rational scientific process.

Although my interest in psychosomatics and psychotherapy played a major role in the onset of this work, you will see that my ensuing research was concerned almost entirely with the speech measure itself. I behaved like parents whose reasons for wanting and having children give way to a consuming interest in the children themselves.

Let us turn now to the beginning of a detailed examination of the "flustering" of speech.

Everyday Disturbances in Spontaneous Speech: General Properties[1]

Are there not very important things which can only reveal themselves, under certain conditions and at certain times, by quite feeble indications? . . . So do not let us under-estimate small indications: by their help we may succeed in getting on the track of something bigger.
—Sigmund Freud (1915–17/1963, p. 27)

Anyone who listens long enough to spontaneous speech notices from time to time that the orderly process of verbal expression has been disrupted. The listener intermittently senses that the speaker has blocked or become flustered, that the speech has become garbled or confused. The following interview excerpts illustrate such instances of flustered speech. The first is from a psychotherapy interview in which a 40 some-year-old male patient is telling the therapist about a pogrom that occurred in his childhood in Russia, following the 1917 revolution. This man had a high school education and was a farmer of sorts. P and T designate patient and therapist, respectively.

P: My uncle had his throat cut.

T: Mhm.

P: And my uncle . . . ah . . . he wasn't killed, but they tortured him. They took him and they slit his throat right . . . the skin . . . just cut the skin right around like this.

---

[1]Most of the empirical data in this chapter were first presented at the Annual Meeting of the American Psychological Association, September, 1956 (Mahl, 1956c).

T: Who did that? (said in a sudden manner)

P: Mmm . . . hulligan . . . holigan . . . huligans, whatever you call them.

T: The who?

P: The . . . ah . . . you know the . . . ah . . . sss . . . he was in . . . the . . . he . . . was dri . . . traveling from one town to the oth . . . next and—

T: Mhm.

P: —he was stopped by a couple . . . ah . . . if you know the situation in the South . . .

(N. B.) T: Were . . . were they . . . were they Russians or were they Bolsheviks?

P: Yes. Yeah . . . mujik . . . mujiks . . . peasants.

In this excerpt, the patient's speech is greatly disrupted.[2] At other times he spoke eloquently. As we saw, the therapist was not immune, either.

The second example is from a radio interview conducted in the 1950s by a husband–wife team with a radio and television newsman who was one of our most famous during and after the second World War. He was a college graduate, renowned for being extremely articulate and for his masculine persona. The excerpt illustrates how the speech of even such a person may be disrupted by anxiety. In her opening remark, the usually assertive female interviewer refers to a series of "couch" questions, ones she used to reveal the deeper aspects of her guests' personalities.

I: Female Interviewer

X-Y: The male public personality X First Name
                                 Y Last Name

I: One last . . . ah . . . couch question for you, X-Y. If you could invite any six people in history to dinner, whom would they be?

X-Y: Let me see. In any period in history?

I: Any period. And you can have current people too. You know, you can combine them.

X-Y: One . . . one would certainly be Sir Winston Churchill. A second one would be H. G. Wells. A third one would be Heinrich Heine. The fourth one, Marcus Aurelius. The fifth, Mr. Lincoln. And the sixth, now it gets really difficult, (I's first name), . . . ah . . . the sixth, I think, would be Beethoven.

---

[2]The excerpt "reads" more disturbed than it originally sounded, mainly because we typically "edit-out" most speech disturbances in our daily interaction.

I: You know something? You selected all men.

X-Y: I wonder why that was. I haven't a clue. I don't know why. I s-(I interrupts)

I: No woman in history, or currently, would interest you?

X-Y: No, no. Th . . . this . . . ah . . . ah . . . you trapped me somehow. I don't know how you did it, but . . . ah . . . ah . . . this—(I interrupts)

I: I didn't say anything about w . . . most men include, well maybe two women anyway and four men.

X-Y: Well, now some psychiatrist is going to conclude something about this but I'm sorry. It . . . I was . . . ah . . . Without warning, I was just saying the people who—(I interrupts)

I: All right. You named Churchill . . .

X-Y: I'm embarrassed.

Following this, the subject resumed his characteristic fluent speech.

Figure 9.1 presents a graph of the frequency of speech disruptions (see the following categories) in the preceding excerpt, save for saying "ah." The interviewer's loaded remark occurred where shown. Before it, the subject had spoken about 2000 words faultlessly (except for the use of "ah"). The effect of the remark is apparent in the transitory "flustering" of his speech.

I turn now to a description of the method we developed for measuring such "flustering" of speech. All the research to be described from here on

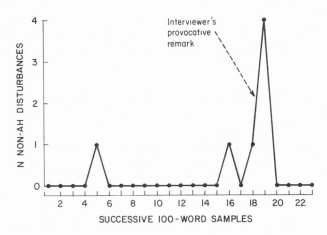

FIG. 9.1.   Speech disturbance graph of X-Y in the radio interview.

was based on tape recordings and verbatim typescripts of psychotherapy or experimental interviews.

THE SPEECH DISTURBANCE MEASURE

Speech Disturbance Categories and Ratios

We began by trying to identify and count clinically-perceived episodes of flustered speech by patients in their psychotherapy interviews. That attempt was based on the (mistaken) assumption that ordinarily a patient's speech procedes smoothly but episodically becomes "flustered." We learned that the reliability with which independent observers identified such episodes was poor. And we learned that the concept of "flustered" speech is too crude. Such episodes consist of various discrete types of disturbances. We developed, empirically, from the study of many tape recordings and typescripts a set of such speech disturbance categories that promised to be generally useful for our purposes. Our final set is presented in Table 9.1, where the categories are defined and illustrated.[3]

We have used the category set in studying the speech of some 500 English-speaking individuals, representing both genders, a wide range of ages, social backgrounds, educational levels, personality structures, and speaking situations. The preceding include patients in psychotherapy, interviewers in initial and therapy interviews, schizophrenic patients in research interviews, college students during role-playing and in investigative interviews, children during research interviews, university faculty members in seminar discussions, and various normal adults in various situations. We have not found it necessary to modify the present set for any particular individuals, samples of subjects, or speaking situations. Several other investigators have also used the set without reporting a need to modify it (Blumenthal, 1964; Boomer & Goodrich, 1961; Feldstein, 1962; and Siegman & Pope, 1965, e.g.,). Thus,

---

[3]Richard Karpe, M.D. (deceased), and I collaborated in the development of the present set of speech disturbance categories. That was exacting, but exciting work. I am grateful to him for the time, energy, and clinical experience which he contributed, often at a sacrifice of his limited leisure time.

In the beginning I was aware only that Freud (1901/1960) had worked with tongue slips. Since then, of course, I've discovered that others had been interested to some extent in phenomena similar to the speech disturbance categories: for example—Baker (1948, 1951), Davis (1940), Froschels and Jellinek (1941), Meringer and Mayer (1895), and Sanford (1942). Dibner (1956) developed a similar category set quite independently, and later workers proposed other sets derived in part from, or related to, ours and Dibner's: Boomer (1963), Krause and Pilisuk (1961), Maclay and Osgood (1959), for example.

TABLE 9.1

Definitions and Illustrations of the Speech Disturbance Categories

Category	Examples
(1) "Ah." Wherever the "ah" sound occurs it is scored. Less frequent variants are "eh," "uh," "uhm."	Well . . . ah . . . when I first came home.
(2) Sentence change (SC). A correction in the form or content of the expression while the word-word progression occurs. To be scored, these changes must be sensed by the listener as interruptions in the flow of the sentence.	Well she's . . . already she's lonesome. That was . . . it will be 2 years ago in the fall.
(3) Repetition (R). The serial, superfluous repetition of one or more words— usually of one or two words.	'Cause they . . . they get along pretty well together. He was . . . he was sharing the office.
(4) Stutter (St).	It sort of well l . . l . . leaves a memory.
(5) Omission (O). Parts of words, or rarely entire words, may be omitted. Contractions not counted. Most omissions are of final one or two parts of words and are associated with sentence change and repetition.	She mour . . . was in mourning for about 2 years before. Then their anni . . . wedding anniversary comes around.
(6) Sentence incompletion (Inc). An expression is interrupted, clearly left incomplete, and the communication proceeds without correction.	Well I'm sorry I couldn't get here last week so I could . . . ah . . . I was getting a child ready for camp and finishing up swimming lessons.
(7) Tongue slips (TS). Includes neologisms, the transposition of entire words from their "correct" serial position in sentence, and the substitution of an "unintended" for an intended word.	We spleat the bitches (for "split the beaches"). He was born in their hou(se) . . hospital and came to their house. The reason that I don't . . . didn't seem to feel the love for him (son) that I felt for J . . (daughter).
(8) Intruding incoherent sound (IS). A sound, which is absolutely incoherent to the listener. It intrudes without itself altering the form of the expression and cannot be clearly conceived of as a stutter, omission, or neologism (though some may be such in reality.)	If I see a girl now I'd like to take out I just . . . dh . . . ask her.

the set is a useful one for describing and measuring commonly found, everyday disturbances of speech.[4]

Hesitations and silent pauses, for example those not filled with "ah," do not appear in the category set, although they too often disrupt verbalization. Initially, their omission resulted from a methodological decision to measure them separately (Kasl & Mahl, 1956). Subsequently, we had sufficient doubt about the functional equivalence of hesitations to the categories of the present set that we did not pursue their investigation. Perhaps the present set could be usefully expanded by the addition of a suitable category for these phenomena. Anyone contemplating such a step, however, must contend with a variety of problems. One of these is distinguishing between pauses that disrupt speech and those that do not. Another is distinguishing "anxious" silence, from other kinds ("hostile" ones, e.g.,).

Speech may be peppered with the various disturbances, but most of them escape the awareness of both speaker and listener. Only when they occur at relatively rapid rates and are "bunched" does the listener perceive them, sensing an episode of "flustered" speech. Independent observers may have different thresholds for judging that rate which constitutes so-called "flustered" speech. If so, their reliability in judging speech as "flustered" suffers. The use of the categories proposed minimizes such problems of observer judgment.

---

[4]Other vocal phenomena come to mind as possibly related to the categories presented here and thus as candidates for inclusion in the category set. These include such things as "nervous" laughs, sighs, lip smacking, the characteristic use of intruding idiosyncratic expressions such as "you see," "see what I mean," "I don't know," "you know what I mean," "understand?," etc. Such phenomena have been studied as expressive behavior by others and ourselves but are not included in our set of speech disturbance categories. We intended the category set to cover the majority of syntactical and lexical disruptions and distortions in spontaneous speech, which result in confused messages when they occur at a rapid rate, not to include all possible expressive behavior accompanying the act of speaking. Nervous laughs, sighs, lip smacking etc. may accompany speech, but they are not uniquely involved in it. They may occur when a person is not speaking or even when he is alone. And neither they nor intruding characteristic expressions regularly, or necessarily, contribute to episodes of confused speech.

Mark Twain, generally acknowledged to be a master of dialect, made frequent use of our speech disturbance categories in the dialogue of *The Adventures of Tom Sawyer* (see chapter 19). (He used there Ah, sentence changes, sentence incompletions, repetitions, and stutters.) Thus, rural Missourians of the last century committed our speech disturbance categories, too. This indicates that these phenomena are relatively time and culture free, for American English. Verón, Korn, Malfé, and Sluzki (1966) developed analogous categories for Spanish. Bond and his co-workers (Bond & Ho, 1978; Bond & Iwata, 1976; Bond & Shiraishi, 1974) did so for Japanese. Nosenko, Yelchaninov, Krylova, and Petrukhin (1977) applied a slight variant of the General Speech Disturbance Ratio to Russian. We cited related observations of Freud, Meringer, and Mayer, which pertained to German. Thus, the speech disturbance phenomena are relatively free from linguistic, as well as cultural, restraint.

Measures of Speech Disturbance Frequency

A useful measure of the general frequency of speech disturbance can be obtained by identifying the various disturbances in a verbatim transcript and then computing the following ratio for any given language sample:

$$\text{General Speech Disturbance Ratio} = \frac{N \text{ speech disturbances}}{N \text{ words in sample}}$$

(The time spent talking can be used instead of N words in the denominator, if that measure is more convenient. We found the correlation between these two ratios to be .91, on the one occasion we compared them.)

I show that the "ah" category should be omitted from the ratio if it is to be used for anxiety measurement. In this case, all the remaining ("Non-ah") categories are used in determining the following ratio:

$$\text{Non-ah Ratio} = \frac{N \text{ Non-ah disturbances}}{N \text{ words in sample}}$$

One can, of course, compute comparable Ah Ratios.

Scoring Speech Disturbances

This is easy and interesting for anyone curious about the details of speech. Only a short training period is required. Our co-workers learned to score by studying a simple manual and practicing scoring the speech of about a half-dozen recorded psychotherapy interviews, each with different patients, showing different degrees of speech disturbance.[5]

The scoring can be done directly from the tape. All ours was done with the simultaneous use of the verbatim transcripts and the tape recordings. Actual hearing of the speech is essential for the most accurate scoring, which sometimes depends on cues of intonation. The simultaneous use of a transcript usually makes for more accurate hearing.

When scoring, the incidence and category of the disturbance are marked directly on the transcript as is illustrated in Table 9.2.

The method of marking the disturbances on the transcript provides for various types of analyses. The frequency can be readily counted, and this

---

[5]The essential parts of the scoring manual consisted of category definitions, illustrations, and scored interview excerpts similar to those presented in the first part of this chapter. The scorers included Jack Austin, Sue Cohen, Stanislav V. Kasl, Katherine McGraw, Sally Green Risberg, Gene Schulze, and myself. I am grateful to the others for their interest and diligent collaboration.

TABLE 9.2
Method of Scoring Speech Disturbances in Transcript

P: My uncle had his throat cut.

T: Mhm.

P: And my uncle.. ⓐʰ ⌐.he wasn't killed, but they
   tortured him. They took him and they slit his
   throat right.⌐.the skin.⌐.just cut the skin
   right around like this.

T: Who did that? (said in a sudden manner)

P: Mmm⌐..hulligan⌐..holigan⌐..huligans, whatever
   you call them.

T: The who?

P: The...ⓐʰ⌐.you know the...ⓐʰ...sss../he was
   in...the..⌐he...was dri.⌐..traveling from one
   town to the oth.⌐..next and -

T: Mhm.

P: -he was stopped by a couple.⌐.ⓐʰ..if you know
   the situation in the South...

T: Were.⌐.were they.⌐.were they Russians or were
   they Bolsheviks?

P: Yes. Yeah...mujik.⌐.mujiks...peasants.

Note. Table 9.1 explains the scoring symbols. "Mmm . . ." was
$O + SC$ on the assumption that patient was starting to say "*mu*jiks".

can be done for various time intervals (successive 2 minutes, for example) or
language samples (successive 200 words of a person's speech, for example)
that can be readily noted on the transcript. Also, many other interesting
questions can be readily studied by scoring directly on the transcript, such
as: the distribution of the disturbances within sentences, the interre-
lationship of various disturbances within sentences, the frequency of disturbances in sentences differing in verbal content, etc.

Reliability of Speech Disturbance Scoring

This is very high. In our own work summarized in Table 9.3, for example,
we have obtained average interobserver correlations of .98 for the Ah-Ratio
and .93 for the Non-ah Ratio. These are the averages for all the correlations
presented in the two right-hand columns of Table 9.3.

TABLE 9.3
Interobserver Correlations of Speech Disturbance Frequencies

Item	Scorers	Nature of Speakers and Situation	Nature of Reliability Sample (N)	Ah	Non-ah
1.	A-B	Psychoneurotics in psychotherapy interviews	65 transcript pages of 3 patients. (65)		.90
2.	A-C	Undergraduates in role playing	Total speech sample of 10 subjects (10)	.99	.98
3.	A-D	Undergraduates in personal interviews (Kasl and Mahl)	36 pages of 5 subjects (36)	.99	.96 (SC.87) (R.97)
4.	A-E	Hospitalized schizophrenic and orthopedic patients telling stories about pictures (Schulze, Mahl, and Holzberg)	12 means of 3 stories from 6 subjects (12)	.97	.99
5.	A-F	Undergraduates in personal interviews under varying auditory and visual feedback conditions	27 pages from 3 subjects (27)		.85
6.	A-F	Undergraduates in personal interviews under varying visual feedback conditions	32 pages from 16 subjects (16)	.96	.90
7.	A-G	Secondary school children giving open-ended responses to questionnaire (Zimbardo, Mahl, and Barnard)	Responses to two questions of 16 subjects (16)		.89
8.	B-C	Psychoneurotics in psychotherapy interviews	56 transcript pages of 6 patients (56)		.91
9.	E-F	Undergraduates in personal interviews under varying auditory and visual feedback conditions	69 pages of 9 subjects (69)		.88
10.	E-F	Adult twins in personal interviews	59 pages from 16 subjects (59)		.86
11.	E-F	Undergraduates responding to TAT inquiries and describing motion-pictures (Schulze)	a) Speech of 5 subjects during 1-minute intervals (X̄ per S = 81)		.89[a]
			b) 25 means of 5 conditions for 5 subjects (25)		.96

Note: Correlations are Pearson r's.
[a] r = average r.

TABLE 9.4
Reliabilities of Speech Disturbance Scoring Reported by Other Investigators

Interscorer	All Categories Combined	Ah	Non-ah	Rep.
Panek and Martin (1959)		.87[a]		.65[a]
		.88[a]		.78[a]
		.98		.94
		.90		.76
Blumenthal (1960)	.53[a]			
	.91[a]			
	.97[a]			
	.98[a]			
Boomer and Goodrich (1961)	.94			
Feldstein (1962)	.98			
Feldstein and Jaffe (1962)	.85[a]			
Feldstein, Brenner, and Jaffe (1963)		.98[a]	.89[a]	
Intrascorer: test-retest				
Feldstein and Jaffe (1962)	.93[a]			
Blumenthal (1961)	.91[a]			

[a]Scored directly from tapes.

In one sample we determined the reliability of Sentence Change and Repetition scores, which were .87 and .97, respectively (Table 9.3, Item 3).

Workers in other laboratories have used our categories, definitions, and examples with the reliability results shown in Table 9.4. The results are in substantial agreement with ours even though scoring often was done directly from the tapes.[6]

The preceding data concerns the scorer reliability for speech disturbance *frequencies*. Those data do not reflect the reliability of *exact* scoring of the individual disturbances making up the frequency measures. We explored the degree of exact agreement in scoring, defined as degree of agreement in the incidence or placement of a disturbance in the transcript *and* in the categorization of it. Three scorers participated in this study; one (A) was considerably more experienced than the other two (B and C) who were about equally experienced. Because "ah" is very easy to score and its inclusion is misleading, we omit reference to it. One study compared the exact agreement of A and C in scoring the Non-ah categories in 34 transcript pages of four psychotherapy interviews of two patients. They agreed exactly in 60% of all the disturbances they both scored. B and C also agreed exactly in 60% of all the

---

[6]Feldstein and his colleagues devised methods for scoring the disturbances directly from the tape onto IBM cards for use with programmed computers (Feldstein & Jaffe, 1963, e.g.,).

Non-ah disturbances they both scored in 44 transcript pages of five interviews from 5 different patients. These percentages represent the agreement in "positive scoring"; they do not reflect the fact that the judges were in very high exact agreement in *not* scoring. This "negative" agreement was not determined for what the unit should be in doing so is not at all clear to us. No matter what it might be—the word, the clause e.g.,—it is obvious that even the degree of exact agreement is better than chance and adequate for investigations concerned with individual disturbances and categories, which are mentioned occasionally. Actually, a great deal of our speech disturbance scoring has been done by one person and then carefully checked in entirety by another person. This was always done in the early work when the basic features of the disturbances were being determined and it was done for all the data cited in the rest of this chapter.

SOME GENERAL PROPERTIES OF EVERYDAY SPEECH DISTURBANCES

Frequency of Occurrence

Judged against the background of everyday speech perception, the frequency of speech disturbances in our materials turns out to be surprisingly high. Table 9.5 illustrates just how frequent they are.

The samples cited there are: (1) a sample of initial interviews of 20 women and 11 men who were applying for psychiatric outpatient treatment; (2) male interviewers who participated in those initial interviews; (3) Yale undergraduates who played the role of a student suspected of cheating on

TABLE 9.5
Seconds of Talking per 1 Speech Disturbance

Sample	N	Mdn.	Q_1–Q_3	Range
Patients in initial interviews	31	4.7	3.5– 5.4	2.8– 8.8
Interviewers A	11	3.8	3.5– 4.3	3.3– 4.9
B	10	6.5	5.9– 8.8	5.5– 9.7
C	10	11.9	8.9–15.6	7.3–16.6
Undergraduate role playing	26	3.9	2.5– 5.2	1.8–11.2
Undergraduate men personal investigative interviews	25	4.0	3.0– 4.9	1.8– 7.9
University faculty	12	5.1	4.1– 6.4	3.2–11.6

examinations who was appearing before a "faculty committee" (also played by undergraduates), which was "unsympathetic" in half the cases but "sympathetic" in the other half; (4) Yale undergraduates who were the subjects of "control", "anxiety", and "anger"—provoking interviewing and (5) faculty members who were engaged in two rather heated seminar discussions on the validity of Rorschach test interpretations.

The data of the table were obtained for each language sample by totaling the number of seconds of talk by the individual and dividing by the total number of speech disturbances in that time.

The medians and quartiles of this frequency measure are very similar for the patients, the undergraduates, and the faculty members. The median of their medians gives an estimate of the general frequency of the speech disturbances: *one disturbance for every 4.4 seconds of spontaneous speech*. Even the data for two of the three interviewers, who because of their roles were much more constrained and less voluble, show a comparable rate.

We are not sure how representative these rates are of more "relaxed" speaking situations, but we believe that even that rate would be surprisingly high.

Awareness of Speech Disturbances

The vast majority of the disturbances in spontaneous speech occur outside the awareness of either the speaker or the listener. This is probably the basis for our surprise at the frequency data just presented.

Our evidence about the speaker's and listener's awareness consists of informal observations only, but they are clear-cut and anyone can readily repeat them. We have never known an interviewer who was not surprised, upon seeing an interview transcription and hearing the tape recording, at the many speech disturbances contained in the speech of both himself and the patient. Subjects, assistants, secretaries, and friends have all reacted with similar surprise when just seeing or working with typescripts and tapes. Beyond surprise, these people have reacted with interest and sudden awareness of disturbances in the speech they subsequently hear in their daily lives. Sudden confrontation with their own speech, in the form of transcripts with the disturbances scored in red pencil, has caused some people to react with disbelief in the accuracy of the typing, disowning their own speech and with despair, shame, and anger. All these responses testify to the lack of awareness of the vast majority of speech disturbances and to the wish not to know of them.

Knowing that they do occur in his speech, one is able to observe them actually taking place in his own speech. He may then notice that the disturbances *happen to him*, so to speak, as if he is passive and they are produced by processes occurring outside his conscious control. If he deliberately commits

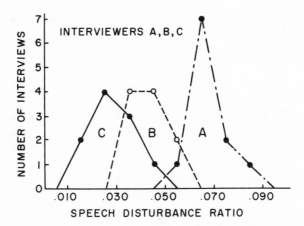

FIG. 9.2.   Frequency distributions of General Speech Disturbance Ratios of three interviewers in initial interviews.

the speech disturbances they will not sound or feel the same as those occurring spontaneously. These subjective experiences are very similar to those accompanying the self-observation of motor tics, compared to the voluntary imitation of them.

Individual Differences in Frequency of Speech Disturbances

The use of the speech disturbance ratios defined earlier reveals these differences. The latter are readily illustrated by Fig. 9.2 that contains the distributions of the 11 different General Speech Disturbance Ratios of Interviewer A in the 11 different initial interviews conducted by him and of comparable distributions for B and C in their 10 interviews each. By analysis of variance, the differences between the three interviewers are highly significant, $p < .001$. These interviewers also differed significantly from one another in their Ah Ratios ($p < .001$) and their Non-ah Ratios ($p < .001$), as determined by simple analyses of variance.

The ratios of the 31 patients taking part in the initial interviews were also subjected to an analysis of variance to test for individual differences. Each interview was divided into successive 2-minute intervals and the ratios for each patient's speech computed for each 2-minute interval. We then determined if the variance in all such 2-minute ratios due to individual patients was greater than the variance within interviews. It was for the General Ratio, the Ah-Ratio, and the Non-ah Ratio, $p < .001$ in each instance. The reader might wonder if the differences between the interviewers and between the patients represent true individual differences or merely reflect correlations between speech disturbance levels of the interviewers and the patients. The latter does not appear to be the case for the average ratios are practically identical for the patients interviewed by the three different interviewers, as the following summary indicates.

	Interviewer		
	A	B	C
Pt's $\bar{X}$ Gen. Ratio	.055	.058	.057
Pt's $\bar{X}$ Non-ah Ratio	.037	.037	.037
Pt's $\bar{X}$ Ah-Ratio	.018	.021	.020

One cannot conclude from these data, however, that there never may be a relationship between their speech disturbance levels when people talk to one another.

Another method of testing for individual differences is to correlate peoples' speech disturbance measures obtained at various times and see if the individuals maintain their relative ranks upon these various occasions. Such an analysis yielded correlations of .85 and .91 between Ah-ratios, and of .81, .82, and .88 between Non-ah Ratios for male undergraduates ($N =$ 25 and 45) interviewed on different occasions (see chapter 12). Blumenthal (1964) found similar correlations of .83, .97, and .90 in schizophrenics' General Speech Disturbance Ratios during successive 5-minute intervals in three different interviews. Both studies demonstrate the existence of stable individual differences.

Intraindividual Variations in Speech Disturbance Frequency

The speech disturbance level of a person varies from time to time about his characteristic level. For example, patients' speech during interviews shows two kinds of such variations: their average level of disturbance varies from interview to interview, and their level changes in a *nonrandom manner* within interviews.

Table 9.6 illustrates *intraindividual variation from interview to interview* for two patients in psychotherapy. The table summarizes the 2-minute General Speech Disturbance Ratios for eight interviews for each patient. Are the variations in the interview averages of these 2-minute ratios significant? To answer this question we used Bartlett's test and a simple analysis of variance to test for the between-hour differences in variability and means. The results presented in Table 9.7 show that there are significant between-hour differences in both variability and means for both measures. Because the variances and the sample N's meet the conditions for which no appreciable error is made in interpreting the F test (L. Jones, 1955), it can be concluded that the differences in means are true differences and not due to the within interview heterogeneity of variance. Similar intraindividual interview-inter-

TABLE 9.6

Summary of 2-minute General Speech Disturbance Ratios
for Two Patients in Psychotherapy

	Mrs. Y				*Mr. Z*		
Interview No.	*N 2' Ratios*	*M*	*SD*	*Interview No.*	*N 2' Ratios*	*M*	*SD*
1	24	.037	.019	2	30	.057	.021
2	25	.041	.014	15	30	.068	.023
5	30	.038	.015	17	31	.060	.040
10	33	.052	.018	20	29	.062	.026
13	28	.042	.015	26	32	.064	.034
17	28	.049	.026	67	30	.055	.029
20	26	.036	.013	83	30	.075	.024
26	29	.048	.024	88	30	.050	.027
	Mean =	.043	.018		Mean =	.061	.028

Note: From Mahl (1956a).

view variations in the Non-ah Ratios have regularly been found in the studies of anxiety to be cited later. We have not tested statistically for the presence of comparable interview variations in Ah Ratios, but inspection of them indicates that they also occur.

The representative graphs of the General Speech Disturbance Ratios in Fig. 9.3 illustrate the variations *within* interviews. These graphs show the variations in the ratios in successive 2-minute intervals for some of the patients having their initial interviews. The inspection of many such graphs strongly suggests that the within-interview variations are systematic instead of "chance" oscillations.

TABLE 9.7

Tests of Between-Interview Differences in 2-Minute
Speech Disturbance Ratios

	Bartlett's Test		*Analysis of Variance*	
Patient	χ^2	*p*	*F*	*p*
Mrs. Y	24.39	<.001	2.7	<.02
Mr. Z	16.14	<.05	2.19	<.05[a]

[a]The violation of the assumption of homogeneous variance might cause this to be spuriously "signficant." The true value might be as high as .07 (see Jones, 1955).

Note: From Mahl (1956a).

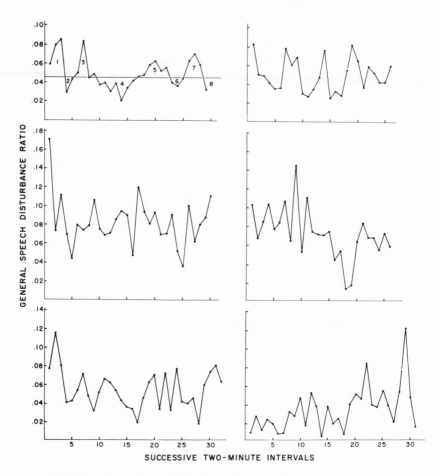

FIG. 9.3.   General Speech Disturbance Ratios in successive 2-minute intervals of initial interviews of six psychiatric outpatient clinic patients. The
speech disturbance level varies from moment-to-moment *within* interviews in
nonrandom fashion.

The appropriate statistical analyses (Wald-Wolfowitz Run Tests; see
Moses, 1952) showed that such variations within the 31 initial interviews
were nonrandom ones for the patients' General Ratios, the Ah-Ratios, and
the Non-ah Ratios ($p < .08$, $< .001$, $< .04$, respectively). (In this test one
compares the number of "runs" above and below the median for each interview [illustrated in the top left graph of Fig. 9.3] with the number expected
by chance.)[7]

---

[7]The writer is grateful to Prof. Robert Abelson for advice on this application of the Wald-
Wolfowitz test.

TABLE 9.8
Category Percentages Based on Data from
Patients in Initial and Therapy Interviews,
Interviewers, Undergraduates, Faculty
Members

Speech Disturbance Category	Average Percentage of all Disturbances
Ah	40.5
Sentence-change	25.3
Repetition	19.2
Stutter	7.8
Omission	4.5
Sentence-incompletion	1.2
Incoherent sound	1.2
Tongue-slip	.7

Similar anslyses were made for the *within* interview variations of the General Speech Disturbance Ratios for the interview samples of Mrs. Y and Mr. Z noted in Table 9.6. These tests, too, showed that the variations within intervews were nonrandom ones. (The details of these analyses will be found in Mahl, 1956a.)

Relative Frequency of Individual Speech Disturbance Categories

There is a great range in the frequency of the individual categories, with "ah" being the most prevalent and tongue slips being relatively rate. Table 9.8 summarizes the relative frequencies in the speech of the 31 patients and the 3 interviewers in the initial interviews, the speech of the 12 faculty members, of the 26 role-playing undergraduate subjects, and the speech of 6 psychoneurotic patients in a total of 25 psychotherapy interviews. The average percentages of Table 9.8 are the averages of the averages of these different groups of speakers. As one can see Ah, Sentence-change, and Repetitions are the most frequent categories and account for 85% of the disturbances.

Individual Differences in Speech Disturbance Predilections

Individuals not only differ from one another in the overall *frequency* of speech disturbances, but also in their *relative predilection* for the most common categories. Some people are predominantly "ah-ers," some predominantly "sentence-changers," and others mainly "repeaters." Speech disturbance profiles, illustrated in Figures 9.4 and 9.5, illustrate this phenomenon. Inter-

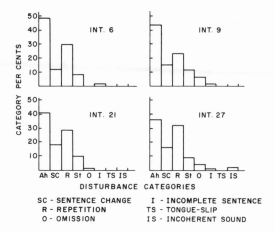

FIG. 9.4.   Category percentages of Interviewer A's speech disturbances in four initial interviews.

viewer A is an "ah-er" and a "repeater", whereas Mrs. Y is a "sentence-changer." (Incidentally, Interviewer A thought he was a "sentence-changer" even after scoring many language samples of other people.) The potential stability of such individual differences is brought out clearly by Table 9.9, which contains the number of interviews in which each of the three initial interviewers and Mrs. Y had all the possible 6 rank-orders of the Ah, Sentence-change, and Repetition percentages. The interviewers differ among

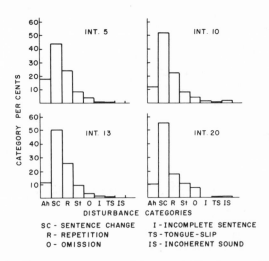

FIG. 9.5.   Category percentages of the speech disturbances of Mrs. Y, a patient, in four of her psychotherapy interviews.

TABLE 9.9
Number of Interviews Falling in the Possible Sets of Rank Orders
of Ah, Sentence-Change, and Repetition Per Cents

Rank Orders of Category %'s	Interviewer A	Interviewer B	Interviewer C	Patient Y
Ah-Sent Change-Rep	2	6	4	0
Ah-Rep-Sent Change	9	1	5	0
Sent Change-Ah-Rep	0	3	1	0
Sent Change-Rep-Ah	0	0	0	7
Rep-Sent Change-Ah	0	0	0	1
Rep-Ah-Sent Change	0	0	0	0
Total	11	10	10	8

themselves and are in marked contrast to Mrs. Y The consistency of the difference between Interviewer A and Mrs. Y is particularly notable when we consider that A's 9 and Y's 7 reflects stability in the rank order of three categories.

SUMMARY

Starting with the attempt to identify episodes of confused or flustered speech, which might be used to identify transitory increases in the patient's anxiety during psychotherapy interviews, we came upon the speech disturbance categories. They promised a useful approach to the measurement of disruption in the flow of spontaneous speech. Speech disturbances can be reliably scored. After scoring considerable material, some of their general properties emerged.

They are surprisingly frequent in spontaneous speech uttered under a variety of conditions by a variety of individuals. Yet the vast majority escape the awareness of both speaker and listener.

Speech disturbances are not merely "random noise"; variations in them manifest regularities of various kinds. People differ from one another in the frequency with which disturbances occur in their speech. And, for a given person, the level of disturbance may change from time-to-time, even from moment-to-moment, in a regular, nonrandom fashion. People differ in the type of speech disturbance most characteristic of them, some showing a striking degree of consistency in this regard.

Speech disturbances are *extralinguistic* phenomena. They are not part of the linguistic code; they have no semantic function. Moreover, they are not subject to tight restraint by the rules of the language. If they were, they would not be so frequent and variable, and speech would rapidly become incomprehensible as their frequency increased. The latter happens only rarely. Being without linguistic function and "free" to vary over a wide range, the frequency and type of speech disturbances become ideal candidates for being functionally related to a variety of extralinguistic variables—such as personality processes and structure, cultural patterning, situational factors, and biological states of the speakers.

The following chapters are concerned with some correlates of the disturbances. Naturally, we are very interested in presenting what we have found about the value of the speech disturbances in the measurement of concurrent anxiety in the speaker. Thus, we turn to that matter immediately. In the following chapter we report on the first of six studies of the relationship between concurrent anxiety of speakers and the frequency of their speech disturbances.

Disturbances in the Patient's Speech in Psychotherapy

10

In chapter 8, I stated that we started to study speech disturbances in search of a nonphysiological measure of transitory variations in the patient's anxiety during psychotherapy interviews. I also presented there our rationale for selecting this particular aspect of speech for this purpose. That rationale included the clinical experience of using episodes of "flustered" or "confused" speech as cues of anxiety in the patient. Having developed measures of speech disturbances and replacing clinical perceptions of the patient's speech with these measures, we were faced with crucial questions: Does our measure of speech disturbance really reflect moment-to-moment changes in the speaker's anxiety? Or is it a monstrous artifact of quantification? To answer these questions we conducted the studies reported in this and the next four chapters.

Our first study chronologically was the one reported in the first section of this chapter. In keeping with the clinical origins and nature of our interests, this first study was derived from clinical materials and its method followed a clinical paradigm. It's method made explicit and systematic, and "purified," what I believe is often the necessarily implicit, haphazard, and "contaminated" method of the practicing psychotherapist.

In the preceding chapter we saw that typically the level of speech disturbance rises and falls in phasic fashion during interviews. This was also found to be true for Mrs. Y, whose therapy interviews provide the material of the following study (Mahl, 1956a). We now wanted to determine if these variations reflect variability in her concurrent anxiety.

A PROPOSED VALIDATION PROCEDURE[1]

Preliminary Findings. During therapeutic sessions and while studying recordings it often appears that interviews are divisible into natural segments or phases, each of which could be assigned to a single theme of content or interaction, and that the patient becomes anxious and conflictful in some but becomes less anxious in others. In some of the latter, it can often be observed that the patient himself has changed the topic or started a new line of interaction with the therapist in such a way that his behavior can be interpreted as a relatively sustained and successful defensive maneuver.

During live interviews or in listening to recordings, judgments of such changes in anxiety as have been mentioned are based in large part upon changes in expressive speech attributes. The assumption underlying the validation procedure and test to be described is that given adequate context for interpretation, it would be possible to judge such phases in typescripts only (not recordings). If this were done validly, and if the Speech-Disturbance Ratio . . . [is a valid index] of patient anxiety, then . . . [this measure] should be greater in the anxious or conflictful phases than in the low anxious or defensive phases. [The measure used was the General Speech Disturbance Ratio defined on p. 169].

A test of . . . [this prediction was made] for Mrs. Y, using interviews 5, 10, 13, 17, 20, 26 as the test hours. Before the test was made, ad hoc clinical evaluations of a similar nature with interviews from Mr. Z and from other patients appeared to give promising results. In addition, almost the same experimental-clinical procedure described later had been followed with still different interviews of Mr. Z from his first 26 sessions. The results were essentially the same as for Mrs. Y and are presented elsewhere (Mahl, 1955a, 1959). They are not described here because the possibility of contaminated phase judgments was not as well controlled as in the test with Mrs. Y's interviews.

With Mrs. Y, the first major problem was to prevent contaminated criterion judgments. The writer had been the therapist, but the test interviews occurred slightly over 2½ years before this validation test was made. The writer had not previously replayed the recordings or studied transcripts of these interviews. After practicing with other interviews, a secretary edited verbatim transcripts and prepared clean scripts that did not contain any

---

[1]This section of this chapter is adapted from George F. Mahl, (1956a), Disturbances and Silences in the Patient's Speech in Psychotherapy," Journal of Abnormal and Social Psychology, 53, 1–15. Copyright 1956 by the American Psychological Association. Adapted by permission of the publisher with slight editorial and stylistic revisions. The excerpted portion is from pp. 6–11 of the published article. The original article reported data about silences, as well as about speech disturbances. Only the latter data are presented in this chapter.

speech disturbances, any annotations concerning pauses, or any explicit reference to silence by the participants. These scripts were no longer exactly verbatim, of course. With these precautions, it was felt that no serious contamination of the phase judgments occurred.

The judgment of the proper anxiety category for the phases of content or interaction requires intimate knowledge of the context. One of the main reasons for this is that the judgment cannot be made on the basis of manifest content alone. The context includes general knowledge of the patient and of the dynamic setting of a given therapeutic session. The development of the context is a major problem. A good deal was known about the patient since the judge had . . . [been her therapist and had participated in] over 100 therapeutic interviews with her. A more immediate context of the test hours was obtained by listening to the recordings for the first 29 interviews, excepting the test hours. Notes made of each of the nontest hours and the complete edited typescripts were then reviewed in sequence. Before the final judging of phases in any given test hour, a rough clinical description of the therapeutic situation at the time was written.

After the interviews were divided into phases and categorized as to anxiety type, the phases were marked off in the original verbatim typescripts. A second person then determined the . . . Speech-Disturbance Ratios for the phases. Just as the phase judge had no prior knowledge of the objective measures, the scorer of the objective measures had no knowledge as to the identity or meaning of the phases.

A total of 19 defensive and/or low anxiety and 19 anxious or conflictful phases were judged in the 5 test hours. For any given interview, however, there had not always been judged an equal number of each type of phase. To control for the confounding of "hour effects" demonstrated earlier [see chapter 9, pp. 176–77], equal numbers of the phase types were randomly selected for each interview. This procedure produced a sample of 15 phases in each group. Table 10.1 contains the pertinent statistical data. . . . [The

TABLE 10.1
General Speech-Disturbance Ratios in Phases of Interviews.
Mrs. Y

	Phase		
Statistic	Low-anxious or Defensive	Anxious or Conflictful	Significance (One-Tailed Test)
N	15	15	
M	.038	.049	$t = 2.68$
			$p < .01$
SD	.013	.009	

186   10. DISTURBANCES IN PATIENT'S SPEECH

General Speech Disturbance Ratio was significantly higher in the anxious or conflictful phases, increasing in them by 29% over the level of the low-anxious or defensive phases.]

Illustrative Interview. The material for Mrs. Y's 13th interview illustrates the kind of interpretive phase judgments involved and the way in which the linguistic measures vary with the phases. Before proceeding to the interview itself, some preliminary information concerning the patient is presented.

Mrs. Y, a college graduate, was in her late 30s at the onset of treatment. She had been married for 11 years. She had two daughters, aged 7½ and 9. A third pregnancy had terminated with a miscarriage some 7 months earlier. The patient sought treatment ostensibly for relief from recurring duodenal ulcers and because of a general feeling of unhappiness and dissatisfaction in her relations with her husband and children. This was consciously related to frustration of strong dependency needs based on a lifelong history of repeated rejection by both of her parents as well as other significant people. As therapy progressed, a strong sex-fear conflict with a great deal of Oedipal flavoring seemed equally, if not more, important in determining her present troubles. This conflict was not only specific to genital behavior but was generalized to many modes of feminine behavior. For example, even though she moved in a fashionable circle and was not restricted in income, she was afraid to buy and wear the kinds of attractive clothing worn by her peers. She always chose "practical" and "adequate" clothes. Although she was aware of "missing the boat" in her sexual relations with her husband, the sexual conflict and the general fearful avoidance of femininity and womanhood was almost completely unconscious in the early stage of therapy.

At the time of the 13th session the patient had been in treatment for a month. During this period she had manifested and felt a positive attachment to the therapist. She was conscious of the dependency aspect of this attachment but not of an inferred unconscious sexual aspect. Consciously she had felt frightened at the dependent attachment, being afraid that the therapist would reject her as her father had done irrevocably and traumatically when she was 10, and as she alleged a previous therapist had done.

There were some unusual aspects of her treatment arrangement that are also pertinent to the evaluation of the 13th session. She knew the therapist was doing research on both recorded therapy interviews and on the psychophysiology of peptic ulcer patients. She also knew that her therapy was included in these studies and that the therapist had accepted her for treatment partially for these reasons. She was aware of the investment of time and energy in each case and the importance of each patient for the research program. In fact, she had felt this as an attraction to enter into treatment with this particular therapist.

Just before the 13th session the patient had been informed by her obstetrician that she was pregnant. The interview is centered on this topic. Becoming pregnant raised many psychological problems for her, but two aspects are particularly prominent in this particular interview. First, she tells the therapist that she is definitely pregnant and, second, she and the therapist explore an irrational fear she has of telling her mother that she is pregnant.

Prior to judging phases in the hour, it was known that both of these aspects were anxiety-laden matters for her. She had suspected some 2 weeks earlier that she might be pregnant and at that time awoke during the nights before her eighth and ninth sessions preoccupied in part with how the therapist would react to this news. She anticipated that if she were pregnant her therapy would be interrupted and this would let the therapist down in his research program. Her thoughts at 3:30 a.m. on the day of the ninth session were:

"Should I tell Dr. Mahl?" She anticipated that he would think "That's just like a woman. There goes my research program. She is gumming up the works." She also said to herself, "Your research program depends in part on me."

Also in the ninth interview she stated that she was afraid to tell her mother she might be pregnant. After the 13th interview her mother came to visit for several days as had been previously arranged. The day her mother came, the patient became "ill" and had to go to bed. Only after this did she tell her mother she was pregnant. (The mother reacted positively.) These observations show that the irrational fear of telling her mother, which is explored in the 13th interview was real and intense.

The 13th . . . interview is now summarized by phases. For each phase, the content or interaction is first summarized, then the category into which the phase was placed and the reasons at the time of the judgment for doing so are stated. The Speech-Disturbance Ratios . . . for the phases are presented in Fig. 10.1.

Phase 1

After spending 30 seconds in idle chitchat about the weather, Mrs. Y abruptly comments: "I got off to a bum start this morning. I'm mad! At least I got mad at my family before breakfast even." She proceeds to state that she woke up with a hollow feeling in her stomach and ate a cracker. She casually interposes the news that since last time she has discovered she is definitely pregnant because she "had an A.Z. test, whatever that is." She immediately goes on to describe in detail her "bum start." Her two daughters had provoked her, one by getting toothpaste on a clean dress and the other by putting on a clean dress instead of one she had worn before. The patient had

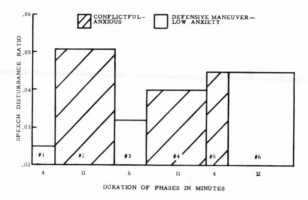

FIG. 10.1.   General speech disturbance ratios in the successive phases of Mrs. Y's 13th session.

become irritated and her breakfast is "sitting right there in a lump." She closes this account by saying that these are more unnecessary things she has to cope with.

Interpretation of the Phase

It is inferred that the patient is afraid of the therapist's reaction to the definite knowledge that she is pregnant. The nature of this fear is the same as she described earlier in the 9th session. This anticipatory fear motivates her to inform the therapist of the A.Z. test results as casually as possible and to induce a sympathetic attitude in him by portraying herself as the "victim" of her daughters. The content of the phase is instrumental in doing these things. By being receptive to the account, the therapist "aids" the patient in doing these things. For these reasons, this is judged to be a relatively successful defensive maneuver in which the anxiety of the patient is minimal. . . . [The speech disturbance measure is at its lowest level in this phase.]

Phase 2

The patient spontaneously changes the subject saying straightforwardly now that she had the A.Z. test and it was positive. Then she says, "Now I'm trying to figure out how I'm going to get through having my mother with me for a week without telling her I'm pregnant. 'Cause I don't want to tell her." She elaborates very briefly saying she knows her mother will be upset and will think the patient shouldn't have any more children, especially so soon after the miscarriage.

The therapist returns to her news of being pregnant by asking the patient how she felt when she heard the A.Z. was positive. She replies that it struck her as amusing because she conceived immediately after she and her husband decided to try again. She adds that she'll be glad to have another child. The therapist asks how this jibes with earlier statements by her to the contrary. With many contradictions, she says that she is glad because her husband wants another child, but that it's not her favorite idea and she wouldn't do it if she didn't feel she should. The patient comments briefly on how she is resigning from several community activities in order to keep her activities at a minimum and prevent another miscarriage.

The therapist asks then for further elaboration of her fear of her mother's reaction. The patient says again she is afraid to tell her mother and that she was always afraid to do so with her previous pregnancies. The therapist remarks: "That's striking, isn't it." The patient acknowledges this and states that although she did, and does, feel afraid, her mother has always expressed surprise when the patient tells her of this fear. Even so, the patient continues, she knows her mother really does disapprove and that she will be critical of her. But then she expresses the belief that there must be something more to this feeling than she has said. The therapist agrees. The patient says she doesn't know what the basis for this feeling could be and would like to know. The therapist states that by thinking about her relationship with her mother now she might start to find out.

Interpretation of the Phase

This is regarded as a phase in which the patient starts to talk about the anxiety-evoking news that she is definitely pregnant. This is the material she was avoiding in part, and preparing for in part, in the first phase. Three things happen that increase her anxiety: (a) she tells the therapist directly that she is pregnant; (b) under some pressure from the therapist, her surface "happiness" at being pregnant is rendered ineffectual as a defense against the anxiety and guilt elicited by her negative feelings; and (c) the defensive aspect of blaming her mother for the anticipatory fear at telling her of being pregnant is partially exposed.

As can be seen in Fig. 10.1, . . . the speech disturbance . . . [measure increases] during this phase.

Phase 3

Responding to the remark of the therapist made at the end of Phase 2, the patient now introduces the theme that her mother has never seemed maternal or supportive, especially when something happens that increases demands upon her. The patient elaborates this with rather detailed descriptions of two instances in which her mother had responded to illness in the family by seemingly becoming upset, excited, impatient, and anxious to escape the situations as soon as possible.

Interpretation of the Phase

This is interpreted as a rather extended defensive maneuver consisting of a well-organized rationalization of her fear of the mother's reaction. Because this is a reinstitution of a defense that had just previously been partially exposed, the anxiety provoked in Phase 2 should now decrease. (The fact that this reinstitution of the defense was necessary here contributed to the judgment of Phase 2 as conflictful or anxious.) It will be seen in Fig. 10.1 that the . . . [speech disturbance level decreases during this phase].

Phase 4

The therapist asks how her mother had reacted to the patient's previous pregnancies in such a way as to account for her present fear. The patient describes her mother as having been interested in the pregnancies, having brought gifts, etc. She repeats how her mother had expressed surprise at the patient's fear of her reaction. The therapist comments that this suggests there hasn't been any basis in her mother's behavior to justify her fear and that maybe the source of the fear lies within herself. The patient asks if the therapist means a feeling between herself and her mother or between herself and the rest of the world. After the therapist replies that he doesn't know the answer to this and that it must come from her, Mrs. Y says: "I'd like to know. I really would like to figure out what it is. I mean whether I'm transferring to my mother some feeling that I have, whether it's a feeling of guilt about having them or what, I don't know." She elaborates this by saying the guilt might be because she doesn't think she is a good mother to her children. The therapist asks if this is an attempt to intellectualize and says this particular feeling could not have been present when she was afraid to tell her mother the first time she became pregnant. Mrs. Y agrees and wonders why she should feel guilty about being pregnant. Shortly she reports feeling blocked in thinking further about it . . .

Interpretation of the Phase

This is a conflictful or anxious phase. The patient should be highly conflictful because the therapist is continually confronting her with the inadequacy of her previous accounts of why she fears her mother's reaction. The patient momentarily gives up the defensive rationalizing, is left blocked in this mode of defensive behavior, and feels repressed near the end of the phase.

It is seen in Fig. 10.1 that . . . the Speech Disturbance Ratio . . . rises in this phase.

Phase 5

When the patient says she feels blocked at the end of Phase 4, the therapist states that this may often happen in her therapy and that although he could offer his thoughts about her fear of her mother, it really wouldn't help. Mrs. Y replies that she realizes that he probably doesn't want to plant ideas in her mind and that "I've gotta dig for it." She goes on to say that this fear of telling her mother is funny, because she doesn't mind telling other people about being pregnant. She feels guilty about telling her mother and she shouldn't have to feel this way. But this is true of other things too, for she hasn't told her mother very much about herself for years.

Interpretation of the Phase

This was judged to be another highly conflictful phase. The therapist was pressing the patient to continue without her defensive maneuvers, and the patient made open acknowledgments that the source of the fear was within herself. In so doing, she was more directly giving up her prepotent defenses. . . . [The speech disturbance measure] rose in this phase, although the *rise* over Phase 4 had not been specifically predicted. That . . . [it] should do so makes sense ad hoc because the therapist was actively prodding the patient when she was already anxious and conflictful.

Phase 6

The patient states that previous attempts to confide in her mother were "flops." When the therapist asks what happened, Mrs. Y responds by recalling in some detail an incident in her teens when she was in boarding school. She had told her mother that she and a boy were corresponding with each other. Shortly afterwards the boy unaccountably stopped writing and the patient was sure her mother had interfered, maybe because she did not approve of men. With collaboration from the therapist, the patient describes other instances of her mother interfering with her dating. In general she depicts her mother as having disapproved of all such adolescent heterosexual activities.

Interpretation of the Phase

This was judged to be a defensive phase in which the patient's anxiety should be decreased from the previous anxiety phase. The content was

regarded as a displaced reference to the basic unconscious fear of giving expression to her feminine sexual desires and needs.
. . . [Fig. 10.1 shows that] the speech disturbance does not decrease[2] . . .

Summary. Linguistic measures of the patient's anxiety in therapeutic interviews can be useful in several areas of research. A working assumption is that the most valid measures will be based on the expressive aspects of speech rather than on manifest content measures. On empirical and theoretical grounds, speech disturbances . . . seem to be expressive attributes that are useful as anxiety indices. [A reliable method for measuring this attribute has been described. See chapter 9.] Motivational phase judgments have been proposed as useful criteria for validating the Speech Disturbance Ratio . . . [as an anxiety measure]. Detailed knowledge of the dynamic context of the interview is necessary to make such judgments of criteria because manifest content is of limited value in this regard. A procedure for acquiring the context without contaminating these judgments has been described. Preliminary results of the proposed validation procedure indicate that the present approach is fruitful. The research and ideas presented here are exploratory and can only be regarded as providing leads that might be of interest to others working in this area so costly of research time.[3]

ANOTHER ILLUSTRATION OF
WITHIN-INTERVIEW VARIATION

Several years after completing the preceding study the writer participated in a demonstration study of the application of various techniques for assessing

---

[2]From my present vantage point, knowing of the substantial amount of evidence validating the speech disturbance measure as an index of anxiety, I conclude that my judgment of Phase 6 was in error. Perhaps Mrs. Y reexperienced fear of her mother's disapproval of her adolescent sexual life.

[3]The General Speech Disturbance Ratio was the measure used in the study just reported. At that time, we had no reason for distinguishing between the Ah-Ratio and the Non-ah Ratio, which were defined and discussed in chapter 9. However, subsequent studies, which are presented in the following two chapters, showed that only the Non-ah Ratio varies with the anxiety of the speaker. Consequently, we reexamined the speech disturbances of Mrs. Y, the crucial subject in the research just described. This reexamination had two results. First, it showed that Mrs. Y used "ah" less frequently than the other common categories. She is the Mrs. Y of Table 9.9 and Fig. 9.5 in chapter 9. Second, the results contained in Table 10.1 are due to a very significant increase in her Non-ah Ratio in the "Anxious or Conflictful Phases." Her generally very low Ah-ratio increased slightly, but not nearly as much as her Non-ah Ratio. The p-value of Table 10.1 ($< .01$) becomes more significant ($< .001$) when Mrs. Y's Non-ah Ratio is used instead of her General Speech Disturbance Ratio. The slight difference in her Ah-Ratio in the two kinds of phases did not reach this level of significance, for its p-value was but .07. (See Fig. 15.1, p. 246).

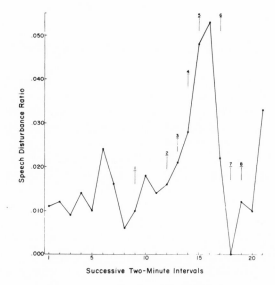

FIG. 10.2.   Variation in a patient's 2-minute Non-ah Speech Disturbance
Ratios during a psychotherapy interview. (From Mahl, 1961a.)

the psychotherapeutic process (Gottschalk, 1961; Mahl, 1961a).[4] This occasion provided an opportunity to make observations similar to those reported previously on material gathered in a completely independent clinic, thus avoiding any possibility of "a self-fulfilling prophecy"—that is any possibility that my interests caused Mrs. Y to speak and communicate as she did in her therapy sessions.

The 18th psychotherapy interview of a young male adult provides this illustration. Figure 10.2 shows the course of the patient's Non-ah Speech Disturbance Ratio (see Chapter 9, p. 169) during successive 2-minutes of the interview. It is apparent that from the 18th to the 36th minute of the interview, the patient's speech disturbance level progressively rises. Then it abruptly falls. Why? In answering, we can show how the disturbance ratio sensitively reflects the therapist-patient interaction and also illustrate further how speech disturbances vary with the types of phases judged clinically in the preceding study. The latter is the case because the first 18 minutes was a low-anxiety phase, the segment from the 18th to the 36th minute was a high-anxiety or conflicted phase, and the segment covering the abrupt drop right after the 36th minute was another low-anxiety phase.

[4]Albert DiMascio, PhD, originated this group study, and Hans Strupp, PhD, organized it. On DiMascio's initiative, the then Research Group at the Massachusetts Mental Health Center provided the group with the recorded psychotherapeutic interviews and associated information.

The patient was a young professional worker in the behavioral sciences whose obsessive-compulsive character disorder had manifested itself partly in work inhibition including procrastination. The therapist's notes about the earlier interviews were available to us and showed that being on time for his interviews was an emotionally charged matter, as one might expect from his history of procrastination in life. The patient was often late and in the past had failed to notify the therapist adequately of absences. His handling of time had all the signs of symptomatic behavior and resistance to therapy. He started this interview by being late. He referred to his lateness at the outset of the interview but then avoided talking further about it for the first 18 minutes. The therapist was quiet during this time. Thus, the patient was successful in avoiding a currently active, emotionally charged issue during this early segment of the interview. His speech disturbance level remained relatively low.

The therapist actively intervened, however, at point 1 in the graph, by stating "You seem not to want to talk about the motivation for your being late today," and "I wonder if we could go into it." Throughout the subsequent minutes when the disturbance curve is rising the therapist maintained a steady, active pressure on the patient to explore his lateness. He did this by commenting at points 2, 3, 4, and 5 in ways that focussed on his lateness and factors that seemed to be related to it. In doing this he was energetically and persistently preventing the patient from defensively avoiding his lateness and the reasons for it. This type of activity by a therapist typically arouses the patient's anxiety. We can reasonably presume this happened in this instance and was manifested in the progressive rise of the speech disturbance curve.

The ensuing decline in the speech disturbance curve was associated with a marked turn of events at point 6. First the patient became briefly angry. The therapist then offered a lengthy interpretation of the patient's lateness, and the patient then experienced an insight and wept as though with cathartic relief. At points 7 and 8 the therapist responded empathically to the patient's tears. This type of interaction is typically reassuring and comforting to patients. Thus, it is fitting that the speech disturbance level reached zero at one point and remained low for several minutes. (See Mahl, 1961a for a more complete discussion of this clinical example.)

INTRICATE RELATION BETWEEN ANXIETY, CONFLICT, AND SPEECH DISTURBANCES

I present the next two examples from my recent clinical work because I believe they reveal in *X-ray fashion* some of the intricacies of anxiety, conflict, and speech disturbance that account for the type of variations within treatment hours that we have been considering. In these two clinical examples we see how such "feeble indications" as a sentence incompletion, or an omission and a sentence change, resulted from conflicts over very important matters.

The speaker is a successful young professional man who was in psychoanalysis with me, where these examples occurred. In each of these, I asked about the speech disturbances, a practice not followed in the research described in this part of the book.

One day when he was speaking about an upcoming vacation trip I asked him where he was going. He said:

> Oh, to B. I have a friend . . . well I planned first to go to A. Then I got the idea of making a circuit by going to B, C, D, and then to A. But when I started to plan the days, I realized it would take 2 weeks to go to all those places. So we'll just go to B.

I then commented: "You said, 'I have a friend . . .' and broke off." He replied along the following lines:

> Well, I was referring to L_____, a woman at Z (where he worked the previous year.) We bedded together and became close friends. She is from B. L_____ was older than me [about 10 years older]. When I first started at Z she seemed prudish, stern, remote. I decided to make her a challenge—to see if I could succeed in getting her into bed and sticking it to her. I did. We did it several times. She became quite fond of me. She was like a mother to me. She used to cook meals for me.

The preceding interchange occurred at a period in his analysis when the patient, with considerable surprise and conflict, was discovering what a significant role his attachment to his mother played in his choice of women as lovers and friends. This conflict, operating with unconscious anticipatory precision, had caused the sentence incompletion—"I have a friend. . . ." Left unremarked, the sentence incompletion would have enabled the patient to avoid this oedipal material.

The speech disturbance was so "innocent" that one would ordinarily attach no significance to it whatsoever. Because the vast majority of speech disturbances are just as "innocent" in external appearance, many people might hesitate to attribute deep, inner significance to them. Our example illustrates how ill founded this hesitancy is.

The same young man committed the disturbances in the following example. These disturbances are less "innocent" because they were less anticipatory—that is, they occurred as conflicted thoughts were on the verge of being spoken, not well in advance of them as in the preceding example. The disturbances may have been more numerous for the same reason.

The young man started his hour one day by lying on his back on the couch, with legs raised, flexed at the knees, feet flat on the couch, and saying: "I feel like a wo . . . This position . . ." here he left the sentence incomplete. He lowered and straightened his legs and shifted to another line of thought, which he followed for some time. Eventually I drew his attention to the omission, sentence change, and incompletion by saying: "You said, 'I feel like a wo . . .' and then veered off to what you've just been talking about. What occurs to you about your phrase, 'I feel like a wo . . .'?"

His associations led to thinking about his previous leg position and to wondering what a woman feels during intercourse. "Believe me," he said, "I don't feel like a woman in relation to you . . . Do you think each of us men has a little of a woman in us; and each woman, a little of a man in her? I do."

It is obvious that these less "innocent" disturbances were indicative of anxiety over thoughts not completely camouflaged by the disturbances. But even these more transparent disturbances did not totally reveal just how conflicted the nature of the related thoughts was.

Our first validation study, reported in the opening section of this chapter, used the *within-person method*. The primary question of the study I describe next was whether or not the use of a *between-persons method* with a larger sample of patients would yield supportive results. In addition, we also studied as secondary questions the possible influence of additional factors in the occurrence of speech disturbances.

Speech Disturbances and Rated Anxiety of Patients During Initial Psychiatric Interviews[1]

11

INTRODUCTION

The primary purpose of this study was to gain further clinical, empirical evidence about the relationship between the speaker's anxiety level and the frequency of disturbances in his spontaneous speech. A secondary goal was to investigate the role of various additional factors in the occurrence of speech disturbances. More specifically, we wanted to answer the following questions.

1. The *within-individual method* employed in the study reported in the first section of chapter 10 showed that as the speaker's anxiety increased so did his/her speech disturbances. This was found to be the case for Mrs. Y in a carefully controlled study, and for Mr. Z in the less well controlled exploratory study. Will the use of a *between-individuals method* with a larger sample yield similar results?

2. Work done after the study described in chapter 10 was completed suggested that "Ah" does not increase with the speaker's anxiety. Can this be demonstrated in this study?

3. Does the identity of the interviewer have a significant effect on the speech disturbances of the patients in initial interviews?

---

[1]This chapter is a revision of a paper entitled "Disturbances in the Patient's Speech as a Function of Anxiety," presented at the Annual Meeting of The Eastern Psychological Association, 1956 (Mahl, 1956b).

4. Is the relationship of speech disturbances to anxiety specific to that emotional state? Will they be influenced by the speakers' hostility as well?

5. Does the gender, age, educational level, or speech rate of speakers influence the frequency of their speech disturbances?

METHOD

The materials of the study were obtained several years earlier for another purpose.[2] Thus they are probably free from subtle, unconscious biases that might arise when materials are obtained for predetermined ends. It is highly unlikely, for example, that the interviewers unwittingly influenced the patients' speech disturbance levels in systematic ways that could account for the results to be presented.

The primary data derive from the initial interviews of 31 representative patients applying for treatment at a psychiatric outpatient clinic. The sample consisted of 20 women and 11 men. The recorded diagnoses were: 18 psychoneuroses, 8 character disorders, and 5 schizophrenics. The ages ranged from 19 to 49. The educational levels ranged from completion of the eighth grade through one or more years of college, but no one had graduated from college.

Two male psychiatric residents and the author conducted and observed the interviews in rotation. One of us interviewed every third patient in the series, while the other two observed the interview through a one-way mirror and heard the verbal interchange over a monitoring system. Immediately after each interview, we independently rated on 5-point scales the degree of anxiety and of hostility manifested by the patient during the interview.

Two of us turned out to be notably more reliable raters of both anxiety and hostility than the third person was. Consequently, the means of these two raters were taken as the anxiety and the hostility measures for each patient. The reliability coefficients for these mean ratings are .83 for anxiety, and .73 for hostility. For reasons that become apparent from the results we returned to examine these reliabilities in more detail and found a marked difference for the anxiety ratings for the men and the women. The reliability coefficient of the anxiety ratings for the 11 men was only .57, contrasted with .86 for the 20 women. Because of the geometric nature of the correlation scale, these coefficients mean that the high reliability for the women was over twice as great as the low reliability for the men.

---

[2]The original purpose for gathering these interviews was to investigate a question of interest to George Andrews, M.D., one of the interviewees: What is the effect on ratings of affect of patients of changing from being the interviewer to being an outside observer? Louis Micheels, M.D. and the author were the other interviewers.

The interviews had also been recorded and the tapes preserved. These were transcribed for the present study. The speech disturbance ratios were scored from the typescripts and tapes in the manner described in chapter 9. All three ratios defined there (p. 169)—General, Ah, and Non-ah—were determined, taking the entire interview as the language sample for each patient.

RESULTS AND DISCUSSION

General Frequency of Disturbances

Averaging across patients yields the following information. There was, on the average, one of the disturbances for every 18 words uttered by the patients. This was equivalent to one disturbance for every 4.7 seconds the patients spent talking. There was one of the Non-ah disturbances for every 27 words or 6.8 seconds talked by the patients. And there was one "Ah" for every 50 words or 12.5 seconds of speech. There were 825 two-minute intervals in the 31 interviews. Only 4, or about .5% of these 2-minute intervals, were free of disturbances in the patients' speech. In short, the disturbances were extremely frequent in the patients' speech. Now, what variables are related to these very frequent phenomena?

Speech Disturbances and Rated Anxiety

Table 11.1 contains the product-moment correlations between the three speech disturbance ratios and the mean anxiety ratings for all 31 patients. There is a significant positive relationship between the Non-ah Ratio and rated anxiety, but a negative correlation approaching statistical significance between the Ah-Ratio and anxiety. The General Speech Disturbance Ratio yields a zero correlation with anxiety. It can be added here that the Non-ah Ratio and the Ah Ratio tended to be negatively correlated ($r = -.23$), although this is not a statistically significant finding ($p < .25$). These find-

TABLE 11.1
Product-Moment Correlations between
Anxiety Ratings and Speech Disturbance
Ratios ($N = 31$)

	Anxiety	p
Non-ah Ratio	.36	<.06
Ah Ratio	−.30	<.10
General Ratio	.08	—

ings indicate that "Ah" does not increase with anxiety, and that it should not be included in the ratio as an anxiety indicator. The remaining results will deal only with the Non-ah Ratio.

The positive correlation of .36 between the Non-ah Ratio and anxiety ratings can be regarded as more significant than $p < .06$ indicates. Because this is a predicted correlation, the statistical significance is more accurately stated to be $p < .03$ (one-tailed). However, the correlation of only .36 was lower than expected on the basis of the research presented in the preceding chapter.

In considering the possible reasons for this discrepancy between the expected and the obtained correlations, the writer recalled how much freer than the men were the women in this sample in manifesting affect in general, but especially distress. Because all interviewers were male, it seemed possible that cultural stereotypes of what is "masculine" interaction might have been constraining anxiety manifestation in the male patients. Accordingly, the correlations between the Non-ah Ratios and the anxiety ratings were next determined separately for the 20 women and the 11 men. Table 11.2 contains the results. It is apparent that the Non-ah Ratio is quite strongly correlated with the anxiety ratings for the women, but not for the men. The most parsimonious explanation of the lack of a significant correlation for the men is that their anxiety ratings were too unreliable. This in turn might be due to the cultural constraint on affect expression just noted.

One way to interpret the correlation of .59 between the anxiety ratings and the speech disturbance measure for the women is to regard it as evidence that the raters, consciously or preconsciously, simply used the speech disturbances themselves as prominent clues of the patients' anxiety. The correlation for the men, however, is not compatible with this interpretation. Nor are the different correlations between the anxiety ratings and the Ah Ratios and the Non-ah Ratios (Table 11.1). After all, prior to this study no one had ever demonstrated such a difference. But more important, it was most unlikely that the observers of these live interviews could have computed the different frequencies of the "Ahs" and "Non-ahs" in the flow of the patients' spontaneous speech. In view of all these considerations, it seems quite unlikely

TABLE 11.2
Product-Moment Correlations between
Non-ah Speech Disturbance Ratios and
Anxiety Ratings in Women and in Men

	Correlation	p
All 31 Patients	.36	<.06
20 Women	.59	<.01
11 Men	−.47	<.16

TABLE 11.3
Comparison of Non-ah Speech Disturbance
Ratios in Men and Women and with
Different Interviewers

	N	M	SD
Interviewer A	10	.037	.015
Interviewer B	10	.037	.012
Interviewer C	11	.037	.016
Men	11	.039	.019
Women	20	.036	.015

that the raters were basing their anxiety assessments on the patients' "Non-ah" disturbances.[3]

Speech Disturbances and Other Variables

The remaining results concern the relationship between the speech disturbances and the other variables mentioned in the introduction.

The first three rows of Table 11.3 compares the Non-ah Ratios for the patients interviewed by the three different interviewers. The speech disturbance levels are the same for the three patient groups. This is quite a striking finding, for there was considerable variation in the "basic personalities" of the three interviewers. And in their speech; one interviewer was born, reared, and educated in Europe and spoke with a slight, but distinct, accent. Why was there no main interviewer effect on the patients' speech disturbance level? The interviewers' professional styles *as initial interviewers* were quite similar; perhaps this was more important for the patients than personality differences between the interviewers. Possibly the personal pressures that drive individuals to initial psychiatric interviews are far more important in determining their behavior during those interviews than is the personality of the interviewer. And this may be especially the case for involuntary, out-of-awareness aspects of their speech, which includes the speech disturbance dimension.

At any rate, in this situation and with these interviewers, the primary source of variation in speech disturbance level appears to reside in the patients themselves. Data presented so far shows that the patient's anxiety is one important source of this variation, accounting for over one third of it, in the women. The patients' gender does not seem to be important in this regard. As the bottom two rows of Table 11.3 show, the Non-ah Ratios of the men and women are the same.

---

[3]The possibility of rater contamination is discussed further in chapter 16.

TABLE 11.4
Correlations between Non-ah Speech Disturbance Ratios
and Other Variables

	All Patients (N = 31)	Females (n = 20)	Males (n = 11)
Anxiety	.36	.59	−.47
Hostility	−.06	−.02	−.04
Education	−.03	.16*	−.33
Age	.05	.01	.10
Words/sec.	.13	−.02	.35

Note: n = 18 for whom education data was available.

The data of Table 11.4 indicate that the other patient variables studied are likewise not important determinants of the Non-ah Ratio. This table contains the product-moment correlations of the Non-ah Ratio with hostility ratings, years of education, age, and rate of talking. (The correlations with the anxiety ratings are also included for ready comparison). None of the former correlations are statistically significant, and most of them are impressively near zero.

SUMMARY

1. This study extends the empirical evidence that the "normal" disturbances of spontaneous speech are positively related to the speaker's anxiety. This is so for the Non-ah disturbances, but not for "Ah." The evidence indicates that only the Non-ah Ratio should be used as an index of the speaker's anxiety.

2. The primary source of variation in the Non-ah Ratio appears to reside in the speaker, for the situation and types of interviewer behavior involved in this study. There was no difference in the Non-ah Ratios for three groups of patients interviewed by three different interviewers.

3. The patients' gender, level of hostility, education, age, and rate of talking were unrelated to the Non-ah Ratio. Variations in these attributes do not appear to impair the usefulness of the Non-ah Ratio as an index of anxiety.

4. The results of this study are relevant to understanding the speech disturbances, as well as to the methodological issue of anxiety assessment.

The studies reported in this and the preceding chapter were both *correlational*. And neither study provided adequate evidence that anxiety and the Non-ah Ratio were positively correlated in males. The next chapter reports the results of an *experimental* investigation of the anxiety-speech disturbance relationship in *male speakers*.

Speech Disturbances and Experimentally Induced Anxiety

12

Stanislav V. Kasl & George F. Mahl
Yale University

INTRODUCTION

Chapters 10 and 11 presented *correlational* evidence that common speech disruptions are positively associated with anxiety in the speaker. In the two studies reported in those chapters the frequency of the Non-ah speech disturbances, defined and illustrated in chapter 9, increased with increments in clinically assessed anxiety. The primary purpose of the study reported in this chapter was to obtain *experimental* evidence concerning the anxiety-speech disturbance relationship and to do so with male speakers.

The confirmation of correlational by experimental data is generally a desirable state of affairs. And such an outcome, if it were to occur, would reduce the uncertainty caused by the inconclusive results for the male patients in the initial interview study reported in the preceding chapter.

Although the primary emphasis here is on the experimental investigation, some additional correlational data about the anxiety-speech disturbance relationship are also discussed, as well as some findings about differences between the Ah and the Non-ah Ratio.[1]

---

[1]The remainder of this chapter is excerpted from Stanislav V. Kasl and George F. Mahl (1965), The Relationship of Disturbances and Hesitations in Spontaneous Speech to Anxiety, *Journal of Personality and Social Psychology*, *1*, 425–433, Copyright 1965 by the American Psychological Association. Excerpted by permission of the publisher and coauthor with slight editorial and stylistic revisions. The main findings were presented at the Annual Meeting of the American Psychological Association in 1958 in a paper entitled, *Experimentally Induced Anxiety and Speech Disturbances* (Kasl & Mahl, 1958).

METHOD

The subjects in the experiment, 25 experimental and 20 control subjects, were Yale undergraduates. They were paid volunteers, recruited from the files of the university bureau, which provides part-time employment for students. The subjects seemed quite homogeneous on intelligence and socioeconomic background. This homogeneity was desirable but not necessary because the speech-disturbance levels do not seem to be related . . . to sex, age, education, or socioeconomic status . . . (Chapter 11).

The experimental procedure utilized an interview sequence in a room with facilities for sound recording and observation (Mahl, Dollard, & Redlich, 1954). The subjects also took the individual form of the MMPI (Hathaway & McKinley, 1951) and their palmar moisture was recorded five times during the entire experiment. The procedure for administering the palm moisture test, described by Mowrer, Light, Luria, and Zeleny (1953), is fully standardized and objective.

The following is a more detailed account of the experimental procedure. The subject is brought into the interview room with facilities for sound recording and observation. After the *first* palm moisture test, the subject is seated in a comfortable armchair and puts on a set of earphones. This becomes the "neutral" interview (Interview A), lasting about 30 minutes. During one half of the interview, the experimenter is in the same room with the subject; during the other half, the experimenter is in the monitor room (separated from the interview room by a wall and a one-way mirror and containing the recording and monitoring apparatus). During the whole interview the subject has on a set of earphones through which he hears the experimenter. The aforementioned procedure is controlled for sequence effects, so that one half of the subjects are alone in the interview room during the first half of Interview A and with the experimenter during the second; for the other half of the subjects, the sequence is reversed. When the experimenter is in the monitor room, he hears the subject through a microphone hidden in a lamp on a table next to the armchair. The subject is told where the microphone is located and that the interview is being recorded. All through Interview A, the subject is put at ease and encouraged to talk freely about school, extracurricular activities, his background, and so on. Direct and "searching" questions are avoided. When Interview A is terminated, the experimenter administers the *second* palm moisture test. Finally, the subject takes the MMPI and then leaves.

The second session, following a period of at least 24 hours after the first one, is started by the administration of the *third* palm moisture test. Thereupon, the subject completes several intellectual tasks, not relevant to this presentation, and the *fourth* palm moisture test is then administered. At this point, the subject is left in the interview room and the experimenter goes into the monitor room. This is the setting for the "anxiety" interview (Interview B). The experimenter manipulated anxiety in two ways: presenting each subject with the same set of anxiety stimuli and suggesting anxiety-provoking topics for discussion. The standard set of anxiety-provoking stimuli included the following: revealing to the subject at that point the presence of the one-way mirror through which he is being observed; remarking that the long test he took was an "adjustment inventory" and then asking him what he remembers about it; announcing that certain topics of the experimenter's choice will now be probed in greater detail; interspersing the discussion with occasional silences at natural breaks in the conversation where the subject might have reasonably expected the experimenter to say something. The other kind of manipulation was not standard across all subjects because the writers believed that the same set of discussion topics would not necessarily arouse anxiety in all subjects. Consequently, the experimenter used his knowledge of each individual subject, gained from Interview A and from the MMPI, to suggest areas for discussion that he believed would prove anxiety-provoking to the particular subject. The probing questions were phrased as invitations to explore some specific issue; direct questions, answerable in short sentences, were avoided. Interview B lasted about 30 minutes and was terminated by the administration of the *fifth* palm moisture test.

At the end of the experiment, each subject was briefly told about its purpose and was assured that all of the experimenter's statements were part of the experiment and were addressed to all of the subjects and that what the experimenter had said had nothing to do with what he really thought of the subject. The subject was then asked to express any feelings, comments, or questions that he might have. Finally, the subject was dismissed when it appeared that any possible aftereffects of the experiment were gone.

Twenty control subjects were included in the design of the experiment. These subjects came for two sessions and went exactly through the same interview sequence as did the experimental subjects, the only difference being that they were given the same freedom of choice of conversation topics during the second session as during the first; that is, both sessions were "neutral." Ten of the control subjects were also given four palm moisture tests before and after Interviews A and B. The control subjects were not given any of the other tests.

The taped recordings of the interviews were transcribed and the typescripts were then corrected for inaccuracies by listening again to the high-fidelity tapes. Thereupon, the speech disturbances were scored, using both the tapes and the typescripts. Three different speech-disturbance measures were used: the Ah-Ratio, the Non-ah Ratio (chapter 9, p. 169), and . . . the ratios for the individual speech disturbance categories. The "ah" measure was isolated from the other categories because previous work had indicated that it behaves in a manner different from that of the other disturbances (chapters 10 and 11). It also merits special consideration because it is the most frequent category (on the average, but not for every subject) and untrained but sensitive listeners are most aware of it in ordinary conversation.

The procedure for recording the subject's palmar moisture yields fingerprints which vary in darkness. The darkness of these prints, reflecting the level of palmar moisture, was measured by a densitometer. This instrument was constructed according to the directions given by Mowrer et al. (1953).

RESULTS AND DISCUSSION

Reliabilities

In order to determine the reliability of the densitometer, the scores for 10 randomly selected subjects were used. This represents 50 separate administrations of the palm moisture test. The reliability of the densitometer is .99, reflecting the agreement between two scorings of the same prints by the same scorer and, of course, suggests that the densitometer does not introduce any perceptible error. The reliability of the palm moisture test itself is not reported by Mowrer et al. (1953) and is not known to the writers. For comparison purposes, however, Table 12.1 may be consulted. It shows the intercorrelations of the palm moisture test for the five administrations and can be viewed as reflecting high stability of individual differences. (The intercorrelations of the first three administrations are based on the data from both the 25 experimental and 10 control subjects. The remaining correlations reflect only the data from the experimental subjects because the conditions were no longer comparable for the two groups of subjects.) The values in Table 12.1, moreover can be seen as a lower bound for a test-retest reliability estimate of the palm moisture measure. This is because in estimating test-retest reliability, one tests under approximately the same conditions,

TABLE 12.1
Intercorrelations of the Palmar Sweat Data

Administration of the Palmar Sweat Test	Second	Third	Fourth	Fifth
First	.82	.70	.62	.64
Second	—	.79	.82	.80
Third		—	.58	.70
Fourth			—	.84
Fifth				—

TABLE 12.2
Intercorrelations of the Major Speech-Disturbance Ratios

	1	2	3	4	5	6
Interview A (experimenter present)						
1. Ah Ratio	—	.49	.85[a]	.39[a]	.91	.64
2. Non-ah Ratio		—	.50[a]	.81[a]	.37	.88
Interview A (experimenter absent)						
3. Ah Ratio			—	.43[a]	.85	.60
4. Non-ah Ratio				—	.33	.82
Interview B (experimenter absent)						
5. Ah Ratio					—	.52
6. Non-ah Ratio						—

Note: Boldfaced correlations reflect the stability of individual differences.
    [a]Correlations are based on all 45 experimental and control subjects. The remaining correlations are based on 25 experimental subjects.

whereas the successive administrations of the measure in the experiment were all under somewhat different conditions, hence the lower bound.

The reliabilities of scoring the speech disturbance ratios are as follows: General Ratio .99, Ah Ratio .99, Non-ah Ratio .96, sentence-change ratio .87, repetition ratio .97. These reliabilities represent the agreement of two independent judges, using the tapes and unscored typescripts of five randomly selected subjects and scoring 36 randomly selected pages of transcripts of these subjects' speech. In other words, the unit here was a double-spaced typewritten page of transcript and the correlation was between the two independent scores for a particular . . . [ratio] for that page . . . The remaining typescripts were scored by one writer and checked by the other. Table 12.2 presents the intercorrelations of the two major speech-disturbance ratios. The 20 control subjects are included in the data for Interview A inasmuch as the interview conditions for the control and the experimental subjects were equivalent.

The mean length of the typescripts of the two interviews for the 45 experimental and control subjects was 6790 words ($SD = 2021$). The experimental and control subjects did not differ much in their average verbal output during Interview A (3687 and 3847 words, respectively) but did show a sizable difference for Interview B (2675 and 3478 words, respectively). The latter difference is a consequence, in part, of the experimental manipulation: during Interview B, the experimenter intentionally allowed occasional silences to develop during the conversation. The absence of the experimenter during one half of Interview A had no effects on the verbal output of the subjects; their average was 1895 words as compared with 1863 words for the other half, during which the experimenter was present. The verbal output of

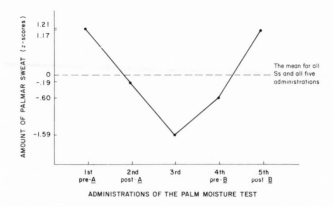

FIG. 12.1.   Mean levels of palmar sweat for the 25 experimental subjects at different stages of the experiment.

the experimenter was minimal and did not differ significantly across the different conditions.

Validation of the Experimental Manipulation

It is being assumed that the palm moisture data reflect the subjects' anxiety levels and that, consequently, they can be used to demonstrate anxiety differences between neutral Interview A and anxiety-provoking Interview B. Figure 12.1 shows the mean palmar sweat values for the 25 experimental subjects during the five separate administrations. The units in that figure are standard scores based on the mean and standard deviation of the raw palmar sweat scores for the 25 subjects across all five administrations.

The experimental manipulation would lead one to expect no change or some decrease in palmar sweat during Interview A and a significant increase during Interview B. The data support these expectations. During Interview A, 17 out of 25 subjects decreased in their palmar sweat ($p < .06$), whereas 18 out of 25 subjects increased in their palmar sweat during Interview B ($p = .02$). The difference between the decrease during Interview A and the increase during Interview B is also significant ($\chi^2 = 6.5$, $p < .02$). The 10 control subjects on whom palmar sweat data were collected showed only random fluctuations in their palmar sweat. During the first interview, 5 subjects showed an increase and 5 subjects a decrease in the amount of sweat. During the second interview 6 out of the 10 subjects showed an increase in the amount of sweat.

A second procedure was adopted to check upon the presence of anxiety in Interview B. Because this method was relatively time consuming, it was applied to only a small subsample of the experimental subjects. The tapes for six subjects were reedited in such a way that a new tape contained ten 1-minute segments of the subject's speech (with the experimenter's questions and remarks erased, and with all speech disturbances edited from the subject's speech), 5 from each interview. These segments were randomly selected and randomly distributed so that the two judges rating the amount of anxiety present would have no clues available to them other than those coming from the subject's speech. The interjudge reliability was satisfactory, albeit not high ($r = .77$); the 30 segments from Interview B were rated significantly higher on anxiety than the 30 segments from Interview A ($p < .04$).

Changes in the Speech-Disturbance Ratios

The major hypothesis of the study predicts a higher frequency of the Non-ah speech disturbances during the anxiety-provoking Interview B than during the neutral Interview A. The results strongly support the hypothesis. Twenty-four of the 25 experimental subjects showed an increase in their Non-ah Ratios ($p < .0001$). Of the 20 control subjects, only 12 showed such an increase from the first to the second interview (ns). The difference between the experimental and the control groups is significant at the .004 level, using Fisher's exact test.

The Non-ah Ratio is a measure which lumps together seven different and distinct speech-disturbance categories (see chapter 9, p. 169). Are all of these categories sensitive to the presumed difference in anxiety between Interviews A and B, or are there only a few of the categories that are primarily responsible for the large increase in the Non-ah Ratio? The data reveal that all seven categories show a significant increase from Interview A to B ($< .01$, using t tests). The increases in the case of the infrequent categories are quite small but consistent enough to yield significant results. This suggests that combining the various speech categories is a meaningful procedure for obtaining a single index, the Non-ah Ratio, which reflects changes in anxiety. The comparable changes for the 20 control subjects showed random variations for all categories except "sentence change": here, the ratios during the second interview were higher than the ratios during the first ($p < .05$). There is no apparent explanation for this isolated finding.

No predictions were made about the Ah Ratio inasmuch as past work . . . [chapters 11, 15, and 18] has suggested that the two kinds of speech disturbances, the Ah Ratio and the Non-ah Ratio . . . are functionally different and may not be equally sensitive to anxiety.

In the present study, the Ah Ratio showed no significant differences, either among the experimental or the control subjects, between the first and the second interviews, that is, the Ah Ratio was apparently not sensitive to the anxiety manipulation. However, an interesting finding comes to light when one compares the effects of the presence versus absence of the experimenter within Interview A. This difference, which leaves the Non-ah Ratio unchanged, has a strong effect on the Ah Ratio: 32 out of the 45 subjects had higher Ah Ratios when the experimenter was away in the monitor room, 2 subjects showed no changes, and only 11 subjects had higher Ah Ratios when the experimenter was present together with the subject in the interview room ($p < .001$). All 45 subjects are used here because the first interview was the same for both experimental and control subjects.

In summary, then, we have two kinds of speech disturbances: the Ah Ratio, which apparently does not change with experimentally produced anxiety but is sensitive to a change from a face-to-face to a telephonelike conversation; the Non-ah Ratio, which is sensitive to anxiety but does not change when one switches from a normal to a telephonelike conversation. The remainder of this chapter is devoted to a more detailed exploration into the meaning of these two ratios.

Non-Ah Ratio and Other Indices of Anxiety

The average increase per subject in the Non-ah Ratio, going from Interview A to B, was 34.2%. Clearly, the experimental manipulation of anxiety had a sizable effect. Two other partial indicators of anxiety can be obtained from the available data: the palm moisture index and the Taylor Manifest Anxiety (MA) scale, derivable from the MMPI (Taylor, 1953).

The palm moisture index is not an unambiguous indicator of anxiety and certain obvious questions arise: does the amount of recorded sweat accurately reflect the sweating during the preceding 5 minutes, 10 minutes, or 30 minutes? Are the absolute values across individuals meaningful or should one use only relative changes in these values? Such questions must be kept in mind as one looks at Table 12.3, which presents the major results concerning the relationship of the frequency of flustered speech to palmar sweat. The Non-ah Ratios during Interviews A and B are related to two indices of sweat: as assessed at the end of each interview and as a derivation from each subject's own basal or "resting" level. (The third palm moisture test was taken as the best approximate indicator of the subjects' "normal" level of sweat. See Fig. 12.1.) The data for Interview A include the 10 control subjects inasmuch as up to that point the test situations were comparable for both the experimental and control groups. The two alternate indices of sweat are only moderately correlated with each other: the correlation is .45 ($N = 35$) for Interview A scores and .32 ($N = 25$) for Interview B scores. This suggests that the alternate measures are not interchangeable.

TABLE 12.3
Relationship of the Non-ah Ratio (Number of Speech Disturbances
per 1000 Words) to Several Indices of Palmar Sweat

| Non-ah Ratio | Amount of Sweat | | df | t |
	High	Low		
Mean Non-ah Ratio during Interview A				
Sweat measured at the end of Interview A	45.8 (N = 17)	39.2 (N = 18)	33	1.19
Sweat measured as the deviation of the value obtained at the end of Interview A from each subject's own basal level	48.2 (N = 19)	35.6 (N = 16)	33	2.45***
Mean Non-ah Ratio during Interview B				
Sweat measured at the end of Interview B	57.2 (N = 13)	44.4 (N = 12)	23	1.62*
Sweat measured as the deviation of the value obtained at the end of Interview B from each subject's own basal level	59.8 (N = 12)	43.1 (N = 13)	23	2.22**
Mean net increase in Non-ah Ratio from Interview A to B				
Sweat measured as the net comparison of the change in sweat during Interview B with that in Interview A	16.5 (N = 13)	8.1 (N = 12)	23	2.27**

*p = .06.
**p = .02.
***p < .01.

The data in Table 12.3 reveal a mild positive association between flustered speech and palmar sweating. Moreover, the last row in that table
demonstrates that subjects who showed a relatively large increase in sweat
during Interview B, as compared with their change in sweat during Interview
A, had a larger increase in the Non-ah Ratio than subjects who showed a
relatively small increase in sweat.

The findings concerning the relationship of the MA scale to the speech
disturbances are a good deal more tentative. The scores on the MA scale
correlated −.53 with the K scale of the MMPI and a statistical correction was
applied (Guilford, 1956, p. 367) to partial out defensiveness, which is pre-

TABLE 12.4

Relationship of the Non-ah Ratio (Number of Speech Disturbances
per 1000 Words) to the Taylor Manifest Anxiety Scale

| Non-ah Ratio | Subjects Reporting: | | t |
	Moderate Anxiety	Either High or Low Anxiety	
Mean Non-ah Ratio during Interview A	46.8	34.0	1.99*
Mean Non-ah Ratio during Interview B	63.1	44.3	2.44**
Mean net increase in Non-ah Ratio from Interview A to B	16.4	10.3	1.53

*$p = .06$.
**$p = .02$.

sumably reflected by the K scale. Henceforth, any reference to the MA scale
means only these scores corrected for defensiveness.

The data reveal no linear relationship between the Non-ah Ratio and the
MA scale. However, if the subjects are divided into three groups with high,
intermediate, and low scores on the MA scale, then a hint of a curvilinear
relationship appears. These data are presented in Table 12.4. The curvilinear relationship was not anticipated and as yet does not particularly
make sense. However, Schwartzburg, Feldstein, and Jaffe (1963) report a
curvilinear relationship between speech disruption and uncertainty contained in the passages that were read. Thus our finding may not be an
isolated one.

Meaning of Ah in Speech

It has been seen that the Ah Ratio, which did not change with experimentally produced anxiety, is highly sensitive to a change from a face-to-face to a
telephonelike conversation: the average change in the Ah Ratio for the 45
subjects is a 41.2% increase from the interview-room situation (experimenter
is present) to the monitor-room situation (experimenter is absent). In this
comparison, sequence effects are randomized and experimentally produced
anxiety remains constant.

The striking increase in the Ah Ratio is a finding that requires some
explanation. One may think of ordinary conversation as a process of communication between two people in which vocal activity constitutes only a part of
the information exchanged. Various facial expressions, movements of the
head, and so on, are all additional cues, which may tell the speaker how he is

progressing and how his speech is understood and received, even though the listener may not actually be saying anything with words. When the experimenter is in the monitor room, the subject is deprived of all these additional cues. The experimenter's silence tells him nothing. Consequently, the subject is more uncertain about the effects his speaking has on his listener and the use of "ah" enables him to pause briefly and determine what he wants to say next. To be sure, the "ah" cannot act as a substitute for the information the listener's many nonverbal cues could give him; it can only enable him to deliberate more carefully. The work of Goldman-Eisler (1958b, 1961) and of Maclay and Osgood (1959) on the relationship of hesitations and pauses to the predictability of words from context tends to support the above interpretation of the function of "ah" in speech. (See chapter 18 for further data and discussion about the meaning of "ah.")

Stability of Individuals' Speech-Disturbance Profiles

It has been the experience of those working with speech disturbances (chapter 9) and hesitations (Goldman-Eisler, 1961; Maclay & Osgood, 1959) that the various speech phenomena under study show stable, characteristic patterns. Moreover, the work of the aforementioned writers suggests that deviations from habitual patterns may be indicative of anxiety and other emotions.

In the present study, the three most frequent categories—the Ah, Sentence change, and Repetition—were used to construct a speech disturbance profile for each individual. Such profiles for Interview A (for the half during which the experimenter was absent) were then compared with those for Interview B. Subjects showing a change in their profiles were those for whom the ordering of the frequency of usage of the three categories did not remain the same across the two interviews. There were 13 subjects who showed such a change. Under the hypothesis that the instability of profiles is in part a function of anxiety, the subjects with stable and unstable profiles were compared on the MA scale and the palmar sweat measures. While the latter indices of anxiety yielded no significant relationships, it was found that on the MA scale, subjects with unstable profiles had higher scores (biserial correlation = .47, $p < .02$).

In investigating the characteristics of subjects with unstable speech disturbance profiles, an additional striking finding came to light. Subjects who are highly labile on the palm moisture test (that is, they show high-intraindividual variation in their scores across the several administrations) are stable with respect to their speech-disturbance profiles, and vice versa (biserial correlation = − .68, $p < .0001$). This relationship suggests that palmar sweat and disruption of . . . speech patterns may be alternate ways in which each subject reacted to anxiety fluctuations which occurred during the experiment.

Speech Disturbance in Anxious Children

13

Philip G. Zimbardo
Stanford University

George F. Mahl
Yale University

James W. Barnard
University of South Florida

INTRODUCTION

This chapter extends the investigation of the Non-ah speech disturbances in three ways. First, it is a second experimental study in which the anxiety of the speaker is sytematically manipulated and the variations in speech disturbance level are observed. The other comparable study was that reported in the preceding chapter. Again, the subjects are male. In the present study, control of the atmosphere of the interview (evaluative-permissive) and the types of questions (positive, negative, or neutral in affective direction) were used to alter the anxiety level of chronically "high" and "low" anxious subjects. Second, the study extends the range of speakers from adults to children. And, third, this study is the first one to attempt a systematic investigation into the interaction of characterological anxiety levels of speakers and experimentally varied, mild anxiety-provoking procedures.

The chapter also illustrates how this expressive speech measure contributes to the understanding of the psychology of test-anxious children, a problem Seymour Sarason and his co-workers investigated for years in their pioneering studies.[1]

---

[1]The following is adapted from P. G. Zimbardo, G. F. Mahl, and J. W. Barnard (1963), "The Measurement of Speech Disturbance in Anxious Children," Journal of Speech and Hearing Disorders, *28*, 362–370, copyright 1963, The American Speech-Language-Hearing Association, Rockville, MD, with the permission of the publisher and coauthors, with slight editorial and stylistic revisions. In addition to being supported by my own NIMH grant, this study was encouraged and supported by Seymour Sarason as part of his Yale Test Anxiety Program under his NIMH grant. We wish to thank Kate McGraw for her valuable assistance in scoring the speech disturbances and with the analysis of the data.

. . . research by Barnard, Zimbardo, and Sarason (1961) indicated that the verbal behavior of anxious children can be differentiated on several dimensions from that of nonanxious children. The speech of highly test-anxious elementary school children (see Sarason et al., 1960) during a structured interview was rated as more "incomprehensible" than that of children whose anxiety was low. Furthermore, high-anxious children used more negative affect in expressing their reactions to other people, situations, and ideas, and used more inappropriate affect than did low-anxious children. These predicted differences between anxiety groups emerged clearly when the interview conditions were experimentally manipulated to create an evaluative atmosphere. However, an unexpected reversal occurred under nonevaluative interview conditions; the verbal behavior of low-anxious children under more "permissive" conditions was similar to that of the high-anxious subjects under evaluative conditions.

This unexpected interaction was investigated further in a subsequent study by Zimbardo, Barnard, and Berkowitz (1963). This second study attempted to replicate the aforementioned result and clarify its meaning by specifying "defensive-denial" as a crucial variable mediating the effects of anxiety on speech within given social environments. Again the interaction was found between anxiety level and interview treatment on the following dimensions of verbal behavior: (1) the expression of affect, (2) the use of inappropriate affect, (3) the use of descriptive adjectives denoting negative evaluation, and (4) incomprehensibility of response. Some of the data appeared to substantiate the importance of defensiveness in mediating the effects of anxiety on speech behavior under permissive but not under evaluative conditions. Briefly, low-anxious children who were highly defensive behaved like high-anxious children. These children have successfully learned to mask their true level of anxiety and not reveal themselves. However, the relatively unstructured nature of the permissive interview conditions made it difficult for them to employ their pervasive (and characterological) defenses. Thus, they behaved more like anxious children whose anxiety was cued off by evalutive (test-like) interview conditions (see Zimbardo, Barnard, & Berkowitz, 1963, for a fuller exposition).

It should be noted that the effects of anxiety upon verbal behavior were most marked for expressive aspects of speech and least marked for the content of speech. No significant differences emerged in either study on a measure of "specificity of information" (number and kind of details mentioned for each answer), nor on a measure of the content of the affect expressed (i.e., the source and topic of the affect). On several measures of speech incomprehensibility, the predicted interaction of anxiety and interview condition (and even the second-order interaction with defensiveness) was demonstrated. However, the measures developed by us were rather crude: (1) a single, global rating of how incomprehensible each answer appeared to a judge rater, (2) the number of words in each answer that could not be decoded, and finally (3) the number of words in each answer which were redundant, or in excess of the minimal information-carrying units.

Because the results of these studies have both practical and theoretical significance, it was hoped to establish them more firmly by subjecting the data to a more thorough and sensitive analysis. . . .

Independent analysis of the data obtained in the study by Zimbardo, Barnard, and Berkowitz (1963) by use of . . . [the Non-ah Speech Disturbance Ratio defined in Chapter 9, p. 169] provided an opportunity both to extend the application of this instrument and to permit a further test of the validity of the interaction effect between anxiety and interview conditions. In addition, it was hoped that use of this more sensitive measure might reveal interactions between anxiety and interview question-types that were predicted but not demonstrated in our previous study. It was expected that high-anxious children would evidence more speech disturbance than low-anxious children when the stimulus questions were less structured (i.e., neutral) than when they were clear in affective direction (i.e., either negative or positive). Moreover, this same disrupting effect of lack of structure should exist for low-anxious, highly defensive children. Thus, the present chapter reports the results of applying . . . [the Non-ah Speech Disturbance Ratio] to samples of the speech of elementary school children under experimentally manipulated interview conditions.

METHOD

Subjects

From a population of over 500 third-grade children tested in 11 elementary schools in Hamden, Connecticut, a sample of 40 males was selected for the present study. Eighteen months prior to the start of this study the entire population received the . . . [Test Anxiety Scale for Children], and the Defensiveness Scale for Children (see Sarason et al., 1960), as well as the Lorge-Thorndike IQ test. Half of our subjects (Ss) were in the highest 15% of the anxiety scale distribution with scores from 16 to 30 and were designated "high-anxious" (HA). The "low-anxious" (LA) Ss were in the lowest 15% of the distribution with scores from 0 to 3. The subjects also varied in their degree of defensiveness. Half of each anxiety group was composed of a subsample with high-defensiveness scores, that is, the top quartile on the defensiveness scale (within each anxiety group), and half with low-defensiveness scores was in the bottom quartile. The Ss in each of the four groups were individually equated on IQ, and the groups were randomly assigned to one of two interview treatments. Thus the research design is a repeated measurement, mixed factorial arrangement: 2 (anxiety levels) × 2 (defensiveness levels) × 2 (interview treatments) with five Ss per cell and three types of interview questions (positive affective direction, negative, and neutral).

Procedure

Interview Administration

The interview, which consisted of a series of questions with standardized probes, was administered individually in a schoolroom by one of two interviewers (who were unaware of the anxiety or defensiveness categories of the Ss). The entire interview was tape-recorded to facilitate complete, accurate recording and scoring. Examples of the questions used and a fuller set of the instructions are given in Zimbardo, Barnard, and Berkowitz (1963).

Evaluative Interview

Because the Ss varied in their degree of anxiety specific to tests and test situations, it was felt that the experimental manipulation of the Ss' perception of the evaluative nature of the interview situation would enable us to observe the effects of the anxiety variable. Accordingly, half of the Ss were led to believe that the interviewer was evaluating them and that they would be given a test following the interview. These expectations were guided by the interviewer's distant and authoritative manner, as well as by appropriate instructions.

Permissive Interview

For the other half of the Ss the interview situation was quite permissive and nonevaluative in terms of instructions, manner in which questions were asked, and frequent reference to S by his first name.

A check on these manipulations revealed that they were effective in producing differential expectations by the Ss of the purpose of the interview. Significantly more of the evaluative children expected to get a test, whereas the permissively treated children expected a game, more talk, or something other than a test ($p < .01$).

Speech Disturbance Scoring

The procedure used to measure speech disturbance was . . . [that described in chapter 9 for determining the Non-ah Speech Disturbance Ratio, using the tape recordings and the verbatim transcripts of relevant language samples of the interviews].

RESULTS

Reliability

Two trained judges independently scored all of the verbal responses to two questions chosen at random from each of 16 subjects. The judges, who were not the interviewers, did not know the anxiety or defensiveness group of the subjects. The reliability of the . . . [speech disturbance] measure, as in other studies, was quite high, the product-moment correlation being +.89 (p < .01). One of these two judges then scored all the material used in this study, furnishing all of the . . . [Non-ah Ratios] used for analysis.

The Relation of Anxiety, Interview and Defensiveness to Non-Ah Ratio

Because it was found that the variances were not homogeneous within the cells, it was necessary to transform the distribution of ratio scores by means of an arc sine transformation before an analysis of variance could be performed. The analysis performed was a repeated-measurements analysis of variance with three independent variables and one correlated variable (question-type).

For the uncorrelated sources of variance, none of the main effects was significant (F < 1). However, as predicted, there was a significant interaction between anxiety and interview condition (F = 4.86, p < .05, df = $\frac{1}{32}$). Table 13.1 reveals that HA children manifest more speech disturbance when they are interviewed under evaluative test-like conditions than when they are treated permissively. On the other hand, LA children react with marked speech disturbance when they are treated permissively but show much less disturbance in an evaluative interview setting.

TABLE 13.1
Mean Speech Disturbance Measures for
Anxiety Groups under Different
Interview Conditions

	Interview	
Anxiety	Evaluative	Permissive
Low	11.9	16.2
High	16.1	13.5

Note: Higher scores indicate greater speech disturbance. Scores are arc sine transforms.

TABLE 13.2
Mean Speech Disturbance of Anxious
Children on Each Type of Question

Question Type	Low Anxious	High Anxious
Negative	13.3	14.4
Positive	14.6	13.8
Neutral	14.1	16.3

The predicted second-order interaction of the aforementioned variables with the defensiveness scale scores was not supported by the data. However, this may be due to artifacts in test administration and the small sample size within each cell . . . [see Discussion]. Closer examination of the data indicates that the trends that emerge are clearly in the direction expected, but that large error variance renders them statistically nonsignificant. Nevertheless, the concept of defensiveness does appear to us to contribute somewhat to our understanding of the interaction of anxiety and interview conditions at least when one considers responses to the different question-types.

It will be recalled that we predicted an interaction of anxiety with question-type in the direction of HA Ss showing more speech disturbance than LA Ss for questions neutral in affective direction as compared to more structured ones with a positive or negative affective direction. The data in Table 13.2 suggest that LA Ss as a total group may not respond differentially to variations in question–type, but HA Ss may—for them, neutral questions elicit most speech disturbance ($F = 2.39$, $p = 10$, $df = \frac{2}{64}$). The mean . . . [Non-ah Ratio] for HA Ss to neutral questions is significantly different ($p < .05$ by two-tailed t-tests) from each of the other group means.

Several provocative findings emerge if we now look more closely at the nonsignificant third-order interaction relating types of question to interview condition, anxiety, and defensiveness ($F = 2.09$, $p = < .15$, $df = \frac{2}{64}$). Across all question-types, the evaluative treatment had a greater disrupting effect on the speech of HA Ss, whereas LA Ss were more disturbed by permissive than evaluative interview conditions. For all groups but one, the biggest difference in speech disturbance between permissive and evaluative interview conditions occurred on questions with a clear-cut affective direction, either positive or negative. The LA, highly defensive children are the exception. Their speech is much more disturbed under permissive than under evaluative conditions when they are responding to neutral questions. Thus we draw the tentative conclusion that these children are most disturbed under conditions, which combine to provide least structure to guide their verbal behavior, such as a permissive interview setting in which neutral questions are asked.

DISCUSSION

The results of the present study can be taken as providing further support for . . . [the Non-ah Speech Disturbance Ratio] as a sensitive indicator of anxiety, detecting anxiety even in young school children and reflecting the consequences of both chronic and experimentally aroused anxiety.

In addition because the results using this measure generally support our previous findings, there is cause for increased confidence in the validity of our earlier finding of an interaction effect upon verbal behavior of anxiety and interview conditions. The data do not offer statistical support for our analysis of this effect in terms of the differential functioning of defensiveness; nevertheless, it may be that the theoretical explanation of the interaction in terms of defensiveness is still satisfactory, but that our study did not provide optimal conditions for its test. It should be recalled that both the anxiety and defensiveness scales used to form the experimental groups were administered a year and a half prior to the start of this study. Unpublished data of a longitudinal study of test anxiety by S. Sarason, Hill, and Zimbardo (1963) indicate that the reliability of these scales with such young children is rather low (test-retest correlations average about .40). Moreover, changes in anxiety level over an 18-month period were shown to be correlated significantly and negatively with changes in defensiveness ($r = -.36, p < .001$ for boys). Thus our failure to demonstrate statistically significant effects of defensiveness may not be due to its lack of association with verbal behavior but rather to the contamination of this variable. Moreover, with our small cell size, unaccountable changes across defensiveness levels could easily attenuate or mask any relation that might exist between our independent variables and speech disturbance.

The role of defensiveness in our study must therefore be viewed cautiously, and we present as worthy of further study the interesting findings that HA Ss show most speech disturbance in answering neutral questions, and that a similar effect is noted for LA, high-defensive children under permissive interview conditions. Thus speech disturbance increases under conditions where the cues as to the appropriateness of one's verbal responses are minimal. The permissive conditions require the child to reveal his thoughts and feelings in a manner which these defensive children have learned successfully to defend against and thereby appear low anxious. But there is not sufficient structure provided under permissive conditions for the child to know how *not* to reveal himself by talking or by being silent, by talking about himself or about others. Moreover, neutral questions which do not have a clear-cut affective direction remove the final situational cue to responses appropriate for self-concealment and for control over anxiety. Under these conditions, the child's habitual use of defenses may be rendered ineffective, and his true anxiety is manifested in expressive aspects of his speech.

Degree of question structure then may play the same role in affecting the verbal behavior of the HA Ss as it does for the LA, high-defensive permissive Ss. This finding is consistent with those of Dibner (1956, 1958) and Pope and Siegman (1962) that there is an inverse relation between (a) degree of structure of psychiatric interview (Dibner) or the specificity of interviewer behavior (Pope & Siegman), and (b) the frequency of disruptions in the patient's speech. Pope and Siegman also used the . . . [Non-ah Ratio], whereas Dibner employed an independently devised scale of nonfluency.

It is noteworthy that the power of the . . . [Non-ah Ratio] permitted detection of the subtle effects of question-types that went completely unnoticed in our earlier study . . . (Zimbardo, Barnard, & Berkowitz, 1963). In addition, this expressive speech measure of anxiety proved effective where several content measures of speech had failed to reveal any effects of anxiety upon verbal behavior.

Our results prompt us to recommend further application of the . . . [Non-ah Ratio] as a valid and reliable indicator of anxiety under a wide range of correlation and experimental uses. The data also suggest that research is called for that focuses upon the behavioral dynamics of a very interesting group of people—those whose measured anxiety is low, but whose defensive denial is high.

SUMMARY

This experiment had three major aims: (1) to determine whether the verbal behavior of test-anxious children was different from that of nonanxious children; (2) to evaluate the efficacy of . . . [the Non-ah Speech Disturbance Ratio] in detecting the effects upon speech of chronic and experimentally manipulated anxiety in young children; and (3) to assess the role of "defensiveness" in contributing to an understanding of the effects of anxiety on speech disturbance.

The independent variables employed were two levels of test anxiety and also of defensiveness (Sarason self-report scales), two types of interview conditions (evaluative and permissive), and three sets of interview questions (varying in affective direction from positive through neutral to negative). The dependent variable was . . . [the Non-ah Speech Disturbance Ratio].

The major results obtained from testing 40 third-grade school boys within the factorial design imposed by the variables just mentioned indicate that there is a significant interactive effect upon speech disturbance of anxiety level and type of interview condition. High-anxious children are more disturbed under evaluative then permissive conditions, whereas the opposite is true for low-anxious children. The expectation that low-anxious Ss who were highly defensive would react in a way similar to truly high-anxious Ss was not supported by the data. The speech disturbance ratio also detected subtle differences in question types, high-anxious Ss showing more disturbance to neutral questions than to those more structured in affective direction. On this measure, the low-anxious children who were also highly defensive showed a more similar effect of lack of structure producing a disruption of verbal behavior.

Speech Disturbances During Induced Psychological Stress

14

Gene Schulze
Consultants for Personal Competence,
Guilford, CT

> *It would be pretty easy for the s-, the son to turn . . . ah . . . the moth- . . . ah . . . the father to turn the son . . . (Laughs) father to turn the mother against the son . . . ah . . . because of the relationship between them.*
>
> —Subject T-11

PREVIEW

Schulze's research extends the investigation of the Non-ah speech disturbances in five ways.

First, it comprises the third and fourth *experimental* studies, reported in this volume, of the effect of anxiety and conflict on the frequency of speech disturbances. The other two were by Kasl and Mahl (chapter 12) and by Zimbardo, Mahl, and Barnard (chapter 13). Thus Schulze increases the ratio of experimental to clinical-correlational data.

Second, Schulze extends our knowledge about the range of speaking situations in which anxiety and conflict can be expected to increase speech disruption. He used two speaking situations that had not been used before: the inquiry into Thematic Apperception Test stories and one in which speakers described films they were observing. The TAT inquiry does call for self-revelation just as the interviews did in the clinical and experimental studies reported in preceding chapters, but it does so in a different context.

223

224   14. SPEECH DISTURBANCES DURING PSYCHOLOGICAL STRESS

Third, this study determines the effect of probing questions with much more precision and rigor than before. In the clinical study reported in chapter 10 probing questions were noted and were often judged to be effective in increasing the level of the patients' anxiety and, hence, speech disturbances. And such questions were included in the experimental manipulations during the anxiety interview in the research presented in chapter 12 and were part of the standardized interview used in the study reported in the preceding chapter 13. In all these instances, however, other variables were known, or could be presumed, to be operating at the same time. In his first experiment, Schulze varies only the nature of the TAT Inquiry questions. Through the use of "low probes," "high probes," and "difficult" questions he is able to determine the effect on speech of presumably anxiety-evoking probing questions and to distinguish that effect from more generalized "arousal," such as might be the result of the "difficult" questions.

Fourthly, Schulze's is the first study that compares the frequency of the disturbances in spontaneous, conflictful, self-revelatory and interactive speech with that in the speech of people who are describing external events, which are potentially anxiety arousing, as they observe them. His findings in this regard raise many questions for future research.

Fifth, this study is the most thorough and sophisticated one to date of the relationship between concurrent physiological changes and speech disturbances. Thus it carries this line of research far beyond correlating speech disturbance level with manual perspiration (chapter 12).

INTRODUCTION[1]

Measures that have been proposed as anxiety indices can be divided into two classes. Those that are relatively stable over time treat proneness to be anxious as a personality trait, whereas those that fluctuate over relatively short periods of time are considered measures of momentary anxiety intensity. The latter have been reviewed by Krause (1961), Krause, Galinsky, and Weiner (1961), Martin (1961), and Mahl and Schulze (1964). One of these proposed measures of momentary anxiety intensity is the Non-ah Speech Disturbance Ratio (NSDR) defined in chapter 9 (p. 169).

The NSDR has been related to a number of stimulus and response variables that were selected because of their hypothetical relation to anxiety. These variables included: body movements (Boomer, 1963), observer rat-

---

[1]The rest of this chapter is a portion of a PhD thesis submitted to Yale University (Schulze, 1964). The research was supported by Mahl's NIMH research grant, by the Veterans Administration, and by NIMH fellowship funds.

ings of anxiety (Boomer & Goodrich, 1961; Mahl, chapters 10, 11), self-ratings of anxiety (Lerea, 1956), physiological measures (DiMascio, 1961; Kasl & Mahl, chapter 12), and antecedent stimulus conditions (Kasl & Mahl, chapter 12; Krause & Pilisuk, 1961; Pope & Siegman, 1962; Schulze, Mahl, & Murray, 1960). However, in similar other studies of the NSDR, negative results have also been reported. Mahl and Schulze (1964) found inconsistencies when they reviewed the results of this body of research. They were led to concur with the conclusion that Boomer and Goodrich (1961) had reached earlier: "In the face of such theoretical complexity the preferred research strategy might be to regard the SDR as a promising measure of certain aspects of anxiety in certain classes of people under certain conditions" (p. 163).

The research reported here was designed to provide further information about the conditions under which relations between the NSDR and other anxiety-relevant variables are found, in order to assess the validity of the NSDR as an index of momentary anxiety intensity and to progress toward determining the realm of that validity. In the present research, two attempts were made at systematic variation of anxiety intensity by stimulus manipulation. The first experiment consisted of administering Thematic Appercep-tion Test inquiry questions, which were *tailored specifically for individual subjects*, with the intent of varying the degree to which the questions probed to elicit expression of anxiety-arousing content. In the second experiment, all subjects viewed and described two motion pictures considered to have varying anxiety-arousing properties. The relation of the NSDR to these conditions, and to several anxiety-relevant response variables, was then examined. These variables were: Verbal Productivity, Anxiety Self-Ratings, and five measures of autonomic response.

The selection of Verbal Productivity was based on the assumption that most people have learned to talk less in speaking situations that make them anxious because cessation of talking is instrumental in terminating anxiety aroused by the content of what is being said, and it is also instrumental in terminating the anxiety-inducing situation as rapidly as possible. The selection of the measures of autonomic response was based on assumptions concerning the effect of drive arousal, per se, regardless of which drive is aroused, on the autonomic nervous system.

Regardless of its validity as an index of anxiety intensity, the NSDR is a reliably measurable behavioral phenomenon, whose fluctuation has been shown to be nonrandom (chapter 9). It is derived from an attribute of speech that usually escapes the notice of both speaker and listener. Identification of the determinants and concomitants of these momentary speech disturbances is likely to yield important information about psychological states of speakers.

The paradigm of the experiments is shown in Fig. 14.1.

Paradigm of the experiments
Session One
Subjects write 9 TAT stories in a group situation; same for all 24 subjects.
Session Two
First Experiment:
1. Orienting instructions,
    attaching electrodes, and
    10 min. habituation.
    Treatment 0. . . . . All 24 Ss
2. Counting silently and
    out-loud . . . . All 24 Ss
3. Describe practice movie. . . . . All 24 Ss
4. Interview
    Treatment I . . . . Difficult Inquiry
                                                                                                    All 24 Ss
                                                                               random
                                                                            assignment
    Treatment II . . . . Hi Probe   Lo Probe
                                                                        12 Ss   12 Ss
    Treatment III . . . . Lo Probe   Hi Probe
                                                                        12 Ss   12 Ss

5. Self-Ratings   random
                                                                          assignment
Second Experiment:
6. Describing movies   6   6   6   6
    Treatment IV. . . . . Hi Stress   Lo Stress
                                                                        12 Ss   12 Ss
    Treatment VI. . . . . Lo Stress   Hi Stress
                                                                        12 Ss   12 Ss
    Treatments V & VII: 5 min autonomic recovery

7. Self-Ratings . . . . All 24 Ss

FIG. 14.1.   Paradigm of the experiments.

FIRST EXPERIMENT: EFFECT OF A PROBING TAT INQUIRY

Problem

The First Experiment had three tasks, which were basically tests of: *main effects* that the experimental manipulation had on speech disturbance rate and the other measures; *intersubject correlations* between speech disturbance rate and the other measures; and *intrasubject correlations* between speech disturbance rate and the physiological measures.

First Task: Main Effects of Experimental Treatments

The purpose of the First Task was to extend, if possible, the generality of an effect whereby probing questions increase the rate of momentary disturbances in the interviewee's speech. Evidence that this effect occurs in the psychotherapy situation was reported in chapter 10, Boomer and Goodrich (1961), and Schulze, Mahl, and Murray (1960, and chapter 17). Evidence that it occurs during experimental interviews about subjects' personal affairs was reported in chapter 12 and Schulze (1961). The generality of the effect was limited by the fact that it was not found in all subjects, and by the narrow range of situations investigated.

In the present study, the situation was an experimental interview based on subjects' fantasy productions elicited by the Thematic Apperception Test. The experimental manipulation consisted of a *High-Probe* Inquiry and a *Low-Probe* Inquiry. Assuming that anxiety intensity would be higher during the *High-Probe* Inquiry than during the *Low-Probe* Inquiry, and that the NSDR is related to anxiety intensity, it was hypothesized that *NSDR would be higher during the High-Probe Inquiry than during the Low-Probe Inquiry.*

Second Task: Intersubject Correlations Among the Measures

The purpose of the Second Task was to test whether the effect of the Probing Inquiry manipulation on NSDR, if found, could be related to effects of the same experimental manipulation on physiological measures, Anxiety Self-Ratings, and Verbal Productivity. The question here is whether any independent presumed evidence of variation in anxiety intensity is consistent in size and direction (as hypothesized) with the evidence of effects on NSDR. This was analyzed by correlating the (directional) size of effects on the NSDR with the size of effects on the other measures, across subjects. This type of analysis had not been done before with the particular response variables studied here. The correlational analyses of the Second Task were based on changes in the measures from one treatment to the next, and also on within-treatment response levels.

Assuming that the *Self-Ratings of Anxiety* would be valid, it was hypothesized that they *would be directly related to NSDR* as a function of anxiety intensity. An *inverse relation between NSDR and Verbal Productivity* was hypothesized, as a function of anxiety intensity. Using the approach-avoidance conflict model (Miller, 1944) it was assumed that subjects would give shorter answers to the more anxiety-provoking questions in order to terminate the anxiety as quickly as possible.

Predominant trends in previous psychophysiological research (reviewed by Duffy, 1962) have indicated direct relations between "level of activation" and Galvanic Skin Potential Level, GSP Positive Deflections, and Heart-rate; and inverse relations between "activation" and both Volume Pulse and Skin Temperature. Assuming that variations in anxiety intensity are one class of variation in Activation, it was hypothesized that *relations between NSDR and both Volume Pulse and Skin Temperature would be inverse; between NSDR and Heartrate, GSP Level, and GSP Positive Deflections, direct.*

Third Task: Intrasubject Correlations

The Third Task was to determine whether intrasubject fluctuations in the NSDR was related to simultaneous fluctuation in the physiological measures. Support of hypotheses subsumed under this task (stated later) would strengthen the case for a relation between NSDR and anxiety intensity because it would indicate a specific correspondence in individual subjects between NSDR and somatic events theoretically interpreted as consequences of variation in drive intensity.

Hypotheses tested in the third task were based on the assumptions that anxiety intensity is one class of variation in Activation, and that the measures of autonomic response are related to anxiety intensity in the same direction as their relation to Activation. It was hypothesized that *Volume Pulse and Skin Temperature would be inversely related to NSDR, and that GSP Level, GSP Positive Deflections, and Heartrate would be directly related to NSDR, as a function of anxiety intensity.*

To summarize the hypotheses of this research, the following are measures that are expected to be *higher* during the *High Probe* (and also High Stress in the Second Experiment, see following) conditions than during the *Low Probe* (and Low-Stress conditions):

NSDR   GSP Level
Anxiety Self-Ratings   GSP Positive Deflections
Heartrate

In both inter and intrasubject correlations, the aforementioned measures are expected to be *directly* related to each other and *inversely* related to the following measures:

Verbal Productivity   Volume Pulse
Skin Temperature

The latter measures are expected to be *lower* during the *High-Probe* (and High-Stress) conditions than during the *Low-Probe* (and Low-Stress) conditions, and *directly* related to each other.

Method

Subjects

The subjects were 24 male undergraduate students who volunteered for the experiment with the inducement of gaining credits to fulfill a psychology course requirement and pay for overtime.

Apparatus

The physiological variables were recorded on a six-channel Grass Model 5 Polygraph. Continuous recording of the physiological indices was obtained throughout the experiment. Subjects sat in a comfortable reclining chair, in semireclined position. An air conditioner maintained air temperature at 24–27 degrees C. Speech was recorded on high-fidelity tape recording equipment, with the microphone placed approximately 1½ feet from the subject's mouth. A specially constructed electrical timing system delivered simultaneous impulses to the tape recorder and marker channel of the polygraph, once a minute, for synchronization of the speech and physiological records. The TAT pictures used in the interview were mounted on a board placed in front of the subject, so they could be viewed without strain or excessive head movement.

Procedure

The First Experiment consisted primarily of an Interview, in which the degree to which TAT inquiry questions, based on TAT stories previously written by the subjects, probed to elicit withheld or avoided story content was varied. It was intended that this manipulation of stimulus conditions would produce variation in anxiety intensity, with anxiety more intense during a *High-Probe* inquiry than during a *Low-Probe* inquiry.

The *High* and *Low-Probe* questions were derived from the subjects' written TAT stories by the experimenter, using a partially systematized procedure of story analysis.

The probe questions had to satisfy the following requirements: (1) They had to provide a systematic variation of the extent to which they probed for avoided content; (2) interest, task difficulty, and familiarity of the topic to the subject had to be kept as constant as possible; (3) the questions could not reveal the nature of the experimental manipulation because this might bias the subjects' later ratings.

The basic assumption on which the derivation of inquiry questions proceeded was that in writing the stories, subjects approached and hinted at ideas that made them anxious, and that in response to this anxiety arousal they avoided fully expressing those ideas in their stories. In reading through the stories, the experimenter attempted to identify instances where subjects were in conflict about whether to include certain anxiety-arousing contents in their stories, and avoided expressing at least part of this content. Examples of this process would include instances where subjects crossed out part of their story; started to say something but left it hanging; hinted at something and then changed the subject; used superfluous emphasis in affirming or denying something; failed to mention feelings or thoughts that, in the story context, were conspicuous by their absence (for example, a victim of assault feeling no emotion.) *High-Probe* questions were those that required the subjects to express avoided, anxiety-laden ideas.

On the other hand, story content that appeared uninvolved in conflict was not rare. Questions that encouraged subjects to elaborate nonavoided ideas were *Low-Probe* questions. These included questions about ideas consistent with the expressed or implied "point" of the story, irrelevant details, and themes that served a defensive function by contradicting or supplanting anxiety-arousing ideas.

The following types of story content were frequently judged suitable for *High-Probe* questions:

1. Desirability of homosexual relations, or intimacy of one male figure with another male figure.

2. Desire of a male figure to enter into a passive, dependent, yielding role in relation to a dominant, assertive female.

3. A male figure's longing to be cared for tenderly by a "mothering" female; longing for intimacy with such a person.

4. Sexual impotence.

5. Painful longing for lost love object.

6. Wish to take things aggressively, demandingness, selfishness.

7. Wish to destroy, kill, mutilate, without justification.

8. Wish to yield to authoritarian demands: for example, sacrificing own preference in in order to comply with parental pressures, in choice of a job or spouse.

This is but a sample of the variety of ideas on which *High-Probe* questions were based, and of course not every occurrence of one of the previous classes of ideas was considered suited for the *High Probes*.

The first step of the story analysis was to read the story through in order to comprehend what the story said at "face value." Then an attempt was made to understand the "point" of the story, or the moral, if there was one. Assuming that subjects were interested in getting the point of the story across to the reader, things consistent with the "point" were usually treated as content not avoided by the subject. Next the experimenter listed contents that appeared to be avoided, and those that appeared to be not avoided. Finally the questions were formulated, taking into consideration the total analysis of *all* the stories told by the particular subject for whom the probes were being designed.

A third treatment, *the Difficult Inquiry*, was introduced to provide another comparison in which anxiety intensity might vary, but with the Level of Activation held constant. Thus, in the comparison of the *Difficult* with the *High-Probe* Inquiry the Level of Activation might be assumed to be roughly equivalent, but not so the level of anxiety intensity. The latter is assumed to be higher in the *High-Probe* Inquiry.

The *Difficult Inquiry* consisted of twelve standard questions, which were designed to confront subjects with a complex intellectual task, involving problem solving and the creation of stories around situations, and in settings, with which the subjects were unfamiliar. The questions were humorous and farcical, with the intent of minimizing anxiety subjects might have about the adequacy of their answers. In this manner an attempt was made to produce high Activation in the subjects by requiring effort but to keep Anxiety at low intensity.

The following questions, asked of each subject.about the story to his first picture, illustrate the *Difficult Inquiry* questions:

(1) Suppose that one of the characters in this picture takes a job as a spy for the European principality of Monaco, and his assignment is to provide Princess Grace with interesting tidbits of gossip about the international Jet Set. Would you describe his experiences on one of those missions? (2) Now suppose that while spying on Ex-King Farouk on the Italian Riviera, he is almost discovered, but succeeds in getting away and reporting back to Princess Grace. Would you make up his report to her? (3) suppose that after his report, Princess Grace asks if he had any close calls. He tells her about how he nearly got caught by Farouk's henchmen, and how he escaped. Would you make up his account of the adventure? (4) After he has finished describing his escapade, Princess Grace decides he deserves to have his heroism rewarded with a distinguished service medal. Would you make up the speech of Prince Rainier, presenting our hero with the medal at the state ceremony?

Each of the three inquiries was based on three of the subject's TAT stories. In order to control for picture-content effects, the order of presentation of the pictures was balanced according to a rotation schedule, to which subjects were randomly assigned.

The *Difficult Inquiry* always came first. Then 12 subjects received the *High–Low Probe* inquiry sequence, and 12 received the *Low–High Probe* inquiry sequence. Subjects were randomly assigned to these treatment sequences. Because each subject went through all experimental treatments, the design permitted each subject to serve as his own control. The order of *High and Low-Probe* inquiries was balanced to control for sequence effects. In administering the *High* and *Low-Probe* inquiries, the experimenter read to each subject the "tailor-made" questions that had already been derived from the TAT stories written earlier by that particular subject. Each inquiry contained 12 questions, four for each TAT card.

Speech disturbance scoring conformed with the procedure detailed in chapter 9, using verbatim typescripts and listening to the tape recordings from which the typescripts were made. The Self-Ratings of anxiety were obtained at the end of the interview, subjects rating each inquiry with respect to the strongest intensity of anxiety experienced during that inquiry. The Verbal Productivity measure was obtained by counting the total number of words in each treatment. Both NSDR and Verbal Productivity were found to be highly reliable, with interscorer reliability coefficients of .80, .85, .87, .92, and .95, for the NSDRs in a sample of five subjects, and higher reliability for the word counts on which the NSDRs were based.

The Volume Pulse measure was an average amplitude of a sample of pulse waves distributed through the minute unit. It was obtained by means of a photo-electric pick-up device that was sensitive to the opacity of the left little finger, on which it was placed. Skin Temperature was measured at the time boundary of each minute. It was recorded from a thermistor placed on the ball of the left index finger. The GSP Level was the average reading in millivolts for the minute, whereas the GSP Positive Deflection measure is the total amplitude of positive-direction deflections cumulated over the minute. Both GSP measures were obtained from the record of the difference in electrical potential between an active electrode on the thenar eminence of the palm, and a reference electrode on the volar surface of the wrist. Scoring of the physiological measures was found to be highly reliable.

The NSDR and physiological measures were based on 1-minute units; Self-Rating and Verbal Productivity measures were based on entire experimental treatments.

Following an approach proposed by Lacey (1956) the measures were corrected to eliminate their dependence on preresponse levels, called initial values. The adjusted response scores are called Autonomic Lability Scores (ALS) for the physiological measures and where the correction procedure was used for nonphysiological measures, the resulting scores are called Regression-Corrected Scores (RCS).

Conversion to ALScores was routinely made for all autonomic response data. In the intrasubject analyses, the dependence of each score on the score from the preceding minute was eliminated. The resulting scores are called *Serial ALScores*. In the intersubject analyses, the mean score of each treatment was corrected to remove its dependence on response level of the minute preceding the treatment. Resulting scores are called *Base-Mean ALScores*.

For the NSDR, the intersubject analysis was based on RCScores whereas the intrasubject analyses were based on Raw Scores. The decision to use Raw Scores followed evaluation of a sample of six randomly selected cases; in these, no general tendency toward dependence of a speech disturbance ratio obtained from a given unit upon that of the preceding minute was found. Self-Rating and Verbal Productivity scores, which were analyzed only on an intersubject basis, were converted to RCScores.

Results

First Task: Main Effects of Experimental Treatments

Effects of Experimental Treatments on NSDR. NSDR Raw and RCScores were significantly higher during the *High-Probe* inquiry than during the *Low-*

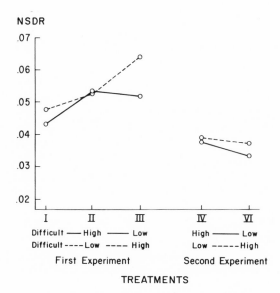

FIG. 14.2.   Treatment means of Non-ah Speech Disturbance Ratio Raw Scores.

Probe inquiry, as hypothesized. The *t*-tests of the mean difference were both significant (*p* < .03 and *p* < .04). The Raw NSDR of 19 of the 24 subjects changed in the hypothesized direction. It is worth noting that in 20 of the 24 subjects, the RAW NSDR was higher in the *High-Probe* Inquiry than in the Difficult Inquiry. The mean NSDR of the Difficult Inquiry was significantly lower than that of the *High-Probe* Inquiry (*p* < .001). These results are shown in Figs. 14.2 and 14.3.

Effects of Experimental Treatments on Self-Ratings.   Anxiety Self-Ratings were significantly higher during the *High-Probe* inquiry than during the *Low-Probe* inquiry, as hypothesized (*p* < .03 for both Raw and RC Scores). This was an effect specific to Anxiety Self-Ratings because additional Hostility and Effort Self-Ratings did not show evidence of a difference. This result is presented in Fig. 14.4.

Effect of Experimental Treatments on Verbal Productivity.   There was no evidence that the experimental manipulation had an effect on Verbal Productivity.

Effects of Experimental Treatments on Physiological Measures.   The results of analyses using Raw Scores and treatment means of Serial ALScores showed no evidence that the experimental manipulation had an effect on the individual measures. Base-Mean ALScores for Heartrate, GSP Level, GSP

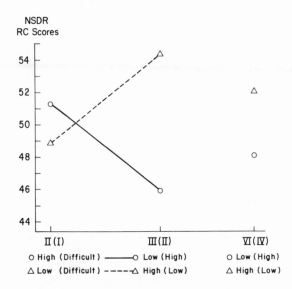

FIG. 14.3.   Treatment means of Non-ah Speech Disturbance Ratios, corrected for regression on means of preceding treatments (RCS). Each point also represents corrected group mean change from preceding treatment. (See *Method:* Law of Initial Values.)

Positive Deflections, and (inverted) Skin Temperature were all higher during the *High-Probe* Inquiry than during the *Low-Probe* Inquiry, as hypothesized. (Volume Pulse omitted because the lack of an absolute scale for the measure prohibits averaging across subjects.) None of these measures individually showed a significant difference, but in combination they support the hypothesis ($p = .003$). Because this result was obtained by multiplying the probabilities together, and selected from three different analysis of the same basic data, it is interpreted as evidence of a weak treatment effect. These results are presented in detailed figures in Schulze (1964).

Second Task: Intersubject Correlations Among Measures

Correlations among the Base-Mean ALScores and Raw Scores of NSDR, Anxiety Self-Ratings, and Verbal Productivity did not support relevant hypotheses consistently over the three experimental treatments. In general, correlations varied in size and direction from treatment to treatment.

Correlations of Change Scores, Treatments III − II: Correlations between NSDR RCScore changes (Treatment III minus II) and: changes in Base-Mean ALScores for Heartrate, Skin Temperature, GSP Level, GSP Positive Deflections, and Anxiety Self-Rating RCScore changes, were generally low

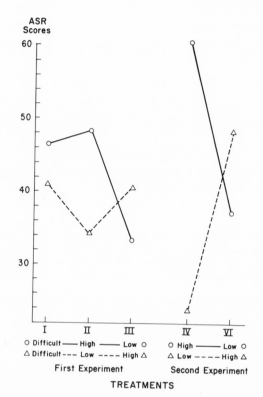

FIG. 14.4.   Treatment means of Anxiety Self-Rating Raw Scores.

and nonsignificant. Only the hypothesized relation between (inverted) Skin Temperature changes and NSDR changes was supported ($r = .43, p = .02$).

Third Task: Intrasubject Analyses

Correlations between Raw NSDRs and Serial ALScores were obtained individually for each subject. The correlation was calculated across the whole interview (Treatments I, II, and III combined); thus it reflects the extent to which the measures covary in their minute-to-minute fluctuation. The 24 correlations (one for each subject) obtained for each pair of measures were then arranged into distributions. The sample was then enlarged by adding comparable correlations from the Second Experiment. The data, when considered collectively, do not support the hypotheses. The number of significant correlations, and the relative numbers of positive and negative correlations do not deviate very far from what would be expected on a random basis.

Reliability of these correlations was estimated by correlating the coefficients obtained in the First Experiment with those obtained in the Second.

The highest reliability coefficients was .208. None of the reliability coefficients was significant.

SECOND EXPERIMENT: EFFECT OF A STRESSFUL MOTION PICTURE

Problem

In the Second Experiment, the stimulus manipulation consisted of a *High-Stress* film, which showed, at close range, subincision of the penis of adolescent Arunta tribesmen, and a *Low-Stress* film, which showed Arunta tribesmen engaged in less dramatic activities, and included no scenes of bodily mutilation.

The Second Experiment had three tasks analogous to those of the first experiment.

First Task: Main Effects of Experimental Treatments

Assuming that anxiety intensity would be higher during the High-Stress film than during the Low-Stress film, it was hypothesized that *NSDR, Heartrate, GSP Level, GSP Positive Deflections, and Anxiety Self-Ratings would be higher during the High-Stress film, and that Volume Pulse, Skin Temperature, and Verbal Productivity would be lower, than during the Low-Stress film.*

The effect that variation of stress using motion pictures has on speech disturbance rate had not been investigated prior to the present study.

Second and Third Tasks: Inter and Intrasubject Correlations

Hypotheses explored in these two tasks were identical to those of the Second and Third tasks of the First Experiment. It was hypothesized that *relations between NSDR and: Heartrate, GSP Level, GSP Positive Deflections, and Anxiety Self-Ratings would be direct; and that relations between NSDR and: Volume Pulse, Skin Temperature, and Verbal Productivity would be inverse,* in both inter and intrasubject analyses.

Prior to the present research, the questions raised in the second and third tasks had not been explored under the stimulus conditions of the Second Experiment.

Method

Subjects

The subjects were the same 24 male undergraduate students who participated in the First Experiment.

Apparatus

The apparatus was the same as that used in the First Experiment. In addition, portions of two silent black-and-white motion picture films were used. The first (*Low Stress*) was the first 8 minutes of the film entitled *Circumcision Rites in the Arunta*. (Nothing suggesting circumcision appears in the portion of the film used.) The second (*High Stress*) was the portion from 2½ to 10½ minutes of the companion film, *Subincision Rites in the Arunta*. These films were made under the auspices of the American Museum of Natural History and were obtained from The Calvin Company, Kansas City, MO. They bear the serial number C-160. The screen was mounted in front of the subject at a distance of 12 feet.

Procedure

The Second Experiment followed immediately after the First, in the same session. Subjects were given the task of describing the films as they were projected; prior to the First Experiment they had practiced doing this on a 2½ minute neutral film.

The attempt to vary anxiety intensity with the selected *High-* and *Low-Stress* film materials was based on previous research by Schwartz (1956), Aas (1958), and Lazarus, et al. (1962), all of whom reported evidence that the Subincision film is an effective stressor. This evidence was derived from self-reports, measures of autonomic response, and TAT story content ratings.

The subjects were randomly assigned to two groups of 12 subjects each. One group received the *High-Stress—Low-Stress* film sequence; the other received the *Low-Stress—High-Stress* sequence. There was a 5-minute recovery period after each film.

The dependent variables were the same for the Second Experiment as for the First and were measured in the same way. NSDR scoring on samples of the subjects' film descriptions were highly reliable. Interscorer reliability coefficients for the NSDR 1-minute ratios from five subjects were .79, .88, .89, .90, and .93.

Results

First Task: Main Effects of Experimental Treatments

Figures 14.2 and 14.3 present the data for NSDR Raw and RC Scores. There was no evidence that the manipulation of stress by motion pictures had an effect on speech disturbance rate.

Anxiety Self-Ratings were significantly higher during the *High-Stress* film than during the *Low-Stress* film, as hypothesized ($p < .001$). The change in

Self-Rating is shown in Fig. 14.4. However, additional ratings of Hostility and Effort were also significantly higher during the *High-Stress* film than during the *Low-Stress* film; thus the effect of the stress manipulation cannot be considered specific to anxiety, if the self-ratings are valid.

Verbal Productivity was significantly lower during the *High-Stress* film than during the *Low-Stress* film, as hypothesized ($p < .001$).

Both the Base-Mean and Serial AL Scores for GSP Level and GSP Positive Deflections were significantly higher during the *High-Stress* film than during the *Low-Stress* film. As in the First Experiment, all the Base-Mean ALScores changed in the directions specified by hypotheses. The three circulatory system measures (heartrate, volume pulse, and skin temperature) were especially sensitive to the difference between the Test Treatments (IV and VI) versus Rest Treatments (V and VII). The two GSP measures, on the other hand, were less sensitive to the Test versus Rest difference but more responsive to the *High* versus *Low-Stress* treatments.

Second Task: Intersubject Correlations Among the Measures

Correlations within Treatments.   Correlations among the Base-Mean AL-Scores and Raw Scores of NSDR, Anxiety Self-Ratings, and Verbal Productivity did not support the hypotheses.

Correlations of Change Scores, Treatments VI − IV.   The hypotheses were supported only by evidence of correlations between NSDR and both Skin Temperature and Volume Pulse Serial ALScores, relations not found in the First Experiment.

Third Task: Intrasubject Analyses

Individual Intrasubject Correlations.   Correlations between Raw NSDR and Serial ALScores for the physiological measures were obtained individually for each subject. The correlations were calculated across the combined film presentation (Treatments IV plus VI). They reflect the extent to which the measures covary in their minute-to-minute fluctuation. The 24 correlations, each based on a sample of 16 pairs of 1-minute scores, were arranged into distributions of product-moment correlation coefficients. These distributions were combined with comparable distributions from the First Experiment to enlarge the sample. The data, when considered collectively, do not support the hypotheses. The pattern of correlations does not deviate very far from what would be expected on a random basis.

The reliability of these correlations was estimated by correlating the coefficients obtained in the Second Experiment with those obtained in the First. The highest reliability coefficient was .208. None of the reliability coefficients were significant.

TABLE 14.1
Group Mean Responses to Successive Film Minutes: Correlations
Among NSDR Raw Scores and Serial ALScores

Response Variable	SkT	GSP Lvl	GSP Pos	Vol Pls	NSDR
Heartrate	−.020	.094	.615**	−.767**	.243
Skin Temp		−.513*	−.198	.264	−.175
GSP Level			.678**	−.448*	.574**
GSP PosDfl				−.811**	.570*
Vol Pulse					−.397

*p < .05 (one tailed; all correlations are in direction hypothesized).
**p < .01 (one-tailed).

Correlations Between NSDR and Autonomic Group Mean Responses to Successive Film Minutes. The fact that the films presented the subjects with a standard stimulus sequence permitted another type of intrasubject analysis of relations between NSDR and the Serial ALScores. This procedure has been used successfully by Lazarus, Speisman, and Mordkoff (1963), in the analysis of autonomic response to the Subincision film. They referred to the procedure as "composite correlation across point means." It consists of calculating a group mean response for each time unit of the films and then correlating different response measures across the time units. Lazarus et al. found correlations between Skin Conductance and Heartrate Raw Scores of +.545 and +.242 for the Subincision and control films, respectively, when these scores were averaged across 50 subjects at 10-second intervals. The present procedure differed in that scores were serial regression-corrected, some different measures of autonomic response were used, the time units were 1 minute in length each, scores were averaged across only 24 subjects, and the control film was a *Low-Stress* section of the Arunta film materials.

Table 14.1 and Fig. 14.5 and 14.6 present the relationships among the measures. All the correlations are consistent in direction with the hypotheses. Six of the 10 correlations among the autonomic measures were significant. The positive correlations of NSDR with GSP Level and GSP Positive Deflections, and negative correlation with Volume Pulse, support the hypotheses. However, this result is almost entirely dependent on the agreement between NSDR and these autonomic measures on the large difference between the first and subsequent minutes of each film. When the first minute of each film is eliminated from the analysis, none of the correlations between NSDR and the physiological measures is significant, and the correlations between NSDR and both GSP Positive Deflections and Volume Pulse reverse direction.

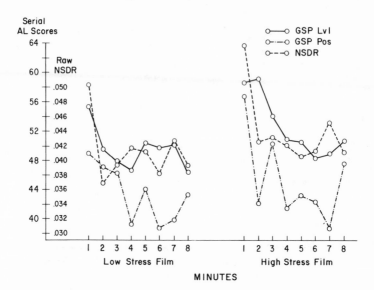

FIG. 14.5.   Group mean responses to successive film minutes: Non-ah Speech Disturbance Ratio, GSP Level, and GSP Positive Deflections (averaged across 24 subjects).

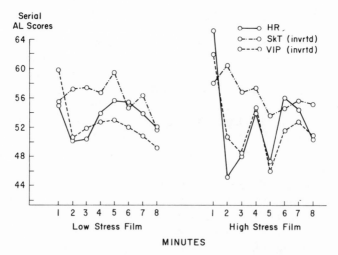

FIG. 14.6.   Group mean responses to successive film minutes: Heartrate, Skin Temperature, and Volume Pulse (averaged across 24 subjects).

TABLE 14.2
Consistency of Group Mean Responses to
Successive Film Minutes: Correlations
Between Subgroups of 12 Subjects Each
($df = 14$)

Response Variable	r	p*
NSDR	.112	NS
Heartrate		
Serial ALScores	.880	<.01
SkinTemp		
Serial ALScores	−.129	NS
GSP Level		
Serial ALScores	.501	.02
GSP Pos Dfl		
Serial ALScores	.625	<.01
Volume Pulse		
Serial ALScores	.855	<.01

*(one-tailed).

Further evidence of the validity of this procedure was found when group mean responses to successive film minutes were averaged separately across the two treatment-order subgroups. This permitted a test of the consistency of the film stimulus effect on a given response variable in the two subgroups of 12 subjects each. Table 14.2 summarizes the intergroup reliabilities (correlated across time) for each response variable. These are significant for Heartrate, GSP Level, GSP Positive Deflections, and Volume Pulse, but not for NSDR and Skin Temperature.

DISCUSSION

Evidence for a treatment effect on NSDR was found in the First Experiment, but not in the Second. The first of these results replicates the effect of a probing inquiry manipulation on NSDR reported by Kasl and Mahl (chapter 12). It also extends the generality of that effect from the direct form of inquiry into private, personal matters (used by Kasl and Mahl) to an indirect form of inquiry into private matters that makes use of the access provided by projective testing. The results do not extend the generality of the Kasl and Mahl finding to conditions where the task is to describe visual events as they are perceived.

The present research produced little evidence that NSDR was related to measures of autonomic response at the 1-minute level of analysis or in treatment means, even when correction is made for regression of response levels on initial values. Although there were significant intrasubject correlations between NSDR and both GSP Level and GSP Positive Deflections in the analysis of group mean response to successive film minutes, these disappeared with the exclusion of the initial minute of each film. In other words, the NSDR agreed with the GSP measures (and to a slightly lesser extent also with Heartrate and Volume Pulse) in differentiating between the initial impact and remainder of each film but was not related to those measures throughout the major portions of the films. There was little evidence of relation between NSDR and the physiological measures in the individual intrasubject analyses, and only sporadic evidence in the intersubject analyses.

Considering the lack of evidence for a treatment effect on NSDR in the Second Experiment, it is possible that the relation between speech non-fluency rate and anxiety intensity is limited in its generality, if it does not hold for situations where an individual *describes* objective and relatively unambiguous stimulus materials. The describing task may inherently offer fewer linguistic choice points and therefore fewer opportunities for indecision and conflict than the task of revealing information about one's internal imagination or self-definition processes.

The NSDRs were markedly lower during both of the film descriptions than during the interview, irrespective of experimental manipulations (see Fig. 15.3, chapter 15). This can be interpreted as an indication that speech, under conditions of describing something external to the subject, is less vulnerable to the disruptive effect of anxiety and conflict than speech that is less stimulus bound. (See also further discussion in chapter 15.)

The main effects that the film manipulation of stress had on the measures of autonomic response can be compared in a rough way with results reported by Aas (1958) and Lazarus, Speisman, and Mordkoff (1962). Despite many procedural differences, these three studies were consistent in finding skin measures (level and response of GSR or GSP) more sensitive to the difference between experimental and control films than circulatory system measures (heartrate, skin temperature, and volume pulse).

The autonomic response main effects reported by Aas and by Lazarus et al. were more dramatic than those found in the present study. Perhaps the most important procedural difference was that in the present study subjects described the films as they were projected, whereas in the Aas and Lazarus studies subjects watched the films silently. This leads to two speculations: (1) The describing task might have diminished the impact of the stress during the subincision film by allowing subjects to take an active rather than passive role vis-a-vis the films, therby faciliating "mastery" of the threatening aspect of the situation, (2) the physical action of talking may have diluted the main effect by providing an additional source of error variance in the physiological measures. In this connection it should be noted that Verbal Productivity was greater during the *Low-Stress* film than during the *High-Stress* film and could thereby have worked against the effect of the stress manipulation.

Evidence that fluctuations in Heartrate, GSP Level, GSP Positive Deflections, and Volume Pulse are consistent in two groups of subjects exposed to the same stimulus conditions adds a new type of support for the efficacy of the composite correlation across point means technique tested by Lazarus et al. (1963).

SUMMARY AND CONCLUSIONS

The research consisted of two experiments administered in tandem, during the same session, to the same subjects, who were run individually. Twenty-four male undergraduate student volunteers served as subjects. In the First Experiment the degree to which TAT inquiry questions probed to elicit avoided content was varied. In the Second Experiment the degree to which bodily mutilation (genital) was portrayed, in motion pictures being described by the subject, was varied. It was hypothesized that both these stimulus manipulations would affect the subjects' speech disturbance rates as a function of variation in anxiety intensity, and that these effects would be consistent with effects on other hypothetical indices of anxiety: Verbal Productivity, Anxiety Self-Ratings, and five measures of autonomic response.

1. Evidence for a treatment effect on speech disturbance rate was found in the First Experiment, but not in the Second.

2. Evidence suggestive of a weak treatment effect on measures of autonomic response was found in the First Experiment. In the Second Experiment there was evidence of a treatment effect on GSP Level and GSP Positive Deflections, but Heartrate, Volume Pulse, and Skin Temperature did not show significant change.

3. Evidence for a treatment effect on Anxiety Self-Ratings was found in both experiments. The effect was stronger in the Second Experiment than in the First. There was no evidence of a treatment effect on Hostility and Effort Self-Ratings in the First Experiment, but evidence of such effects was strong in the Second Experiment.

4. There was no evidence of a treatment effect on Verbal Productivity in the First Experiment, but there was strong evidence of such an effect in the Second.

5. Thus, the main effects of the experimental manipulations on speech disturbance rates were consistent with main effects on Self-Ratings, and the

suggestion of a main effect on physiological measures, in the First Experiment; but the main effects on Verbal Productivity, Self-Ratings, and the GSP measures were inconsistent with the lack of evidence for a treatment effect on speech disturbance rate, in the Second Experiment. However, the direction of change in all these measures in the Second Experiment was consistent.

6. In general, there was little evidence that speech disturbance rates covaried with any of the other measures, either in Intersubject Treatment Means, Intertreatment changes in those means, or Intrasubject minute-to-minute fluctuations when analyzed separately for individual subjects.[2]

---

[2]The original doctoral dissertation, upon which this chapter is based, presents the study in greater detail. It is available in the Sterling Memorial Library of Yale University. The numbers of the figures and tables in this chapter correspond to the dissertation numbers listed here.

Chapter Numbers	Dissertation Numbers
Figures:	Figures:
14.1	1
14.2	3
14.3	4
14.4	5
14.5	23
14.6	24
Tables:	Tables:
14.1	14
14.2	13

15

Everyday Speech Disturbances and Anxiety: Summary

In the preceding chapters we have reported six studies of the relationship between the everyday speech disturbances and the speaker's concurrent (state) anxiety. We now summarize the results of those investigations.

The studies used a variety of subjects and speaking situations. The procedures included various correlational and experimental methods. These factors combine to enhance the generalizability of our findings.

The accompanying figures summarize the results of the six studies. Figure 15.1 illustrates the results reported in chapters 10, 11 and 12. Figures 15.2 and 15.3 show the results reported in chapters 13 and 14, respectively. In five of the studies, the speaker's anxiety was positively associated with the Non-ah speech disturbance level. The speaking situations of those five studies had at least one thing in common: They called for self-revelation by the speakers, either in psychotherapeutic or in personal investigative interviews.

Schulze's film study was the one negative instance. The failure to obtain a difference in speech disturbances with the film manipulation may be due to various factors. First, it may be an actual instance where increased anxiety in the speaker is not accompanied by increased speech disturbances. Secondly, it may be due to the fact that the subincision film created higher stress, rather than creating a relatively pure increase in anxiety. Thirdly, *the verbal behavior of the subjects during both film presentations consisted of description of external scenes rather than revelation of internal, personal matters, as occurred in the Thematic Apperception Test interviews.* Figure 15.3 shows that the speech disturbance levels during the description of *both* the Low- and High-Stress films

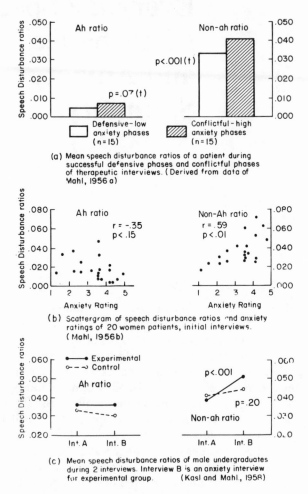

(a) Mean speech disturbance ratios of a patient during
successful defensive phases and conflictful phases
of therapeutic interviews. (Derived from data of
Mahl, 1956 a)

(b) Scattergram of speech disturbance ratios and anxiety
ratings of 20 women patients, initial interviews.
(Mahl, 1956b)

(c) Mean speech disturbance ratios of male undergraduates
during 2 interviews. Interview B is an anxiety interview
for experimental group.   (Kasl and Mahl, 1958)

FIG. 15.1.   Summary of the results reported in chapters 10, 11, and 12.

were markedly lower than during *both* the Low- and High-Anxiety Probe
interviews. This suggests that description of external scenes results in a
generally lowered level of speech disturbances and may prevent that level
from changing as a result of changes in the emotional state of the speaker.
One possible reason for these effects is that description may involve fewer
conflicted choice points in the process of verbalizing than does spontaneous
self-revelation. Hopefully, future research will decide which of these possibilities, or another, was responsible for the lack of change with the film
manipulation.

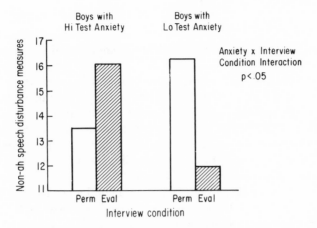

FIG. 15.2.   Summary of the results reported in chapter 13.

In one study (chapter 12) we determined the effect of the speakers anxiety on each of the Non-ah categories. It was positive in each instance.

Three of our studies also investigated the relationship between the Ah-Ratio and anxiety. Figure 15.1 shows that in no instance was the relationship significant.

On the basis of these results, we conclude that the Non-ah Ratio is a valid indicator of the speaker's concurrent anxiety. We also conclude that the Ah-Ratio is not such an indicator. Data presented in chapters 12 and 18 indicate that "Ah" and the Non-ah disturbances follow different behavioral laws.

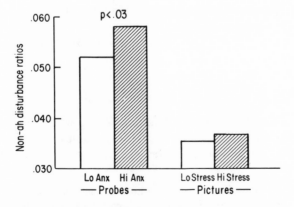

FIG. 15.3.   Summary of results reported in chapter 14.

THE WORK OF OTHERS

In the last 30 years many investigators have contributed to the growth of a substantial literature concerned with the relationship between transient anxiety and nonfluency. This growth started with the simultaneous and independent work of Dibner (1956, 1958) and ourselves (Mahl, 1956a) on nonfluencies in the speech of patients in interviews and that of Lerea (1956) on nonfluencies during public speaking. Our Non-ah Ratio is the single most researched measure of nonfluency in the subsequent literature we have located. Table 15.1 summarizes those studies by others of the relationship between transient anxiety and the Non-ah Ratio.

Additional studies of transient anxiety and nonfluency have involved analogues of the Non-ah Ratio or modifications explicitly made in it. Table 15.2 summarizes this group of studies. Dibner's (1958) Cue Scale I is nearly identical with our Non-ah Ratio, consisting, as it does, of the categories *breaking in with a new thought, sentence incompletion, sentence change, repetition, stutter,* and *'I don't know.'* In the one study (Krause, 1961a) that compared the two measures, they were highly correlated, $r = .91$. Lerea's (1956) measure of "speech fright" is nearly identical with the General Speech Disturbance Ratio (Ah plus Non-ah, see chap. 9, p. 169) consisting, as it does, of *pauses,* repetition, sentence change, sentence incompletion, and prolongations. Edelmann and Hampson (1979, 1981) used the General Speech Disturbance Ratio in their two studies.[1] All but one of the remaining studies cited in Table 15.2 used a slightly modified version of the General Speech Disturbance Ratio, such as one that also included fillers like "I don't know," "I mean." The one anomalous study just mentioned was that of Horowitz, Sampson, Siegelman, Wolfson, and Weiss (1975). Its Discomfort Quotient consisted of a core of the Non-ah categories, *plus* filler words, nonverbal sounds (sniff, laugh, cough, knuckle cracking, marble clicking), instances of unintelligible speech, and silence.

Tables 15.1 and 15.2 speak for themselves. We make only a few comments about them.

Validity of Speech Disturbance Measure of Anxiety

Table 15.1 indexes 16 studies, counting separately the two reported by Brady and Walker (1978). Twelve of these studies confirm our findings concerning the Non-ah Ratio, one was inconclusive, and three failed to show

---

[1]The reader might infer from the content of Edelmann and Hampson (1979) that the Non-ah Ratio was used in that experiment and in the later, related one (Edelmann & Hampson, 1981). However, the General Speech Disturbance Ratio was used in both (Edelmann, Personal Communication, April, 1986).

TABLE 15.1

Summary of Studies by Others of Non-ah Ratio and Transient (State) Anxiety

Investigators	Subjects and Speech Samples	Type of Study	Type of Anxiety Manipulation	Anxiety Measure Correlated	Results (Positive, + Negative, − Inconclusive, I)
Blass & Siegman (1975)	Female nursing students speaking in research interviews	Experimental	Personal questions		+
Blumenthal (1964)	Hospitalized male schizophrenic patients speaking in research interviews	Experimental	Nonunderstanding interviewer		+[a]
Boomer (1963)	Speech excerpts from psychotherapy interviews of one patient[b]	Correlational		Nonpurposive body movements	+
Boomer & Goodrich (1961)	Selected interviews from psychotherapies of 2 female patients	Correlational		Judgements of high-low anxiety phases of interviews	I
Bradac, Konsky, & Elliott (1976)	College students speaking in research interviews[b]	Experimental	Low question specificity, high-status interviewer, arousing topic		+

(Continued)

249

TABLE 15.1
(Continued)

Investigators	Subjects and Speech Samples	Type of Study	Type of Anxiety Manipulation	Anxiety Measure Correlated	Results (Positive, + Negative, – Inconclusive, I)
Brady & Walker (1978)	1. Male and female *Australian* college students discussing an interesting experience with E	Experimental	Evaluation of social competence by unseen observers		+[c]
	2. Similar subjects doing same but with a peer	Experimental	Same as above		+[c]
Cook (1969)	Female and male *Oxford University* students speaking in research interviews	Experimental	Sensitive topics and probing of embarrassing, worrisome matters		+
Feldstein, Brenner, & Jaffe (1963)	Male and female outpatient psychotherapy patients speaking in research interviews	Experimental	Personal problems topic		+
Geer (1966)	Female college students talking about a test they had taken	Experimental	Talking to unseen audience of 5 vs. speaking to tape recorder		–

Study	Subjects/Task	Design	Stress condition		Effect
Meisels (1967)	Female college students telling TAT stories	Experimental	E's manner "cold" and unsupportive, evaluative situation		+
Musumeci (1975)	Fifth grade boys and girls telling stories	Experimental	Test, evaluative situation		+
Pope, Blass, Siegman, & Raher (1970)	Female and male hospitalized psychosomatic psychiatric patients in free-associative monologues	Correlational		Nurses' daily anxiety ratings	
Pope, Siegman, & Blass (1970)	Female nursing students speaking in initial interview analogue	Experimental	Evaluative situation		+
Siegman & Pope (1965)	Female nursing students speaking in initial interview analogue	Experimental	Personal topics		+
Reynolds & Paivio (1968)	Male and female college students defining nouns	Experimental	Increasing audience size		−

[a]Interaction effects.
[b]Subject gender not specified.
[c]Type of speech disturbance ratio inferred from bibliographic references.

251

TABLE 15.2

Summary of Studies by Others of Speech Disturbance Ratio Analogues and Transient (State) Anxiety

Investigators	Subjects and Speech Samples	Type of Study	Type of Anxiety Manipulation	Anxiety Measure Correlated	Results (Positive, + Negative, − Inconclusive, I)
Dibner (1956, 1958)	Male hospitalized psychiatric patients speaking in clinical evaluative interviews	Experimental	Ambiguous behavior of interviewer		+
Edelmann & Hampson (1979)	Male and female English college students speaking in research interviews with trained interviewer	Experimental	Unexpected remark by interviewer designed to embarrass S		+
Edelmann & Hampson (1981)	Female and male English college students speaking in research interviews with unfamiliar peers	Experimental	Intimate questions		+
Eldred & Price (1958)	Female patient speaking in psychotherapy interviews	Correlational		Clinical judgments of anxiety	+
Horowitz, Sampson, Siegelman, Wolfson, & Weiss (1975)	1. Male patient speaking in psychoanalytic interviews	Correlational		Emergence of warded-off material	+
	2. Same	Correlational		Neutrality-Nonneutrality of analyst	+

Study	Subjects	Method	Variable		Result
Horowitz, Weckler, Saxon, Livaudais, & Boutacoff (1977)	Female and male college students speaking in interviews about incidents of anger	Experimental	Degree of associated discomfort		+
Krause & Pilisuk (1961)	Male and female college students describing possible reactions to disastrous situations	Correlational		Degree of stress in the situations	+
Lerea (1956)	College students' initial and final speeches in public speaking course	Correlational		Decrease in reported speech fright	+
Levin, Baldwin, Gallwey, & Paivio (1960)	10–12 year-old girls and boys (high and low in exhibitionism and self-consciousness) telling stories	Experimental	Size and unfamiliarity of audience		+[a]
Levin & Silverman (1965)	10–12 year-old boys and girls (high and low in need-achievement and self-consciousness) telling stories	Experimental	Audience of 4 adults vs. tape-recorder		−
Nosenko, Yelchaninov, Krylova, & Petrukhin (1977)	1. Russian technicians[b] speaking during psychological testing	Experimental	Presence of authority figures, evaluative situation, criticized for prior test performance		+

(Continued)

253

TABLE 15.2
(Continued)

Investigators	Subjects and Speech Samples	Type of Study	Type of Anxiety Manipulation	Anxiety Measure Correlated	Results (Positive, + Negative, − Inconclusive, I)
	2. *Russian* applicants[b] to technical school speaking in interviews, tests, and class meetings	Correlational		Inefficiency in test performance	+
Paivio (1963)	4th and 5th grade girls and boys (high and low on exhibitionism and audience anxiety) telling stories	Experimental	Social isolation before story telling		−
Panek & Martin (1959)	Male and female patients speaking in psychotherapy interviews	Correlational		Psychogalvanic skin responses	+

[a]Interaction effects.
[b]Subject gender and technical specialty not specified.

254

that speech disturbances rose with a manipulation intended to increase the speaker's anxiety. One of the latter (Meisels, 1967) obtained the anomalous finding of decreased Non-ah Ratios with the experimental manipulation. We comment later on this fact. Pooling the studies cited in Table 15.1 and ours yields 22 studies, 17 of which demonstrate that the Non-ah Ratio increases with transient anxiety.

Table 15.2 treats of 15 additional studies, counting separately the two experiments in both Horowitz et al. (1975) and in Nosenko, Yelchaninov, Krylova, and Petrukhin (1977). Thirteen of these 15 yielded positive results. The negative results of two exceptions were failures to find an increase in speech disturbances upon the experimental manipulation.

The studies noted in the two tables involved a variety of methods, speakers, and situations, just as our work did. The combination of our studies with those cited in these two tables provides a corpus of 37 studies, 30 of which gave positive results, despite the complexities involved. The evidence is overwhelming that measures of nonfluency are valid indicators of transient anxiety.

Distinction Between *Ah* and *Non-ah*

Seven of the studies cited in Table 15.1 examined the relationship between the Ah-Ratio, as well as the Non-ah Ratio, and concurrent anxiety. Six of them (Blass & Siegman, 1975; Cook, 1969; Feldstein et al., 1963; Pope, Blass, Siegman, & Raher, 1970; Pope, Siegman, & Blass, 1970; Siegman & Pope, 1965) confirmed our findings that the Ah-Ratios did not increase with the speakers' anxiety, whereas the Non-ah Ratios did. Meisels (1967) obtained the anomalous finding that the Non-ah Ratio *decreased* with the anxiety manipulation (an interaction effect), whereas the Ah-Ratio was unchanged. (Viewing Meisel's study in the context of the body of research summarized earlier suggests that his finding was a spurious one. He discusses various reasons why his experimental procedure might have misfired.) Again, the work of others confirms our findings.

Cross-Cultural Nature of the Speech Phenomena

We noted earlier (chapter 9, p. 168 fn. 4) that our speech disturbance categories are applicable to English, German, Japanese, Spanish, and Russian. Now we can state that there is some evidence that the relationship between the speech disturbance phenomena and transient anxiety is a cross-cultural one. Thus it has been demonstrated in Russians (Nosenko et al. (1977), in English-speaking Australian college students (Brady & Walker, 1978), and in English college students (Cook, 1969; Edelmann & Hampson, 1979, 1981) as well as English speaking subjects of the United States. We commented earlier on the significance of freedom from linguistic restraint for the vocal-verbal measurement of anxiety (pp. 181–182). It will be very interesting to see the extensions of and limits to the cross-cultural dimensions that might emerge in future research.

Comments About Particular Studies

1. Boomer and Goodrich (1961) attempted a meticulous and rigorous replication of our first study of anxiety and speech disturbances (1956), which we reported in chapter 10. They expanded the methodology by having independent judges identify the motivational phase units. The judges consisted of the therapists who treated the patients and other experienced therapists as well. Boomer and Goodrich obtained inconclusive results. In one of the cases, using the therapist's judgments of the motivational phases confirmed our findings. But when the nontherapist judgments were used in this case, there was no difference in the speech disturbance levels in the two types of phases. In the second case, there was no difference in the disturbance levels for the two types of phases for either the therapist's or the nontherapists' judgments.

It is not possible on the basis of present information to account for the discrepancy between our findings and those of Boomer and Goodrich. There may have been residual, concealed differences in methodology between the two studies—such for example as in the method and individual capacity for making the phase judgments. Or, the relationship between anxiety and speech disturbances in interview phases of high- and low-conflict or anxiety may hold for some patients in psychotherapy and not for others. Possibly our case and the first of theirs were patients for whom the positive relationship held and yet only the therapist has the capacity to make the motivational phase judgments with sufficient accuracy to yield positive results. Possibly their second case is a person for whom the positive relationship simply isn't valid. Obviously our reasoning here is ad hoc; it raises questions that can only be answered by further attempts at replication. The widespread agreement in the accumulated literature reviewed here diminishes the significance of this failure to fully replicate the results of our initial study.

2. Edelmann and Hampson's study (1979) tickled us for two reasons. First, because it amounted to a systematic replication of the second observation with which we introduced the speech disturbance phenomena (chapter 9, pp. 164–165). There a provocative female interviewer caught her male celebrity off guard by noting that he had thought of only men to have for a memorable dinner. His speech was abruptly and momentarily disrupted

(Fig. 9.1). Edelmann and Hampson exposed their subjects to very similar interviewer behavior with identical results. A subject was first shown a series of pictures and asked which one he or she *liked least*. Then an interviewer, who was uninformed of the hypothesis of the study, asked the subject a series of 15 questions about his attitude toward the picture he had liked least and about art in general. The eighth question was "Would it interest you to know that the picture you chose was in fact drawn/painted by me." The preceding and subsequent questions were nonembarrassing ones. Fifteen of the 22 subjects said they had been embarrassed by the eighth question. The Speech Disturbance Ratios of these subjects tripled in their responses to the eighth question and then subsided to their preembarrassment level during questions 9–15. (Edelmann and Hampson use a felicitous term to describe this kind of interaction: *a failure of meshing.*) Secondly, the speech of these subjects delighted us for the way it, as did that of our radio interviewee, illustrates the delicate sensitivity with which speech disturbances manifest fleeting anxiety. (See also the clinical vignettes on pp. 194–196).

3. Horowitz et al. (1975) provide yet another paradigm for studying the anxiety—speech disturbance relationship with psychotherapeutic interview material. Working with the first 100 tape-recorded psychoanalytic hours of a male analysand, they did two things of particular relevance here. First, they rigorously identified episodes in Hours 41–100 in which the patient verbalized matters that he had previously warded off. They compared the Discomfort Quotient of the patient during these episodes and a control sample of passages not involving the expression of previously warded-off material. The Discomfort Quotient was significantly higher in the former episodes. This substudy is in essence comparable in method and results to our first clinical validation attempt (chapter 10). Secondly, they compared changes in the patient's Discomfort Quotient in passages following emotionally neutral and nonneutral behavior by the analyst. Neutral behavior by the analyst was followed by a decrease in the patient's Discomfort Quotient, but nonneutral behavior was followed by an increase.

4. Studies of audience anxiety and speech disturbances contributed disproportionately to the group failing to yield positive results, as the following tabulation of the corpus of 37 studies shows.

	Results	
	Positive	Inconclusive or Negative
Audience anxiety	2	4
Other anxieties	28	3

The two "positive" audience anxiety studies are those of Lerea (1956) and Levin, Baldwin, Gallwey, and Paivio (1960) summarized in Table 15.2.[2] The four "negative" ones are those of Geer (1966) and Reynolds and Paivio (1968) cited in Table 15.1 and those of Levin and Silverman (1965) and Paivio (1963) cited in Table 15.2. We have no convincing, uniform explanation for this anomalous situation of the audience anxiety studies. That must await future research.

Trait Anxiety and Speech Disturbances

Speech disturbance measures do what they were designed to do: reflect state anxiety of the speaker. In contrast twelve attempts to examine the relation of speech disturbances and trait anxiety have yielded inconclusive results. Table 15.3 summarizes these studies. Five positive associations (including interaction effects) between trait anxiety and speech disturbances have been found, but in seven instances that was not so.

Other Emotional States and Speech Disturbances

Are increases in the Non-ah Ratio specific to increases in state anxiety and conflict? Or do they also occur with other transient emotional states? Unfortunately, very few studies of speech disturbances and other emotional states exist. We know of three involving anger, all of which indicate that the Non-ah Ratio does not increase with transient anger. We found no correlation between hostility ratings and the Non-ah Ratio in our initial interview study (chapter 11). When Kasl (1957) angered his subjects, they did not increase their Non-ah disturbances. When Feldstein and Jaffe (1962) induced anger in their subjects, the latter did not increase their Non-ah Ratios. Pope, Blass, Siegman, and Raher (1970) found no correlation between the Non-ah Ratios and daily ratings of depression in hospitalized patients. These are the only studies we know of concerning speech disturbances and other emotional states besides anxiety. They suggest that the Non-ah disturbances might be specific to anxiety. But much additional work concerning this matter needs to be done.

---

[2]Baker (1964) showed that participation in a basic college speech course resulted in a significant decrease in the Non-ah Ratio. Unlike Lerea (1956), however, he did not measure independently experienced changes in "stage fright." Given that omission I have not included Baker's study in Table 15.1, nor in the evaluation of the validity of the Non-ah Ratio as an anxiety indicator. It is possible that the decrease in speech disturbances of his subjects reflects only increased fluency resulting from the speech course and not concomitant decreased anxiety.

TABLE 15.3
Summary of Studies of Trait Anxiety and Speech Disturbance Measures

Investigators	Trait Anxiety Measure	Results (positive, + negative, −)
Brenner, Feldstein, & Jaffe (1965)	Test anxiety	+
Cook (1969)	Taylor MAS[a] McReynolds AS[b]	− −
Geer (1966)	Audience anxiety	−
Kasl & Mahl (1965, chap. 12)	Taylor MAS[a]	−
Levin, Baldwin, Gallwey, & Paivio (1960)	Audience anxiety	+
Meisels (1967)	Test anxiety	−
Musumeci (1975)	Spielberger Trait Anxiety	+
Ragsdale (1976)	Welsh Anxiety Index	+
Reynolds & Paivio (1968)	Audience anxiety	−
Siegman & Pope (1972)	Taylor MAS[a]	−
Zimbardo, Mahl, & Barnard, (1963, chap. 13)	Test anxiety	+

[a]Manifest Anxiety Scale.
[b]Assimilation Scale.

Knowing how substantial the evidence is concerning anxiety and speech disturbances, it is appropriate that we now reexamine the wisdom of our original rejection of manifest verbal content analysis, as described in chapter 8. We do this in the next two chapters.

Speech Disturbances and Emotional Verbal Content In Initial Psychiatric Interviews[1]

16

INTRODUCTION

We are now returning to some of our initial assumptions mentioned in chapter 8. There we advanced certain working hypotheses about the relationships between emotional states, manifest verbal content, and extralinguistic attributes of speech. Now that we have presented evidence in the intervening chapters that the Non-ah speech disturbances are positively related to the transient anxiety of the speaker we are in a position to begin to test those hypotheses. We are primarily interested in two basic questions:

1. What will be the relative validities of manifest content measures and the Non-ah Ratio as indices of the speaker's anxiety level? Is it true that the Non-ah ratio will be the more valid measure?

2. What is the relationship between the frequency of the Non-ah disturbances and the simultaneous utterance of emotional manifest verbal content? Is it true that this relationship will be very weak or nonexistent?

In this and the next chapter we see what the answers to these questions are when two different types of content measures are used. This chapter

[1]This chapter is a revision of a paper presented at the Annual Meeting of The Eastern Psychological Association, 1957 (Mahl, 1957). I wish to express my appreciation to Frank Auld for his collaboration in the verbal content scoring procedures. He taught the author the rules for sentence unitizing, which he had developed (Auld & White, 1956), and he scored the manifest verbal content in the reliability sample. The verbal content data used in the present chapter is a portion of a slightly larger collection used for other purposes by Auld and Mahl (1956).

concerns the relationship between the Non-ah disturbances and the Discomfort-Relief content analysis method developed by Dollard and Mowrer (1947).

METHOD

Sample

The speech material for this study consisted of the 31 tape-recorded and transcribed initial psychiatric interviews described in chapter 11.

Measures

Non-Ah Speech Disturbances

These were scored on the typescripts by simultaneously reading them and listening to the recordings in the manner described in chapter 9. Non-ah speech Disturbance Ratios for entire interviews, as well as for certain samples of sentence collections to he described, were computed in the usual way (Chapter 9, p. 169). The interscorer correlation for ratios of individual pages was .91.

Discomfort-Relief Quotients

To obtain the verbal content measures, each typescript was first unitized into sentence-units according to the rules developed by Auld and White (1956). Then the typescript was scored by the Discomfort-Relief Quotient method (Dollard & Mowrer, 1947). In this procedure, each sentence unit is classified on the basis of the manifest verbal content alone as expressive of a discomfort, a relief, or a neutral feeling. A sentence is scored as a Discomfort unit if its manifest verbal content refers to mounting drive tension or various forms of distress (anxiety, for example). In a Relief unit, the manifest verbal content refers to decreased drive tension or decreased distress. A Neutral unit is one in which the manifest verbal content refers to neither discomfort-distress nor relief. A Discomfort-Relief Quotient (DRQ) for each interview as a whole was obtained by the formula.

$$DRQ = \frac{N \text{ Discomfort Units}}{N \text{ (Discomfort + Relief Units)}}.$$

One judge unitized and scored the content of all 31 typescripts. His scores were used in obtaining the results. An independent judge unitized and scored the content of 21 interviews. A secretary independently unitized 10. The reliability of the sentence unitizing was determined by comparing the secretary's unitizing with that of the two judges. There was agreement on placement of more than 95% of the unit markings. The correlation between the two sets of DRQ's was .90. The degree of agreement in scoring individual units as either discomfort, relief, or neutral was determined for 10 interviews. There were 5,660 sentence units in these 10 interviews, and the two scorers agreed exactly in 75% of them. In only 3% of the units had one judge scored a unit in the discomfort category that the other judge had scored as a relief unit. Twenty-two percent of the units had been scored as neutral by one judge, but as either a discomfort or a relief unit by the other judge.

Anxiety Ratings

The anxiety level of the patients during their initial interviews was rated on a 5-point scale by independent raters as described in chapter 11. The same mean anxiety ratings for the two reliable raters that were noted in chapter 11 were used in this study. As already stated the reliability coefficients of these mean anxiety ratings was .86 for the women patients, but only .57 for the men.

In short, the speech disturbance scoring, the verbal content scoring, and the anxiety ratings of women provide quite reliable measures. The reliability of the anxiety ratings of the men is poor.

RESULTS

Let us first consider the relative validities of the verbal content measure of discomfort and of the Non-ah Ratio as indices of the concurrent anxiety level of the speaker. Table 16.1 contains the intercorrelations between the anxiety ratings, the Non-ah Ratios, and the DRQ's for the 20 women patients. As can be seen, the speech disturbance measure, but not the verbal content measure, is significantly and positively related to the anxiety ratings. (Table 16.2 contains the same data for the 11 men. In their case, neither the speech

TABLE 16.1
Product–Moment Correlations in Initial Interviews
of 20 Female Patients

	Discomfort-Relief Quotient	Non-ah Speech Disturbance Ratio
Anxiety rating	.11	.59*
Discomfort-Relief Quotient		.39**

*$p < .005$ (one tail test).
**$p < .05$ (one tail test).

TABLE 16.2
Product–Moment Correlations in Initial Interviews
of 11 Male Patients

	Discomfort-Relief Quotient	Non-ah Speech Disturbance Ratio
Anxiety rating	−.08	−.47*
Discomfort-Relief Quotient		.00

*p = .16 (two-tail test)

disturbance nor the verbal content measure is correlated with the related anxiety. The low reliability of the men's anxiety ratings has been noted.) The adequate data, that of the women, clearly indicates that the Non-ah Ratio is a superior index of anxiety than is this particular verbal content measure.

The nature of the relationship between the Non-ah disturbances and the type of verbal content uttered is also shown in Tables 16.1 and 16.2. One can see that there is a modest, significant correlation between the DRQ's and the Non-ah Ratios for the women but not for the men.

Because these two correlations of .39 and .00 are for the measures for the interview as a whole, neither one of them tells us anything precise about the frequency of speech disturbances in the very utterances themselves that fall in the three different content categories. To determine that, we made the following analysis. We obtained for each patient a 25% unbiased sample of the discomfort sentences, a 25% unbiased sample of the neutral sentences, and a 100% sample of the relatively much less frequent relief sentences. For each patient, the frequency of the speech disturbances was then determined for the separate samples. Averages across patients were then computed. Table 16.3 summarizes the findings. For the women, the mean Non-ah Ratio is the same for the utterances in the three content categories. The

TABLE 16.3
Summary of Sentence Analysis of Initial Interviews

	Subjects	Discomfort Sentences	Relief Sentences	Neutral Sentences
Mean Non-ah Speech	20 women	.038	.036	.038
Disturbance Ratio	11 men	.041	.044	.035
Mean N				
sentences	20 women	90	51	74
analyzed	11 men	65	40	70

disturbance levels for the men are very similar for the discomfort and for the relief sentences. The mean disturbance level is lowest for the neutral sentences with the men, but it is not significantly lower than for the other two categories.

DISCUSSION

The possibility of contamination in the findings of this study and that reported in chapter 11 exists, for the author was one of the two anxiety raters and his speech disturbance and verbal content scoring provided the other data of these investigations. Could unconscious biases have caused him to rate and score in such a way as to produce spurious results? This seems highly unlikely, for the following reasons:

1. His anxiety ratings, speech disturbance scoring, and verbal content scoring were highly correlated with those of independent judges. And these independent judges were different individuals for each of the three measures.

2. The recurring sex differences in the correlations between all three measures are inconsistent with the contamination hypothesis. The author would have had no reason to produce negative findings about anxiety and speech disturbances in the men, for example, nor a positive correlation between the Non-ah Ratio and the DRQ in the women and not in the men.

3. The most important reason, however, is that the conclusions about rated emotion and the DRQ are the same when the DRQ scoring of the independent judge is used, as they are when the author's scoring is used (Auld & Mahl, 1956). This independent judge did not share the author's biases about the use of verbal content for assessing emotions.

Although these observations make the possibility of contamination extremely remote, they do not rule it out completely. The study to be reported in the next chapter does control rigorously for this possibility.

Why was there no correlation between the DRQ and the anxiety ratings? In the case of the men, one could attribute this to the poor reliability of the anxiety ratings. But this would not account for the same finding for the women, whose ratings were quite reliable. One possibility is that the DRQ is not a specific measure of anxiety, nor was it intended to be by Dollard and Mowrer. All kinds of tension references are scored as "discomfort" in this method. Auld and Mahl (1956) found that pooling Anxiety, Hostility, and Dependency ratings resulted in a significant correlation of .41 with DRQ's for a larger sample of 26 women patients, which included the 20 involved in the present study. But similar results did not obtain for male patients. Thus this possibility remains a viable one, about which the results are inconclusive.

An examination of the scattergram of the anxiety ratings and DRQ's reveals that the DRQ's were restricted to the high end of the scale, ranging from .77 to .97. The anxiety ratings, however, ranged over the entire 5-point scale. The relative homogeneity of the DRQ's may have contributed to the absence of a correlation between the two measures. It could not account entirely for it, however, for it did not prevent the DRQ's from being positively correlated with the Non-ah Ratios in the women.

Why the DRQ's were restricted to the high end of the scale may be understood when the function of verbal content in the initial interview is considered from the instrumental viewpoint (see chapter 8). It may be the result of a process analogous to a child saying "I'm scared, Mom," when he is not frightened but wants his mother to hold him. Verbal "distress" messages are entirely appropriate to the initial psychiatric interview situation. First, the interview is usually aimed at eliciting a description of his suffering. Second, the patient has come to obtain help with his psychic distress. He or she must reasonably assume, consciously or preconsciously, that the utterance of discomfort units will maximize the likelihood of obtaining that help. The patient wants help and, in effect, cries "help," engaging in suitable instrumental behavior. And right at that moment he may feel comfortable and relieved because he is being heard, tended to, and feels future relief lies ahead.

Related considerations can also explain the absence of any difference in the Non-ah Ratio when the three classes of verbal content are being uttered. The discomfort-relief-neutrality dimension by which the utterances were classified is one based on the conventional meanings of the words. But, as Freud (1901/1960) showed long ago for tongue slips, it must be the private and motivational significance of the utterances that determines whether they are to be disrupted by the speech disturbances. For example, a superficially neutral statement of fact—such as where he lives, or what his occupation is—may be a transitory source of anxiety for a status-minded patient. Here would be a neutral DRQ unit subject to speech disruption. Likewise, as suggested previously, distress utterances may be unconflicted responses if they are instrumental in achieving the goal the patient has set to be accomplished in the initial interview. One can easily multiply such examples of the private intrapsychic and interpersonal significance of utterances from the three content categories. We return to this matter in the Discussion of the following chapter.[2]

---

[2]In executing this study, I would often listen to the tape recording of the particular interviews after scoring the corresponding typescripts for the verbal content categories. Often the vocal signs of the emotional state of a patient and the manifest content I had scored in the typescript were markedly discrepant. For example, a patient might sound relaxed while uttering a long run of Discomfort sentences pertaining to his or her symptoms; or a patient might sound quite distraught while uttering such Neutral manifest content as where he or she lived and worked.

What about the correlation of .39, for the women, between the DRQ and the Speech Disturbance Ratio for the interview as a whole? The findings from the sentence analysis show that this correlation reflects the association of two behaviors occurring *at different times* in the interview. It is not surprising that patients with higher anxiety (indicated by higher speech disturbance) might utter more distress content at some point in the interview than less anxious patients. But it is surprising that this would only be true of women, and not of men. Thus, the reasons for the correlation in the women and for the gender difference are unclear to us.

SUMMARY

1. This study concerned the interrelationships of one verbal content measure of emotional tension (the Discomfort-Relief Quotient), the Non-ah Speech Disturbance Ratio, and rated concurrent anxiety of patients during initial psychiatric interviews.

2. The verbal content measure of emotional tension was not significantly correlated with rated anxiety, whereas the Non-ah Ratio was. The latter was the case for the female patients, but not for the male patients whose anxiety ratings were of low reliability. Thus the speech disturbance measure was here a more valid indicator of rated anxiety than the Discomfort-Relief Quotient.

3. For the interview as a whole, the Discomfort-Relief Quotients and the Non-ah Ratios were moderately, positively correlated for the women patients, but not for the men. However, there was no difference in the frequency of speech disturbances in samples of discomfort, relief, or neutral sentences for either male or female patients.

4. The instrumental viewpoint about verbal content renders these findings intelligible.

Do the results of this study have general implications for the assessment of anxiety and for understanding the speech disturbance phenomena, or are they limited to data obtained by the particular method of manifest verbal content analysis used? The research presented in the next chapter helps to answer this question, for it concerned a different method of content analysis.

17

Speech Disturbances and Manifest Verbal Content in Psychotherapeutic Interviews[1]

George F. Mahl
Yale University

Gene Schulze
Consultants for Personal Competence, Guilford, CT

Edward J. Murray
University of Miami

INTRODUCTION

This is the second chapter concerned with the relationship of the Non-ah speech disturbances described in chapter 9 and manifest verbal content. We are interested in this topic on two counts. First, it bears on our working hypothesis, presented in chapter 8, that nonlexical extralinguistic features of speech provide more useful measures of the emotional state of the speaker than does the manifest verbal content. Secondly, the study of this relationship can contribute to the understanding of the speech disturbance phenomena themselves. Extending this understanding is just as important as is the methodological issue about the measurement of the speaker's emotional state.

The preceding chapter presented data relevant to both of the points just noted. There it was shown that the Non-ah speech disturbances, but not the amount of tension or discomfort referred to in manifest verbal content, were significantly correlated with the rated anxiety of female patients in initial psychiatric interviews. It was also shown that the frequency of these speech disturbances did not differ in samples of sentences containing "discomfort," "relief," or emotionally "neutral" manifest verbal content. The primary focus of the present chapter is on pursuing the latter finding by investigating

---

[1]This chapter is a revision of a paper entitled "Speech Disturbances and Content Analysis Categories as Indices of Emotional States of Patients in Psychotherapy" (Schulze, Mahl, & Murray, 1960) presented at the Annual Meeting of The American Psychological Association, 1960.

the relationship between the Non-ah disturbances and categories of manifest verbal content that are more fine grained than "discomfort," "relief," and emotional "neutrality." Because no independent assessments of the speakers' anxiety were made in this study, the data cannot directly test the hypothesis that the Non-ah Ratio is a more sensitive indicator of anxiety than verbal content. But in view of the evidence presented in chapters 10 through 15 that the Non-ah Ratio does increase with both judged and induced anxiety, the data can bear indirectly on the hypothesis that manifest verbal content analysis is not a useful method for assessing the speaker's anxiety.

METHOD

Subjects and Materials

The subjects were three individuals engaged in psychoanalytically oriented psychotherapy. All were diagnosed as "psychoneurotic." *Mr. Z* (also referred to in chapters 9 and 10) was 40 years old and married. He entered psychotherapy for relief from anxiety attacks and duodenal ulcer. His course of therapy involved two or three interviews a week for a total of 102 hours extending over a calendar year. Eight of his interviews, ranging from the second to the twenty-first, were used in this study. *Mrs. T* was 26 years old and married. She sought psychotherapy because of anxiety, depression, and frigidity. Her therapy involved 17 interviews, once a week. Her first 4 interviews were used. *Mr. S* was 22 years old and single. He suffered from impotence and feelings of depression. He was seen once a week for a total of 29 interviews. Five of his interviews distributed through the first 20 were used in this study.[2]

All three subjects were white and middle class. Mr. Z was self-employed, well read beyond his formal high school education. Mrs. T had attended college and was the wife of a young professional man. Mr. S had a high school education and worked as a clerk.

Every therapeutic hour of these three people had been tape-recorded on high-fidelity equipment in a specially designed interviewing room (Mahl, Dollard, & Redlich, 1954). Multiple copies of verbatim typescripts had been prepared for the interviews used in this study. These tapes and typescripts were the raw material for this study. The only criterion for inclusion of particular hours in this study was the availability of the typescripts for verbal content scoring by Murray at the time of his extensive study (Murray, 1956).

---

[2]The first author was the therapist of Mr. Z. Merton Gill, M.D. was the therapist of Mrs. T and Mr. S. We are grateful to him for providing the materials for these two people.

Verbal Content Analysis

Using one set of copies of the typescripts, Murray scored the manifest content according to categories he developed for assessing the underlying drives and conflicts of patients during psychotherapy (Murray, 1956). Murray's content scoring was independent of the speech disturbance scoring. He did it while we were developing the speech disturbance categories and doing our first studies with them. He had no knowledge of the speech disturbance scoring of any of the interviews, nor any belief that the disturbances reflected in the typescripts were indicative of the patients' emotional states.

Murray first divided the patients' speech into sentence units according to the rules presented in his paper. Then he assigned each unit to one of the categories in his content analysis system.

Wishing to have as objective a system as possible, Murray constructed categories that require relatively little inference by the scorer and that reflect chiefly manifest content. His choice of categories was also guided by psychoanalytic concepts and Neal Miller's Approach-Avoidance Conflict Theory (Dollard & Miller, 1950; Miller, 1944). Murray's system includes categories for statements expressing a need (Approach Categories), for statements expressing anxiety about a need (Anxiety Categories), and for statements expressing hostility on account of frustration of a need (Hostility Categories). The needs included are: sex, affection, dependence, independence, and "unspecified" drive. Thus the total array of Murray's categories include Sex, Sex Anxiety, Sex Hostility, Affection, Affection Anxiety, Affection Hostility, etc.

In this study we are primarily concerned with the groups of Approach and Anxiety Categories. Murray found that both of these groups of categories could be rated reliably, the respective reliability coefficients being .89 ($p < .001$) and .77 ($p < .001$).

Speech Disturbance Scoring

The Non-ah disturbances, defined and illustrated in chapter 9 (pp. 167–169) were scored while reading a second copy of the typescripts and listening to the tapes. The interjudge reliability of the scorer in this study had been tested on three previous occasions.[3] Her Non-ah Ratios had reliabilities of .86, .88, and .90.

Just as Murray's content categorizing had been done without knowledge of the speech disturbance scoring, so the latter was done completely without knowledge of the former.

---

[3]Mrs. Sue Cohen scored the speech disturbances. We wish to express our appreciation for her careful, dependable work and for other technical assistance in organizing the data of this study.

Data Analysis

Two main comparisons were made between the Non-ah Ratios and content measures.

In the first comparison, we grouped together the Anxiety Content units in each hour and the Approach Content units in each hour and computed the Non-ah Ratios for each sample of units. From these hour measures we then computed each patient's average Non-ah Ratios for these two broad content groups and evaluated differences in these average ratios by t-tests.

In the second main comparison, we broke each hour down into blocks of consecutive sentence units with just over 200 patient words per block. In this way we approximated interview segments comparable in size to the 2-minute intervals that we found to be useful ones in our previous work (chapters 9, e.g.,). There were from 15–20 sentence units per block and the blocks, in sequence, covered the whole hour. For each block we computed the Non-ah Ratio and an Anxiety Content Proportion. The latter is the proportion of sentence units in the block that were scored Anxiety by the content method. A correlation between the two measures was then computed for each hour.

We also made a third comparison to explore the frequencies of the speech disturbances in all of Murray's individual content categories. To do this we formed blocks of sentence units of the same category (of sex, dependency, etc.). Each block contained enough consecutive units of the same content category to bring it to just over 100 words. Although given category units were grouped consecutively, it was not required that they be adjacent, that is, units of other categories might have been interspersed between some of them in the original transcript. Non-ah Ratios were then determined for each of these blocks, and a mean Non-ah Ratio for each content category for each patient was obtained by averaging over the appropriate blocks.

RESULTS

Speech Disturbances and Anxiety Content

Table 17.1 presents the mean Non-ah Ratios for each patient's nonanxious, Approach Content Categories and for his Anxiety Content Categories. These data show that the frequency of the speech disturbances is no higher in the Anxiety Content Categories than in the nonanxious, Approach Categories. In fact, for one patient the opposite is true; Mr. Z's disturbance level was significantly lower when he uttered manifest Anxiety Content.

Table 17.2 contains the product-moment correlations between the Non-ah Ratios and the Anxiety Content Proportions for each therapeutic hour of the three patients, and the mean correlation for each patient. It is clear that there is no overall stable correlation between these two measures. Nine of

TABLE 17.1
Mean Non-ah Speech Disturbance Ratios for Approach and Anxiety
Content Categories

Patient	Approach	Anxiety	t	p
Mr. Z	.0545	.0416	2.97	<.01
Mrs. T	.0539	.0618	0.87	N.S.
Mr. S	.0529	.0489	0.67	N.S.

the hourly correlations are negative, and 8 positive. It is interesting to note that the 4 "significant" correlations ($p < .05 - .01$) are negative. There is a slight trend towards a more negative relationship between these two measures in the cases of Mr. Z and Mr. S.

Speech Disturbances and Individual Content Categories

The average Non-ah Ratios for each of the content categories used by the three patients are presented in rank order in Table 17.3. The various specific Anxiety Categories tend to accumulate in the lower rankings for all 3 patients.

The data of Table 17.3 reveal the striking fact that open content utterance by all 3 patients of Dependence needs is associated with the greatest

TABLE 17.2
Correlations between Non-ah Ratios and Anxiety Content Proportions

Patient	Therapy Hour	n	r	p	Mean r	p
Mr. Z	2	34	.10	N.S.		
	3	31	.01	N.S.		
	6	35	−.43	<.01		
	7	25	−.30	N.S.		
	8	25	−.21	N.S.		
	9	27	−.01	N.S.		
	17	23	−.43	<.05		
	21	27	.03	N.S.	−.15	N.S.
Mrs. T	1	20	.38	<.10		
	2	24	.31	N.S.		
	3	25	−.44	<.05		
	4	21	.18	N.S.	.08	N.S.
Mr. S	1	31	.09	N.S.		
	2	34	−.19	N.S.		
	8	27	.05	N.S.		
	14	23	−.30	N.S.		
	20	35	−.32	<.05	−.14	N.S.

TABLE 17.3
Verbal Content Category Profiles of Non-ah Ratios
for Individual Psychotherapy Patients

Mr. Z	Mrs. T	Mr. S
.0686 Dependence	(.0922^a) Dependence	.0711 Dependence
(.0535) Dependence-Hostility	.0793 Sex-Hostility	.0583 Unspecified Anxiety
.0477 Affection	(.0701) Independence-Hostility	.0575 Unspecified Hostility
.0473 Dependence-Anxiety	.0698 Unspecified Hostility	.0499 Independence
(.0466) Independence-Hostility	(.0693) Independence-Anxiety	.0463 Affection
.0448 Sex	(.0671) Dependence-Hostility	.0459 Affection-Hostility
(.0447) Sex-Hostility	.0661 Affection	.0452 Affection-Anxiety
.0440 Unspecified Anxiety	.0626 Affection-Hostility	.0382 Sex-Anxiety
.0435 Unspecified Hostility	.0625 Sex-Anxiety	(.0357) Independence-Hostility
.0421 Affection-Anxiety	.0611 Affection-Anxiety	(.0336) Independence-Anxiety
.0410 Sex-Anxiety	(.0576) Unspecified Anxiety	
.0363 Independence-Anxiety	(.0512) Sex	
(.0334) Affection-Hostility	.0406 Independence	

^{a}Parentheses indicate Mean Non-ah Ratios with low reliability due to small samples of sentence units in the verbal content categories or to unreliability of content scoring for Dependence Hostility and Independence Hostility. Categories not listed for a given patient were completely lacking in the hours scored.

disturbance of speech. For each patient, the difference between the Non-ah Ratio associated with the Dependence Category and that of the next ranking category considerably exceeds all remaining ratio differences between adjacent categories, except for one instance in the case of Mrs. T. Thus Dependence manifest verbal content, rather than Anxiety content, is associated with the highest levels of speech disturbance in these particular samples.

The stability of the rank orders of Mr. S and Mr. Z was evaluated by splitting each of their sample of therapy hours into two groups and correlating the newly computed mean Category Non-ah Ratios of these groups with each other. For Mr. S, the correlation between his mean Category Non-ah Ratios averaged over hours 1 and 2 versus hours 8, 14, and 20 was .46. In Mr. Z's case, we correlated the Category ratios averaged over hours 2, 7, 8, 21 versus hours 3, 6, 9, and 17. His correlation was .39. Thus, both of these correlations are in the positive direction. Neither is statistically significant, however, with the small number of category entries involved. Nevertheless, the correlations do suggest that there is some stability to the rank ordering of categories by the degree to which their utterances are punctuated by speech disturbances. (The sample of Mrs. T was not adequate in size for this type of analysis).

DISCUSSION

Two types of data analysis revealed that the frequency of Non-ah speech disturbances did not, as a rule, increase in utterances of Anxiety manifest verbal content by three patients in their psychotherapy interviews. This finding is consistent with that of the study reported in the preceding chapter and is an extension of it. The previous study showed that the voicing of various kinds of "discomfort" verbal content entailed no more disturbance of speech than did the uttering of "relief" or emotionally "neutral" content. In considering those results, we raised the possibility that they could be attributed to the crudeness of the three content categories. It remained an open question as to whether or not specifically Anxiety Content might be associated with speech disturbance. The results of the present study show that this was not the case with the particular materials and content analysis system used. Also, the methodology of the present study was more rigorous than that of the preceding one in that the scoring of the verbal content and of the speech disturbances were done completely independently. One can be even more confident that these results are not spurious.

The results revealed a tendency for the Non-ah speech disturbances and Anxiety Content to be negatively related. This was clearly the case for Mr. Z, whose mean Non-ah Ratio was significantly lower in his Anxiety units than in his Approach units. How can one understand such results?

This finding did not surprise us, for the experience of one of us as Mr. Z's psychotherapst had been one of the important reasons for skepticism about the usefullness of manifest content measures as indices of emotional states. We still remember an interchange between Mr. Z and his therapist, which may contain part of the explanation of why his Anxiety units had fewer speech disturbances than his Approach units. For several interviews Mr. Z had spoken in detail about many frightening experiences in his life. The therapist finally asked Mr. Z if he didn't feel anxious as he spoke of his frightening experiences. Not at all, Mr. Z answered. He had felt comfortable, believing that he had aroused the therapist's interest, sympathy, and concern. Clearly, the instrumental function for Mr. Z of Anxiety Content made him feel more comfortable. This in turn could account for his more fluent utterance of such content.

We do not know whether this particular interpersonal function of Anxiety Content also operated at times for the other two patients. If it did, it need not be the only process that could mediate the negative relationships between Anxiety Content and speech disturbances. It is possible, for example, that the utterance of Anxiety Content reduces the speaker's anxiety for reasons other than those verbalized by Mr. Z and thereby decreases speech disturbances. At one time, verbalizing anxiety might be a step towards its mastery, for example; at another time, it might have the significance of portraying the speaker as a brave or strong person, etc. It is also possible that some people can sometimes speak of being frightened or anxious when they feel relatively less anxious, which in turn could be indicated by a lowered frequency of speech disturbances. Once we know that Anxiety Content may be at times associated with decreased speech disturbance it is easy to think of possible explanations for the phenomenon. Obviously, however, this is a question that can only be settled by further research.

So far we have considered only one side of the coin. It is also important to note the converse relationship between verbal content and speech disturbances revealed by this study: utterances by patients in psychotherapy devoid of references to anxiety, i.e., the Approach Categories, is just as likely to be disrupted by speech disturbances as is Anxiety Content. More likely, in fact, in some instances. This was most clearly shown by the finding that verbal content openly stating Dependency needs was by far the most disrupted content for all 3 patients.

Are there plausible explanations for such findings that are consistent with the evidence presented in chapters 10 through 15 that the Non-ah Ratio is an index of current anxiety? Some come to mind. It is common clinical knowledge that the expression of needs is frequently the source of anxiety and conflict for adults seeking psychotherapy. So it is not surprising that the voicing of needs (in the Approach Categories) should be just as disrupted as the Anxiety Content.

What is surprising, and still left unaccounted for, is that the expressions of Dependency needs should be associated with the highest frequency of speech disturbances in each patient. It might be that the heightened anxiety, indicated by more disturbed speech, causes people to experience and voice dependency needs, just as a frightened child feels the need to be cared for by his parents. It is even possible that both the utterance of dependent needs and the increased speech disturbance are the result of that inner sense of helplessness, which Freud (1926/1959) posited as the "basic" anxiety.

Thus it is possible to offer plausible explanations for the data about the Approach Categories, and for the finding that Dependence was characterized by a higher frequency of speech disturbances than any other verbal content category. As is true for the possible explanations of the Anxiety Content-speech disturbance relationship, only future research can tell which, if any, of them are valid. But the mere fact that such further questions are raised by the data is regarded as an important outcome of this study.

The rank ordering of the speech disturbance data for the various Content Categories raises another possibility for future research into the psychotherapeutic process. Although there was a trend towards some within-patient stability in the rank order of the categories, the variability in the rankings was greater than the stability. Research aimed at discovering the reasons for this variability is obviously in order. One direction it might fruitfully take would be to see how the rank orders of various patients vary over the course of psychotherapy, and to what the variations might be related. Would it be found, for example, that the speech disturbance level of Sex Content, relative to that of other categories changed in any uniform way in a sample of psychotherapies of patients with sexual conflicts as their chief complaint? Would it tend to decrease in the later phases of "successful" therapies, and not in "unsuccessful" ones? What attributes of therapy might be related to these different courses of events?

SUMMARY AND CONCLUSIONS

1. This study concerned the relationship between the frequency of the Non-ah speech disturbances and the Verbal Content Categories developed by Murray for use with psychotherapy interviews. Typescripts and tape recordings of 17 psychotherapy interviews of 3 patients were scored independently by the two methods.

2. The speech disturbances were not higher during the utterance of Anxiety Content than during the utterance of other, "nonanxious" content. In fact, the speech disturbances and Anxiety Content tended to be negatively related. These findings are consistent with, and extend, those reported in chapter 16 concerning disturbed speech and "discomfort" content.

3. In all 3 patients, the utterance of Dependence-need Content was more disrupted by speech disturbances than was the utterance of any other content scored in Murray's system.

4. Various possible explanations for the observed relationships between speech disturbances and the manifest verbal content categories are discussed. These raise questions for further research.

5. The specific contribution of the study is the extension of empirical data about the association of verbal content and the Non-ah speech disturbances. An auxiliary contribution is the implication of the results that manifest verbal content does not provide direct, simple measures of the concurrent emotional state of the speaker. This implication arises when one views

the findings of the present study in the light of the evidence presented in chapters 10 through 15. That evidence predominantly indicated that the Non-ah Ratio is positively related to the concurrent anxiety of the speaker.[4]

---

[4]In a small demonstration study (Mahl, 1961a), we found that the Non-ah disturbances were not related with still a third method for assessing "anxious" verbal content. This was Gottschalk's method (Gottschalk, Springer, & Gleser, 1961).

18

The Use of "Ah" in Spontaneous Speech[1]

The focus of the preceding eight chapters has been the relationship between the Non-ah speech disturbances and the speaker's concurrent anxiety. In these next four chapters we widen our perspective to look at some of the disparate speech phenomena that attracted our attention over the years.

The first of these disparate phenomena is saying "ah." Two hints have appeared in earlier chapters that this is not merely an annoying speech habit, but a lawful event. Chapters 10, 11, and 12 uniformly showed that the frequency of saying "ah" did *not* increase with the speaker's anxiety, as do the Non-ah disturbances. (See Fig. 15.1, chapter 15). In chapter 15, we cited a similar finding in six additional studies by others. And in chapter 12 we demonstrated that saying "ah" increased markedly in a telephone-type situation versus the usual face-to-face condition. This did not happen with the Non-ah disturbances. That finding led us to speculate briefly that saying "ah" served to provide the speaker with time to decide what to say (chapter 12, pp. 212–213). In this chapter, we examine in detail some of the research that formed the background for that speculation.

We have seen that, in general, "ah" is by far the most frequent of our eight speech disturbance categories. It accounts for some 40% of everyday speech disturbances. Then follows, in decreasing order, Sentence change, Repetition, Stutter, and what we will call here the "rare" categories (Omission, Sentence incompletion, Incoherent sound, and Tongue slip). (See

---

[1]This chapter is a revision of a paper presented at the Annual Meeting of the Eastern Psychological Association in 1955 (Mahl, 1955b).

chapter 9, Table 9.1 for definitions and examples of the categories, and Table 9.8 for the overall category percentages.)

RELATION BETWEEN "AH" AND SENTENCE CHANGE WITHIN INTERVIEWS

The present study is based on 26 psychotherapy interviews of six psycho-neurotic patients, using the procedures described in chapter 9. It started when individual variations in the category percentages were noticed. These can be seen with the construction of profiles of the percentages of a person's disturbances in the various categories. Figure 18.1 contains such profiles for two patients. Both are women college graduates. The language samples are two psychotherapy interviews for H and eight for Y. The profiles of the percentages of their disturbances in the Repetition, Stutter, and Rare categories are quite similar. But their "ah" and Sentence change profiles are almost mirror images. These data suggested that the percent "ah's" and percent Sentence changes might be negatively correlated.

Rank order correlations for all the possible pairs of category percentages were determined for the 6 patients. The results are summarized in Table 18.1. Looking first at the second column of this Table, it can be seen that the percent "ah"-Sentence change correlation by patients is −.75. "Ah" was also negatively correlated with the other categories but to a lesser degree. ('Ah'-Repetition −.21, 'Ah'-Stutter −.48, 'Ah'-'Rare' −.31). There were no consistent relationships between the various Non-ah categories.

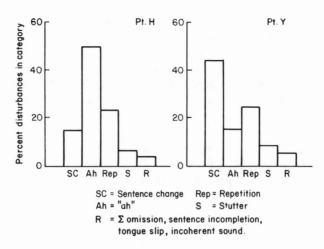

SC = Sentence change   Rep = Repetition
Ah = "ah"   S   = Stutter
R = Σ omission, sentence incompletion,
     tongue slip, incoherent sound.

FIG. 18.1.   Speech disturbance profiles of two patients.

TABLE 18.1
Rank Order Correlations of Speech Disturbance Category Percentages

	Order Correlations		
Samples	Ah-Sentence change %	Ah-Remainder %	Sentence Change Remainder %
By patients			
$n = 6$	−.75	−.37	−.19
By interviews			
Pt. Z, $n = 8$	−.80	−.64	.16
Pt. Y, $n = 8$	−.95	.76	−.90

Note: The relevant %'s were as follows:

	Ah %	Sentence change %	Remainder %
6 Pts.	35	30	45
Pt. Z	41	34	25
Pt. Y	16	44	40

Eight interviews had been scored for two of the patients and similar rank order correlations were computed for the interview percentages within each of the two patients. Here again, high negative correlations between the "ah" and Sentence change percentages were obtained, −.80 for Z and −.95 for Y. No consistent correlations in the two patients were found between the other category pairs.

In short, high negative correlations between "ah" and Sentence change percentages were found both across six patients and across interviews within two patients.

The evaluation of these high negative correlations is complicated somewhat by two things:

1. These are correlations between percentages.
2. "Ah" and Sentence change, on the average, make up 65% of the speech disturbances.

Are the direction and size of the correlations only a function of these two factors? Negative evidence for this possibility appears, first, in correlating the "ah" percentage with a Remainder percentage that is obtained by pooling the Repetition, Stutter, and "Rare" percentages together, and, secondly, in correlating the Sentence change percentage with this Remainder percentage. In this way comparably sized percentages are being correlated. The results of such procedures are shown in the two right-hand columns of Table 18.1, with the actual percentage values being appended in the note of the table.

A comparison of the direction and size of the correlations with the size of the percentages indicates that the high negative "ah"-Sentence change correlations are not just spurious effects of correlating large percentages. For example, the three correlations of percentages across six patients are on comparable percentages, yet they systematically decrease by large differences. The same lack of relationship between the direction or size of the correlations and the size of the percentages on which they are based is also true for the within-patient correlations.

We conclude at this point that *when these patients made speech disturbances* there was a high negative relationship between the occurrence of "ah" and of Sentence change. The remainder of the chapter is likewise limited to *samples of disturbed speech.* The analysis that follows offers further evidence for this conclusion, but it is concerned principally with the mechanism underlying the negative relationship.

RELATION BETWEEN "AH" AND SENTENCE CHANGE WITHIN SENTENCES

Because Sentence change by definition involves the sentence as a unit, the first question raised is whether the negative relationship that appears across patients and across interviews will also appear across disturbed sentences within patients. For this analysis, 100 consecutive sentences each of which contained one or more speech disturbance regardless of type were selected for each of the six patients. "Sentence" here was defined in accordance with the grammarian's rules systematized by Auld and White (1956), with the exception that they are broadened to include Sentence changes within a sentence unit.

If a sentence contains "ah" it will be called an 'ah sentence,' if it does not it will be called a 'non-ah sentence'. Using the 100 sentence sample, the number of 'non-ah sentences' was matched with the number of 'ah sentences' produced by each patient.

Table 18.2 shows for the group of six patients the mean percent of 'ah' and 'non-ah sentences' that contain the other disturbances. All percentages were transformed into radians before determining the significance level by the t-test. If 'ah' is present in the sentence, the sentence is less likely to contain a Sentence change, a Repetition, or a Stutter. To see if these group findings would also be true for the individual patients, Chi-square tests of independence of "ah" and the other categories were made for each patient. In these tests the complete 100 sentence sample for each patient was used. The results are presented in Table 18.3. A tetrachoric correlation is presented for each test only where the Chi-square analysis yielded a p-value of .05

TABLE 18.2

Mean Percentage of 'Ah sentences' and 'Non-ah sentences'
Containing other Types of Speech Disturbances

Category	"Ah" Present in Sentence	"Ah" absent from Sentence	p-Value
Sentence change	29	54	.02
Repetition	11	30	.01
Stutter	8	25	.08
Rare	9	17	—

Note: All sentences contain one or more disturbances. N 'Ah' and 'Non-ah' sentences matched per patient. N patients = 6.

or less. The negative "ah"-Sentence change relation still appears within five of the six patients across disturbed sentences. And this is the most uniformly occurring negative relation indicated in the table.

Another question was now asked: Do "ah" and Sentence change substitute for each other within the structure of the sentence? To answer this in a preliminary way, ten consecutive sentences containing only "ah," only Sentence change, or Repetition and so forth were collected for each patient. The location of these disturbances was then categorized as to whether it occurred at the onset of the sentence, in the subject, or in the predicate of the sentence. The onset is defined as extending to the second word of the sentence. The findings were that "ah" occurred at the onset of the sentence in 62% of the sentences, whereas on the average the percentage of sentences

TABLE 18.3

Tetrachoric Correlations Between Ah and Other Disturbance
Categories in 100 Consecutive Sentence Units Containing
One or More Speech Disturbances

Patient	Ah- Sentence Change	Ah- Stutter	Ah- Repetition	Ah- Rare
D	−.57	—	−.37	−.56
Z	−.60	—	—	—
F	−.54	−.59	—	−.36
Y	−.49	—	—	—
T	−.37	−.71	—	—
H	—	−.52	—	—

Note: Correlations presented only where Chi-square test yielded *p*-value of .05 or less.

with disturbances at the onset was 35%. None of the other categories showed this predilection for occurring at the onset of the sentence.

With these findings in mind, we return to the sample of 100 disturbed sentences for each patient. Now the question asked is: Do the previously shown effects of "ah" vary with the position of "ah" in the sentence? To answer this, for each patient equal numbers of consecutive sentences were selected from the 100 unit samples that (1) contained "ah" only at the onset of the sentence, (2) did not contain "ah" at the onset, but did elsewhere in the sentence, (3) did not contain "ah" anywhere in the sentence. For five of the patients, there were 15 of each type of sentence, whereas for the sixth patient there are only eight of each type.

Then the percentage of each class of 'ah sentence' that contained the other disturbances was computed for each patient. The means of these are presented in Table 18.4. When the data are transformed into radians to insure homogeneity of variance within each "ah"-condition, and the data subjected to a simple analysis of variance, it is found that the "ah"-condition significantly affects the occurrence of Sentence change, Repetition, and the "Rare" categories. In each instance that gives a significant F, "ah"-onset is significantly superior to the "ah"-elsewhere for Sentence change and Repetition. "Ah"-elsewhere is significantly different than non-"ah" only for Repetitions. In the case of Sentence change, then, it is the onset-"ah" that is of primary significance. Dichotomizing sentences into "ah"-onset and non-"ah"-onset sentences and repeating the type of individual Chi-square tests performed earlier the findings contained in Table 18.5 are obtained. A significant "ah"-onset effect on Sentence change is found for each of the six patients. In four patients the correlation is greater than the comparable ones in Table 18.3. For some patients, there is also a significant negative relation between "ah"-onset and other forms of disturbance, but the uniformity of the Sentence change effect is clearly greater.

TABLE 18.4
Mean Percentages of Various Types of 'Ah-sentences' Containing
Other Types of Disturbances

Category	"Ah" at Onset of Sentence	"Ah" Elsewhere in Sentence	"Ah" Absent From Sentence
Sentence change	14	40	56
Repetition	2	19	34
Stutter	6	12	20
'Rare'	4	9	20

Note: All sentences contain one or more speech disturbances. N sentences of the various types matched per patient. N patients = 6.

TABLE 18.5
Tetrachoric Correlations Between "Ah" at Onset of Sentence
and Other Disturbance Categories in 100 Consecutive Sentence Units
Containing One or More Speech Disturbances

Patient	*"Ah" Onset-* *Sentence Change*	*"Ah" Onset-* *Stutter*	*"Ah" Onset-* *Repetition*	*"Ah" Onset-* *'Rare'*
D	−.72	—	−.57	−.71
Z	−.34	—	—	—
F	−.47	−.48	—	−.49
Y	−.76	—	—	—
T	−.63	−.68	—	—
H	−.31	−.46	—	—

Note: Correlations presented only where Chi-square test yielded *p*-value of .05 or less.

SUMMARY

To sum up, in disturbed language samples:

1. There is a rather strong negative relation between the occurrence of "ah" and of Sentence change. This appears in correlating across patients, across interviews of a given patient, and across sentences within patients.
2. The maximal effect of "ah" in this regard results if "ah" is at the onset of the sentence.
3. The use of "ah", particularly the onset "ah", is also negatively correlated with the other disturbances, but this effect does not appear as uniformly in individual patients as does the negative "ah"-Sentence change relation.

HYPOTHESIS OF DETERMINING TENDENCIES

We conjecture a hypothesis to account for these findings. When we describe speech, we are likely to think of the word-to-word progression. But it is also possible to think of the sentence-to-sentence, phrase-to-phrase, or thought-to-thought progression. Let us assume that the structure and content of any given sentence unit, or long phrase, is determined at the outset of the sentence and that on the basis of this prior determination the specific word-to-word sequence is emitted. Still conjecturing, under certain conditions this prior determination of entire sentence units may be impaired. Perhaps "ah" is likely to be used under such circumstances. If it is used at the onset, the sentence unit—the structure and content of the sentence—is more likely to be determined at the outset. If this has taken place the least likely disturbance in the subsequent utterance of the sentence is Sentence change. Other disturbances, such as Repetitions, Stutter, Omission and so on, will occur with greater frequency than Sentence change, for they are not alterations in the structure or content of the sentence and thus not made as improbable by the prior determination of the sentence. In the case of very long sentences, of course, this type of hypothesis would include prior determination of phrase units. In short, it is being conjectured that the differential effect of "ah" on the other disturbances and the differential effect of "ah" at the onset of sentences are indications that there are *determining tendencies* for sentences, and that in spontaneous speech there is a succession of such determining tendencies as well as the succession of specific words and uttered sentences.[2]

Why "ah"? Why would the speaker voice "ah" while determining what to say? Perhaps there are two reasons. The first could be an intrapsychic one: to release tension that mounts during the momentary inhibition and delay that occurs during the moment of deciding or planning what to say. This might be a phenomenon analagous to the tail switching of a cat waiting and deciding to pounce on its prey. The second reason for voicing "ah" might be an interpersonal one: to forestall the other participant from interrupting the speaker, as the latter might do during a *silent* pause. Thus "ah" may be analogous to a "Do not disturb" sign. In short, "ah" may have simultaneous, multiple functions that protect the integrity of the speech process.

SOME REMAINING QUESTIONS

The research presented here has only scratched the surface of the significance and determinants of saying "ah." In the course of our explorations, we came upon two interesting possibilities for further research. In one study, we found that early weaning was very strongly, positively associated with increased frequency of using "ah" in young adulthood (Mahl & Kasl, 1958). The time of weaning was that recalled and reported by the mothers in completing questionnaires. Our later attempt to verify that striking finding by interviewing mothers of different speakers was unsuccessful. We should have, but didn't, pursue this issue to a final solution.

---

[2]On completely independent grounds, Miller, Galanter, and Pribram (1960, see especially pp. 139–158) reached a similar conclusion about the role of anticipatory "plans" in speech. Our "determining tendency" harks back to Ach (1905) and is an elementary analogue of the highly elaborated concept of *Plan* articulated by Miller et al. (1960). For a related discussion see also the discussions of "central programming" in speech in Osgood and Sebeok (1954, especially pp. 57–60, 71–73).

In another study (Mahl, 1958), we conducted an "armchair factor analysis" of those items of the Minnesota Multiphasic Personality Inventory (Hathaway & McKinley, 1951) that were especially characteristic of very frequent "Ah-ers" and those of very frequent "Sentence changers." The items forming a *coherent pattern* for these two groups are listed in Table 18.6. It seems quite likely that intelligible personality characteristics exist for these two types of speakers, and that the type of upbringing by parents contributes to these particular speech characteristics. We have presented these very exploratory findings, as well as those concerning weaning, in the hope that they will spark the interest of some future investigators.

TABLE 18.6
Personality Items Forming a Coherent Pattern Reported by High "Ah'ers"
and High "Sentence changers"

"Ah'ers"	*"Sentence Changers"*
I usually have to stop and think before I act even in trifling matters. *	I have more trouble concentrating than others seem to have. *
I have often lost out on things because I couldn't make up my mind soon enough. *	I find it hard to keep my mind on a task or job. *
When I am cornered I tell that portion of the truth which is not likely to hurt me.	When in a group of people I have trouble thinking of the right things to talk about. *
I cannot keep my mind on one thing.	In school I found it very hard to talk before the class. *
I am unusually self-conscious.	It is unusual for me to express strong approval or disapproval of the actions of others.
I feel anxiety about something or someone almost all the time.	I seldom "lay my cards on the table" with people that I am trying to correct or improve.
I frequently find myself worrying about something.	It takes a lot of argument to convince most people of the truth.
I must admit that I have at times been worried beyond reason over something that really did not matter.	It is not always a good thing to be frank.
I worry quite a bit over possible misfortunes.	I am unusually self-conscious.
It takes a lot of argument to convince most people of the truth.	I am certainly lacking in self-confidence.
My parents and family find more fault with me than they should.	I am not entirely self-confident.
The man who had most to do with me when I was a child (such as my father, stepfather, etc.) was very strict with me.	It makes me feel like a failure when I hear of the success of someone I know well.
	I am easily embarrassed.
	I frequently have to fight against showing that I am bashful.
	Sometimes I am sure that other people can tell what I am thinking.

* "Face validity" items.

19 Everyday Speech Disturbances in *Tom Sawyer*

When I was immersed in the preceding studies of everyday speech disturbances, I was looking for them everywhere, including dialogues in fiction and drama that I encountered in daily life. My informal searches produced two surprises. First, some fictional dialogue includes fictional speech disturbances. Thus, I often saw "er . . . er" where "ah" or "uh" or "uhm" occurs in real speech. Sometimes "er . . . er" indicated stuttering. Yet I cannot recall ever observing ". . . er . . ." in the extensive corpus of spontaneous speech we have investigated (see chapter 9, p. 166). Second, I saw that masterful dialogue may rarely contain everyday speech disturbances. Thus, I noticed that Ernest Hemingway rarely used them.

Although interesting, these two findings were disappointing. Naturally, I had hoped to find that some writers used our speech disturbance categories in their dialogue and used them, moreover, to portray states of anxiety and conflict in their characters. Such findings would enhance the generality and credibility of our approach by supplementing our scientific findings with evidence of quite a different nature. This would provide esthetic as well as intellectual pleasure.

Hemingway came to the rescue. He directed me to Mark Twain by praising him as the source of all modern American literature.[1] I reread *Tom*

---

[1] In *The Green Hills of Africa*, Hemingway (1935) wrote:

All modern American literature comes from one book by Mark Twain called *Huckleberry Finn*. If you read it you must stop where the Nigger Jim is stolen from the boys. That is the real end. The rest is just cheating. But it's the best book we've had. All American writing comes from that. There was nothing before. There has been nothing as good since. (p. 22)

286

Sawyer and *Huckleberry Finn*, and researched the former. This chapter presents the results of that research.

PURPOSE

Mark Twain closed his Preface to *The Adventures of Tom Sawyer* (1876/1982a) with the following words:

> part of my plan has been to try to pleasantly remind adults of what they once were themselves, and of how they felt and thought and *talked* [around 1840; italics added], and what queer enterprises they sometimes engaged in. (p. xvii)

Every critic agrees that Twain achieved his goals, including the one of especial interest to us—showing how people talked in 1840, in the Southwest. In achieving the latter goal, he used his generally acclaimed unparalleled talent with vernacular. DeVoto (1932) wrote "the voice [in his dialogues] is recorded by the most sensitive ear ever devoted to the study of American speech" (p. 266). Kaplan (1966) extolled this talent as follows "his ear for the rhythms of speech was unsurpassed, and he demanded in dialect and social notation nothing short of perfection" (pp. 179–180). Warfel (1965) spoke of Twain's "masterly control over the English language in its standard and Western dialect forms" (p. ix). In his critique of Twain's life's work, Cox (1966) included an evaluative survey of the vicissitudes of Twain's use of dialect and vernacular beginning with *The Celebrated Jumping Frog of Calaveras County* and continuing into his final writings. He argues, as apparently all other critics do, that Twain's greatest success in the use of vernacular and dialect was the dialogue in *Huckleberry Finn* (Twain, 1884/1960).[2] The critics, however, explicitly or implicitly praise Twain's use of this talent in *Tom Sawyer* as well.

In reading *Tom Sawyer* one sees that Mark Twain manifested his 'most sensitive ear for American speech' in multiple ways. The following is an illustrative, not an exhaustive, account of this fact. Most prominent is his ubiquitous use of vernacular in the sense of the "lower" or illiterate language. In addition, he used dialect. And he frequently employed idiomatic terms, as when he used *evening* for *afternoon* (Twain, 1876/1982a, p. 3) and when he distinguished between a *marvel*, an *alley*, and a *tow* (p. 12; a marble, one of alabaster, and a large fancy marble, respectively). Moreover, Twain often controlled the *form* of dialogue to vividly portray the course of interaction. In the following example, he rapidly telescoped the exchange between Tom and the stranger so that it ended with the exchange of verbal jabs.

---

[2]See also Smith (1958) and Stegner (1960).

Neither boy spoke. If one moved, the other moved—but only sidewise, in a
circle; they kept face to face and eye to eye all the time. Finally Tom said:
"I can lick you!"
"I'd like to see you try it."
"Well, I can do it."
"No you can't, either."
"Yes I can."
"No you can't."
"I can."
"You can't."
"Can!"
"Can't!" (pp. 5–6)

The minister gave out the hymn, and read it through with a relish, in a
peculiar style which was much admired in that part of the country. His voice
began on a medium key and climbed steadily up till it reached a certain point,
where it bore with strong emphasis upon the topmost word and then plunged
down as if from a spring-board:

Shall I be car-ri-ed toe the skies, on flow'ry *beds*

of ease,

Whilst others fight to win the prize, and sail thro' *blood-*

-y seas?

He was regarded as a wonderful reader. At church "sociables" he was

THE CHURCH CHOIR.

always called upon to read poetry; and when he was through, the ladies would
lift up their hands and let them fall helplessly in their laps, and " wall " their
eyes, and shake their heads, as much as to say, " Words cannot express it; it is
too beautiful, *too* beautiful for this mortal earth."

FIG. 19.1a. The printed version of the minister's reading of the hymn.
Adapted from Twain (1876, pp. 54–55), courtesy of The Collection of American Literature, Beinecke Rare Book and Manuscript Library, Yale University.

Twain also resorted, with great delight, I presume, to the plastic portrayal
of a vocal quality already described textually. Figures 19.1a and 19.1b[3]

[3]The illustrations from the holograph manuscript of *The Adventures of Tom Sawyer* are used
with the permission of the Georgetown University Library's Special Collection Division (Washington, D.C.). They appear in the two volume facsimile edition of the holograph manuscript
published by University Publications of America, Frederick MD, and the Georgetown University Library, Washington, D.C. (1982).

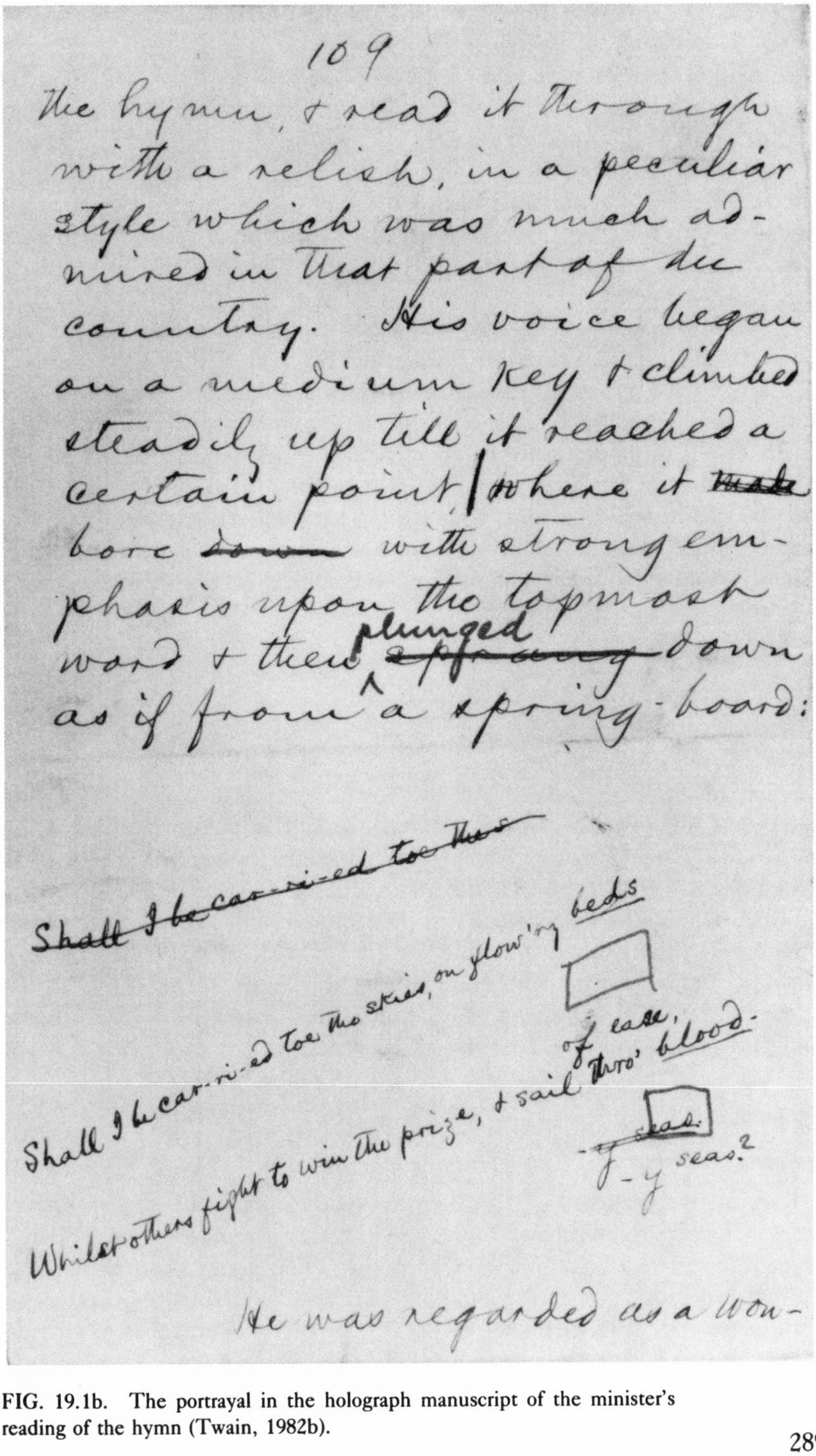

FIG. 19.1b. The portrayal in the holograph manuscript of the minister's reading of the hymn (Twain, 1982b).

illustrate this portrayal in the first edition of *Tom Sawyer* (Twain, 1876) in his holograph manuscript (Twain 1982b). Note the care Twain took in writing "the picture" of the minister's voice.

Mindful of Twain's desire to show how people talked in Hannibal (St. Petersburg), of his generally acclaimed ability to do so, and that he used various devices to achieve that goal, we are in a position to state the primary questions of the study reported in this chapter. They are:

1. Will Twain also use everyday speech disturbances in his dialogue? Did he write them in the first draft of *Tom Sawyer*, or "revise" them into the text?

2. If he used everyday disturbances, how will they compare with our findings in the spontaneous speech of contemporary speakers? Will they consist of our categories, and compare with the frequencies, which we reported in chapter 9? (The pursuit of the question of frequency raised an important additional question, which will be introduced later.)

3. If Twain does have his characters use our everyday speech disturbances, will he have them doing so in psychological contexts which seemed to be operative in our speakers?

PROCEDURES

Materials

A variety of "modern" editions of *Tom Sawyer* exist. The truly authoritative one, based directly on Twain's original manuscript, is a recent publication by The Mark Twain Library (Twain, 1876/1982a). Because this study was started in the 1970s, speech disturbances and word counts, which comprise the basic data of this study, were first determined from several of the earlier "modern" editions (Twain, 1876/1959b, 1876/1965, 1876/1976). The final data reported here were determined from the authoritative Mark Twain Library edition. We also examined a published facsimile of the original holograph manuscript of *Tom Sawyer* (Twain, 1982b).

Dialogue Scoring

Speech Disturbances

I scored the dialogue of *Tom Sawyer* twice for everyday speech disturbances. Twelve years elapsed between the two scorings, during which I never referred to the originally scored text. The comparison of the two scorings provides a test-retest reliability measure. We tabulated the speech disturbances per story character and also pooled all disturbances to provide an overall measure of their frequency. For certain purposes, we also computed overall measures for successive chapters of the book, and for successive 200-word segments of Tom's dialogue.

Dialogue Word Counts

Two assistants[4] independently counted the number of words spoken by those characters who did speak. One person completed a single count; another performed two independent counts. These word counts were tabulated by the speaking characters. I compared these tabulations and reconciled the few differences in the character totals. The word counts of the two-time counter were also tabulated by character by chapter. I reconciled the few differences in the two tabulations.

The criterion for "dialogue" was that words be spoken aloud. With rare exceptions such words were part of an interchange between people. If someone spoke aloud but to his or herself (implicitly to the reader), as Aunt Polly does at the outset of chapter 1, the utterance was considered "dialogue." Words presented in quotes which were thought, but not spoken, were not considered dialogue.

Psychological Context of Speech Disturbances

Sometimes Twain indicated this context, more or less explicitly. At other times, the writer made a judgment about the context. Usually such judgments were obvious ones.

Use of the Holograph Facsimile

We inspected this manuscript for two reasons. First, we wanted to see if the speech disturbances appearing in the published *Tom Sawyer* were written by Twain in the very first draft of his manuscript or were added during revision of it. Secondly, we wanted to compare the frequency with which Twain had revised the manuscript for the first 18 chapters with that for the last 17 chapters. Why we wanted to do this is stated later in the context in which the question arose.

RESULTS AND DISCUSSION

General Finding

Our most general, and to us most important, finding is that Mark Twain did use everyday speech disturbances in his dialogue and all those he used are included in our categories. This finding is important to us for two reasons. First, it gives further support to "the reality" of our categories. Twain's perceptions of American speech and the results of our early work in develop-

[4] I am grateful to Steven B. Ford, Yale '68, and Carmel Lepore for their uncomplaining dedication to this tedious chore.

ing our category set are in essential agreement on the variety of everyday speech disturbances. Secondly, the overall finding increases the generality of our category set, extending it to the Southwestern vernacular spoken by a wide variety of people 150 years ago. It is further evidence of the freedom of these extralinguistic phenomena from sociocultural restraint, which we have noted previously (as in chapter 9, fn. p. 168).

Test-Retest Reliability

A total of 100 speech disturbances were scored in the two scorings separated by 12 years. There was exact agreement (for both incidence and category type) in 89 instances, i.e., an 89% agreement for exact scoring. This degree of intrascorer agreement compares very well with the average interscorer correlations of .98 (Ah Ratio) and .93 (Non-ah Ratio) reported in chapter 9 (p. 170). A full appreciation of the significance of the 89% exact agreement comes with the knowledge that there are 21,631 words of dialogue in *Tom Sawyer*. Thus, the statistical opportunities for disagreements in repeated scoring are quite numerous.

The high reliability is primarily the result of the obviousness of the phenomena in Twain's dialogue and merely attentiveness to them by the scorer. They are not elusive, subtle phenomena. Nor does their perception often require interpretation of the text.

Twain's Usage of Speech Disturbances: General Aspects

The reconciliation of the discrepancies in the repeated scorings, yielded a final total of 50 speech disturbances, (47 from the first, and 3 from the second scoring.)[5]

General Quantitative Features

Table 19.1 presents basic data about the 50 disturbances: their categories, and their distribution among the story characters. These data show several facts about Twain's use of speech disturbances. First, Twain's disturbances fall within five of our categories. He did not use all our categories, however. His dialogue contained no Tongue slips, no Omissions, and no Incoherent Sounds (See chapter 9, Table 9.1). Secondly, the dialogue percentages for Σ Ah, Sentence Change, Repetition and for the "Rare" categories (Incompletion, Stutter, Ommission, Incoherent Sound) are comparable to those in our contemporary samples. Thirdly, Twain's characters committed many fewer speech disturbances than people do in reality. Extrapolating from our samples, we would anticipate conservatively that Twain would have included at least 1000 speech disturbances, in contrast to the actual 50. The former

---

[5]The writer will provide the identity and exact location of these 50 disturbances upon request.

TABLE 19.1

The Nature of the Speech Disturbances and Their Distribution
among Story Characters

Character	Speech Disturbance Categories						% Grand Total	General[a] Ratio × 1000
	Ah	Sentence Change	Repetition	Sentence Incompletion	Stutter	Total		
Tom	11	6	16	3	—	36	72	4.4
Huck	—	2	1	—	—	3	6	.7
Aunt Polly	—	1	—	2	—	3	6	1.4
Becky	—	—	1	1	2	3	6	3.7
Schoolteacher	—	—	1	—	—	1	2	10.0
Joe Harper	—	—	1	1	—	1	2	1.9
Muff Potter	—	—	—	1	—	1	2	2.0
Mrs. Harper	—	—	—	1	—	1	2	6.8
Anonymous playmate[b]	—	—	—	1	—	1	2	8.5
Total	11	9	19	9	2	50	2	2.3
% Σ Ah, S.C., Rep.		78						
% Σ Inc., St.				22				
Comparable % Contemporary Speakers[c]		85		15				

[a] General Speech Disturbance Ratio × 1000 = $\dfrac{\Sigma \text{ Speech Disturbances}}{N \text{ Words Dialogue}}$ × 1000.

[b] Based on dialogue of all anonymous children.

[c] Based on Table 9.8.

293

would be the equivalent of a General Speech Disturbance Ratio ($\times$ 1000) of
46.2, compared with the actual one of 2.3, which is presented in Table 19.1.
There is a good reason for this discrepancy. Twain used speech disturbances
for artistic effect, and he would have sacrificed that effect if he had increased
their frequency. The latter might have put off the reader, as verbatim records often do and would have weakened the impact of the disturbances on
the reader. The single disturbance of the schoolteacher (Twain, 1982a) has a
marked effect on the reader, partly because of its rarity in this man's speech.
It occurred in response to Tom's (crafty) admission that he was late for school
because:

> "I STOPPED TO TALK WITH HUCKLEBERRY FINN!"
> The master's pulse stood still, and he stared helplessly. the buzz of study
> ceased. . . . The master said:
> *"You—you* did what?" [italics added]
> "Stopped to talk with Huckleberry Finn."
> There was no mistaking the words. (p. 53)

The schoolteacher's Repetition is the verbal enactment of his emotional
shock, helplessness, and disbelief. Its emphatic power is the greater because
of the schoolteacher's otherwise usual composure. *Mark Twain used speech
disturbances to promote his artistic creation, not to make his dialogue read like a
verbatim transcript of tape recorded interchange.* As Smith (1958) claimed for
Twain's use of dialect in *Huckleberry Finn* the frequency of Twain's use of
speech disturbances in *Tom Sawyer* is in the service of "establishing the
illusion of accuracy, in making the reader accept a character's speech as
lifelike" (p. xxiii). Twain penned these speech disturbances as a painter
brushes accenting colors.

Speech Disturbances and Story Characters

Thirty identified characters and assorted anonymous individuals utter the
21,631 words of dialogue in *Tom Sawyer*.[6] Only 9 of these characters, howev-

---

[6]The following tabulation presents our dialogue word counts for the identified and anonymous characters.

Tom	8,241	Ben Rogers	202	Mrs. Thatcher	75
Huck	4,611	Alfred	192	Mary Austen	60
Aunt Polly	2,087	Defense Lawyer	188	Minister	53
Welshman	985	Mrs. Harper	148	Lawyer for	
Injun Joe	945	Widow Douglas	143	Prosecution	43
Becky	801	Mr. Walter	133	Dr. Robinson	29
Joe Harper	533	Mary	133	Billy	7
Muff Potter	511	Anon Adults	129	Susy Harper	5
Sidney	378	Anon Children	118	Gracie Miller	4
T'Other	355	Schoolteacher	100	Sheriff	4
Judge Thatcher	326	Jim	90	Sally Rogers	2

Σ 21,631

er, commit speech disturbances, as Table 19.1 shows. The narrative significance of the character seems to be the primary determinant of the distribution of speech disturbances amongst the story characters. With the exception
of the anonymous playmate, the characters listed in Table 19.1 are among
the chief characters in the narrative. And those leading the list in Table
19.1—Tom, Huck, Aunt Polly, and Becky—are certainly the leading actors
in the story. Tom, of course, is the paramount figure in both regards. Yet
character significance is clearly not the exclusive determinant of whether his
or her dialogue contains speech disturbances. This is shown by the fact that
as "insignificant" a character as "an anonymous playmate" commits a
speech disturbance, although Injun Joe does not. The playmate's
disturbance[7] underscores the emotionality of the recalled premonition of
Tom's death as well as indicating that the boys' "deaths" affected their
playmates as well as Mrs. Harper and Aunt Polly. Disturbances in Injun Joe's
speech would not be consistent with his uncomplicated and unconflicted
emotional makeup.

Tom commits the greatest number of speech disturbances and also has
the largest share of the dialogue. This observation raises the question as to
whether the distribution of the speech disturbances amongst the characters
was significantly influenced by the sheer quantitative variations in the
number of words of dialogue allotted by Twain to the various characters. A
comparison of the data of Table 19.1 and the dialogue word counts (see
Footnote 5) shows clearly that this was not the case.

These considerations of the manner in which Twain distributed speech
disturbances among his story characters again indicates the artistic dimension
to his use of this attribute of speech.

Speech Disturbances: Originals or Revisions?

A comparison of the published *Tom Sawyer* (Twain, 1982a) with the holograph manuscript of it (Twain, 1982b) yields an astonishing finding: *Twain
wrote 49 of the 50 speech disturbances in Tom Sawyer in his free-flowing first draft;
only 1 disturbance being directly "revised into" the text.*[8] This finding is striking

---

[7]Chapter 17 opens with the narration of the sad anticipation of the morrow's funeral for
Tom, Joe Harper, and Huck (who are cavorting on Jackson's Island). The account in Twain
(1982a) includes the following passage:

Then quite a group of boys and girls,—playmates of Tom's and Joe's—came by, and
stood looking over the poling [schoolyard fence] and talking in reverent tones of how
Tom did so-and-so, the last time they saw him . . . and each speaker . . . added something like . . . and he smiled just this way—and then something seemed to go all over
me, *like—awful*, you know—and I never thought what it meant, of course, but I can see
now! [italics added to mark the Sentence Incompletion] (pp. 129–130)

[8]On one occasion, Twain did make an immediate revision of several lines of his manuscript
in which revision he included a speech disturbance (Twain, 1982b, p. 286). I regarded this as an
"original" not a "revised-in" disturbance, for it itself was not a revision.

testimony to the facile, natural control Twain had over this aspect of speech. It is especially impressive that every single speech disturbance in the two passages where they are extremely frequent was an "original." The two passages in question were Tom's attempt to recall for Mary the Beatitudes and the "dream" he lied to Aunt Polly (Twain, 1982a, pp. 26–27 and 134–136, respectively). In the former, there are 19 speech disturbances in 11 printed lines. (Figure 19.2a and 19.2b presents the holograph and printed versions of this passage.) In the second passage, there are 10 disturbances in 35 printed lines.

The single exception to the "originality" of writing the speech disturbances is instructive. In chapter 7, right after Tom and Becky become engaged, Tom unintentionally let's Becky know that she is not the first—he and Amy had been engaged before. Tom tries to console her by saying, "Becky, I—I don't care for anybody but you" (Twain, 1982a, p. 62). The original holograph version of this statement is shown in Fig. 19.3. There you can see that Twain committed a pen slip. He omitted his intended repetition of *I* (clearly indicated by the dash in "I—") and unintentionally anticipatorily started to write *don't*. Twain was so vigilant to the writing of speech disturbances, however, that he cut *don't* off with the written *do . . .* , tried to immediately blot away the pen slip, and inserted the originally intended repetition of *I*. Twain not only wrote all but one of the speech disturbances in "the original" but was so alert to his pen slip that he "revised-in" the one exception before the ink had dried. We can conclude that the speech disturbances of *Tom Sawyer* were on the tip of Twain's tongue and his pen when he wrote the original manuscript draft. The disturbances came forth with remarkable facility.

Twain's Usage of Speech Disturbances: Their Psychological Contexts

We determined the psychological contexts of the speech disturbances in two ways. First, we accepted as definitive all explicit references and/or allusions by Twain to the psychological state of the speaker at the time of his or her utterance containing a speech disturbance. Examples of explicit references are found in the text for Speech Disturbance 1 by Aunt Polly (see Table 19.2) when Twain (1982a) wrote, "She did not finish [the sentence] . . . *she needed breath* [italics added]" (p. 1), and in that for Speech Disturbance 22 by the schoolteacher when Twain wrote, "The master's *pulse stood still*, and he stared *helplessly* [italics added]" (p. 53). Examples of allusions by Twain are found in the text for Speech Disturbances 3–21 by Tom. I regarded the statements by Tom "Oh I don't know what it is!" (p. 27, line 9) and "Why don't you tell me, Mary?—what do you want to be so mean, for?" (p. 27, lines 13 and 14) as allusions to a state of helplessness and being upset.

Secondly, when Twain did not define the psychological state I inferred it from the immediate context. Thus, I inferred that Mrs. Harper and Aunt Polly left their sentence incomplete in Speech Disturbances 32 and 33 because they were 'conflicted over uttering unspeakable grievous thoughts.' Table 19.2 presents Twain's references and my inferences about the psychological states for the various disturbances. With the information in the table, the reader can locate each disturbance and form his own judgment about the psychological state of the speaker.

The following tabulation summarizes the information of immediate interest in Table 19.2.

Psychological state of speaker	N speech disturbances
Emotional neutrality	1
Struggle at recall	18[a]
Struggle at recall, helpless, upset	12[b]
"Anxious": Helpless, uncertain, conflicted, anxious, frightened, fearful	18
Melancholic	1
	50

[a]Includes that portion of Tom's struggle to recall Bible verse before Twain's allusion to Tom's feeling helpless and upset, Tom's feigned struggle to recall "dream," and Joe Harper's effort at recall.

[b]Includes that portion of Tom's struggle to recall Bible verse after Twain's allusion to Tom's feeling helpless and upset.

As the summary shows, Twain had 49 of the 50 speech disturbances occurring under psychological conditions of tension. And these were states of tension that were on the negative side, either outrightly so, or negatively tinged. In no instance was a disturbance associated with a positive emotion. Two general psychological states accounted for the vast majority of the disturbances: a struggle to recall (real or feigned) and an "anxious" condition. These results are similar to our findings that anxiety and conflict are significantly, but not perfectly, correlated with the everyday disturbances in the spontaneous speech of psychotherapy or investigative interviews. Moreover, all the adults and children in *Tom Sawyer*, except for Joe Harper, who did commit speech disturbances, did so at some point when "anxious." This

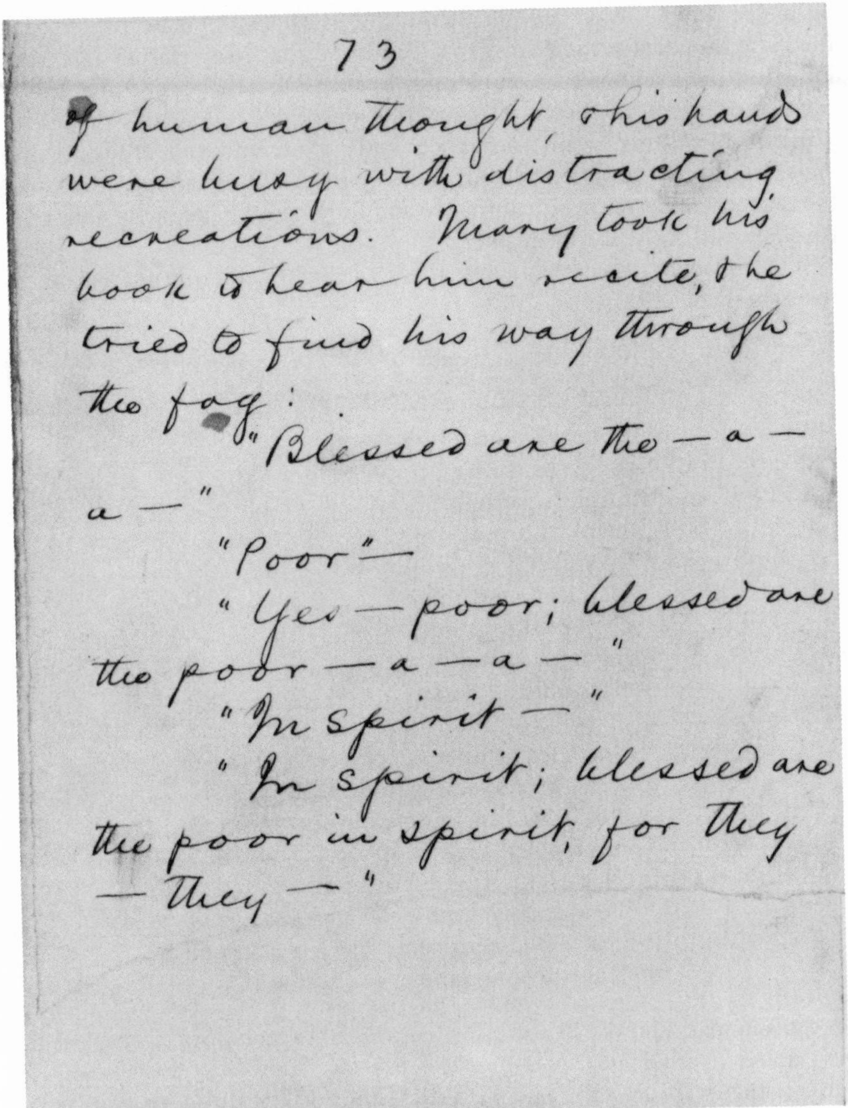

73

of human thought, & his hands
were busy with distracting
recreations. Mary took his
book to hear him recite, & he
tried to find his way through
the fog:
     "Blessed are the — a —
a — "
          "Poor" —
          "Yes — poor; blessed are
the poor — a — a — "
          "In spirit — "
          "In spirit; blessed are
the poor in spirit, for they
— They — "

FIG. 19.2a.   Holograph manuscript version of Tom's struggle to recall Bible
verses (Twain, 1982b).

74

"*Theirs* — "

"For *theirs*. Blessed are the poor in spirit, for *theirs*, is the kingdom of heaven. Blessed are they that mourn, for they — they — "

"*Sh* — "

"For they — a — "

"*S, H, A* — "

"For they S, H — Oh I don't know what it is!"

"*Shall*!"

"Oh, shall! for they shall — for they shall — a — a — shall mourn — a — a — blessed are they that shall — they that — a — they that shall mourn, for they shall — a — shall *what*? Why don't you tell me, Mary? — what do you want to be so mean, for?"

Then Tom girded up his loins,
so to speak, and went to work to
"get his verses." Sid had learned
his lesson days before. Tom bent all his energies to the memorizing
of five verses; and he chose part of the Sermon on the Mount because
he could find no verses that were shorter. At the end of half an hour
Tom had a vague general idea of his lesson, but no more, for his mind
was traversing the whole field of human thought, and his hands were
busy with distracting recreations. Mary took his book to hear him
recite, and he tried to find his way through the fog:
"Blessed are the—ⓐ-ⓐ—"
"Poor—"
"Yes—poor; blessed are the poor—ⓐ-ⓐ—"
"In spirit—"
"In spirit; blessed are the poor in spirit, for they⊣they—"
"Theirs—"
"For theirs. Blessed are the poor in spirit, for theirs—is the kingdom
of heaven. Blessed are they that mourn, for they⊣they—"
"Sh—"
"For they—ⓐ—"
"S, H, A—" *SC*
"For they S, H⊣Oh I don't know what it is!"
"Shall!"
"Oh, shall! for they shall⊣for they shall—ⓐ-ⓐ—shall mourn—
ⓐ-ⓐ—blessed are they that shall⊣they that—ⓐ—they that shall
mourn, for they shall⊣ⓐ—shall what? Why don't you tell me,
Mary!—what do you want to be so mean, for?"

FIG. 19.2b.   Printed version of Tom's struggle to recall Bible verses. Adapted from Twain (1982a, pp. 26–27). a = ah; SC = Sentence change; R =
Repetition; Inc = Sentence incompletion (See Table 9.1, chapter 9).

generality, too, is similar to our research findings that the positive anxiety-
speech disturbance relationship seems to be a very general one in the
population.

Twain's prominent use of speech disturbances to depict the struggle to
recall merits some discussion. We know that at times in our interviews,
patients and subjects tried to recall repressed material and committed speech
disturbances in the process. We regarded such disturbances as the result of
the anxiety and conflict aroused in that emergence into awareness of unconscious material. The "struggles to recall" depicted by Twain were of a
different nature, however. Tom's struggle to recall the Beatitudes was an
effort to remember what he had never really learned. Joe Harper's effort to
recall a line from *Robin Hood* was of the same nature. Tom's feigned struggle
to recall a supposedly "real" dream approaches the feigned recall of the
repressed but is not really in that category. There is nothing in "the dream"
that could be regarded as conflicted and thus the target of repression. Apparently, Twain believed that the struggle to recall simply forgotten, benign
material involved disrupted trains of thought and that these would be manifested in hesitant, disrupted sentences. And apparently he believed that
such a struggle could have negative emotional repercussions if it spelled

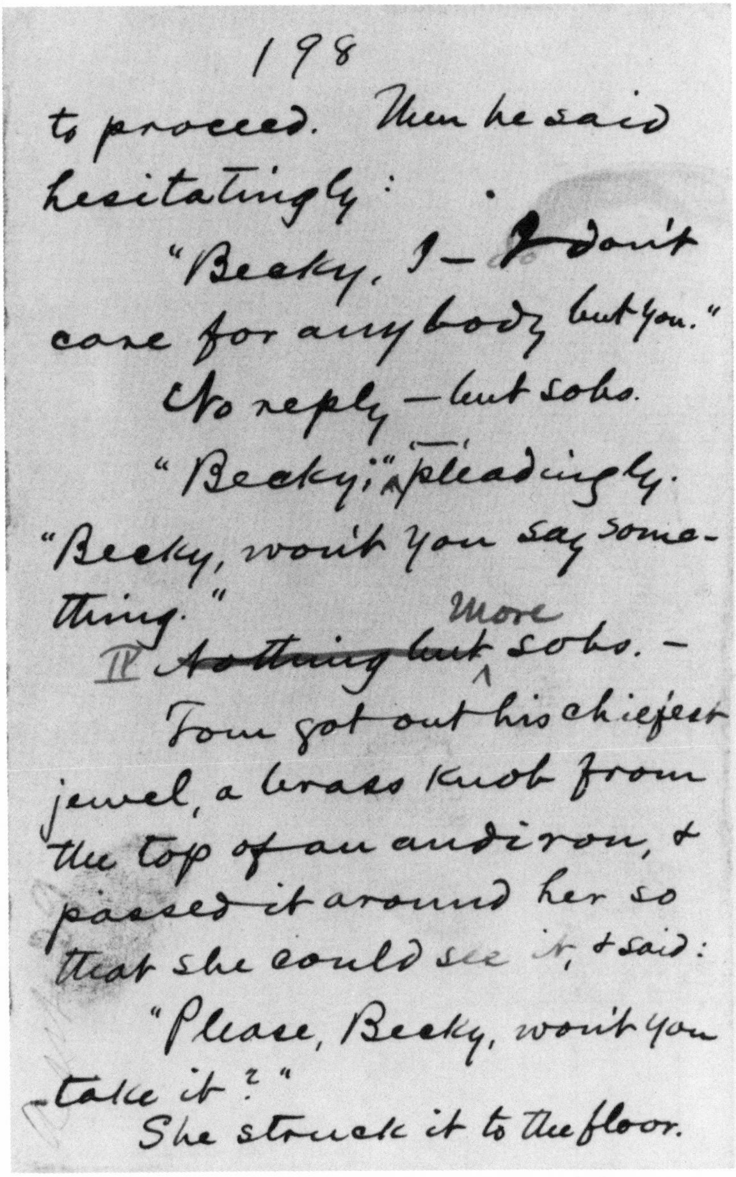

198

to proceed. Then he said
hesitatingly:

"Becky, I— I don't
care for anybody but you."

No reply—but sobs.

"Becky," pleadingly.

"Becky, won't you say something."

¶ ~~Nothing but~~ More sobs.—

Tom got out his chiefest
jewel, a brass knob from
the top of an andiron, &
passed it around her so
that she could see it, & said:

"Please, Becky, won't you
take it?"

She struck it to the floor.

FIG. 19.3. Illustration of the only speech disturbance in *Tom Sawyer* resulting from a revision (Twain, 1982b).

TABLE 19.2
The Psychological States of Speakers When Committing Speech Disturbances

Speech Disturbance Number	Location in Text[a]	Speaker	Psychological State Identified by Twain[b]	Speech Disturbance Category and Frequency[c]	Psychological State Inferred by This Author from Context
1	1.21	Aunt Polly	Saving her breath. (Emotionally neutral)	Inc 1	
2	15.1	Tom		SC 1	Feigned conflict
3–21	26.24–27.13	Tom	Struggle to recall Bible verses that he never learned. Helpless, upset	Ah 11, SC 1, R 6, Inc 1	
22	53.13	School-teacher	Helpless, pulse affected	R 1	
23	60.9	Tom		Inc 1	Uncertain, conflicted
24	60.13	Becky		St 1	Anxious
25	60.17	Becky		St 1	Anxious, conflicted
26	61.15	Tom	Confused, uncertain	Inc 1	
27	62.14	Tom	Uncertain	R 1	
28	66.38	Joe Harper	Struggle to recall	R 1	
29	81.18	Tom	Frightened	R 1	Uncertain, frightened
30	82.14	Huck		R 1	

			Fearful, hopeless			
31	89.1	Muff Potter	Fearful, hopeless	Inc	1	
32	116.23	Mrs. Harper		Inc	1	Conflicted over unspeakable grievous thoughts
33	116.31	Aunt Polly		Inc	1	
34	130.7	Play-mate		Inc	1	Conflicted over the unspeakable
35	133.29	Tom		SC	1	Uncertain, conflicted
36–45	135.1–135.37	Tom		SC / R	3 / 7	Feigned struggle to recall a "real" dream.
46	172.6	Tom		R	1	Conflicted
47	179.2	Huck		SC	1	Conflicted
48	228.10	Becky		Inc	1	Conflicted over unspeakable thought
49	252.8	Aunt Polly	Uncertain	SC	1	
50	257.1	Huck	Melancholic	SC	1	
				Total	50	

[a] Page number and line of Twain (1982a). For example, 1.21 is reference to page 1, line 21.
[b] Identified by explicit words or by obvious allusion.
[c] Categories: Ah (rendered *a* by Twain), SC (Sentence change), R (Repetition), Inc (Sentence incompletion), St (Stutter, Stammer), see chapter 9, Table 9-1.

failure, as in Tom's inability to recall the Bible verses, but would not have them if the struggle was successful, as in Tom's ability to "recall" the entire "dream" about the mournful meeting of Aunt Polly and the others on the eve of the "funeral" of Tom, Joe Harper, and Huck. In our research, we never seriously entertained the possibility of such an anxiety-free and conflict-free struggle to recall as Twain apparently believed could occur. I am not ready to simply dismiss Twain's implicit claim on this point, for I have developed too high a regard for his knowledge of human behavior. Twain's emphasis on the role of a relatively emotionally neutral, cognitive struggle to recall, as well as on the role of anxiety and conflict, in the production of speech disturbances is a subject deserving careful investigation. Is there such a thing as a relatively neutral struggle to recall? Do the speech disruptions occurring in such a presumed struggle reflect merely neutral disrupted trains of thoughts, or do they reflect the anxiety and conflict aroused by the occurrence of disrupted trains of thoughts? We need empirical answers to these questions.

While awaiting those answers, we can be sure that Twain did deliberately use speech disturbances to depict the struggle to recall. This is clear from the sheer quantity of them in the two episodes involving Tom mentioned earlier. In addition, a close examination of Tom's "dream" report shows that Twain used speech disturbances *with precision* to depict the course of Tom's feigned struggle to recall. Tom's efforts to recapture the "dream" take some time, involving 372 words of dialogue by him that are spread over nearly three pages of text (Twain 1982a, 134.17–136.19). This recall procedes in two stages. In the first, Tom's recall is very sluggish and he commits 7 disturbances while uttering but 131 words. Suddenly his memory clears: "Oh, it's all getting just as bright as day now" (p. 135.22). Thereafter, as his memory improves markedly, Tom's speech becomes notably more fluent. Now he nearly doubles his verbal output to 241 words but commits only 3 speech disturbances. And as Tom's memory becomes perfect, his speech becomes flawless. Again, we can see the artistic deftness with which Twain pens speech disturbances.

One other finding emerges from a study of the episodes involving a struggle to recall: Only here does Twain put "ahs" in the mouth of a speaker. All the "ahs" in the entire text are committed by Tom when he struggles to recall his poorly learned Bible verses. At no time does any speaker say "ah" when "anxious" or conflicted. Yet 18 of the 39 Non-ah disturbances are committed by speakers when in a state of anxiety, unaffected by a struggle to recall. (And Tom commits 5 more of them when he feels helpless and upset while trying to recall his verses.) *Thus, Twain makes a clear distinction between "ah" and the Non-ah disturbances that is in agreement with our own research findings that "ah" and the Non-ah disturbances follow different psychological rules.* I find this agreement most striking.

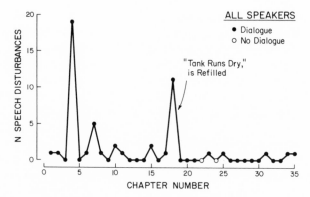

FIG. 19.4. Total speech disturbances by all speakers in successive chapters of *Tom Sawyer* (Twain, 1982a).

Variation in Speech Disturbances in the Course of the Narrative

Most of the speech disturbances in *Tom Sawyer* occur in the first 18 of the 35 chapters. Thus Fig. 19.4 shows that there is a sustained decrement in the frequency of disturbances following chapter 18, with 45 of the 50 disturbances occurring before and 5 after that point. Figure 19.5 shows that this change is due to the changing frequency of disturbances in Tom's dialogue. The two peaks in both graphs represent the effects of Tom's struggle to recall his Bible verses and his feigned struggle to recall the "dream," respectively.

Our study of *Tom Sawyer* had reached this point many years ago. At that time I speculated as to why the marked decrease in speech disturbance frequency occurred in the second half of the book. My speculations focused on possible changes in the psychology of Tom that Twain was portraying by

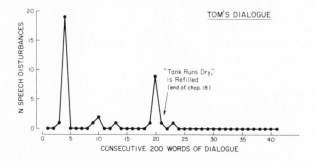

FIG. 19.5. Number of speech disturbances by Tom in successive 200 word segments of his dialogue in *Tom Sawyer* (Twain, 1982a).

the speech disturbance decrement. Thus, I theorized that Twain was showing indirectly the effect on Tom of his decision not to lie again after telling
the "dream lie" to Aunt Polly in chapter 18, as well as the related effect of a
possible decrease in Tom's battle with his conscience, which played an
important role in the first half of the book. Because I was unconvinced by my
own speculations I placed the entire study on the shelf, uncertain as to
whether I would ever be able to solve this puzzle. Maybe I have done so
now.

A few years ago I read Twain's autobiography (Twain, 1917/1959a).
There I found Twain's description of the lesson he learned while writing
Tom Sawyer. On page 400 of the original manuscript, he said his "tank ran
dry": *he* was writing the story instead of the story writing itself. So, he
claimed, he laid the manuscript aside for 2 years during which he worked on
other writings. When he returned to *Tom Sawyer,* the story readily flowed
out: "The tank had refilled." (Apparently, the 'tank refilled' in a few
months.[9]) I could hardly wait to consult the manuscript (Twain, 1982b) to
see if the tank had run dry and had been refilled at the end of chapter 18. *It
had!* The point at issue occurs in the next to last paragraph of chapter 18, in
the second line of p. 143 (Twain, 1982a). Although possible, it seems improbable that the timing of this significant event in the creation of *Tom
Sawyer* and the decrement in speech disturbance frequency was merely coin-
cidental. The timing suggested that a change in Twain's psychology after
the interruption, rather than one in Tom, might account for the concurrent
decrease in speech disturbances.

How might Twain have changed? Under the mistaken impression that the
interruption lasted 2 years, as Twain stated in his autobiography, I hypothesized that when he returned to the manuscript he might have worked under
a sense of urgency to finish it, a pressure that didn't exist during the writing
of the first half of the story. In turn, he might have been slightly less
attentive in his writing, causing him to take less care in including speech
disturbances in the dialogue of the second half of the tale. As an independent test of this hypothesis, I compared the frequency with which Twain
revised the manuscript before and after the interruption. I assumed that a
sense of urgency to finish the manuscript would cause him to make fewer
revisions, especially "immediate" revisions made during the original writing
in contrast to revisions made in later rereading of the entire manuscript.
(Variations in ink and pen points make this distinction between "immediate" and "later" revisions a relatively easy one. See Fig. 19.1a, 19.2a, and
19.3.)

---

[9]The essential point, but not the specifics, of Twain's recollection of this experience is
correct. He interrupted his writing of *Tom Sawyer* with the annotation on the back of manuscript
page 500, "condemn rest of chapter." However, the duration of the interruption seems to have
been a matter of months, not of 2 years (see Baender, 1982, pp. xii–xiii).

RESULTS AND DISCUSSION 307

TABLE 19.3
Quantitative Aspects of 20 Percent Sample of Holograph Manuscript Pages of *Tom Sawyer*

	Complete Text of ms Pages		Dialogue of ms Pages	
	Ms Pages Before Tank Ran Dry	Ms Pages After Tank Refilled	Ms Pages Before Tank Ran Dry	Ms Pages After Tank Refilled
N pages	93	69	48	42
Σ words	7957	6088	2312	2225
M Revision Index/page[a]	18	20	14	14
% Words dialogue			29	36

$$\text{[a]Revision Index/page} = \frac{N \text{ lines text revised on page}}{N \text{ words on page}} \times 1000.$$

I made two such comparisons of immediate revisions in samples of every fifth page in the holograph manuscript (Twain, 1982b). The first comparison was based on the complete text on those sampled pages. The second comparison was based only on the dialogue contained on those sampled pages. Table 19.3 contains the results. Twain made immediate revisions equally often before his "tank ran dry" and after it was refilled. Our initial hypothesis for the coincidence of the interruption in the writing of *Tom Sawyer* and the decrement in speech disturbances is not substantiated.

What other change in Twain might have occurred during the interruption? I have one suggestion: Twain might have returned to the manuscript with a different plan for *Tom Sawyer* than he had beforehand. One meets the observation about *Tom Sawyer* that it is largely an account of unrelated escapades in the life of its hero, lacking in a coherent, unifying plot (Elliott, 1959, p. 223; Warfel, 1965, p. xii).[10] I believe that characterization of the story is especially true of those pages written before Twain's interruption. There he seems to be exclusively interested in thinly fictionalizing recollections of his childhood days in Hannibal: There is room for depicting such isolated episodes as Tom's playing hooky, stealing sugar, picking a fight with a "new boy" in town, changing white-washing a fence from a punishment into an entrepreneurial achievement, releasing pinchbugs in church, courting the "new girl" in town, running-off to play pirates on Jackson Island, etc. And

---

[10]*Tom Sawyer* was Twain's first independently attempted novel. His earlier, first novel, *The Gilded Age* (Twain, 1873) was a collaborative attempt with Charles Dudley Warner. Twain wrote the dialogue; Warner the plot. Kaplan (1966) includes relevant comments on Twain's handling of plot in *Tom Sawyer*. He says, "[Twain] began it with no clear idea of where it would end" (p. 178). And he refers to "Clemens' characteristic method of improvising from chapter to chapter" (p. 179).

there is room for such episodes, peppered with speech disturbances, as trying to memorize his verses for Sunday School and faking a dream recall as he lies to Aunt Polly to relieve his sense of guilt and raise her spirits. Although still apt, that characterization of the story is less appropriate for the part Twain wrote after he returned, replenished. Nearly all the chapters to follow are more or less loosely entwined on a story line involving Tom, Huck, and Injun Joe. Injun Joe and the graveyard murder appear in chapters 9, 10, and 11. They lie fallow until Twain resurrects them in chapter 22. Thereafter, the "Injun Joe" theme plays a role in every chapter until the final chapter 35. With Twain's return to his manuscript he changed *Tom Sawyer* from a recounting of escapades unrelated by a story line into a more coherent tale of adventurous action. He introduced a narrative line that culminated in the fated death of Injun Joe and the triumph of Tom and Huck in finding the hidden treasure once possessed by Injun Joe. There was no place in the second half of the story for Tom to be involved with real and feigned struggles with a faulty memory, events that caused the majority of the speech disturbances in the book.

I offer the preceding hypothesis about the effect of Twain's interruption on the composition of *Tom Sawyer* very tentatively; I am neither a literary critic, nor a learned scholar of Twain's works, including *Tom Sawyer*.

SUMMARY

Mark Twain, an acknowledged master of speech portrayal, used our speech disturbances in the dialogue of *Tom Sawyer*. Thus, he informs us that our categories were used in Southwestern America nearly 150 years ago. All but one speech disturbance was an "original." Only one was revised-in, and that was done instantaneously.

Twain employed the speech disturbances to create artistic effects, not to imitate verbatim typescripts of tape recordings. Thus, he used them to highlight his story characters and to achieve special narrative effects.

All but one of the speech disturbances in *Tom Sawyer* occurred when the speaker was under "negative" psychological tension. In Twain's hand, there were two psychological states predominating the production of speech disturbances: a real or feigned struggle to recall and a variety of "anxious" conditions. "Ahs" only occurred in the struggle to recall, never when a speaker was "anxious." But a very sizable proportion of the Non-ah disturbances were associated with anxiety and conflict. Twain's usage of "ah" and the Non-ah categories parallels remarkably our research findings that "ah" and Non-ah disturbances are functionally different. The cooccurrence of Non-ah disturbances and "anxiety" among various adults and children in *Tom Sawyer* is in agreement with our research findings of great generality of the positive relationship between Non-ah disturbances and anxiety-conflict amongst our various speakers in psychotherapy and investigative interviews.

A prominent, sustained decrement in speech disturbances in Tom's dialogue occurs after chapter 18. Speculations focused on possible changes in Tom's psychology do not result in convincing explanations for the decrement. The decrement coincides with the interruption in Twain's creation of the story when his "tank ran dry." I tentatively suggest that Twain's story plan changed, after his tank refilled, in such a way as to render pointless episodes of Tom's struggle with his memory, and thus to remove one of the major conditions for speech disturbances in *Tom Sawyer*.

The results of this study of the dialogue created by an *artistic* genius adds to the generality and empirical basis provided by our *scientific* investigations of the spontaneous dialogues of real people.

Dialect, Stress, and Identity Feelings

20

George F. Mahl
Yale University

Arthur S. Bender, M.D.
University of Virginia Medical School

> *All the answers that occurred to him came forward in slang, and a feeling for the proprieties suggested to him that he speak French, but everyone knows that in trying moments it is the mother tongue that prevails.*
>
> —Jean Genet, 1943/1963, p. 288

> *"Come here to me you," she told him from the register, "I want to show you funny theeng." Her English had no Spanish accent unless she were under emotional stress; he should have taken warning from that. "A funny theeng—look!"*
>
> —Nelson Algren, 1956/1984, p. 58

> *"I can't tell if that play's any good or not. I can't tell any more, anyway." Whenever he was unsure, his Southern accent became more noticeable.*
>
> —James Baldwin, 1960, p. 286

So far in this section of the book we have been concerned with the psychology of an *extralinguistic* attribute of speech—the everyday disturbances in it. We did propose in chapter 8, however, that under certain conditions *linguistic* elements of speech might also function as expressive behavior, that is, they too might reflect nonlinguistic, psychological states of the speaker. We believe the phonemes of dialect might be among such linguistic elements. Here we report a study in which we explored this possibility, trying to gain experimental control of phenomena, which we subsequently discovered are common knowledge to creative writers.

THE PROBLEM

The question of the effect of stress and a sense of personal identity on dialect usage arose out of an observation made during a psychoanalytic society scientific meeting. A well-known English male psychoanalyst was speaking in America, where he was presenting a "new viewpoint." At the beginning his dialect was strongly British, but as he progressed his "accent" became less noticeable.

We drew several inferences from this incident. First, we hypothesized that his strong dialect at the beginning of the lecture resulted from stress he might have felt during the early part of his speech: He was addressing strangers and they might reject his new ideas. We postulated that as he continued the speaker felt less stress and consequently the strength of his British dialect decreased. We also hypothesized that the initially strong dialect was also partly a result of a transitory intensification of the speaker's already strong identity as an Englishman. We wished to see if the "hunches" about the Englishman could be confirmed experimentally.

Specifically, we tested two basic hypotheses in the present experiment: (1) induction of stress will cause an increase in the degree of regional dialect spoken; and (2) individuals who show a greater dialect increase will manifest stronger feelings of identity with their native region.

METHOD

Subjects

The subjects were upperclassmen enrolled in Yale College. Only students whose home was in the Boston, Massachusetts metropolitan district or the Charleston, South Carolina and Atlanta, Georgia areas were considered. Students who listed either of the aforementioned locations with the college as their official residence were sent questionnaires. These questionnaires contained items of a biographical nature such as hometown, length of time lived there, and time spent in other geographical locations. Items also asked for volunteers for an experiment. Students were chosen from Boston, Atlanta, and Charleston because these areas are well represented at Yale and because the dialects spoken there are easily distinguishable from the "general American" dialect that predominates at Yale.

Twenty subjects participated in the experiment. They were obtained at random from the number volunteering to participate in the study. Ten subjects came from the Boston metropolitan district, whereas the other ten were from the Charleston or Atlanta area. Both the Bostonian and Southern subjects were assigned randomly to control and experimental groups.

Procedure

The experiment was described to the subject, on his arrival at the interview room, as a test in reading comprehension. He was told that the experimenter was interested in his comprehension of written material when read silently and when read aloud. Thus, we avoided any focusing of attention on the subject's dialect. Everything said during the interview was tape-recorded. These recordings were later used for measuring both dialects and the subject's identity feelings.

Next, the subject was told that he would be given stories to read, some of which would be read silently, others aloud; and that after each reading of the story, he would be given a question to answer on the content of the story.

Practice Story

After those instructions, the experimenter gave a practice story to the subject and asked him to read it silently. This story contained four, double-spaced typed pages. Following the silent reading, the subject was handed a question on the content of the story and asked to write out his answer. Upon completing his answer, the subject was given the same story to read, but this time he was instructed to read it aloud to the experimenter. After reading the story aloud, the subject was given the same question to answer. After completing his answer, the subject was asked to read the story aloud, again, to the experimenter and was then given another question to answer on the content of the story.

Readings of this story were not used to analyze dialect. Rather the practice readings served to familiarize the subject with the act of reading aloud under these circumstances, thus hopefully reducing initial feelings of stress caused by the surroundings.

Test Story

After finishing his answer to the final question about the practice story, the subject was given the test story (see Appendix) to read silently. Upon completion, he was given a question to answer on the content of the story. Then he read it aloud. Following this reading, the subject was given the same question to answer, as before.

Induction of Stress

After writing his answer, the subject returned the question sheet. The experimenter, a fellow upperclassman, then read carefully both this answer and the answer submitted after the silent reading. Then he said to the subject, "You have gained absolutely nothing from reading the story a second time. You have added no new information. In fact you have omitted some details in your second answer. Everyone else, under the same conditions, added a great deal more information after the second reading." Because most college students take pride in their ability to comprehend written material, it was expected that criticism of their comprehending ability would stress the subjects. After inducing stress, the experimenter asked the subject to read the story aloud for the second time, requesting him to "do much better" in answering the question following the reading.

Stress was induced only in the experimental subjects. The control subjects proceeded with the second reading of the test story aloud without interruption.

After the second reading aloud, both the control and the experimental subjects were given the same question to answer for the third time. The experimenter then left the room to change the recording tape.

Removal of Stress

Stress was removed when the experimenter returned to the interviewing room and explained the nature of the experiment and his reasons for reprimanding the subject. He told the subject he would have been reprimanded for his lack of comprehension regardless of the completeness of his answers, and that the reprimands in no way reflected his comprehension ability. The experimenter explained that by his disapproval he had attempted to stress the subject, because the experiment dealt with the effect of stress on dialect rather than the subject's ability to comprehend written material.

Determination of Stress Feelings

Following rhe removal of stress, an indication of the subject's feelings of stress was gained by the self-report method. The subject was handed a short questionnaire requesting indications of the relative amounts of "stress and nervousness" felt by the subject during the four times he read the two stories aloud. The method used to score these indications is presented later.

Determination of Identity Feelings

Following administration of the stress questionnaire, the experimenter said he wanted to discuss with the subject his feelings of identification with the South (Boston area) in order to understand more fully the effect of stress on dialect. The discussion did not take the form of a rigidly ordered interview. Rather, the subject was allowed to talk freely around several topics dealing with his identity. These topics were: (1) his length of residence in the South (Boston area), (2) his parents' length of residence in the South (Boston area), (3) whether he prefers dating girls from the South (Boston area), (4) whether he has an image of himself as a Southerner (Bostonian), and (5) whether he feels personally identified with the South (Boston area). As soon as the experimenter felt enough had been said about a particular topic, a new one was introduced. Following the discussion, the subject was asked to avoid talking about the experiment with his friends, in order to prevent contamination of future subjects. This concluded the interview.

Scoring

In the present experiment three aspects of the subject's behavior were measured: (1) the amount of stress felt during successive readings of the stories, (2) the amount of dialect shown by the subjects during each reading aloud of the test story, and (3) the subject's feelings of identification as a member of a regional group.

Stress Scores

To indicate the amount of stress felt during the reading of the stories aloud, the subject was asked to rank the readings from one, least stressed, to four, most stressed. If the subject felt equally stressed or unstressed in two or more readings, he was instructed to indicate this equality by using the same number. In this experiment, only the subject's stress feelings in the first and second readings aloud of the test story were of consequence. Simple subtraction determined the stress difference between these two readings. Questionnaires were administered to both experimental and control groups in order to determine whether the prolonged reading of stories aloud had a stressing effect.

Dialect Scores

In order to measure dialect and dialect change, a number of key words were woven into the text of the test story. These key words were selected because they contained features of the Boston and Southern dialects most easily distinguishable from the dialect that predominates in the Yale community. Although the "Yale dialect" is not homogenous, it is possible to recognize distinctly Southern or distinctly Bostonian sounds among the students. These distinct sounds were used to determine degree of dialect.

Key words appearing in the test story were phonemically transcribed according to the methods used by Francis (1958). The phonemicization of the key words was done with reference to dialect atlases. In all cases the phonemic form chosen was the one used by well-educated Bostonians or Southerners. Table 20.1 contains these forms. The authors "took a course" with an advanced graduate student in linguistics to learn the phonemics involved.[1] They did the dialect scoring in the following manner.

After deciding on a phonemic form for each word, a phonemic judgment was made of each of these words as the subject read them in the story. If the

---

[1] We express our appreciation and indebtedness to A. Richard Diebold for his careful, patient linguistic instruction and advice.

subject's pronunciation corresponded to the Southern (or Bostonian) phonemic form, the word was given a "plus" score. The total dialect score for each reading was the sum of these "plus" scores.

In order to prevent contamination of the dialect scores, a coding system was used. All readings of the story were copied onto new tapes in a coded order unknown to the scorers. The coding prevented them from knowing either the subject who was reading or the condition under which the story was being read.

To facilitate the scoring of intrasubject differences, two tape recorders were used. The coded tapes were divided into two groups, A and B. The stories, although randomized both as to control and experimental subjects and first and second readings, were arranged so that the first story on tape A was read by the same subject who read the first story on tape B, etc. This arrangement of stories permitted listening to both readings in a paired comparison fashion, thus facilitating the direct comparison of words.

One author, the experimenter (A.S.B.) was one judge; the other author (G.F.M.) was the independent judge. The latter judge had no previous contact with the subjects and could not be influenced by previous knowledge of either the reader or the conditions under which the story was read.

Identity Scores

Each "identity" topic introduced during the interview following the readings attempted to elicit a measurable aspect of the subject's conscious identification feelings. Every answer to the questions was assigned a score, with the highest scores assigned to the answers showing the strongest identification feelings. Table 20.2 illustrates the rating scales used. Answers to the two final topics of self-image and identification feelings were given double weight in the scoring because they were felt to be the best indicators of conscious identification feelings.

RESULTS

Reliability of Dialect Scoring

In order to determine the reliability of dialect scoring, the experimenter and the independent judge both scored every reading of the test story. Interscorer correlations for each measure presented in the results are given in Table 20.3.

All correlations are significant with the exception of the difference score calculated for the Bostonians. The difference score is the score obtained by subtracting the number of key words pronounced in the dialect during the

TABLE 20.1
Test Words Used to Measure Dialect

Key Word	Dialect	Phonemic Transcription	Key Word	Dialect	Phonemic Transcription
afternoon^r	Bo	/aftɛ(h)'nuwn/B/æf.../s	crop	Bo	/krɔp/
air^r	Bo	/ɛh/	dearer^r	Bo	/'diːrə/B/dɛhrə/s
aunt	B	/ant/	dinner^r	Bo	/'dinə/B/'dinə ~ dinə/s
bait	S	/beht ~ beyt/	dog	S	/dɔhg/
barn^r	Bo	/baːn ~ bahn/B/bahn/s	drain	S	/drehn/
bath	Bo	/baθ/B/bæ·θ ~ bæhθ/s	due	S	/dyuw/
bear^r	Bo	/beh/	ear^r	Bo	/ih/B/eh/s
beard^r	Bo	/bihd/	eight	S	/eh/
beer^r	Bo	/bih/	fair^r	Bo	/feh/
because	Bo	/bɪ'kɔz/B/bɪ'kɔz/s	father^r	Bo	/'fadə/B/'fadə(h)/s
bird^r	Bo	/bəːd ~ bəhd/B/bəhd/s	fear^r	Bo	/fih/B/feh/s
boil	S	/bɔhl/	fire^r	Bo	/'fayh ~ fay-ə/B/fayhə/s
boat	S	/boht ~ bowt/	flour^r	Bo	/flaw-ə/
boor^r	Bo	/bɔh/B/buh ~ boh/s	fog	Bo	/fəg/B/faːg ~ fɔːg/s
boot	S	/but/	forty^r	Bo	/'fɔhtiy ~ fɔːtiy/B/fɔːtiy/s
bore^r	Bo	/bɔh/	four^r	Bo	/fɔːh ~ fɔː/B/foh/s
bout	S	/bæwt/	fourteen^r	Bo	/foh'tiyn ~ fɔːitiyn/
boy	S	/bɔy/	glass	Bo	/glas/B/glæːs ~ glæhs/s
burr^r	Bo	/bəː ~ bəh/B/bəh/s	greasy	S	/griyziy/
calm	S	/kæhm/	haunted	Bo	/'hɔːntid/B/'hɔːntid/s
careless^r	Bo	/'kɛhlɪs/	hoarse^r	Bo	/hohs/
caught	B	/kɔːt/	horse^r	Bo	/hɔhs/

316

Word	Dialect	Phonemic transcription
coop	S	/kup/
cot	Bo	/ka:t/ᴮ /kaht/
jury	S	/'jariy/
loud	S	/'læwd/
law	S	/lɔh/
lot	S	/lot/
marryʳ	S	/'mæhriy/
Mary	Bo	/'mɛ:riy/ᴮ/'meyriy/ˢ
merryʳ	S	/mehriy/
mirrorʳ	Bo	/'mirə ~ mirə/
morningʳ	Bo	/məhiyn(ŋ)mɔ:n . . . /ᴮ ɨ/ˢ
mountain	S	/mæwntin/
mourningʳ	Bo	/mohniyŋ ~ moiniyn/ᴮ /mohniyn ~ mɔ:niyn/ˢ
Mrs.	S	/miziz/
new	S	/nyuw/
night	S	/na:yt ~ nəyt/
on	Bo	/ɔn/
oxen	S	/'ɔksin/
pa	S	/pæh/
poorʳ	Bo	/poh/ᴮ/poh/ˢ
house	S	/həws/
hurryʳ	S	/'hə(h)riy/
post	B	/pohst/
pot	S	/pɔt/
pretty	S	/pritiy ~ pritiy/
road	B	/rohd/
root	B	/rut/
scissorsʳ	Bo	/sizəz/ᴮ/sizəz ~ sizəz/ˢ
sisterʳ	Bo	/sistə/ᴮ/sistə ~ sistə/ˢ
sorry	Bo	/'sɔriy/ᴮ/sɔ:riy/ˢ
starry	S	/stariy/
story	S	/storiy/
Thursdayʳ	Bo	/'θəhzdey ~ 'θə:zdey/ᴮ /θə:zde(h)/ˢ
Tuesday	S	/Tyuwzde(h)/
waterʳ	Bo	/'wɔtə/ᴮ/'wɔhta ~ 'wɔ:tə/ˢ
without	S	/wiθæwt/
worry	S	/'wəriy/
woreʳ	Bo	/wɔh/ᴮ/woh/ˢ
yardʳ	Bo	/yahd/
yourʳ	Bo	/yɔh/ᴮ/yoh/ˢ

Note: In the column labeled "dialect," B indicates a word used to analyze the Boston dialect; S, a word used to analyze the Southern dialect; and Bo, a word used to analyze both dialects. The superscripts in the column labeled "phonemic transcription" have the same connotations.

ʳDenotes an "r-less dipthong" word, a word that is pronounced without the retroflexed /r/, in either the Bostonian or Southern dialect.

: Denotes *length* in the phonemic transcription.

TABLE 20.2

Rating Scales Used to Measure Conscious Identity Feelings

I. Length of Residence

1[a]	2	3	4
one–five years	six–ten years	eleven–fifteen years	sixteen—

II. Place of Parental Residence

0	1	2
not from the area (of the subject's residence)	from near this area	lived their entire lives in this area

III. Residence after College

0	1	2
definitely not going to reside in the area	uncertain of their future place of residence	might live in the area, but only because of business connections
	3	4
	definitely live in the area, but because of business connections	definitely live in the area, with or without connections

IV. Dating

0	1	2
does not enjoy dating girls from his area	this factor is of little importance	prefers dating girls from his area

V. Self-Image

0	2	4	6	8
no image	slight image	moderate image	strong image	very strong image

VI. Identification Feelings

0	2	4	6	8
no identification	slight id.	moderate id.	strong id.	very strong id.

[a]The numbers indicate the point values assigned to each response.

first reading from the number pronounced during the second reading.[2] This low reliability puts in question all results using the Bostonians' difference score.

Because the experimenter administered the readings, it would have been possible for him to remember both the subject and the condition under which the subject was reading, despite the coding of the tapes. The contamination factor that could have been caused by this previous knowledge was eliminated by using the outside observer's scores in all of the results presented later.

[2]In the remainder of this chapter, "first" and "second" reading will refer to the pre and poststress readings *aloud*.

TABLE 20.3
Inter-scorer Reliability of Dialect Scores

Scores	Bostonian Subjects	Southern Subjects
Sum scores, first Reading	$r = .90$ $p < .01$	$r = .85$ $p < .01$
% "r-less" words spoken first reading[a]	$r = .91$ $p < .01$	$r = .80$ $p < .01$
Difference scores[b]	$r = .37$ $p < .14$	$r = .82$ $p < .01$

[a]% "r-less" words, obtained by totaling the number of these words pronounced by the subject, and dividing this number by the total number of "r-less" words in the list of key words.

[b]Difference score was obtained by subtracting the number of key words said in the dialect in the first reading from the number said in the second reading of the test story.

Effectiveness of Stress Induction

It is necessary to discuss first the effectiveness of the stress induction method. The method was based on the hypothesis that college students will become stressed if their ability to comprehend written material is questioned, even by a peer. The results of t-tests showing differences in self-reported stress feelings between the stressed and relaxed readings of the test story appear in Table 20.4.

TABLE 20.4
The Difference in Amount of Stress Reported by the Subjects in the First and Second Reading of the Test Story

Group	Bostonian Subjects	Southern Subjects
Experimental	$M = 1.0$ $S.D. = 1.4$	$M = 1.2$ $S.D. = 1.1$
Control	$M = -0.1$ $S.D. = 0.74$	$M = 0.6$ $S.D. = 0.89$
t	1.5	0.9
p	$< .07$	$< .18$

The p-values shown in Table 20.4 are for two-tailed tests. They are in the direction indicated by the experimental procedure. Also, it must be remembered that measures of stress were obtained at a conscious level only. Preconscious and unconscious indications of stress were not included, thereby possibly reducing the accuracy of the method.

Differences in Dialect Between the Experimental and Control Groups

The most important finding of the study is presented in Table 20.5, which compares the difference in dialect change between the experimental group and the control group for both Bostonians and Southerners.

The difference in dialect change between the Southern experimental and control groups is significant, showing that the stress induced caused a definite increase in the Southerners' degree of dialect. The difference for the Bostonians, although in the predicted direction, is not significant. Two-tailed tests were used.

The Effect of Stress and Identity on Dialect Change

There was no correlation between the reported amount of stress and degree of dialect change between first and second readings, for either Southerners or Bostonians. Nor was there any correlation between identification feelings and dialect change, for either dialect group.

TABLE 20.5
Dialect Change Due to Stress[a]

Group	Bostonian Subjects		Southern Subjects	
Experimental	$M =$	0.8	$M =$	1.4
	$S.D. =$	3.0	$S.D. =$	2.3
Control	$M =$	-0.6[b]	$M =$	-5.8
	$S.D. =$	4.4	$S.D. =$	5.4
t		0.6		2.8
p	$<$	.28	$<$	.02

[a]Difference scores used to measure dialect change.

[b]A minus score indicates that the subject read more words in his dialect during the first reading than he did during the second reading.

TABLE 20.6
Comparison of Differences between Southerners and Bostonians[a]

Groups	Amount of Dialect Change Under Stress[b]	Total Identity Score[c]	% of "r-less" Words Pronounced In First Reading
Bostonian	$t = 0.6$ $p = .60$	$M = 14.0$ $S.D. = 5.2$	$M = 13.7$ $S.D. = 15.9$
Southern	$t = 2.8$ $p = .02$	$M = 20.2$ $S.D. = 4.7$	$M = 31.4$ $S.D. = 17.7$
t	1.7	2.0	1.7
p	$< .11$	$< .06$	$< .11$

[a]Two-tailed t-tests.
[b]Difference scores used; experimental vs. control groups.
[c]Experimental and control groups combined.

Differences Between Southerners and Bostonians

Table 20.5 revealed a significant difference in dialect change between experimental and control Southerners, but an insignificant difference between experimental and control Bostonians. Although the difference between the two groups is not significant, as the p-value of $<.11$ in column 2 of Table 20.6 indicates, some explanation for the difference is necessary. The dissimilarity cannot be accounted for by differences in the amount of stress induced by the experimenter. Perhaps the most important factor is the low interscorer reliability of the dialect differences for Bostonians.

Relation of Identity Feelings and Dialect Present Before Stress

Column 4 of Table 20.6 shows the difference between the Bostonians and Southerners in the percentage of "r-less" words pronounced during the first reading. The first reading occurred before stress was induced, and was, therefore, independent of the experimental effect. "R-less" words were used as a measure of strength of dialect for two reasons. Firstly, the loss of the retroflexed /r/ is one of the easiest characteristics to notice in the dialects studied. Secondly, it is a distinguishing feature of both Southern and Bostonian dialects, thus serving as a common ground for comparison.

The larger difference in original dialect on the part of the Southerners, and their correspondingly larger identity scores indicates that there very possibly is a relationship between strength of identification feelings and initial amount of dialect present. This indication is corroborated by Table

TABLE 20.7

Correlation between Identity Score and
Dialect Present before Stress[a]

Bostonians	Southerners
$r = .80$[b]	$r = .43$[b]
$p < .01$	$p < .07$

[a]Dialect present measured by the % of "r-less" words pronounced in the first reading of the test story.
[b]The difference between these correlations is not signnificant, $p = .24$.

20.7, which shows the correlation between the original strength of an individual's dialect and his total identity socre. For Bostonians, the correlation is definitely significant. For the Southerners the p-value is of borderline significance. The difference between the two correlations is not significant.

DISCUSSION

The present experiment yielded two important findings. The first of these concerns the difference in dialect change between Southern experimental and Southern control subjects. The Southern experimental subjects showed a slight increase in dialect during the reading of the test story under stress. The Southern control subjects, however, showed a marked decrease in dialect between the first and second reacings of the story. The slight increase recorded for the experimental subjects, and the marked decrease recorded for the control subjects, led to the establishment of a significant difference between dialect change in the two groups.

An explanation for this slight increase for the experimentals, and marked decrease for the controls must involve the initial amount of stress present during the first reading of the test story. Despite the practice story, designed to relieve initial stress feelings, we believe that confrontation with a new story to be read aloud raised the stress level of the subjects during the first reading. The induction of stress in the Southern experimental subjects either maintained or increased slightly the initial amount of stress present, causing a slight increase in dialect. The Southern control subjects, on the other hand, were not subjected to stress induction, and therefore, the level of stress present in the first reading declined, and the subject's dialect decreased correspondingly.

The dialect change for the experimental Bostonians, however, was not significantly different from the change recorded for the control Bostonians, although the differences occurred in the prediction direction. The lack of significant differences for the Bostonians could easily have been a reflection of the low reliability of the difference scoring for them. An alternative explanation for the lack of a significant difference concerns the Bostonians' conscious identification feelings. It could be said that their identification feelings were not strong enough to manifest themselves through dialect change. Still another alternative would be that the Bostonians were not placed under enough stress to show a significant change. Yet Southerners, under the same conditions, did show a significant change. The difference in dialect change between the two groups, and the significant difference between the identity scores, suggests that perhaps the strength of the Southerners' identity feelings were partly responsible for their dialect change under stress. The conclusion that strong identification feelings do cause an intensification of dialect under stress cannot be presented with certainty, because the differences in dialect change between Bostonians and Southerners were not significant and the difference scoring for Bostonians was not reliable.

The experimenter himself was an upperclassman with a Boston dialect: The effect of this on the Boston-Southern group difference should be investigated further. A design that included both Bostonian and Southern subjects and experimenters would be required for this purpose.

The association of speech dialect with other aspects of behavior is not new in psychological literature. Krapf (1955) stated: "The common denominator of the motivations that underlie the choice of language in polyglot psychoanalysis is in general a tendency to avoid anxiety. The individual uses the language that in a particular situation is least likely to provoke a feeling of anxiety, or conversely, most likely to give him a feeling of security" (p. 356). Krapf's study was based on the selection among different languages by polyglot analytic patients. His reasoning can be applied to regional dialects, as well. It was felt that an individual who has lived in more than one dialect area would use his dialect in the same way a multilingual individual uses his language, i.e., to avoid or reduce anxiety. In the present experiment, stress was induced to arouse anxiety, and the effect of this anxiety on the strength of the subject's dialect was noted. The subject was expected to reduce anxiety by making his dialect more similar to the dialect of his identification figures. The subject who showed strong identification feelings for his native region of the country was expected to show a greater increase in dialect change under stress.

A question left unanswered concerns the reason why an increase in the manifestation of personal identity was expected to reduce anxiety. We hypothesize that when an individual is stressed, his ego integrity is threatened;

and to withstand this threat, the individual automatically manifests more of the actions that form the central core of his character—his identifications. In this experiment there is a paradigm of regression, and it is impossible to distinguish its effects from the effects of identification feelings. Regression could also account for the experimental findings. The two concepts are by no means incompatible, but establishing a connection between them is left to another study.

Although the findings concerning the effect of identification feelings on dialect change under stress were inconclusive, a significant relationship was found to exist between amount of dialect present before stress induction and the strength of identification feelings. Although this finding may not be surprising, it gives an empirical base to a behavioral dimension that might be useful in further studies of identification.

A final word must be added about the method of dialect scoring. The study was done on a phonemic, not a phonetic, level. A phonetic analysis, because of its finer discriminations, might have yielded more conclusive results concerning the effect of stress on dialect change.

CONCLUSION

The present experiment was designed to show relationships between stress, identification feelings, and dialect usage. Results showed that stress produced a significant change in the dialect of the Southern subjects. This change, although not clearly related to conscious identity as measured, was compatible with findings presented showing stronger identity feelings in the Southerners than in the Bostonians. In addition, a significant correlation was found to exist between conscious identification feelings and the amount of dialect present before the induction of stress.

Perhaps the chief value of this exploratory study consists of its indications that the relationship between stress, identity, and dialect is researchable and worthy of further study.[3]

APPENDIX

Bostonians' Test Story

(Words scored for *Bostonians* italicized.) Early one Tuesday *morning, Mary,* a pretty girl, climbed out of bed and put on her clothes hastily. Glancing quickly in the *mirror,* she ran downstairs and out into the *yard* and the fresh *air* without stopping to

---

[3]In the following chapter (pp. 343–345) we present further data about dialect.

greet her *aunt* who was stirring the oatmeal in front of an oaken *pot*. She went over past the drain and across the dirt road to the *barn* where she could pat her *horse* and water her pet oxen. She collected the milk pails, which her *sister* had forgotten, and returned to the house where her pa had already come down to the breakfast table.

There were *four* of them now, instead of five. Her older brother, who was only *fourteen*, had been *caught* setting *fire* to their neighbor's *crop* the night before and was now in the pit the law calls a jail, waiting until *Thursday* before seeing the jury. This had cut deeply into her *father's* pride. They were *poor* folk, but her pa was a just man, and expected his whole family to be the same way.

They were indeed a *sorry*-looking lot, and an air of *mourning* hung over the entire household as Mary walked in.

"Yeah," she heard her father say, "I can't post bail for that boy of mine, and I'm not going to worry about him either. I've fought to bring my family up right for *forty* years. If they don't learn, then it's their fault."

Mary thought her father a *boor because* he was saying these things. Yet she couldn't help thinking that he might be right.

She was brought out of her reverie by the *hoarse* voice of her father asking for a *glass* of *water*. She became *careless* and spilled a little *on* him, but he said nothing.

There was no conversation at the table, and Mary passed the time looking out the window at the distant mountain which appeared so calm in spite of what was going on at home.

She was almost in a complete *fog* when her father's voice boomed next to her *ear*.

"Guess I'm about due for a shopping trip today," he mused in a loud voice, attempting to start a conversation.

"Yes," replied Mary enthusiastically. "We need new wire for the coop, some *flour*, some cooking grease, *scissors*, some lard. . ."

Her father cut her off in the middle.

"Enough, enough" he said, scratching his *beard*. "We'll both end up in the poor house this way." He said it kindly as he had always felt that Mary was *dearer* to him than the others.

"I'll be home about five, in plenty of time for *dinner*," he said, walking out.

That left the three of them. Mary, her sister, and her aunt, Mrs. Corcoran, or Aunt Ida, as they all called her.

Ida Corcoran was a strange woman. Her husband had been killed some eight years ago while hunting *bear*, and the *fear* of losing another husband *haunted* her so much that she swore she would never marry again. When Mary's mother died, it was only natural for Ida to live with them.

There were times when she would tell a marvelous story, which would buoy up the spirits of the whole household, but there were other times when she could be a dreadful *bore*. She had only a soft *burr* of an Irish accent left, but she was still Irish enough to have an occasional glass of *beer* with the menfolk.

The fire in the stove had heated the coffee to a boil, and Ida rose to pour it. Mary didn't drink coffee yet, so only her older sister and Aunt Ida drank from their greasy cups.

Mary was musing again, and her aunt reprimanded her sharply. "Get that starry look out of *your* eyes," she almost screamed at Mary.

Ida was a person always in a hurry, and she couldn't stand for anyone being different. Mary left the table with a start, and the feeling of fear she always felt with her aunt arose in her.

She stepped outside onto the front steps. It was a wonderfully *fair* day giving promise of a warm *afternoon*. Somewhere in the distance a merry *bird* twittered, and Mary could hear her dog barking playfully. That's my dog, she mused happily, and no one can take him from me.

Still she didn't know where he was, so she called inside, "Where did my dog go, Aunt Ida?"

"He just came around to the backyard," she said, coming away from the window.

Mary ran around to find him, and she saw him amusing himself with the springs of an old army *cot* which had been thrown out years before. He beat his tail happily on the ground when he saw Mary and ran towards her.

She found an old boot which she *wore* as a child on the rubbish heap, and threw it over his head. He loved to retrieve, and would playfully bite Mary's hand upon returning.

After tiring of this, they had a playful wrestling bout near the *root* of the big tree which shaded their house. Then they set off looking for bait for an afternoon's fishing, using the hull of an old toy boat as a container and looking forward to their *bath* in the lake after a day in the hot sun.

Southerners' Test Story

(Words scored for *Southerners* italicized.) Early one *Tuesday morning, Mary,* a *pretty* girl, climbed out of bed and put on her clothes hastily. Glancing quickly in the *mirror,* she ran downstairs and out into the *yard* and the fresh *air without* stopping to greet her aunt who was stirring the oatmeal in front of an old oaken pot. She went over past the *drain* and across the dirt *road* to the *barn* where she could pat her *horse* and water her pet *oxen.* She collected the milk pails which her *sister* had forgotten and returned to the *house* where her *pa* had already come down to the breakfast table.

There were *four* of them now instead of five. Her older brother, who was only *fourteen,* had been caught setting *fire* to their neighbor's *crop* the *night* before and was now in the pit the *law* calls a jail, waiting until *Thursday* before seeing the *jury.* This had cut deeply into her *father's* pride. They were *poor* folk, but her pa was a just man and expected his whole family to be the same way.

They were indeed a *sorry*-looking lot, and an air of *mourning* hung over the entire household as Mary walked in.

"Yeah," she heard her father say, "I can't *post* bail for that boy of mine, and I'm not going to *worry* about him either. I've fought to bring my family up right for *forty* years. If they don't learn, then it's their fault."

Mary thought her father a *boor* because he was saying these things. Yet she couldn't help thinking that he might be right.

She was brought out of her reverie by the *hoarse* voice of her father asking for a glass of water. She became *careless* and spilled a little *on* him, but he said nothing.

There was no conversation at the table, and Mary passed the time looking out the window at the distant *mountain* which appeared so *calm* in spite of what was going on at home.

She was almost in a complete *fog* when her father's voice boomed next to her *ear*.

"Guess I'm about due for a shopping trip today," he mused in a *loud* voice, attempting to start a conversation.

"Yes," replied Mary enthusiastically. "We need new *wire* for the *coop*, some *flour*, some cooking grease, *scissors*, some lard. . ."

Her father cut her off in the middle.

"Enough, enough," he said, scratching his *beard*. "We'll both end up in the poor house this way." He said it kindly, as he had always felt that Mary was *dearer* to him than the others.

"I'll be home about five, in plenty of time for *dinner*," he said, walking out.

That left the three of them. Mary, her sister, and her aunt, *Mrs.* Corcoran, or Aunt Ida, as they all called her.

Ida Corcoran was a strange woman. Her husband had been killed some eight years ago while hunting *bear*, and the *fear* of losing another husband *haunted* her so much that she swore she would never *marry* again. When Mary's mother died, it was only natural for Ida to live with them.

There were times when she would tell a marvelous *story*, which would buoy up the spirits of the household, but there were other times when she could be a dreadful *bore*. She had only a soft *burr* of an Irish accent left, but she was still Irish enough to have an occasional glass of *beer* with the menfolk.

The fire in the stove had heated the coffee to a *boil*, and Ida rose to pour it. Mary didn't drink coffee yet, so only her older sister and Aunt Ida drank from their *greasy* cups.

Mary was musing again, and her aunt reprimanded her sharply. "Get that *starry* look out of *your* eyes," she almost screamed at Mary.

Ida was a person always in a *hurry*, and she couldn't stand for anyone being different. Mary left the table with a start, and the feeling of fear she always felt with her aunt arose in her.

She stepped outside onto the front steps. It was a wonderfully *fair* day giving promise of a warm *afternoon*. Somewhere in the distance a *merry bird* twittered, and Mary could hear her *dog* barking playfully. That's my dog, she mused happily, and no one can take him from me.

Still she didn't know where he was, so she called inside, "Where did my dog go, Aunt Ida?"

"He just came around to the backyard," she said, coming away from the window.

Mary ran around to find him, and she saw him amusing himself with the springs of an old army *cot* which had been thrown out years before. He beat his tail happily on the ground when he saw Mary and ran towards her.

She found an old *boot* which she *wore* as a child on the rubbish heap and threw it over his head. He loved to retrieve and would playfully bite Mary's hand upon returning.

After tiring of this, they had a playful wrestling *bout* near the root of the big tree which shaded their house. Then they set off looking for *bait* for an afternoon's fishing, using the hull of an old toy *boat* as a container and looking forward to their *bath* in the lake after a day in the hot sun.

People Talking When They Can't Hear Their Own Voices[1]

21

The situation of spontaneous speech usually includes two ubiquitous conditions: people hear themselves as they talk and they see their interlocutors. Primarily, this chapter concerns the role of the auditory feedback in the control of spontaneous speech and interaction, and in determining subjective experience. Very secondarily, it also deals with the role of the visual input from the audience.

LITERATURE REVIEW

The significance of feedback in the regulation of behavior has been recognized implicitly or explicitly for a long time. On the physiological level, for example, the early work of Bell (1826), Bernard (1858), and Sherrington and Mott (1895) demonstrated the critical role of proprioceptive feedback in the regulation of voluntary motor activity. The clinical condition of *tabes dorsalis*

[1]Adapted from G. F. Mahl (1972), People Talking When They Can't Hear Their Voices. In A. Siegman and B. Pope (1972, Eds.), *Studies in Dyadic Communication*. New York: Pergamon Press. (chapter 10, pp. 211–264). Adapted with permission of the editors and publisher, with slight editorial and stylistic revisions. The author presented a summary of the basic observations reported in this chapter at the 16th International Congress of Psychology, Bonn, 1960 (Mahl, 1961b).

The author's interest in feedback is an old one. As mentioned in chapter 7 (fn. 2), his first publication concerned a technique for providing visible signs of muscular activity (Snodgrass & Mahl, 1941). And during the early 1950's he explored the effect of playing back to patients tape recordings of their psychotherapy interviews.

did the same. Cannon's elucidation of homeostatic mechanisms (1932) often dealt with complex feedback systems.

Viewed retrospectively, it is clear that Freud's psychological models also included feedback systems although they were not articulated as such. This is most apparent in the regulatory role Freud ascribed to *self-observation*. To mention a few major instances, Freud explicitly or implicitly dealt with this process in his hypothesis of *Cs* as a sense organ that monitors the workings of the psychic apparatus (1900/1953a) pp. 615ff.); in his concept of dream censorship (1900/1953a); in his hypotheses of the self-observing, self-evaluating, and self-critical functions of the Super-ego (1914/1957a, 1923/1961); and in his revived and revised theory of anxiety and defense (1926/1959). One could say with some validity that one thing Freud did as he developed his theory was to articulate in more detail feedback processes involved in self-observation and self-regulation and to attribute greater significance to them. The relevance of psychoanalytic theory to feedback concepts and to this chapter is clearly implied in Freud's brief statement (1901/1960, p. 101) that "we may hear the stifled voice of the author's self-criticism" in the speech disturbances of everyday life and in contorted writing. In the Discussion, we consider further the relation of this chapter and psychoanalytic theory.

Wiener (1948, 1950) pointed out the early application of feedback principles in the use of the governor and the steering machine for the control of the speed of the steam engine and the position of the rudder. He cites Maxwell's paper (1868) on governors as the "first significant paper on feedback mechanisms" (1948, p. 19). One does not have to agree with this judgment to realize that in both the practical use and the theoretical understanding of machine behavior, "feedback" has a long history.

In spite of this history, as well as that indicated for physiology and psychology, it was Norbert Wiener who articulated the feedback concept and with his colleagues (Rosenblueth, Wiener, & Bigelow, 1943) pioneered in showing the relevance of feedback theory to the behavior of machines and of man.

With the appearance of *Cybernetics* (Wiener, 1948) and Lee's related discovery of the effects of delayed auditory feedback (1950a, 1950b, 1951), a previously latent, and only sporadically manifested, interest in the role of auditory feedback in speech regulation gained momentum. The speech deficit of the deaf had always provided dramatic evidence that auditory feedback was critical for speech development and regulation. But it is largely due to the research of the past 30 years that a more exact picture of the feedback regulation of speech has begun to emerge. We review this research by summarizing the findings of studies in which (a) the temporal aspect of auditory feedback has been altered, (b) other aspects of auditory feedback have been changed, (c) auditory feedback has been abolished or masked.

Effects of Changing the Timing of Auditory Feedback

Delayed Auditory Feedback (DAF)[2]

. . . Black (1954), himself a pioneer investigator in this area, observed that Fletcher's notes contained a brief reference in 1918 to this problem as it might arise with increasing distance of side-tone transmission over telephone circuits. But Lee's paper (1950a), which was actually a "letter to the editor," is generally regarded as the first report on the effects of DAF. Nine years later Chase, Sutton, and First (1959) listed 101 references in their DAF bibliography; Smith's integrative reviews (1962; Smith, Ansell, & Smith, 1963) contain additional references. There is obviously a voluminous DAF literature. The reader is urged to consult Lee's original papers and to use the bibliography of Chase et al. and Smith's reviews as guides to this literature, for only the major findings are cited here.

Lee (1950a, 1950b) discovered that if a person's speech was returned to his ears through earphones at an amplified level and delayed by one-eighth or one-quarter second, the individual stuttered, spoke slower, increased the pitch or volume of his speech, and sometimes stopped speaking. A delay of only one-fifteenth second had little or no effect, which indicated that the time factor was critical. Marked speech disruption only occurs if the delayed feedback *replaces* normal feedback. The use of earphones and amplification of the signal produces this condition, for the former decreases normal air-borne feedback and the latter masks bone-conduction feedback as well as any airborne feedback still effective through the earphones.

Lee also observed other effects. Some subjects developed "a quavering slow speech" reminiscent of cerebral palsy. Emotional arousal was indicated by reddening of the face. Extension of the DAF condition for more than 2 minutes caused physical fatigue. Individual differences in all the DAF effects were apparent.

Subsequent research has confirmed and refined Lee's original observations. The work of Fairbanks (1955) and Fairbanks and Guttman (1958) is particularly relevant. They verified the critical significance of the time factor, finding that the general peak disturbance of speech during oral reading occurred with a delay of .2 seconds. They also demonstrated, however, that different types of articulatory disturbances were maximal with slightly different delay intervals. This finding emphasized *the intricacy of the feedback control of speech*.

Chase, Sutton, First, and Zubin (1961) compared the effect of DAF on the impromptu speech of children 4–6 years old and 7–9 years old. DAF caused the children of both age groups to repeat more words and syllables, to prolong more syllables, and to speak slower. The last two effects, however,

---

[2]Also sometimes called "delayed sidetone."

were significantly greater in the older than in the younger children. Correlated with this age difference, the older children indicated in an Inquiry greater dependence on and sensitivity to auditory feedback than did the younger children. Nearly all the older children recognized their own voices through the earphones in both control and DAF conditions; only half of the younger children did in both conditions! The children were asked how the voice they heard in the DAF condition differed from that of the control condition. Half of the older children showed some awareness of the delay factor, but not a single one of the younger children did!

Accelerated Auditory Feedback

It takes time for normal auditory feedback to reach one's cochlea. Peters (1954) cites Stromstra's estimate that normal bone-conducted feedback takes at least .0003 seconds and normal air-conducted feedback at least .001 seconds. Peters then investigated the effect on reading rate of decreasing these normal delay intervals to .00015 seconds by electronic means. This accelerated feedback *increased* the reading rate, whereas delayed feedback decreases it.

Effects of Changing Other Dimensions of Auditory
Feedback

If the timing of the speaker's auditory feedback is left untouched, but feedback is altered in other ways, his speech will still be affected. The speaker will vary the *intensity* of his voice inversely with the intensity of his feedback (Black, 1950a; Lighttoot & Morrill, 1949). The intelligibility of heard speech varies directly with the intensity of it and also depends on the high-frequency components in it. A speaker will increase the *intelligibility* of his speech if the intensity of his feedback is lowered (Black, 1950a; Black, Tolhurst, & Morrill, 1953) or if the high-frequency component is filtered o   f his feedback (Peters, 1955).

In the preceding studies, the feedback was delivered to the speakers' ears through earphones and was altered electronically. Black (1950a, 1950b) also manipulated feedback characteristics by varying the acoustical environment in which subjects spoke. He found that people spoke louder in "dead" than in "live" rooms. Moreover, their voices became progressively louder in the "dead" rooms but softer in the "live" rooms. Wiener (1950, p. 170) mentions a related phenomenon: when people use a "dead" telephone system, in which their own speech is not fed back to their ears through the receiver, they start shouting into the telephone.

In short, speech appears to change in ways that compensate for experimentally produced variations in auditory feedback. *Again, the feedback regulatory system emerges as a very intricate one.*

Effects of Abolishing or Masking Auditory Feedback

Speech Changes in the Deafened

Congenital or early deafness seriously impairs the development of speech. Of special interest here is the fact that the individual who suffers a hearing loss after he has learned to talk manifests several characteristic changes in his speech: a deterioration of precision of enunciation, a flattening of the intonation patterns, and a loss of control of loudness of his voice (Carhart, 1960). The latter varies with the etiology of the hearing loss. In conduction-deafness, where there is damage primarily to the middle ear and not to the inner ear, the individual speaks very softly. Because his bone-conducted auditory feedback has not been impaired while air-conducted input has, his own voice sounds louder to him that the voices of others. He compensates for this differential "ear experience" by lowering the intensity of his own voice. In perception-deafness (nerve deafness), where there is damage to the inner ear or the auditory neural pathways, the individual speaks very loudly. He compensates for the total loss of auditory feedback. Thus the painful experiment of nature provided in the deafened individual demonstrates that the maintenance of acquired speech patterns depends on the presence of auditory feedback.

Experimental, Temporary Hearing Loss

Prolonged exposure to loud noises and tones results in temporary hearing loss of the perception type (Davis, Morgan, Hawkins, Galambos, & Smith, 1950, e.g.,). Black (1951) studied the effects of such temporary deafness on speech intensity by comparing the voice intensity *following exposure to loud noise* for 2 hours with that preceding such treatment. He confirmed the production of a temporary hearing loss by appropriate auditory measurements. His subjects spoke louder immediately following the exposure to noise and their voices decreased in intensity as their auditory thresholds recovered.

Masking of Auditory Feedback

This may be accomplished by means of loud low-frequency tones and especially broad-band noises, which include low-frequency components; that is, by the same techniques that mask perception of the speech of other people (Miller, 1951). When such tones and noises are administered through earphones to *both* ears, a speaker's auditory feedback may be partially or completely masked. The actual extent of the masking varies with the intensity and frequency composition of the noise, assuming that it is continuous. Such masking interferes with both bone-conducted and airborne feedback. The work of Galambos and Davis (1943, 1944), as well as that of Lowy (1945), strongly suggests that this masking is due to neural processes in the cochlea itself.

One well-known effect of masking feedback is an increase in voice intensity. This is the Lombard effect (Lombard, 1910), which forms the basis of one procedure used to identify nonorganic deafness. Hanley and Steer (1949) found that as a binaurally administered, "airplane type" masking noise was systematically increased in intensity, speakers increased the loudness of their speech, lengthened syllables, and decreased their word rate. Winchester and Gibbons (1958) obtained similar results for word rate but their data failed to reach statistical significance. Their study, however, was not an exact replication of Hanley and Steer's.

Wood (1950) observed subjectively the speech changes during oral reading by 20 college students when a "high-level white noise" completely masked their auditory feedback. He judged that every subject increased his voice intensity and decreased his speech rate with this experimental treatment.

Wood believed that the masking condition also caused changes in the pitch, resonance, and intonation patterns of the voice. We refer to his description of these effects later in the Discussion.

Four different investigators, apparently quite independently, discovered that the masking of auditory feedback *improves* abnormal speech. Kern (1932), Shane (1955, research done in 1946), and Cherry and co-workers (Cherry & Sayers, 1956; Cherry, Sayers, & Marland, 1955) found that binaural masking produced a striking decrease in stuttering. Cherry and Sayers demonstrated, furthermore, that the effect of a low-frequency masking noise was much greater than the effect of a high-frequency noise (cut-off point was 500 c.p.s.). This finding is important for it indicates that feedback masking is the crucial factor and not the mere use of noise. Only with the low-frequency noise is complete masking achieved. The masking techniques of Kern and Shane utilized low-frequency sounds. Birch (1956); Birch and Lee, (1955) masked the speech of patients with *expressive aphasia* with a low-frequency tone of 256 c.p.s. and found that, "In approximately 75 percent of the patients tested, [verbal] performance was decisively improved" (Birch, 1956, p. 3851).

Conclusions From Literature Review

The speech deterioration of the deafened provides clear evidence that continual auditory feedback plays a significant role in the preservation of developed speech patterns. The effects on speech of experimentally produced temporary hearing loss and of binaural masking underscore the dependence of speech patterns on auditory feedback. Habitual speech changes within seconds or minutes when feedback is masked. An increase in loudness of voice is the most well-documented change. The literature is scant as far as other changes are concerned, but what there is suggests that feedback masking effects a broad spectrum of the dimensions of speech: rate of speech, pitch, vocal quality, and intonation, and those factors involved in the abnormal speech of stuttering and expressive aphasia. As meager as the data are in these respects, they too suggest that the feedback control of speech is an intricate matter. The DAF literature and the manipulation of nontemporal aspects of feedback pointed in the same direction. *It appears that multiple attributes of speech are delicately regulated by corresponding, multiple channels of auditory feedback. And these feedback sub-systems are all integrated in the regulation of the entire speech pattern.* The literature supports the increasingly complex feedback models proposed by Lee (1950b), Fairbanks (1955), and Smith (1962).

The feedback literature also poses a challenge. A sketchy outline of the *aural monitor* has been emerging during the past 15 years. Most of the information on which the sketch is based has come from studies of delayed auditory feedback, but the temporal is only one aspect of feedback. A great deal of work needs to be done on other aspects of auditory feedback to verify, correct, and extend what is now known or believed. This will not only result in a more detailed picture of the aural monitor and how it works; there is a strong possibility that future work on feedback in speech will be of more general significance because feedback control is such a prevalent behavioral phenomenon.

PRESENT STUDY

Purpose

Originally, this experiment was designed to determine the role of auditory feedback from one's own voice and visual input from interlocutors in the occurrence of common disturbances of spontaneous speech [chapter 9]. . . As the experiment was conducted for the original purpose, it became apparent that the masking of auditory feedback had many striking, grossly observable effects, many of which have not been reported in the literature or at least are not generally known. The purpose of this chapter is to present a survey of those effects and to consider their potential theoretical significance. The chapter is exploratory. It does not test any general hypotheses; that doesn't seem fruitful at present. It does, however, lead to some hypotheses for further research.

The paper is related to the research reviewed above in the following ways:

a. The auditory feedback manipulation is *complete binaural masking*.

b. The effects on *normal, spontaneous,* and *extended speech* of a speaker engaged *in a dialogue* are studied. When this research was conducted, only Wood (1950) had studied the effect of complete binaural masking on normal speech, as far as we know, and his subjects read in a monologue for a maximum of 3½ minutes. With only rare exceptions, the previous feedback studies have utilized the monologue, oral reading of brief phrases, or sentences.

c. The effects of binaural masking on *the more general psychological state* of the speaker are studied, as well as the effects on speech.

Method

Overall Plan

College students were interviewed under four different conditions: (a) when they sat in the usual face-to-face situation (F); (b) when they faced the interviewer but could not hear themselves because of the administration of a masking noise through earphones they were wearing (F-N); (c) when they were not facing the interviewer and thus could not see him because he sat behind them (B); and (d) when they could neither see the interviewer nor hear themselves talk (B-N). Exploratory work demonstrated the feasibility of these interview conditions. Students and associates and the writer himself spoke under the projected conditions without physical or psychological discomfort after an initial period of adaptation. The writer found he could interview under the projected conditions and gained familiarity with doing so.

To distinguish between initial effects due to the pure novelty of the experimental conditions and the effects due to the essential nature of the conditions, each subject was interviewed three times. All interviews were tape-recorded and transcribed. The clinical and objective study of the tape recordings and interview transcripts, as well as recorded reports by the subjects during an inquiry at the close of each interview, provide the basic data of the study. The subjects took the Minnesota Multiphasic Personality Inventory (MMPI) and were given the Wechsler Adult Intelligence Scale (WAIS) between interviews. Home interviews with the mothers of each subject occurred after he had completed his interviews; they are not relevant to the present chapter but are mentioned for the sake of completeness.[3] In the following paragraphs, the Method is described in more detail.

Subjects

A psychology professor at a then small state university, primarily concerned with training public school teachers, recruited the subjects from his second

---

[3] I am grateful to the following people for their contributions to this project: the subjects, Drs. Richard Waite and William Trinkaus, Naomi Miller, Irene Bickenbach, Judith Tillson, Genoveva Palmieri, Gene Schulze, Sue Cohen. Susan Ehrlich, and Ruth Johnson.

and third year classes. He stated that a psychologist at Yale was seeking both male and females subjects, whose parents lived within an hour's drive of the school, for an experiment involving several interviews, psychological tests including the WAIS, and interviews with their mothers. He stated that the subjects would receive, in return, the experience, a small fee, and the results of the WAIS, which he himself would convey to them.

Seventeen students, eight male and nine female, volunteered. Fourteen intended to become schoolteachers. Their ages ranged from 20 to 27, fourteen being 20 to 22 years old. The group was above average in intelligence and of higher verbal than performance ability, as the following summary of the WAIS scores shows.

Scores	M	$S.D.$
Vocabulary Scale	13	1.4
Verbal IQ	117	6.5
Performance IQ	113	8.2
Full Scale IQ	116	4.4

No precise social class indexing was carried out, but nine of the subjects seemed to be of lower middle-class background, seven from upper middle-class households and one from a lower-upper class household. The ethnic home background of the sample was quite heterogeneous, as is indicated by the following tabulation of the nationality or ethnic membership of the subjects' parents:

Ethnic Influences in Home of Origin	N
Anglo-Saxon ("American")	4
Italian	5
Jewish	2
Irish-American	1
Greek	1
Czech	1
Hungarian	1
Irish-American and Jewish	1
Polish and Anglo-Saxon	1
	17

All subjects were white and had been born and spent their entire lives in the United States. English was the native language for all subjects. Some had limited familiarity with the original language of their parents where this was other than English. No subject gave any gross signs of speech pathology or "foreign accent."

The Interviews

Each subject went through the following schedule: Interview I, Inquiry, followed immediately by the self-administered, individual form of the MMPI; Interview II, Inquiry, followed immediately by WAIS; Interview III, Inquiry. The home interviews with the mothers occurred within 7 weeks after Interview III, except in one case when it took place on the day of Interview II. Interviews I, II, III occurred on different days, being distributed over spans of 4 to 16 days, with a modal span of 8 days for 7 subjects. They took place in a room especially designed for high-fidelity sound recording of interviews [Mahl, Dollard, & Redlich, 1954].

The personal, psychological interview, modeled after the initial psychiatric interview, was used in the belief that it would afford equally for interviewer and subject the most meaningful and useful situation for sustained repeated interaction.

The following outline sketches the essentials of the three interviews: further following comments describe certain features more fully.

Interview I, (familiarization) about 50 minutes long.
Introductory phase: 5 to 10 minutes
Interview proper: 30 minutes
  Continuous topics: interests, family, academic choice
Conditions, fixed sequence: F, F-N, B-N.
Inquiry: 10 minutes

Interview II, about 50 minutes long.
Discontinuous topics: fixed sequence
  1. Current activities in school, work, hobbies.
  2. Most significant person in current life: nature of the person and relationship with subject.
  3. Most significant person in past life:
     nature of the person and relationship with subject.
  4. MMPI experience
Conditions: sequence varied by subject
  F   10 minutes
  F-N   10 minutes
  B   10 minutes
  B-N   10 minutes
     (one topic per condition)
Inquiry: 10 minutes

Interview III, about 50 minutes long.
Topic content and schedule ordinarily the same as in Interview II.
Conditions: same as in Interview II, except that each subject
starts with what was his second condition in Interview II.

Interview I: Familiarization   This interview opened with the first meeting
between the interviewer and the subject. They sat face-to-face and spent
approximately the first 5 minutes discussing the nature of the scheduled
procedures, time arrangements, and payment of fees. The essence of what
the interviewer told each subject about the nature and purpose of the study
was as follows:

> In this experiment, I'm interested in people's reactions when they are talking
> under different conditions. First, when you're talking with me like this, face-
> to-face, under the usual conditions. Then, when you can't hear yourself talk
> because of a noise playing through earphones in your ears. The noise will not
> be painful, but it is loud enough and has such characteristics that you won't be
> able to hear yourself talk. The next condition is when you're not looking at me.
> In that case, I just turn your chair around and I sit behind you. The final
> condition is when we are talking and you can't hear yourself because of the
> noise while you are sitting with your back to me.
> I am doing this study now with well-functioning people like yourself and
> the other students. Later I may compare the reactions of all you people with
> hospitalized psychiatric patients.
> Another thing I'm interested in is how different kinds of people react to
> these situations. We are all different and we all have different reactions to
> things. To help define the difference between yourself and your classmates,
> I'll also ask you to take the Wechsler intelligence test and a personality test,
> and I'd like to have an interview done with your mother. In all of these
> interviews, tests, etc., I'm not interested in how smart you are or whether you
> have such and such a complex. I'm only interested in seeing how you're
> different from the others and if your reactions to these conditions are related to
> these differences between yourself and the others.
> Today you can get used to the conditions while we talk and I can get to
> know a little bit about you. We'll talk sitting like this, then with the noise, and
> then with the noise while you're facing away from me. In the next two inter-
> views, we'll use all four of the conditions and they'll be in a different order
> each time. We'll be more systematic then.

The instructions were designed to orient the subjects to *their general reactions*
when talking under the different conditions rather than to the specific details
of the speech process itself. In his responses to the initial questions asked by
the subjects, the interviewer attempted to reinforce this general emphasis
and it was further reinforced by the general nature of the Inquiry questions.
Following the introductory phase, the interview proper began with this
remark by the Interviewer: "I'd like to begin by finding out something about

you—how old you are, what your interests are, how you came to go to teacher's college, about your family, and so on." This comment defines the areas covered in Interview I, proper, which lasted for about 30 minutes. The goal of this interview section was to familiarize the subject with the various conditions under which he would be speaking, with the interviewer in this particular role and he with the subject and with the general situation of a personal interview.

The Inquiry always consisted of an open-ended exploration of the following questions:

1. How did you feel in the different conditions? What was your inner experience like when you spoke with the noise on? When facing away from me? And when these two were combined?

2. What did the noise remind you of?

3. How would you rank the conditions for comfort or discomfort? For ease of talking?

4. When we were talking in the various conditions you might have had some peripheral, fleeting thoughts you didn't have a chance to mention. Do you recall any? Could you tell me about them?

5. Is there anything else you think of that would shed light on how you experienced the different conditions?

Interview II.   This included all four conditions of talking and a somewhat restricted schedule of four general topics, one topic being considered in each condition. The topic sequence was the same for all subjects, but the sequence of the conditions was varied systematically from subject to subject. The topics mentioned in the aforementioned outline were explored in an open-ended manner.

The sequence of conditions for Interview II was determined in the following manner. A basic sequence of F, F-N, B, and B-N, in that order, was designated. The subjects were listed according to the order in which they were scheduled for their first interview. The first subject started the basic sequence in F condition, the second subject in F-N, the third in B, the fourth in B-N, the fifth in F, etc. This system provided four condition sequences, with four subjects in three sequences and five in the other.

N Subjects	Sequence			
	F	F-N	B	B-N
5	1	2	3	4
4	4	1	2	3
4	3	4	1	2
4	2	3	4	1

Interview III.   It also included all four conditions. Now each subject started one step over in the sequence he followed in Interview II. Again, four subjects followed three of the sequences and five the other sequence. The topic schedule was more variable in this interview. Because the maintenance of "natural" and spontaneous interchange was the principal goal, the interviewer played it by ear. Although he basically attempted to renew discussion of the topics of Interview II in the same sequence, he did deviate from this approach whenever he felt it resulted in constrained interaction or seemed forced and artificial. In such cases, he pursued something from the preceding portions of this or the first two interviews, which the subject seemed interested in discussing further.

The Masking Noise

This consisted of frequencies up to 500 c.p.s. in equal intensities. This particular masking noise was chosen for several reasons. It is very effective in masking all auditory feedback, both bone and air conducted. Cherry and Sayers (1956) had demonstrated that the use of this masking noise produced a striking reduction in stuttering. And such a noise is somewhat less noxious than one containing higher frequencies.

The noise, produced electronically and permanently recorded on tape, was administered into the subjects' ears through padded earphones simply by playing the tape on a recorder. The author operated the recorder by means of a foot switch. In the noise conditions, the masking noise was administered at all times except when the interviewer spoke. The subject could hear the interviewer easily when the noise was stopped even though he was wearing earphones. The interviewer, of course, could always hear his own speech and that of the subject.

The subject first donned the earphones after the introductory phase of Interview I. Thereafter, he wore them in all conditions except during the inquiries. The noise playback volume was variable, being set and maintained at that level reported by the subject to produce complete masking of his voice. The average volume was approximately 93 db above the reference level of .0002 dynes/cm². The important thing is that, generally speaking, subjects had no awareness whatever of their voices with this procedure. There was a total of six noise conditions for each subject in the three interviews.

Study of the Tapes and Transcripts

Externally Observable Effects of Interview Conditions.   The author observed certain effects of the masking procedure during the exploratory work, during the actual interviews of this study, and in listening to all the interview tapes. From these observations, he established a set of categories used in a careful restudy of the recordings and transcripts. The categories, listed in Table

21.1, are of two general classes: one class refers to *speech attributes* per se, such as loudness, pitch, etc.; the other refers to *more general psychological changes* inferred from or manifested in verbal behavior. Nearly all the raw data of this study pertaining to externally observable effects of the masking noise are *judgments* by the author. In some cases, supplementary, more objective data were obtained by procedures that are more appropriately described when these additional data are presented in Results.

Subjective Experiences of Subjects.   The open-ended inquiries were summarized and then coded with a set of categories, some of which generally convey the things frequently reported by the subjects and others of which provide information about the subjects' experience of certain of the phenomena that could be observed externally.

Results

The externally observable effects of the masking noise are described first. In the course of doing so, the subjective experiences especially relevant to the observable changes are cited. The final section of Results consider the subjective experiences as a whole.

Externally Observable Effects of Masking Noise

The masking noise condition produced the effects summarized in Table 21.1. As far as could be determined by the gross observational method employed, these effects were the same in the F-N and B-N conditions. The following comments elaborate and illustrate the data of Table 21.1.

Linguistic Changes.   *Loudness.* All subjects spoke louder with the masking noise. This change was usually sustained throughout a given condition, but the level of loudness was not constant. Occasionally, the voice would become dramatically loud, and a few subjects momentarily spoke with subaudible intensity. Voluntary control of voice volume was apparently minimal in the masking conditions, for subjects persisted in speaking very loudly even though the interviewer told them they were doing so and that he would be able to hear them clearly if they lowered their voices.[4]

Intonation. The subjects characteristically showed some degree of flattening of the intonation pattern of the English sentence. In extreme instances, sentences showed very little variation in pitch or stress.

Voice style. This term refers to a variety of changes. The specification of the exact details of the change is a task for the trained phonologist and

---

[4][He did this to reduce the possibility of excessive fatigue of the subjects.]

TABLE 21.1
Observable Linguistic and Behavioral Changes During Masking of
Auditory Feedback

Category	Nature of Change	N of the 17 Subjects Showing the Change	Average N Noise Conditions per Subject in Which the Change Was Judged to Occur. (Highest possible 6)
A. Linguistic			
Loudness	increase	17	5.8
Intonation	flattens	17	5.5
Voice style	changes	17	4.9
Prolongation	increase	17	4.6
Pitch	changes	15	4.5
	(higher	9)	
	(lower	6)	
Vocal Noises	increase	15	3.4
Slurring	increase	12	1.5
Rate	changes	12	1.8
	(decrease	7)	
	(increase	5)	
Phrasing	more distinct	10	1.8
B. Behavioral-Psychological			
Affect expression	increase	14	2.1
Associative response	freer	14	2.1
Cognitive confusion	increase	11	1.2
"Thinking aloud"	increase	5	.5

linguist; all the writer can do is present here for each subject, terms and images that occurred to him as he listened to the tapes. The following summary itemizes changes judged to have occurred in each subject with the masking noise and the number of noise conditions in which the change occurred. If this number is less than four, the interview will also be given. Generally, the changes noted were characteristic of most or the entire duration of the condition.

Female Subjects

Subject 1. Voice loses whispering quality (6 conditions).

Subject 2. Loss of subdued, voiceless quality (5 conditions) and, in addition, voice is piercing and clear (2 of these conditions).

Subject 3. Voice is more nasal (5 conditions).

Subject 4. Voice is more nasal (4 conditions).

Subject 5. Voice is more nasal, and loses its whispery, wistful, soulful tone (4 conditions). Also, speech sounds less cultured (1 condition of Interview II).

Subject 6. Voice is more nasal and sounds less cultured, causing this listener to think of speech of Molly Goldberg and Jack Benny's telephone operator (4 conditions).

Subject 7. Voice loses whispering quality (1 condition, Interview I) and sounds more nasal (1 condition, Interview III).

Subject 8. Sounds "voiceless" and boyish at times (1 condition, Interview III).

Subject 9. Sounds "voiceless" and hollow at times (1 condition, Interview II).

Male Subjects

Subject 10. Denasalization occurs causing the subject to sound less cultured; like he has a "code in the head" and to remind the listener of the stereotype of the "punch drunk" fighter (6 conditions).

Subject 11. Voice sounds less hoarse or raspy, and speech becomes telegraphic and uncultivated (6 conditions).

Subject 12. Voice sounds less hoarse and "growly"; sounds "mouthier" and speech is less cultured (6 conditions).

Subject 13. Voice is less "picky"; sounds harsher and more aggressive and masculine; dialect is less cultured (6 conditions).

Subject 14. Voice quavers (5 conditions).

Subject 15. Sounds more resonant (5 conditions) and "tougher" (2 conditions—one each in Interview I and II).

Subject 16. Increased nasality (3 conditions: 2 in Interview I, and 1 in Interview II).

Subject 17. Sounds less "froggy" and less strained (2 conditions, Interview I).

A shift toward lower social status dialect, that is, in phonological features, was the principal determinant of the impression that six subjects sounded "less cultivated" when speaking in the masking conditions. Thus, Subject 13, American born of Italian immigrant parents, characteristically said the sound /θ/ in "*th*ink, *th*rough, etc." more like "*t*ink, *t*rough" in the masking condition, and the voiced sound /ð/ in "*th*at, *th*is" more like "*d*at, *d*is." He also showed shifts toward the lower social status phonetic position of the vowel /ô/ in words like c*au*ght, t*a*lk, th*ou*ght, and s*a*w.

TABLE 21.2
Frequency (Percentage) of "th" Variants in Speech of Subject 13
in the Four Conditions

Variants	Facing-No Noise	Facing Away-No Noise	Facing-Noise	Facing Away-Noise
θ,ð (*th*ink, *th*at)	86.5	75.9	74.5	68.8
t, d (*t*ink, *d*at)	13.5	24.1	25.5	31.2
	100.0	100.0	100.0	100.0
N Occurrences	333	261	541	362

The author *heard* such changes in the speech of Subject 13 as the masking voice conditions were introduced. In this particular instance an analysis by a linguist, Professor William Labov. . . who has studied intensively social class dialect on the Eastern seaboard (Labov, 1966), provides invaluable data. Labov carefully analyzed the tape recordings of this subject's speech during the four experimental conditions in all three interviews. Table 21.2 summarizes the frequency with which Labov observed the subject using the standard variants, /θ/ and /ð/ (as in *th*ink and *th*at), and the substandard variants, /t/ and /d/ (as in *t*ink, and *d*at), in the four conditions. Table 21.2 shows that both the masking noise and the interruption of visual contact with the interviewer were associated with a shift towards the lower class forms. Thus, in the face-to-face condition without the masking noise, only 13% of this subject's 'th' variants were of the lower class forms; but when the masking noise was introduced, 25% were of the lower class forms. There was a similar increase from 24 to 31% when the noise was introduced into the "facing-away" condition. Changing from the face-face conditions to the facing-away conditions was also associated with comparable increases in the use of the lower class forms. The author had not detected *this* effect. Thus it is possible that a more refined analysis of all the tapes would reveal effects of the change in the visual condition of the interview, which the author did not observe in his more global assessments.

Occasionally there was increased use of entire word-forms characteristic of less cultivated English speech. Subject 13, for example, uttered the vocative form "see" 14 times in his first masking condition of Interview I, after he had spoken throughout the preceding nonmasking condition without a single instance of this form. This differential use of "see" in the masking–nonmasking conditions did not occur in subsequent interviews, where the form appeared at most twice in a given condition. Subject 6, a young woman born in this country of Jewish parents and reared in the Jewish community, showed the Yiddish feature of starting utterances with "so, ____," in contexts where an American English apeaker might say "And ____," but when neither conjunctive form is essential to the meaning of the utterance. In all the masking conditions, she used this form 49 times; but in the nonmasking conditions the frequency was only 35, ($\chi^2 = 2.33$, $p = .07$ t_1). Thus the frequency of this form increased 40% in the masking condition. This subject also responded twice to interviewer queries in one masking condition with the expressive introductions to her replies, "Don't ask me." In the same condition she also said, "So he said to me 'what am I thinking about.'" Such striking idiomatic expressions never occurred in the nonmasking conditions. All these usages were among the cues that reminded the author of "Molly Goldberg's speech."

Prolongation. This was a phenomenon of intermittently increasing the duration of sounds. When it did occur it was usually at the end of phrases or sentences and consisted of protracting the phonation of single syllable words or the endings of longer words, as in the following example from the speech of Subject 13:

I mean, she . . . ah . . . didn't wanta be alooone. Like if . . . ah . . . my mother and father went out, why she would call them up where they were and say come on hooome. Y'know. I don't like to be left alooone. Little things like that.

The combination of prolongation and flattened intonation often imparted a marked singsong quality to the speech.

Pitch. All but two subjects spoke at different pitch level in the masking conditions than in the nonmasking conditions. Nine subjects raised their general pitch level whereas six lowered it. Whenever a change in pitch occurred it was consistently in the same direction for a given subject.

Vocal noises. When speaking with the masking noise all but three of the subjects produced guttural sounds. These were "noises" in that they are not English phonemes and did not sound like the usual vocalizations—ah, uh, etc. Some were similar to "croaking" or "choking," strangulation noises. These metaphorical terms might create the impression that the subjects were straining in an effort to talk when they produced the noises. That would be erroneous. They did not seem to be doing so to the interviewer. The noises could occur in the absence of any visible sign of effort and were not disruptive of speech. These noises occurred either during pauses or upon the onset of a word, phrase, or sentence. The following interview excerpts illustrate the positions and linguistic contexts in which they occurred. An "x" indicates the occurrence of a noise approximately the duration of a syllable.

The following subject was unusual in that one of his noises replaced the word "she," illustrated in the first passage, and some of his noises lasted several seconds as in the second passage.

Subject 11

First excerpt

Interviewer: I wonder if you could give a picture of what she's like? (i.e., subject's wife).

Subject: Well, (omits "she") . . . (*xxxx*) is wonderful, and a very good wife, and a very good girl, a good Catholic, uncomplicated. And . . . uh . . . (*xxx*) she's not overly intelligent, but I mean in the affairs of everyday life she's . . . (*xx*) well, she's down to earth. And . . . uh . . . well, she's . . . uh . . . uncomplicated.

Second excerpt

And . . . uh . . . I dunno what age they (i.e., mother and father) were when they got married. —(*xxxx* . . . *xxxx* . . . *xxxx*)—. Anyway, we lived in B— for awhile, and I was born in B—, etc.

Slurring. Unusually indistinct articulation occasionally occurred in the masking conditions. Only one subject showed increased slurring in all six masking conditions; he spoke the least distinctly of all the subjects without the masking noise as well. Six subjects slurred only in the third interview and four subjects did it for the first time in the second interview. Only two subjects slurred in the first interview. Thus this was a late-appearing phenomenon, which fact may account for its low incidence in Table 21.1.

Rate. No sharp distinction was made between articulation rate when speaking and overall word-rate per unit time in judging rate of speech. As Table 21.1 indicates, some subjects spoke slower and some faster in a small number of the masking conditions. There was no relationship between the incidence of rate changes and slurring.

The following tabulation shows that the male and female subjects differed considerably in this effect of the masking condition.

Kind of Rate Change

	Faster	Slower	None
Males	0	6	2
Females	4	1	4

Phrasing. This term refers to the fragmentation of a continuous utterance into a discontinuous series of phrases demarcated by noticeable but brief pauses. The net effect was the impression that the subject was speaking in phrases and not in sentences.

General Behavioral-Psychological Changes.   Affect expression. Fourteen subjects manifested greater affect in one or more of the masking-noise conditions than in any of their nonmasking conditions. The *types of changes* observed included: variations in laughter, greater general spontaneity of affect expression, increased excitement, anger, and sensuality or erotism.

In the masking conditions, the laughter was more frequent, of longer duration, louder of course, sometimes more paroxysmal and more erotic. Changes in laughter were largely characteristic of the female subjects, being apparent in seven of them but in only one of the men.

In some cases, the change in affect expression was general throughout a condition. Male Subject 13, for example, characteristically sounded assertive and aggressive in the masking conditions but obsequious and somewhat effeminate in the nonmasking conditions. The lower upper class young woman, Subject 4, characteristically spoke with greater vitality and spontaneity with the noise, causing the listener to be more interested in what she was saying and to find greater enjoyment in hearing her speak than was true when she spoke in the nonmasking conditions.

At times, intense affect was expressed in relation to the personal content being discussed by the subject. Female Subject 9, who was usually quite pleasant and easygoing, sounded exceedingly angry and spoke in an extremely loud shouting voice as she recounted having been angered several years earlier by an unreasonable high school teacher. No comparable intensity of affect was observed in the nonmasking condition.

An especially interesting increase in content-related affect was shown by female Subject No. 7 as the following interchange took place in one of the masking conditions. Just before this fragment of the interview the patient was speaking about her religious conversion at an Evangelical Bible Camp 3 years ago ("vocal noises" also indicated by *x*):

Interviewer: But did you have any kind of an emotional experience?

Subject: Yes I did.

Interviewer: What was that like?

Subject: (Subject characteristically seemed excited when speaking with masking noise. In this passage her excitement increased and her face started to become red.) Well, . . . ah. . . I'm very emotional anyway when it comes to sad things so I can't say this is just a sad experience or a happy experience or an emotional experience. I feel as if the Holy Spirit really touched my heart and made me want to repent. And take Christ as my personal saviour. And . . .

ah . . . it brought tears to my eyes. But I don't want to believe that this is just an emotional experience. I . . . because that's not enough.

Interviewer: Uhuh.

Subject: Because if it was, it wouldn't last. So it's something that you (x) take for life. In other words, your eternal life begins right then, instead of beginning when you die. Begins right on earth.

Interviewer: Uhuh. What did it seem like when you had that experience? You felt that the Holy Spirit had touched your heart?

Subject: (With the following utterance, her excitement becomes very intense, face becomes redder, and toward the end of it her upper lip is curled back on one side.) Well, I felt like a very (x) insignificant sinner who had been forgiven by my decision. And I felt very happy. Extremely happy. Although it's no bowl of cherries because (x) most anyone who has any type of . . . ah . . . strict religion, is usually persecuted in some way. And as a Christian, I know I'd be persecuted. In fact, I know I haven't really been persecuted enough, because I haven't stood up for what I should. That's one of the reasons I feel I have back-slidden—because I haven't stood up for what I really believe, in many situations.

(As he listened to this psychotically flavored content and observed her increasing level of agitation, the interviewer thought he should determine her immediate capacity for "testing reality" and coping with her paranoid ideation. He felt somewhat alarmed and was considering bringing the experiment to a close for this subject.)

Interviewer: Uhuh. How do you think the . . . ah . . . how are the Christians persecuted?

Subject: (sounding quite surprised) Pardon me?

Interviewer: You know, you said that you felt that you hadn't been persecuted enough. Can you explain that to me? . . . I'm interested in finding out.

Subject: At first when I had this conversion experience and took Jesus as my saviour—

Interviewer: Yeah.

Subject: (x) A lot of people laughed at me, and

Interviewer: Uhuh.

Subject: And you know . . . not laughed, but at school you're different. You are no longer a worldly person. And . . . ah . . . people noticed it. And now I feel as if I've become very worldly again. I'm not living the type of life I should, and. . . Not that I want people to laugh at me. I don't. And I don't think that's the idea of becoming a Christian, just to be persecuted. I think as a Christian you—

Interviewer: Yeah.

Subject: Spread the message and you show your love. You don't go around being self-righteous. That's not what I mean. But (x) I. . . I. . . I feel as if I. . . (x). . . I'm not standing up to what I really believe enough.

Interviewer: (Feeling now that a crisis was past, perceiving the subject quieted as she progressively reassessed and negated the paranoid ideation.) Uhuh. That's interesting, I'd like to talk more about that in some of the other interviews.

This young woman became excited in five of the six masking-noise conditions and on two other occasions her excitement reached a high level as she spoke about specific content: once when speaking of her boyfriend when she also laughed in a "devilish and libidinal" manner, and again when she uttered a loosely organized, symbolically toned, almost incoherent statement about her teaching aspirations.

This subject's MMPI scores were all within normal limits, but they showed the typical "schizophrenic cluster" on the paranoid, psychasthenic, and schizophrenic scales and these scale scores all fell very close to the upper limit of the normal range. Apparently her definite capacity for heated thought, psychotically toned both in form and content, springs from her general psychological status at the time of this investigation. In the non-masking conditions she frequently negated paranoid thoughts. Several times, for example, she said of her present life circumstances, "I'm not the victim of circumstances." But in the masking conditions, the underlying psychotic affective and ideational tendencies episodically became more manifest.

At times, the increased affect expression consisted of direct emotional responses to the interviewer. In evaluating the examples about to be presented, the reader should picture the interviewer through the subject's eyes: he's visibly 20 years older, a stranger, and a gray-haired, pipe-smoking "professor" of psychology at a university that overshadowed the subject's college.

Some of the emotional reactions toward the interviewer were openly positive or thinly veiled erotic ones. Thus one of the young women, No. 1, spoke affectionately as she said the following in a masking condition in the third interview:

Subject: (After a long description of her not completely satisfactory relationship with her boyfriend, including episodes of his being inconsiderate, she suddenly laughed.) I'm thinking of you sitting over there (laugh).

Interviewer: What are you thinking?

Subject: I was just watching you smoking. You look so calm and relaxed.

Interviewer: Well, what did you think?

Subject: I was. . . I was thinking you looked so. . . ah. . . well, I guess I should use the word 'understanding' again. You look so understanding sitting there and. . . I just felt like talking. (laugh) I've nothing in mind to say, but you are the type of person that people can talk to.

Interviewer: Thank you.

Subject: You are really. (laughs). I'm not trying to give out compliments but, I mean, it. . . (*xx*). . . I think that's a wonderful trait for a person in your field to have because you really need it.

Interviewer: I like to talk with people.

Subject: You can see you do.

Subjects also expressed anger toward the interviewer. Thus a female subject, No. 5, *suddenly and sarcastically* spoke as follows in one of the masking conditions:

Subject: You're quite comical (laughing).

Interviewer: What?

Subject: You're quite comical (laughing).

Interviewer: Why? Why?

Subject: The position you have.

Interviewer: Oh? Why? T. . . tell me about that. How did it seem comical to you?

Subject: (Pause) Well, I don't know (laughing), it's just the idea that you're interfering.

Interviewer: How. . . ?

Subject: (interrupting) Can't you hear me?

Interviewer: Yeah.

Subject: Oh, can't you hear me?

Interviewer: Yeah, yeah, sure.

Subject: You're interfering in my train of thought.

Interviewer: How?

Subject: By pressing it, of course (laughing). [i.e., pressing the foot switch controlling the masking noise]

Interviewer: (laughs) But you said my position was comical. What did you mean?

Subject: Yes. You're sitting there with a pipe, just like. . . ah. . . I don't know, some English gentleman I suppose (laughing).

Associative response. This term refers to the flow of utterances by the subject during the interviews. "Freer associative response" means that the subject talks more readily, a change, which he may manifest in several ways. He may say more in response to the interviewer's comments; he may respond more quickly to the interviewer; and the interviewer may find that it is not as necessary to ask questions and that simple acknowledgements that he is listening are all that are necessary on his side to maintain a continual stream of utterances from the subject. At times this effect of the masking condition was very impressive, for the subjects would continue talking at such length that the interview transcripts would run two or three pages consecutively with only one comment per page by the interviewer, and often none at all.

Quantitative measures reflect more objectively the "freer associative responses" observed in the clinical survey of the interviews. The interview typescripts followed the format of the interview excerpts that have been presented throughout this chapter and the page margins were fixed. Upon inspecting this format it is apparent that a count of the number of words uttered by the subject per page provides an index of the quantitative aspect of what we have called the "associative response." Therefore, we tabulated the words per page under the masking and nonmasking conditions for each subject. These tabulations were carried out only for Interviews II and III. The inclusion of Interview I would have introduced a constant bias in the results because the nonmasking condition was always the first condition of that interview and at the same time it was always one in which the interviewer was most active. The interviewer's relatively high-activity level in itself would automatically lower the subject's page word count in the nonmasking condition of Interview I. The effect of the masking condtion was clearly to increase the verbal productivity for the group as a whole ($p < .001$); *the average change in average words per page was 24%.*

One also gained the distinct clinical impression that a qualitative difference in the associative response occurred, as well as the quantitative change just reported. The subjects revealed fairly intimate, personal material in these interviews, and often to a greater degree in the masking conditions. The following instance illustrates this apparent phenomenon. During one of the masking conditions, a male subject, when asked to tell the interviewer about his family, told the following in detail. When he was a very young child his father, a factory worker, brought a male friend to his home. Soon this man became a roomer in the household. He and the subject's mother became lovers and would have intercourse upstairs at night, while the father would become drunk downstairs. This home situation persisted for many years and resulted in one illegitimate child, a half brother of the subject. In the Inquiry, this subject said he preferred the masking condition of this interview because he didn't hear the unpleasant things he was saying.

Eleven subjects, six females and five males, spontaneously (!) referred during the Inquiries to the externally observable changes in associative response. Their comments revealed an awareness by them of both the quantitative and qualitative effects of the masking conditions. Three subjects felt they "rambled" during the masking conditions. Eight subjects stated quite directly, although in various ways, that they felt less inhibited when talking in the masking conditions.

One subject felt an "urge to confess" and felt less inhibited but, at the same time, "resistant at letting out all these intimate things."

Another said he had told something he had never told anyone before—i.e., his complex private feelings about the appearance of his acne-marred face.

Two subjects felt they said "too much," "revealed too much."

One sensed an increase in her ability to recall memories of her past life and in the vividness of the memories. Another thought "maybe I admit things I wouldn't ordinarily bear to think" in the noise condition. Still another subject said she had discussed things she ordinarily wouldn't discuss.

The final subject said that during the masking conditions he felt he had a lot to say and wanted to tell so much that there wasn't enough time.

Cognitive confusion. This category includes relatively minor variations in normal syntax, simple forgetting of what one was talking about, and disorganized sequence of utterances.

The following excerpt from masked speech illustrates some of the *minor, but unusual, syntactical variations.* Subject No. 2 said:

I took piano and he took accordion. And . . . uh . . . I guess I took about 8 or 9 years lessons.

The following interchange with another subject, No. 10, contains a more complicated syntactical confusion; it involves the underlined "quite often," not the many normal sentence changes. The solid and dotted arrows are discussed later.

The *"quite often"* occurs out of context but it was uttered without a break in tempo. Possibly the "quite often" migrated from the end of the preceding statement, as indicated by the solid arrow; the reconstructed, "She and I go to the beach quite often," is meaningful. But it is also possible that it migrated from some earlier point in time, such as that indicated by the broken arrow. This reconstruction also "makes sense." (The fact that the

Interviewer: Do you see a lot of her?

Subject: Well, I have more during the . . . since we've been out from school. Wh . . . when I went to school, I had one . . . I was in one class with her. But other than that I . . . I saw her perhaps for 5 or 10 minutes   ?
a day. So the only time we've ever got to go out would be on a Friday or Saturday. So . . . however since the . . . uh . . . school's been let out, I've seen a lot more of her. Wh . . . she . . . uh . . . she and I go to the beach   We went

to the beach yesterday *quite often.* I expect to see her tonight. And we're
                                (lower volume)
going to go to X_____ and maybe I'll see her . . . uh . . . well, Saturday,
maybe tomorrow night.

"quite often" was uttered at a lower volume level suggests another possibility: that it was the subject's intention to inhibit these words. The basis for this speculation becomes clear when more definite examples of "thinking aloud" are examined later.)

There were many instances in the masking conditions where *subjects lost their train of thought, forgot what they were talking about,* and simply acknowledged that fact and fell silent. Sometimes the subjects coped with their loss of train of thought by repeating earlier words or phrases. They reported this device enabled them to proceed with only a minimal amount of confusion.

Sometimes the loss of train of thought was obviously due to the sudden intrusion of other trains of thought. Vacillation between different lines of thought often produced a series of utterances confusing to the listener. This happened in the following interchange, at the end of which the subject (No. 11) picks up the original train of thought. The instances of "cognitive confusion" caused by intruding thoughts are underlined and asterisked. Except where indicated the subject is speaking very loudly.

Interviewer: Mhm. What kind of things do you do together?

Subject: Well, before the baby came we just. . . ah. . . went to the movies, played cards. . . ah. . . went swimming, went for rides, and. . . ah just spent our time together at home, *xx* (vocal noise) and television. And. . . ah. . . now we don't get to go out much. We spend most of our nights at home watching television or . . . she'll help me study for a test, . . . but . . .ah . . . our social life is pretty limited now.

Interviewer: Get along okay together? (i.e., subject and his wife)

Subject: We get along very good. I mean . . . ah . . . *I get along* (much lower volume) . . . ah . . . we get along fine. I mean . . . ah . . . she's a little . . . ah . . . gets a little tired and cross at times because she has to . . . ah . . . stay in. I mean she doesn't like to go out all the time, but she likes to meet people. She's a very friendly girl. She makes friends with . . . ah . . . everyone she meets. And she gets a little lonely because she's . . . for all of her life she's worked in an office and had a lot of girl friends. And she comes from a big family, so it gets a little lonely at times for her. And I'm not financially . . . or . . . ah . . . ah . . . *I don't have enough time* * *to . . . ah . . . go out dancing or go to the . . . movies . . . or spend as much time away from my studies as I would be if I wasn't married.* But . . . ah . . . *xxx* (vocal noise) . . . *as far as doing* **things together . . . ah . . . getting along, that's it, getting along (silent laugh) . . . ah . . . we get along in an uncomplicated way.*

In the last passage, the subject spent most of his time talking about his wife's feelings. As he was doing so, however, statements referring to his own sentiments intruded out of context on two different occasions. And as he spoke of how he and his wife got along together, a statement about their doing things together intruded, apparently being the product of the perseveration of the line of thought relevant to the *preceding passage*. The subject himself showed awareness of his cognitive confusion in the last utterance of the excerpt.

Another type of cognitive confusion consisted of an *exceptional degree of fragmentation and syntactical disorganization of utterances,* such as occurred in the following excerpt.

Interviewer: What was it about her (i.e., a former teacher) that you liked?

Subject No. 7: Well, *x* (vocal noise) at the time I . . . I didn't really know what a good teacher was and what a bad teacher . . . their teaching methods. She seemed to be a fairly good teacher, in . . . in the actual teaching, and yet she was a very nice person. She was a person to be expected . . . respected, and she's a person that . . . ah . . . in a wh . . . She inter . . . within her teaching program . . . ah . . . within teaching us she . . . ah . . . intramingled . . . ah . . . the teaching of democracy and teaching of high principles for us as citizens. Yet it didn't sound corny, it sounded very good, and I think *x* (vocal noise) that's one reason I like her, because I respected her so much as a person.

The subject remembered this episode in the inquiry at the end of the interview. She felt she needed help putting the words in the right order.

In all, *14 subjects reported experiencing "cognitive confusion" at some time during the masking conditions.* Twelve subjects experienced losing their train of thought or forgetting what they wanted to say; nine subjects reported a sense of having difficulty in expressing their thoughts such as finding the right word, keeping their words in the right order, or coherently organizing their thoughts.

"Thinking aloud." In this rare but striking event, subjects said aloud things that they were thinking but apparently were not aware of and/or did not

intend to be audible. One instance occurred in the following interchange, at the asterisked point. The subject, No. 1, is speaking of a recent event: her boyfriend did not take her to a veterans' group party after all.

Subject: Well, it's strange. All along I assumed that I was going. He kept saying, "I'm not taking anyone to this." He kept saying, "I . . . I wouldn't take a dog there" (laughs). He said, "I don't like the locality, I don't like the neighborhood." It's a very tough neighborhood. And he . . . he kept saying that he thought it would just end up into be a . . . being a beer brawl. And he said he didn't want me around. But I thought he was kidding all the time. And so up until Friday I thought I was going, even though I wasn't. (laughs) So I talked to him Friday and it became more clear to me what was happening, because he said he was going to give out drinks all night. And . . . ah . . . so I realized that he wasn't just fooling around. In the beginning though I just thought he was just joking. Because we go every place together.

Interviewer: Uhuh.

*Subject: And, -?-?-?-? (incomprehensible, low-volume mutter)

Interviewer: What did you say then?

Subject: What did I say then? *Oh, I was just thinking about the party.* He was telling me. . .

Interviewer: What . . . what were your thoughts?

Subject: I was thinking about the beer party.

Interviewer: Yeah.

Subject: I was just thinking about the beer party. Because he said that they were nine deep at the bar and he said he couldn't give out the beer fast enough (said laughing).

The incomprehensible, low-volume mutter occurred at a time when the subject was "just thinking." To that extent, she thought out loud.

Early in the first interview, a 27-year-old male subject (No. 16), a Jew, said, "And my father's been dead for 20 years," while speaking without the masking noise. The next reference to "father" occurred in the following interchange when the subject was speaking under a masking condition of the same interview.

Interviewer: When was this that you lived in X_____ and Y_____?

Subject: I lived in X_____ when . . . I musta been about 1 or 2 years old. Then we moved to Y_____ and . . . ah . . . lived there for 2 years. And then my father got a position in Z_____, and . . . ah . . . we moved to Z_____. And that's where he died.

Interviewer: What kind of work did your father do?

Subject: Well my father, *av'sholom,* was a rabbi.

Interviewer: Mhm. Ah . . . you sa . . . you said a word there. You said, "My . . .

Subject: Oh. Ah . . . that means . . . ah . . . "may he rest in peace." In . . . in . . . when . . . in . . . Je . . . when you're Jewish, whenever you speak of a dead person, you always say that—which means "may he rest in peace."

The subject had not, however, said "av'shalom" as he spoke earlier of his father, even of his father's death, when he could hear himself. Nor did he ever use this expression again when speaking upon several occasions about his father.

His father, who died when the subject was 7, was "an extremely Orthodox Jew." The subject regarded himself as a Conservative Jew, for he kept a Kosher home and observed the Holidays. In the third interview, the subject was aware of thinking but not saying "av'sholom" as he spoke of his dead, Orthodox aunts. As he thought about the incident of the first interview he realized that he did not use this expression when speaking with someone who was not a Jew, and that upon meeting the interviewer he had preconsciously categorized him as not Jewish. Finally, the verbatim extract shows how the subject's speech became very "flustered" when the interviewer asked about the use of "av'sholom." These facts suggest that this subject always said "av'sholom" when speaking of the dead, but to himself when speaking with a non-Jew, and that he only spoke it aloud with the interviewer because of the influence of the masking condition.

The next-to-last example of cognitive confusion contained an instance of "thinking aloud" that is more complicated that the preceding ones. It is the utterance out-of-context, and at low volume, of the thought fragment, "I get along." (see p. 353) The schematization of Fig. 21.1 illustrates what is assumed by the author to have happened after the interviewer asked: "Get along okay together?" The intended statements, those at the top, are unified both syntactically and acoustically. The "I get along" is a syntactic and acoustic foreign element. It seems to belong to an inhibited, conflicted line of thought, concurrent with the intended statements. The instigation to utter the inhibited line of thought seems to have become stronger with the passage of time. This produced another conflict, one between uttering the intended statements and those belonging to the inhibited line of thought. The conflicts are manifested in the pausing behavior and the conjoined "I get along." From the subject's standpoint, the conflicts were resolved in favor of his intended statements. For the moment only, however. A rereading of the entire passage excerpted earlier will show that as the subject

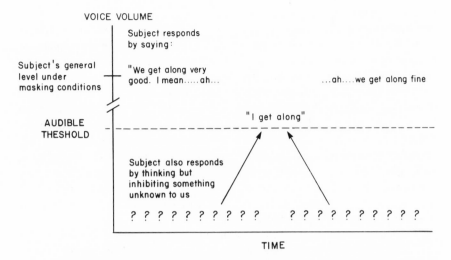

FIG. 21.1 Schematization of processes hypothesized to account for subject's thinking aloud, "I get along," which is spoken at a barely audible intensity and out-of-context.

continues he speaks of how his wife feels. But then there occurs the statement:

> And I'm not financially . . . or . . . ah . . . ah . . . I don't have enough time to . . . ah . . . go out dancing or go to the . . . movies . . . or spend as much time away from my studies as I would if I wasn't married.

which is completely unrelated to what he has been saying, causing the listener to be confused. It seems quite possible that this statement is a result of, and thus further evidence of, the private inhibited line of thought we have inferred to be accompanying the public, intended statements.

Changes Over Time of Externally Observable Effects of Masking Noise. The precise determination of changes over time was not attempted in this study. This could only be done through a great deal of additional scrutiny of the tapes where this determination was the sole purpose. Nevertheless, the writer did form some definite impressions. Those pertaining to the degree to which effects were sustained during individual noise conditions were presented in the discussion of the individual effects. Two further impressions were formed.

Immediacy of Speech Changes. Speech changes dramatically *the moment* the masking noise is administered. Colleagues and audiences who have heard excerpts of the tapes have been struck by this fact. Immediate increased loudness, flattening of intonation, and changes in "voice style" are especially striking. The second generation Italian–American, male subject (No. 13) who has been mentioned (p. 343) illustrates the immediacy of change very clearly. Before the masking noise was first administered he spoke softly and precisely and sounded effeminate and obsequious. The moment the masking noise was administered he spoke loudly, with flattened intonation, and sounded harsher, more masculine and aggressive. And his lower social status dialect characteristics immediately became noticeable. Before the masking he sounded like an "overly refined young man"; the moment the masking occurred he sounded like a "tough kid." The masking noise was deliberately turned on and off for brief periods in one of the noise conditions of the third interview to obtain a record that would demonstrate the immediacy of its effects. His two styles of speech changed regularly, *as though they were being switched on and off.*

In all the subjects, the return to normal speech with cessation of the masking noise was just as striking as the masking-induced change. Occasionally, a definite transition period of about 30 seconds could be observed. One got the impression in these instances that the subject was in the process of regaining his auditory feedback, as though his auditory threshold was decreasing over a brief period of time.

Adaptation. The category showing the most noticeable evidence of adaptation over the three interviews was loudness. Subject 17 was even able to talk in Interview III with only a little difference in volume in the masking and nonmasking conditions. He had set volume control as a definite goal for himself. Although he finally approached it, he didn't completely achieve it.

Generally, however, signs of adaptation were not remarkable nor consistent. By the end of the third interview a few subjects gave a general impression of some adaptation, but most did not; and a few subjects became increasingly affected by the masking conditions. Furthermore, trends over interviews were not always in the same direction in all categories. Some subjects who showed adaptation in loudness, for example, made more vocal noises in the third interview than earlier. The late occurrence of slurring was noted previously.

Subjective Experiences in Masking Conditions

The subjective report data were sometimes congruent with the externally observable behavior discussed earlier and sometimes they were not. Generally speaking, the subjects' *reported* experience of the masking conditions was negative, more so initially than after the first interview. Some important exceptions are cited later. Also, the inquiry data is compared with the impression formed by the interviewer of the subject's general reactions to the masking conditions.

Fifteen of the 17 subjects felt it was easier to talk without the masking noise in Interview I. Nine subjects felt this way in the third interview. The major reported aversive qualities of the masking conditions included the noise itself, the physical effort of talking in its presence, the inability to hear oneself, the interference with cognitive processes of "keeping one's train of thought" and verbal articulation, a sense of loss of contact with oneself or the interviewer, and negative affects. It is not surprising that nearly a third of the subjects felt angry during the masking conditions of the first interview. The aversive qualities were especially marked at that time; nearly all of them were reported considerably less frequently after the first interview. Correlated with this change was the report of considerable adaptation to the masking condition by every one of the subjects and an increase from two subjects at the time of the first interview, to eight in the third interview who did not find it more difficult or unpleasant to talk with the masking noise. This is the general outline of the reported subjective experiences in the masking conditions.

The overall picture conflicts in two important ways with the impression produced in the interviewer by the overt verbal, vocal, and general behavior of the subjects. First, the subjects did not appear to be "suffering" as much as is suggested by their reports, even in the first interview. In fact, some of them seemed to enjoy the experience even in Interview I and certainly in the investigation as a whole. The interviewer was more struck with how easily the subjects talked than with initial or episodic disturbances in talking. As a group, the subjects impressed the writer with their involvement in the interview transactions and in the experiment. *Not a single subject postponed, arrived late, or missed an appointment.* Secondly, there is no agreement between the "objective" signs of adaptation and the subjective sense of it on the part of the subjects. Although every subject reported considerable adaptation to the noise as a stimulus and to the lack of auditory feedback, few subjects gave objective evidence in their speech behavior of progressively and extensively adapting. In fact, four of the subjects distinctly appeared to be more affected in the second or third interviews than in the first. Yet one of these said it was easier to talk with the noise than without it in Interviews II and III.

Turning now to illustrate and examine in more detail the *negative subjective experiences*, we begin with the stimulus properties of the noise itself. The noise reminded the subjects of rushing air or water, various mechanical sounds, and of radio or telephone static. When the noise was experienced as a noxious stimulus, as it was for fourteen subjects in Interview I, it was primarily because of its intensity and of its intrusive quality, both of which preempted the subject's attention. The following paraphrased comments illustrate this kind of reaction to the noise in the first interview.

It was a hostile sound coming in on you. It wasn't welcome. It was distracting to have that noise going around in my ears. It was like this was inside my head. When I start talking my brain doesn't grasp onto the thought and right away the noise becomes the most prominent thing.

Some subjects, six in Interview I and two in Interview II, complained that talking with the masking noise was effortful. Some of their comments were:

You had to force your thoughts to take place and to express yourself in words rather than just talk naturally. The first time I was worn out after I left. I was too pooped to pop.

Not every subject complained about the fact that he couldn't hear himself, but 12, 8, and 2 did so in Interviews I, II, and III respectively.

Difficulty in cognitive organization and syntactic expression was reported nearly as often as the noxious properties of the noise in Interview I and more frequently in Interviews II and III. Subjects often attributed this difficulty both to the intrusive-preemptive quality of the noise and to the feedback deficit, as the following paraphrased reports demonstrate.

Subject No. 7: I felt as if I couldn't express myself in any way possible because I couldn't hear myself. I wasn't sure I was using the right words, verb forms, and sentence structure. And I think I was more inclined to forget what I had just said.

Subject 9, Interview I: In the beginning it really distracted me. I couldn't think of what I was saying. I had a sensation that I wasn't really speaking. I almost felt that I was thinking of this. (i.e., instead of speaking). That was when I coughed and realized I was speaking. I wasn't quite sure of what I was doing. *Interview II:* I didn't find the noise as distracting this time as last time. I still had to fish around a few times for a particular word I wanted. Maybe it's because I can't hear it and I don't know whether I'm saying it right or not. That's why with that word *"sick"*—I was trying to say "afflicted" and I didn't know whether it was going to come out right so I just didn't say it.

Some subjects reported what we have come to call *"Loss of Contact with Self or Interviewer"* during the masking condition. This experience was most frequently reported in Interview I and when the subject was deprived of both auditory feedback from his own voice and visual contact with the interviewer. The following paraphrased remarks indicate the nature of the experience.

Subject 1, Interview I: It's harder to talk with the noise. But it was easier when you were in front of me than behind me, because at least there was some contact with something—something you could see, something concrete.

Whereas when you're behind me it's very astract. I felt there was no one there to talk to really even though I realized you were behind me.

Subject 8, Interview I: With the noise I felt like I was talking to myself. I talk but I don't seem to have a part in what I'm saying. It's even funnier facing away from you. It's like talking to no one; it's like nobody's there. *Interview II:* It's a lot harder to talk with the noise on. You don't know how you're saying things; you don't even know what you're saying; you sort of forget things; you don't know if you did or didn't say something. It leaves you with an empty feeling. And the noise seems to push you back. It seems to put you out of reality in a way. It feels like you're talking through clouds or something.

Subject 10, Interview I: It made me feel like I was sitting in a big room and the room was so big that as I was talking I wasn't getting any rebound off the walls and my ears. I was just talking into emptiness.

Subject 11, Interview I: It took me away from reality. It was like being separated from everything, being in some kind of ether. I mean some never-never land. It was more subjective. I was all alone with the sound. (In B-N condition.)

All of the preceding negative aspects of the masking-noise condition were stated or implied to be causes of general discomfort for the subjects. Except for the physical effort required in talking, these negative aspects were also the causes for the more specific affects of anxiety and tension, and for anger as well. It is worth noting that the reports of anxiety and tension were the only ones of the "negative reactions" that did not decrease from Interview I to Interview III.

The general decrease in frequency of negative references about the masking conditions was associated with reports by every subject of considerable adaptation by the third interview. Even the nine subjects who stated that it was easier to talk without noise than with it in the third interview reported considerable adaptation by that time.

Six subjects specified certain "positive" features of the masking conditions. And at one time or another during the interview series, four subjects preferred talking in the masking condition whereas five others reported having no preference between the masking and the unmasking condition. For seven of these nine subjects, the masking condition achieved its preferred or neutral status only in Interviews II and III, indicating the importance of experienced adaptation.

A most unusual and informative case was Subject 5, a young woman, who from the first interview preferred the masking condtions—even though she found the noise itself a noxious stimulus in that interview and complained that it interfered with thinking and verbal expression. She insisted that she didn't like to hear her own voice and felt more relaxed and at ease when the masking noise prevented her from doing so. Her singular reaction is consistent with the total picture that emerges from observing her speech style and considering it in the light of her social context and personal history. This young woman persistently tried to speak the dialect of the American stage and theatre. Her normal speech style reminded the interviewer from the beginning of Bette Davis'—in caricature. She spoke with exaggerated articulatory movements and strenuous attempts at acoustic precision. Yet she came from a lower middle class Italian–American background. The total impression was one of affectation. This configuration of factors indicates that she was concerned with how she sounded. One determinant of her speech style was an avowed aspiration to be an actress. Another, fully conscious, determinant was an "obsession for perfection" in action and speech, which she attributed to her mother's perfectionism and to her own sense of worthlessness. Her relevant remarks, paraphrased and condensed, were:

Subject: My mother required perfection. She always reprimanded me for the way I acted or the way I talked. My sister was a year older and she mastered things before I did and spoke better. And before I knew it, nothing was quite right anymore in the way I walked, the way I talked, or the way I did things.

Interviewer: Why don't you want to hear your voice?

Subject: I have an obsession for perfection. I don't like my voice. I don't feel it's good. It comes from my mother pestering me all these years about the way I speak, about my voice and my diction.

The subject also reported that when she talked with the masking noise she felt more relaxed generally, *and her mouth seemed to move more freely* than was true without the noise.

We infer the following from these data. The subject had internalized her mother's observing and critical functions. When she spoke under normal conditions she was continually trying to be "perfect" and was continually listening to her speech to see if it was "perfect," that is, as good as her rival older sister's and as good as her actress ideals. She judged it negatively but continued trying to speak perfectly. Tension and effortful speech were some of the results. The caricature that resulted may also have had a hostile component directed toward her mother, for even her "perfect" speech angered her mother. When the subject couldn't hear herself speak, she was spared both the sense of worthlessness prompted by what she felt were "imperfect" qualities of her voice and diction and the strenuous attempt to overcome this low self-esteem. Now she could relax and articulate more freely.

One might expect this subject, normally so self-conscious about her speech, to become anxious instead of comfortable when she couldn't hear herself speak because she then had no way of knowing if she sounded "perfect" or not. The reason this did not happen may be related to her report that talking with the masking noise, while facing away from the interviewer, "was close to sitting and daydreaming." This was another positive aspect of the masking condition for her. Talking in the masking condition was not like talking, it was like being half divorced from reality in fantasy, when she would have no reason to be concerned with how she sounded. Apparently the capacity of the masking condition to decrease contact with reality and herself brought positive relief from such concerns to this subject, not discomfort, even panic, as it did in the instances of negative reactions discussed above.

Subject 14 was also unusual in that he had no preference for masking or nonmasking in any of the interviews. He enjoyed hearing the noise, at least in Interview I, because it had a hypnotic quality for him. He compared it pleasantly with static he used to pick up with his short-wave radio as a boy that he used to fantasy was the sound of the surf on some island shore far off in the ocean. He experienced talking in the masking condition in Interview II as a comfortable state akin to fantasy. He said it was "like musing" and that then the interviewer became just part of his "own imagination." Apparently these positive elements were balanced by negative ones, some of which he specified. He felt he skipped syllables occasionally with the noise and "felt a spasm of resistance at letting out all these intimate things" which he attributed to "an urge to confess" in the masking conditions.

Other subjects reported positive experiences similar to those of the preceding two subjects. Subject 1 preferred the masking-noise conditions in Interview III because she felt as though she were "escaping reality," and she felt "more secure" because she experienced "less fear of criticism" for what she said when she couldn't hear herself. Subject 11 reported greater comfort with the noise in Interviews II and III. He specified in Interview II that with the noise he didn't have to hear unpleasant things he said, by which he meant certain personal details of his life causing him shame and embarrassment, which he felt an inner compulsion to tell. His comment in the Inquiry of Interview III, "the sound is an old friend," implies that the same sense of security was produced by the masking condition in that interview also and was a reason for preferring that condition then.

Subject 8 experienced increased visual vividness of, and greater accessibility to memories of her childhood in the noise conditions of Interviews II and III. She seemed to enjoy being thus "pushed back by the noise."

Seven subjects reported an interesting phenomenon at one time or another: the intensity of the noise seemed lower when they talked than when they were silent. We will call this the "attention phenomenon."

Subject 5: You can deafen the noise with your own thoughts.

Subject 8: When the noise was on, you sort of wanted to keep talking so you wouldn't hear the noise. You couldn't hear yourself anyway, but at least you had something to think about when you were talking.

This phenomenon raises a question about the mechanism responsible for the increased verbal output in the masking conditions. In our choice of the category label "freer associative response," we implied that a mechanism of disinhibition was responsible for the increased output. The phenomenon now discussed, especially as formulated by Subject 8, raises the possibility that the increased verbal output may occur because speaking is rewarded by decreasing the aversiveness of the masking condition. The following comparison of the increase in verbal output in the masking conditions for those seven subjects reporting this phenomenon with that for those subjects not reporting it bears on this question. These data are inconsistent with the avoidance hypothesis.

	Mean % increase in verbal output in masking conditions of interviews II and III
Subjects reporting attention phenomenon	17%
Subjects not reporting attention phenomenon	28%
	$p = .20$ (t_2)

Discussion

Many striking changes were observed in the speech and in the more general behavior of our subjects during the masking conditions. The fact that the subjects were as a group quite intelligent and of high-verbal skills perhaps makes the changes all the more impressive. We do not claim to have observed all the effects of the experimental condition. This survey only deals systematically with those effects that originally caught our attention as we conducted the interviews and screened the tape recordings. Others approaching the interviews with different perspectives might find additional effects of the experimental manipulations.

In the following discussion we consider the reliability and generality of these observations, the probable cause of the changes associated with the masking conditions, the possible role of feedback in "ego-functions," and some miscellaneous ideas and questions suggested by this study.

Partial Confirmation in the Work of Others

How *reliable* are the observations of the linguistic and psychological changes associated with the administration of the masking noise? This question arises because many of the observations consist of the "subjective" judgments and inferences of a single observer. How *general* are the presumed effects of the masking noise? Are they unique to these subjects, to the interview situation involving this particular interviewer, etc? Although we are aware of only a few other studies of completely masked speech, their results and ours appear to be very similar.

Changes in Speech. Several investigators have noted various changes in the speech process. Shane (1955) and Cherry and Sayers (1956) found that stutterers spoke much more fluently when their speech was masked by noise. Birch (1956) and Birch and Lee (1955) observed a similar change in the disturbed speech of expressive aphasia. These findings are comparable to ours in showing that speech in general is altered by masking. They also bear on our observations of a possible disinhibition process, as is discussed later.

Most of the specific categories listed in Table 21.1 as "linguistic changes" have been observed by others: increased loudness, flattened intonation, and prolongation of syllables have been reported by Wood (1950) and Klein (1965). Wood, Klein, and Shane also observed changes in "voice quality." Also, Wood noted increased pitch; Klein and Shane, slurring; and Shane as well as Holmes and Holzman (1966), changes in rate of speech. The only "linguistic" categories in Table 21.1 not reported by others are those of vocal noises and more distinct phrasing, although the latter may very well be a manifestation of "increased editing" observed by Klein in some subjects. These two phenomena were so apparent when they occurred that the lack of confirmation by others is not regarded as a serious matter. Wood noted, as we did, that the most varied speech changes occurred immediately, or nearly so, upon the onset of masking.

Behavioral-Psychological Changes. For the purposes of this discussion we group together the externally observable changes listed under this heading in Table 21.1 and the subjective experiences reported by the subjects in the inquiries. Here, too, most of our important basic observations have also been noted by others.

Friedhoff, Alpert, and Kurtzberg (1962) investigated the *expression of affect* in voice intensity when subjects were required to lie repeatedly to the experimenter. The intensity of these subjects' voices did not change upon lying when they could hear themselves. But it did change if the subjects could not hear their own voices because of a masking noise. Upon lying, under this condition, the voices consistently became louder or softer, depending on the individual concerned. If one regards these vocal changes as manifestations of affects associated with lying, then these findings are comparable to our observation of increased affect expression in the masking conditions of the interviews.

Our *associative response* category referred to both the quantity of talking and a variety of qualitative attributes, such as the degree of spontaneity, of defensiveness, and the readiness to reveal intimate and personal material. We judged from external criteria that the associative response was freer during the masking conditions. Certain of the subjects reported that they experienced this change. Klein (1965) observed similar phenomena when subjects were asked to respond to paintings, Rorschach cards, and stimulus words under normal hearing and masked auditory-feedback conditions. The introduction of a white masking noise increased the quantity of responses, the vividness of imagery, and the number of drive-related contents in the imagery. The subjects experienced their imagery as livelier and more vivid. Holmes and Holzman (1966) asked subjects to tell about a very embarrassing experience using only a nonsense language of their own invention instead of English. Under white noise masking, the subjects spoke in significantly longer utterances and tended to begin speaking sooner than under normal conditions. Thus the associative process became freer in both of these studies.

Although no investigator has reported observations exactly like our *thinking aloud* category, as far as we are aware, the fate of English words that the subjects of Holmes and Holzman had to inhibit and translate into nonsense language was that they were frequently "thought aloud" in our terms; that is, more English words crept into the accounts spoken in nonsense language during the white noise than during the normal condition.

Cognitive confusion phenomena, apparently quite similar to those observed in and experienced by our subjects, were also noted by Klein.

Increased affect expression, freer associative responding, "thinking aloud," as well as the preference of some subjects for speaking with the noise when they couldn't hear their (to them) unpleasant voices and the distressing things they were saying, were among the reasons for our hypothesizing (Mahl, 1960) that disinhibition took place in our subjects under the masking conditions. We discuss this hypothesis in more detail in a moment. We mention it here because the studies by Klein (1965) and Holmes and Holzman (1966) and others, bear on it. The quantitative changes reported in the first two of these studies are consistent with this hypothesis, as are the qualitative changes in the responses of Klein's subjects. So is the difference in English word usage observed by Holmes and Holzman (1966).

Stanton (1968) studied a more familiar form of disinhibition. He asked subjects to utter as many taboo words as possible to standardized listeners under masking and normal conditions. The subjects said many more such words when they could not hear their own voices. The majority of Stanton's subjects expressed a preference for uttering taboo words under the noise condition. But we cannot we sure if this finding is comparable to similar reports by some of our subjects, for Stanton's control subjects who never experienced the noise condition expressed the same preference as did his experimental subjects.

If one assumes that the subjects of Friedhoff, Alpert, and Kurtzberg (1962) were attempting to conceal vocal clues of their lying, then the appearance of changes in voice intensity with the introduction of a masking noise is also a case of disinhibition. And so is the increased fluency of stutterers observed by Cherry and Sayers (1956), if one assumes that speech inhibition is the crucial factor involved in stuttering.

In short, there are several results from other studies in addition to the present one that are compatible with the inference that an underlying process of disinhibition occurs when people speak during the masking-noise condition. Why disinhibition might occur is considered in a moment.

Three other findings remain to be checked against the results of others: the loss of contact with self or interviewer, the attention phenomenon, and adaptation, both observed and experienced, to the masking condition. There have not been reports on the latter two phenomena. Klein's (1965) preliminary report suggests that some of his subjects, too, felt a change in sense of self and reality. Thus, he notes that some subjects reported uncertainty about what they were saying and he comments on a "feeling of isolation" that may have been induced partly by the masking noise and partly by the physical isolation of his subjects in a darkened room. On the whole, there is less confirmation of our findings concerning the subjective experiences than of the externally observable changes in linguistic and more general processes. This may be due to the fact that the other investigators have not studied the subjective experiences in great detail. This appears to be the case.

The fact that most of our basic observations have also been reported by others is important on two counts. First, it indicates that these observations were reliable, for in effect ours were *independent* ones. Until several years later, we did not know of any of the studies reviewed except that of Cherry and Sayers (1956) and those of Birch (1956; Birch & Lee, 1955). The papers by Wood (1950) and Shane (1955) were published in obscure places; the others were reported after this study was completed. Second, the basic phenomena listed in Table 21.1 appear to have a high degree of generalizability across samples of people and various speaking situations. Most of the linguistic changes, for example, have occurred if the subjects read aloud as they did for Shane (1955) and Wood (1950), or if they spoke spontaneously as they did for us and for Klein (1965). Furthermore, both linguistic changes and the rather striking, more general psychological changes have not only been observed in the interview situation used here, but in the various situations used by Holmes and Holzman (1966), Klein (1965), and Stanton (1968), each of which was markedly different from the others. It is quite obvious that some genuine phenomena have been observed in these studies.

Cause of the Phenomena: Noise Input and/or Feedback Deficit?

This question raises many theoretical alternatives. To begin, the masking condition introduces two distinct elements: the stimulus input of the noise and the deficit in feedback of auditory cues from the subject's own speech. Either element might produce one or more different internal states: (a) The stimulus input, for example, might increase the general level of activation or arousal, or it might specifically stress the subject. Or the noise input might cause the subject to automatically make an erroneous unconscious inference: that the interviewer also heard the noise. After all, in his previous experience, any loud noise that interfered with his hearing also affected others present and required loud speech; (b) The significance of the feedback deficit, for example, might consist simply in the fact of the deficit, of there being something missing that is essential for normal or customary functioning. Or the deficit might be a stressor because it disrupts the organization of the organism on many levels: the relationship to reality and to himself, cognitive organization, normal speech patterns, for example; (c) Various factors, arising either from the noise input or the feedback deficit of auditory feedback, might operate simultaneously. And they might do so either convergently so that every observed effect is multiply caused, or heterogeneously, so that different effects result from different features of the masking condition. In addition, some or all of the effects might be direct results of the factors mentioned or they might be indirect results of attempts to cope with the states engendered by the masking condition. Finally, different causes or mechanisms may be operative in different individuals.

Some of these various conceivable attributes of the masking condition appear capable of explaining certain results. The input-arousal hypothesis, for example, could account for the greater loudness, affect expression, and verbal productivity. The simple deficit hypothesis can also account for these phenomena. Ideally, we should present at this point a detailed examination of the various interpretations, concluding with a statement of those alternatives, which seem the most likely, and then await the results of experimental testing of these conclusions. Instead of engaging in that exercise, we will present a provisional "armchair" evaluation of the alternatives that seems quite plausible, leaving the final explication and testing of the various alternatives where they belong—to future controlled empirical analysis.

Considerable *experienced* adaptation to the masking noise occurred over the course of the six exposures to it in the three interviews. Every subject reported experiencing some adaptation. There was also a decrease in the frequency of negative references about the masking condition and in the number of subjects who stated it was more difficult to talk with the noise. Some subjects even developed a preference for the masking condition and some preferred it from the start. The observable phenomena, however, did not show a parallel change. They not only did not systematically decrease but actually became more prominent in some cases. These observations suggest that neither the novelty nor the stress caused the speech and other behavioral effects. Furthermore, a test of a stress-related hypothesis concerning increased productivity yielded negative results.

When they spoke in the masking conditions, the subjects sounded like individuals who have become deaf after learning to talk. These people sound alike in at least two respects: in loudness and the flattening of intonation. The similarity is so striking that the speech of one would be mistaken for the other. This resemblance strongly suggests that the feedback deficit was a critical factor. But there is no reason why auditory feedback would function only in the regulation of loudness and intonation. It seems quite possible thaf the feedback deficit was also responsible for other linguistic changes: the prolongation, pitch changes, the vocal noises, slurring, rate changes, and exaggerated phrasing. These are all aspects of the speech skill that the delayed auditory feedback literature (Chase, Sutton, & First, 1959; Lee, 1950a, b) has shown to be dependent on normal feedback.

Viewed from the standpoint of either learning theory or psychoanalytic psychology, the remaining observable results—the cognitive confusions, the changes in voice quality, increased affect expression, freer associative response, and "thinking aloud"—could also be due to a deficit in auditory feedback. One must merely assume that the control of these aspects of behavior—one's vocal style, the degree and quality of affect expression while talking, spontaneity and freedom in verbalizing, and cognitive organization—is a negative feedback system. According to this assumption, any *deviations* in the auditory feedback from the vocal style, etc., which the individual characteristically "sets" for himself, constitute signals that activate modulations and defenses that inhibit the audible deviations or the underlying processes instigating such deviations. In learning theory terms, such deviations in the auditory feedback would function as Hullian response-produced cues (r→s) to which inhibitory responses and/or their drives were conditioned. In psychoanalytic theory, such deviations would function as self-produced stimuli perceived by the self-observing and self-evaluating superego functions that, in turn, instigate ego regulation and defense.

Hypothesis: Disinhibition Due to Deficit in Auditory Feedback.   The results and the reasoning in the preceding paragraphs suggest that disinhibition due to the deficit in auditory feedback was a central result of the masking-noise condition. Here we summarize the evidence and arguments in favor of this hypothesis.

In the present study, the behavior during the masking-noise conditions included such phenomena as:

1. increased loudness,
2. less cultured speech,
3. more ethnocentric speech,
4. increased laughter,
5. freer expression of positive and negative affect and thought, which sometimes concerned the interviewer,
6. increased amount of talking, reaching monologue proportions at times,
7. revelation of very intimate personal information,
8. the voicing of thoughts meant to be silent,
9. the misplacement of thought fragments in the flow of speech.

This all adds up to "strange" behavior under any conditions, especially on the part of college students interacting with a stranger and a "college professor" at that. The assumption of a process of disinhibition makes this strange behavior understandable. As we noted earlier, the results of other independent investigators are compatible with this assumption.

Several considerations suggest that this disinhibition is due to the deficit in auditory feedback and not to the noise input per se: (a) The failure to actually adapt to the masking condition in spite of the subjective experience of adaptation to the *noise* and the similarity of the subjects' speech to that of the deaf are highly suggestive in this regard, (b) The immediacy of the behavior change and the exquisite "off–on" nature of the relationship between the changes and the use of the masking noise seem more compatible with the deficit hypothesis than with the input hypothesis, (c) As we have shown, it is theoretically conceivable that the disinhibition could be due to the deficit in auditory feedback, (d) Many of the subjects' reports support this interpretation, for the relief from anxiety and self-criticism based on auditory feedback appeared to be the major reason why some subjects preferred to talk under the masking condition. The fact that some subjects were distressed by the noise condition is not evidence against the feedback deficit hypothesis. Indeed, such a deficit appears to be frightening for some people for the very reason that it appears to be preferred by others, i.e., its disruption of the customary drive-defense balance. In addition, the disturbance in customary modes of thought and speech and in the sense of self and reality could be indirect noxious results of a sensory deficit for some people.

Thus the hypothesis provides a relatively coherent explanation of the observable phenomena and many of the major experiential reports by the subjects. This hypothesis is consistent with conclusions about the role of sensory feedback derived from studies of distorted auditory feedback and the extensive studies of sensory deprivation. Indeed, our general behavioral categories are reminiscent of findings of the latter, as Klein (1965) has also pointed out. But the hypothesis clearly needs empirical testing.

Stanton (1968) has made the first attempt at such empirical testing, in the study cited earlier. His design included a normal no-noise condition, and two noise conditions. In one of the latter, a white noise of complete feedback masking intensity was used; in the other, the noise was loud, but not quite loud enough to cause feedback masking. His subjects did not utter more tabooed words in the latter noise condition than in the no-noise condition. But they did utter more tabooed words in the masking-noise condition than in either the control-noise condition or the control no-noise condition. Thus Stanton's results not only demonstrated disinhibition when subjects could not hear themselves but also showed that a loud noise per se was not sufficient to produce this disinhibition. Further studies of this type are needed to determine which of the full range of behaviors observed by ourselves and others are functions of a feedback deficit and which might be caused by noise alone.[5]

The Possibly General Role of Sensory Feedback in Ego Functioning

It is now well known that sensory feedback from the organism plays a crucial role in complex skills (e.g., Smith, 1962). Speech is simply a particularly interesting and important case in point. The results of this study, and those of Holmes and Holzman (1966), Klein (1965), and Stanton (1968) suggest that other ego functions may also be part of complex feedback systems. This discussion has emphasized the possibility that defense and other forms of inhibitory control are aspects of negative feedback systems. Klein's (1965) discussion emphasizes the role of auditory feedback in secondary process thinking.

One naturally wonders, next, if the role of actual *sensory* feedback is not more extensive in ego functioning than is realized. There are two aspects to this question, both of which suggest problems for future research. On the one hand, one can ask: *"What is the range of sensory feedback signals involved in any particular ego function?"* Consider the process of defense against aggression, for example. Is it possible that proprioceptor feedback from the skeletal musculature, somesthetic feedback from the autonomic musculature (the

---

[5]Janis (1959, p. 214) proposed that the use of a masking noise might result in "verbalization [that] would more closely approximate his own silent thoughts than if he could hear himself talk." On this basis, Janis and Terwilliger (1962) obtained subjects' associations to fearful communications under masking-noise conditions, but they did not test the underlying premise.

"heat" of anger and the felt pounding of the heart, or their absence, for example), visual feedback from one's overt actions, auditory feedback from one's voice, as well as the feedback of one's thoughts, all play a crucial role in defense against aggression? Is it possible that deviations in such *feedback signals* from those body sense perceptions one has come to tolerate are critical for the instigation and maintenance of defense? Is the essence of defense the minimization of such deviations from one's customarily tolerable feedback sense perceptions?

On the other hand, one can ask: *"What is the range of ego functions in which sensory feedback from the organism's activities plays a significant role?"* Some of our observations suggest that other complex ego functions, in addition to the processes of defense and organized thought, may be just as dependent on feedback as are sensory-motor skills. Feeling "empty" when deprived of auditory feedback, as some subjects did, suggests that sensory feedback is critical for one's *basic sense of being.* An inability to maintain the presentation of oneself as the realization of a fantasied cultivated actress with the loss of auditory feedback, as well as the return of less cultured and more ethno-centric speech in several young adults striving for upward social mobility and greater acculturation, suggest that one's *sense of identity* may depend on orga-nismic feedback. Perhaps the *basic mechanism of achieving identifications* is a negative feedback process in which the individual is continually monitoring the most assorted sensory feedback from himself and is continually minimiz-ing all deviations in this feedback from that totality of sense impressions arising from his memories and fantasies of the person with whom he is identifying. By such a process one could transform himself into a replica of the identification object. This would merely be a complex, generalized form of the process by which a hearing child presumably comes to speak as his parents do. *Self-observation, self-evaluation, and self-regulation* appear to be major ego functions having general significance. But what is the basic mate-rial that is observed, and what is the observing, evaluating and regulating agent? The observations from studies of masked speech suggest that the basic material may consist, to a significant degree, of concrete sensory feed-back and that the observing, evaluating, and regulating agent is the brain and its sensory-perceptual and memory systems. Thus studies of the role of feedback in complex ego functions may bring together Freud's conceptions of personality functioning set forth in chapter 7 of *The Interpretation of Dreams* (1900/1953a) and *The Ego and the Id* (1923/1961) and modern neurophysi-ology, to the mutual advantage of both approaches (see also chapter 4).

These conceptions presume that extremely complex and intricate feed-back processes operate in behavior. This seems quite possible in view of the intricate, multifaceted feedback regulation of speech revealed by the studies that were reviewed in the introductory section of this chapter.

Miscellany

A few other aspects and implications of the study merit some brief comments.

1. *The effect of the masking condition varied with the individual.* Klein (1965) found the same to be true in his study. This implies that people vary in the degree to which auditory feedback is involved in the regulation of their behavior. This, in turn, raises a number of questions for further investigation. Some of them are: What accounts for these individual differences? Are they a function of personality differences? Does this individual variation reflect variation in the degree of "internalization" of behavioral controls? What other cues or mechanisms can replace those involved in auditory feedback?

2. We have noted but not discussed the fact that *some aspects of language were essentially unaffected by the feedback deficit.* This seems very interesting in view of the other marked effects it has. It would appear that some aspects of speech in adults are independent of auditory feedback. Some of them, such as the phonetic-articulatory, may be primarily dependent on kinesthetic feedback. Perhaps there are other aspects of language that can be, and have been—over and over again—performed silently and thus become independent of auditory feedback. All through life a person "thinks" in the grammatical forms of his language. Such patterns can become independent of auditory feedback, in contrast to the strictly vocal, audible aspects of language. This consideration has two obvious research implications: one developmental, the other cross cultural. Would the masking noise have greater effects on the "basic" linguistic patterns with younger subjects simply because of the parallel decreased frequency of silent practice? Would feedback deficit have greater effects on the basic linguistic patterns as the different modes of silent practice varied? In children unable to read and write, for example, or in illiterate cultures?

3. Subjects reported that when they talked the noise did not sound as loud as when they were not talking. This could be an "attention phenomenon." The subjects' reports supply striking confirmation of certain aspects of Freud's (1900/1953a) theory of consciousness and attention as stated in chapter 7, *The Interpretation of Dreams,* and elsewhere. David Rapaport (1960, pp. 227ff) provided a brilliant, and the most useful, synthesis of this theory and a historical perspective of Freud's thinking about it. Of the fourteen proposition (pp. 228–9) Rapaport derived from Freud's formulations, the following are especially relevant here:

1. The subjective conscious experience is determined by the distribution of a limited quantity of mental energy termed attention cathexis.

3. Attention cathexis is part of the energy of the system Cs-Pcs (in present-day terminology, the ego) which is termed hypercathexis.

4. Excitations within the mental apparatus (internal) or on the receptor organs (external) attract attention cathexes proportionately to their intensity.

5. Attention cathexis, if so attracted and if exceeding a certain amount (threshold), gives rise to the conscious experience of the excitation.

6. Simultaneous or contiguous excitations compete for the limited quantity of attention cathexis.

9. Defenses and *other processes* utilizing great amount of hypercathexes diminish the quantity of attention cathexis available. (Italics ours. In psychoanalytic theory, "other processes" would include the ego functions of speech and secondary process-thinking such as our subjects were engaging in during the interviews.)

When our subjects talked in the masking conditions they were doing two things that, according to Freud's theory of consciousness, *should have* caused the masking noise to decrease in loudness. First, they were producing receptor-excitation (proprioceptive) and "internal" excitation (ideational content of verbal images) that completed for attention cathexis with the auditory excitations from the masking noise (Propositions 1, 4, 5, 6). Secondly, when talking, the subjects were utilizing "ego energy," hypercathexes (Propositions 1, 3, 9). Not only is Freud's theory of consciousness supported by the raw data, it thereby provides one explanation of them.

Aside from the relation to psychoanalytic theory, the subjects' reports of the basic phenomenon have some interesting implications. Generalizing from their reports, one would have this proposition: There is an inverse relationship between talking and the perceived intensity of receptor stimulation. Talking decreases it and not talking increases it. This implies something potentially important about human interaction: that when a person talks he is less aware of cues emanating from his interlocutor than when he is silent. The generalization also implies something about intrapsychic functioning: that when a person talks he is less aware of stimulation arising from within himself than when he is silent.

Common clinical observations and everyday experiences seem to be consistent with these ideas. The "compulsive talker," for example, is inaccessible to the ordinary external influences in interaction and appears clinically to talk in order to defend himself against inner sensations of anxiety. The latter is a form of resistance (defense) well known to the psychoanalyst. Under the guise of free associating par excellence, a patient may actually be successfully avoiding experiencing his anxieties. The increased self-awareness that often comes with silence may be due, in part, to the mechanism underlying the attention phenomenon. It is obvious that this phenomenon suggests a wide range of problems for further investigation. Is the interpretation of the subjects' experiences as an attention phenomenon valid? What actually are the intrapsychic consequences of simply talking or not talking, disregarding content? What are the interactional consequences? Do nonverbal interactional cues, for example, have greater influence during brief pauses—when one is the listener, not the talker?

4. The vocal noises generally occurred during pauses and at the onset of sentence and phrases. Although some of them were described as resembling "straining" sounds, it should be emphasized that the subjects did not show visible signs of making greater physical effort at these particular times. Nor were the sounds part of a speech-block pattern. The sounds, in their speech contexts, gave one the impression they resulted either from resting, aimless activity of the speech musculature during pauses, or from motor preparation for articulation at the onset of sentences or phrases. Obviously, slow muscular contractions or tensions in the speech apparatus produced them. Perhaps the same tensions are occurring regularly during normal speech, but at subaudible intensities.

The findings of this study and their interpreation result in a view of the internal states of talking people that is somewhat different than one suspects from their normal overt speech. Subaudible muscular tensions in the speech apparatus; silent speech, often unrelated to or in conflict with audible utterances and even unknown to the speaker; reined dispositions to use seemingly discarded idiolects and dialects; stronger affects and impulses than are manifested overtly; promptings to talk at length and to say more personal things; perpetual self-observation and self-regulation; the continual maintenance of a sense of self and of reality—all these must form part of the current of behavior flowing silently beneath the rippling surface of the stream of overt speech.

Summary

Seventeen college students, male and female, participated in three individual personal interviews that were tape-recorded. During the interviews the subjects spoke under four different conditions: (a) in the usual face-to-face situation; (b) when they couldn't hear their own voices because of a masking noise administered through earphones; (c) when they couldn't see the interviewer who was sitting behind them, but could hear themselves; and (d) when they could neither see the interviewer nor hear themselves talk. Each interview concluded with an open-ended inquiry. The tape recordings and typescripts were primarily studied by the systematic, clinical-observational method; some supplementary quantitative procedures were used.

This report focuses on the effect of the masking-noise conditions. During these conditions, all subjects spoke in a much louder voice, with flattened intonation and, at times, lengthened syllables—all of which gave their speech a "sing-song" nature. All subjects also showed changes of various kinds in their "voice quality." Some of these changes were of a general phonological nature, such as increased nasality, whereas others included social class dialect shifts of a "regressive" nature. Changes in pitch, meaningless vocal noises, slurring of articulation, changes in rate of speaking, and more distinctive phrasing also occurred in the masking conditions, in decreasing frequency.

More general behavioral changes also occurred, including: increased affect expression; freer associative response, indicated quantitatively by increased verbal productivity and qualitatively by increased spontaneity and the communication of highly personal information; increased cognitive confusion; and "thinking aloud." The latter, rare but striking, phenomenon consisted of the unintended and unconscious utterance of content often just above the audible threshold. In one instance, a subject disclaimed even the "thoughts" involved.

All subjects reported experiencing considerable adaptation to the masking conditions, but there was no consistent external evidence of it. Control of loudness of the voice showed the greatest adaptation.

Most subjects, especially in the first interview, preferred to talk without the noise. A small number, however, preferred talking with the noise and the nonnoise preference decreased as the interviews progressed. The major aversive qualities of the masking conditions included: the noise itself, the physical effort of talking in its presence, the voice feedback deficit, interference with cognition and articulation, a sense of loss of contact with oneself and the interviewer, and negative affects. Many subjects reported that the noise sounded less intense when they talked than when they didn't. The generally negative portrayal of the subjects' experience contradicts the external impression of the subjects' behavior during the interviews. No subject failed to complete the experiment and all appointments were kept.

"Positive" reports about the masking condition included statements that the noise induced relaxation, a state akin to daydreaming, relief from reality, and self-criticism.

It is important to note that the basic linguistic patterns persisted in the masking conditions: The subjects could still "speak English."

An evaluation of various mechanisms that might have mediated the effects of the masking conditions leads to the conclusion that the feedback deficit was crucial and that normal auditory feedback plays an important role in the regulation of many *vocal* dimensions of language behavior, in the control of the vocal expression of affects and thoughts, and in the maintenance of a sense of self and of reality. Various additional implications of the findings were discussed.[6]

ADDENDA, (1986)

We have examined the auditory feedback literature that has appeared since the preceding article was written, and we have reexamined some of the preexistent literature. Our search failed to locate any study replicating our use of white noise masking during extended, interactive, spontaneous discourse. Yet there has been sustained investigation of exposure to loud noise and other related procedures. Generally these studies have involved brief episodes of speech and often the reading aloud of printed passages. Two notable exceptions are the studies of Holzman and Rousey (1971), in which subjects produced Thematic Apperception Test (TAT) stories, and Garber and Martin (1974), in which subjects uttered spontaneous monologues in 50-minute experimental sessions. Holzman and Rousey replicated the findings of their earlier study (1970), cited in our original article, that white noise masking caused an increase in impulse-related themes and a decrease in defensive themes on the TAT. Except Holzman and Rousey's, the studies have been concerned with strictly vocalization processes. Four emphases emerge from this literature: the effect of exposure to masking noises on stuttering, the effect of such noise on voice loudness (the Lombard effect), the effect of amplifying auditory feedback (sidetone amplification) on voice loudness, and developmental aspects of auditory feedback.

Noise Exposure and Stuttering. The early observations that exposure to loud masking noise decreased stuttering (Cherry & Sayers, 1956; Cherry, Sayers, & Marland, 1955; Kern, 1932; Shane, 1946, 1955) provided the major stimulus for our study. Subsequent research has provided substantial confirmation of those pioneering observations (Adams & Hutchinson, 1974; Adams & Moore, 1972; Burke, 1969; Conture, 1974; Conture & Brayton, 1975; A. D. Dewar, 1984; A. Dewar, A. D. Dewar, & Barnes, 1976; Garber & Martin, 1974, 1977; Maraist & Hutton, 1957; May & Hackwood, 1968; Murray, 1969; Sutton & Chase, 1961; Webster & Dorman, 1970). Although Cherry and Sayers concluded that the low-frequency band "red" noise (cut-off at 500 c/s) was much more effective than high frequencies in reducing stuttering, subsequent research indicates that high-frequency noise may be effective (Conture, 1974; May & Hackwood, 1968). Nearly all the studies cited, however, used a wide frequency band "white" noise.

---

[6]For a rigorous study and further discussion of the disinhibition hypothesis, the reader is referred to a later study by Holzman and Rousey (1970), published when these pages were already set in type.

The nearly universal assumption among the researchers just cited is that the effect of the noise on stuttering is a direct consequence of interference with the auditory feedback of the speaker, which is assumed to be "hyper-salient" for the stutterer (Lane & Tranel, 1971) for whatever reasons. (We made the same assumption in our discussion of this phenomenon.) Several workers have challenged this assumption on various grounds. Sutton and Chase (1961) questioned it because they found that noise stimulation only during pauses in speech reduced stuttering just as much as noise stimulation during phonation or continuously during the testing session. Webster and Dorman (1970) replicated that finding. These findings do not necessarily negate the role of interference with auditory feedback. Noise stimulation during pauses could have produced temporary increased threshold shifts that interfered with auditory feedback. In our own study, we occasionally noticed shifts in speech upon turning off the noise that could be accounted for by recovery from such threshold shifts (see p. 358). Noise stimulation during pauses might also have distracted the speaker's attention from his own au-ditory feedback. Barr and Carmel (1969) found that high-frequency noise of moderate intensity reduced stuttering, even though the noise properties were such that it did not in itself completely mask auditory feedback. They tested each subject twice: The reduction in stuttering was much greater in the first test. Such results might be due to the distracting effect of the noise, for it might well have been greater in the first test, when its novelty would be greater. Thus, the results of these three studies do not rule out the pos-sibility that the masking of auditory feedback is the principal factor mediat-ing reduced stuttering upon noise stimulation.

Noise Exposure and Vocal Intensity.   Speakers automatically talk louder when stimulated with a loud noise—the Lombard effect (Lombard, 1910). This effect has been repeatedly confirmed in *normal speakers* in the literature we searched (Dreher & O'Neill, 1958; Gardner, 1964, 1966; Korn, 1954, Kryter, 1946; Pickett, 1958; Siegel & Kennard, 1984; Siegel, Pick, Olsen & Sawin, 1976; Siegel, Schork, Pick, & Garber, 1982; Webster & Klumpp, 1962) *and in stutterers as well* (Adams & Hutchinson, 1974; Adams & Moore, 1972; Conture, 1974). Wingate (1970) based another alternative to the feed-back-masking hypothesis upon this Lombard effect. He proposed that the reduction in stuttering under noise stimulation might be mediated simply by the increased vocal intensity of the speakers rather than by the reduction in auditory feedback. He did not test this hypothesis, nor have others who adopted it merely on the basis of the co-occurrence of increased loudness and reduced stuttering as general effects of noise stimulation (Adams & Hutchin-son, 1974; Adams & Moore, 1972). Conture (1974) did determine the cor-relation between such changes in vocal intensity and stuttering: the two were highly correlated, .98, when one anomalous subject was omitted from the analysis. These group and individual associations between increased vocal intensity and decreased stuttering do not prove that the former caused the latter. Auditory feedback masking could have caused each of them.

Garber and Martin (1977) compared the frequency of stuttering when subjects spoke with a normal level and an increased level of loudness, both with and without noise stimulation. Speaking in a loud voice did not decrease stuttering in either quiet or noise, but all subjects reduced their stuttering in noise compared with the quiet condition.

Thus, the hypothesis that increased vocal intensity mediates the decrease in stuttering upon noise stimulation has not yet been confirmed. That hypothesis does raise a comparable question about our findings. Could the increased loudness with which our subjects spoke under the masking noise conditions have mediated any of the other concomitant changes? That seems unlikely because adaptation in loudness, when it did occur, was not always related to adaptation in other phenomena. Future research, however, should address that question.

Sidetone Amplification.   In the introduction to our study we noted that two investigations (Black, 1950a; Lightfoot & Morrill, 1949) had found that increasing the intensity of a speaker's auditory feedback (sidetone amplification) causes the person to lower the intensity of his voice. Our subsequent search of the literature has shown that this phenomenon has been repeatedly demonstrated (Lane, Catania, & Stevens, 1961; Siegel & Kennard, 1984; Siegel, Pick, Olsen, & Sawin, 1976; Siegel, Schork, Pick, & Garber, 1982).

Intraindividual Feedback or Social Communicative Loops.   As was the case in accounting for the effect of loud noise exposure on stuttering, investigators have been nearly unanimous in attributing, explicitly or implicitly, the Lombard effect and the results of sidetone amplication to changes in auditory feedback. Lane and Tranel (1971) provided a notable exception. In their tightly reasoned, trenchant paper, they concluded that both of these effects resulted from automatic attempts of the speaker to maintain a voice loudness level that is favorable for intelligible communication with the participant. Lane and Tranel argue, for example, that upon noise stimulation the speaker assumes that the hearing of the audience is impaired as his is and speaks more loudly to improve the ability of the listener to understand what he is saying. Analogously, they argue, a person speaks more softly when the experimenter amplifies this sidetone in order to obviate the assumed altered communication caused by his assumed loud voice. Thus Lane and Tranel shift the explanation from modifications in auditory feedback to changes that the speaker assumes have occurred in the reception and comprehension of his speech by the listener. They have replaced the emphasis on an intraindividual feedback loop with emphasis on the interpersonal communicative loop.

Investigators of auditory feedback have neglected the proposal of Lane and Tranel. We found only one study that attempted an explicit test of it. Siegel et al. (1982) had speakers talk in various feedback conditions and they determined the intercorrelations of speech changes caused by those conditions. Of particular relevance here was the finding that there was no correlation between the voice intensity changes caused by the Lombard procedure and those caused by sidetone amplification. The reasoning and conclusion of Lane and Tranel require a significant correlation between the two types of changes.

This single negative result does not destroy Lane and Tranel's hypothesis. Perhaps the changes in the social communicative loop will be shown to contribute to the Lombard and sidetone amplification effects. But it seems highly unlikely that those inferred changes are the only ones that occur upon auditory feedback masking. Most of the changes observed in our subjects seem unrelated to attempts to maintain intelligible communication, or seem even contrary to such an aim. They seem related to disinhibition (see p. 369). Others have reached similar conclusions (Holmes & Holzman, 1966; Holzman & Rousey, 1970, 1971; Klein, 1965; Stanton, 1968). Perhaps the intraindividual feedback and the social communicative loops interact in ways yet to be determined.

Developmental Patterns. Near the end of the discussion in our chapter, we raised the issue of possible developmental patterns in the role of auditory feedback and of possibly differential roles for different aspects of speech. Our subsequent examination of the literature shows that these developmental issues have received some attention, with as yet inconclusive results.

The relevant developmental studies have been almost exclusively concerned with the effect of *delayed auditory feedback* (DAF) on *temporal* aspects of speech. There are some 10 such studies that have yielded contradictory findings, with about half showing a decreasing effect of DAF with increasing age and the other half showing the opposite effect. Differences in ages of the subjects and in procedure make it difficult to draw any general conclusions from these studies. The reader is referred to a recent paper by Siegel, Fehst, Garber, and Pick (1980) for a discussion of those studies, as well as the report of their own research into the issue.

A few studies have been concerned with the developmental pattern of the Lombard and sidetone amplification procedures. Siegel et al. (1976) found that college age subjects were affected more than preschool children by sidetone amplification. Both age-groups were equally susceptible to the Lombard effect. The latter result is compatible with the finding of Crary, Fucci, and Bond (1981) that 6–9 year-old children and 19–25 year-old adults were equally likely to prolong vowels with auditory masking. Such findings, that different types of feedback changes seem to show different developmental patterns, led Siegel and his co-workers (Siegel et al., 1980; Siegel et al., 1976) to suggest that there may well be multiple feedback loops involved in speech that might follow different developmental courses.

22 Questions for the Future

I have suggested some questions for future research at various places in the preceding chapters. In this chapter I discuss three areas of research that seem especially important to me: the potential use of the Non-ah speech disturbances to measure psychotherapeutic change, the psychological functions of the individual speech disturbance categories, and the developmental vicissitudes of the speech disturbances.

THE USE OF SPEECH DISTURBANCES TO MEASURE PSYCHOTHERAPEUTIC CHANGE

One of my original interests was this potential use of the speech disturbance measure. However, the combination of several factors caused me to indefinitely postpone pursuing it. (Those factors were primarily the pressure to validate the measure as an index of anxiety and conflict, the need to substantiate our choice of an extralinguistic dimension over manifest verbal content, and the emergence of my interest in nonverbal behavior.)

A serious need for good outcome studies of psychotherapy persists. Objective indicators of therapeutic change are crucial for the execution of such studies. I believe investigating the potential of the speech disturbance measure for such purposes is worthwhile for several reasons. First, the measure is viable and impeccably objective. Second, it reflects events that nearly always occur outside the speaker's awareness and conscious control. Thus they are relatively free of influence by demand characteristics that threaten the usefulness of improvement measures based on self-reports by patients or on

382

their manifest verbal content in assessment interviews. Third, the research reported in chapters 10–15 shows that the Non-ah speech disturbance measure is a very sensitive indicator of anxiety and conflict in self-disclosing or self-expression. Most researchers would agree that decreases in such anxiety and conflict would indicate successful outcomes of psychotherapy. Fourth, the speech disturbances are manifestly disturbances in clarity and directness of communication. A fair number of clinicians would regard a manifest improvement in these attributes of communication as an indicator of significant improvement in mental health.

I suggest two starting points for this proposed research: (a) the quest for general, overall decrements in the Non-ah speech disturbances, and (b) the search for more specific content-related decrements.

General Decrements in Non-Ah Speech Disturbances

It is possible that one outcome of successful psychotherapy is a general reduction in the level of anxiety and conflict and that this change would be reflected in a general decrease in the frequency of the Non-ah speech disturbances. Such a decrease might be found by comparing the speech of patients in standardized, comparable interviews before and after psychotherapy judged independently to be successful. Of course, a similar comparison should be made for some type of "control" patients, such as those not treated at all or those whose psychotherapy appeared to be unsuccessful.

Because the research we summarized in chapter 15 was inconclusive concerning the relationship between trait anxiety and speech disturbances, one might be inclined to discount the value of even attempting this particular kind of outcome research. This reaction would be premature, however, for that research relied completely on self-reportable measures of trait anxiety obtained at one point in time *across* subjects. It remains to be seen if psychotherapy-induced change in the general level of anxiety and conflict would be reflected *within* subjects by changes in their general speech disturbance level.

Specific Content-Related Decrements in Non-Ah Disturbances

Perhaps successful psychotherapy has more specific effects on the patient's anxiety and conflict, ones restricted to specific psychodynamic issues. Thus future research might well focus on the possibility that psychotherapy might result in decreases in the Non-ah disturbances when the patient is talking about, or giving verbal expression of, specific psychodynamic categories such as various types of wishes and feelings. This possibility could be investigated by scoring speech disturbances when the patient talks about, or gives utterance to, such things in standardized interviews before and after treatment. One could compare, for example, the speech disturbance levels in pre and posttreatment samples of voicing the various need categories of Murray's (1956) verbal content analysis system described in chapter 17 or the interpersonal wish components of Luborsky's (1977, 1984) *Core Conflictual Relationship Themes.* Specific patients might show specific treatment effects. One patient, for example, might manifest a significant decrease in speech disturbances when voicing sexual material, whereas another patient might do so with hostile material. And, of course, one would be very interested in seeing whether these idiosyncratic changes were in areas that were originally the most distressing for the person. [Horowitz et al. (1977, pp. 1041–1042) independently made very similar suggestions to those we have proposed here.]

The purpose of the proposed research would be to arrive at one outcome measure to be included in a battery of measures.

THE PSYCHOLOGICAL FUNCTIONS OF THE INDIVIDUAL SPEECH DISTURBANCE CATEGORIES

What psychological functions are common to the various speech disturbances categories we delineated (see Table 9.1) and what functions might be unique to individual categories? We have made a beginning towards answering these questions but there is much to be done.

The finding we have achieved so far that has the most substance is that "Ah" and the Non-ah disturbances follow different rules. (Mark Twain apparently knew this long ago. See chapter 19.) The results of three studies dealing with the issue showed that anxiety and "Ah" were unrelated, but that anxiety significantly increased Non-ah disturbances (See Fig. 15.1). In chapter 15 we cited six studies by others that obtained similar results. In addition, the study reported in chapter 12 shoed that the change from a face-to-face to a telephone-type speaking situation had no effect on the Non-ah disturbances but caused a marked increase in the frequency of "Ah's." We proposed therefore that one function of "Ah" was interpersonal in nature—to "hold the floor" and to cope with the uncertainty that might be caused by the absence of visual feedback from the other participant. The study reported in chapter 18 revealed another, intrapsychic, function of "Ah"—to fill a pause during which the plan for the ensuing phrase or sentence was formulated. We then proposed that "Ah" served both to release the tension accompanying this formulation *and* to "hold the floor" while doing so.

I believe it would be very fruitful to conduct further research on the relationship between anxiety and conflict and the Non-ah disturbances. In only one study did we investigate the relationship between anxiety and the individual Non-ah categories. We cited results in chapter 12 that showed that anxiety increased the frequency of each Non-ah category. Attempts to replicate this finding are in order. (Perhaps we could begin to do this by reanalyzing the raw scoring of the transcripts for the studies reported in chapters 10–14.) Assuming replications would be forthcoming, the next matter requiring study is the determination of the intracacies of the relationship between anxiety and the individual categories. This research should begin with the two most frequent Non-ah categories—Sentence change and Repetition. And it might profitably begin with the questions: How does anxiety cause these disturbances? Do these types of disturbances enable the speaker to cope with that anxiety, and, if so, how?

I am not sure how best to approach these questions. But my own inclination, influenced no doubt by my psychoanalytic bent, would be to develop a method based on obtaining "free associations" (broadly defined) of the speaker to concrete Repetitions and Sentence changes, which he or she has committed; that is, I would develop a method that took as its point of departure the phenomena contained in the two clinical examples presented in the closing section of chapter 10 (pp. 195–196). There we saw that by presenting a person with Sentence changes and asking for his associations evidence emerged indicating that the utterance prior to the Sentence change aroused anticipatory anxiety related to what might follow and that the Sentence change avoided the unfolding of that utterance and associated material.

1. Conduct recorded personal, investigative interviews with a sample of subjects.

2. Score the speech disturbances in the transcripts of the interviews.

3. Select samples of the Repetitions and Sentences changes in the transcripts. And select a sample of control points in sentences free of speech disturbances, the points being comparable to the sites of the Repetitions and Sentence changes in the sentences involved.

4. Present to each speaker the utterance preceding the Repetitions, Sentence changes, and control points and obtain their associations to those utterance fragments. Or one might begin by conducting the inquiry as a sentence-completion test, asking the speaker to complete the utterance, clocking the reaction and completion times as well as noting the content of the completion. Then the completed sentence could be used as the stimulus for free associations. These proposed procedures are analogous to the projective Thematic Apperception Test where pictures are used to elicit story telling. Here sentence fragments are used to elicit completed sentences and a stream of associative material.

Would one obtain data indicating that anticipatory anxiety was more frequent for the pre-Repetition and pre-Sentence change fragments than for those preceding the control points? Such data might consist of the finding that the content of the associative material for the Repetition and Sentence change was more anxiety provoking than the content that followed those very disturbances in the interview and than the associative material for the precontrol point utterances.

Would the data reveal different responses to the anticipatory anxiety in the case of Repetitions and Sentence changes? For example, would an examination of all the Sentence change verbal material—the pre-Sentence change fragment, the post-Sentence change utterance in the original interview, and the associative material of the postinterview inquiry—indicate that Sentence changes were characteristically abrupt inhibitions and avoidance of anxiety evoking and thus conflictual material? (That seemed to be the case in our clinical illustrations of chapter 10.) And would an examination of all the Repetition material indicate that Repetitions implement other responses to the anticipatory anxiety, such as a less abrupt, less obvious glossing over conflictual material?

No doubt the researcher who tries to come to grips with the question of the intricate relation of Repetitions and Sentence changes to the speaker's anxiety and conflict by following the procedure of his choice will come upon nitty-gritty details that will provide some surprises as to the nature of that relationship. In any case, it seems likely that this line of research will add to our knowledge about the process of spontaneous speech and about methods of coping with anxiety and conflict.

DEVELOPMENTAL VICISSITUDES OF SPEECH
DISTURBANCES

The speakers involved in our studies have ranged from 8 to 49 years of age. All of them committed speech disturbances. Other researchers have found that even 1-year-old children may spontaneously "repair" their speech as our speakers did when committing Sentence changes (see Clark's [1982] report of such findings and a review of similar findings by others). A few additional workers have investigated the occurrence of other disfluencies in children's speech. The pioneers in this effort were students of Wendell Johnson. Because of their interest in the etiology of stuttering they focused on Repetitions by preschool children (Branscom, Hughes, & Oxtoby, 1955; Davis, 1939). Because tape recorders were yet to be developed, their data base consisted of written records of speech. Recently others have used modern tape recordings and have included additional types of disfluencies such as interjections, phrase revision and incompletions, pauses, and dysrhythmic phonations (Colburn, 1979, 1985; DeJoy & Gregory, 1985; Haynes & Hood, 1977; Wexler & Mysak, 1982; Yairi, 1981). Three general trends emerge from the research cited here. First, disfluency is a general phenomenon of the speech of preschoolers. Second, the disfluencies generally decrease in frequency from 2 to 5 years of age. Third, there is a strong suggestion that syntactical disfluencies, such as those involved in sentence formation, tend to increase with age during early childhood.

All the aforementioned raise the question of the developmental vicissitudes of our speech disturbance categories. I believe pursuit of this question will surely result in a significant extension of our knowledge about speech disturbances and conjointly about developmental aspects of important domains of psychology—speech, language, and psychological conflict.

There are many possible types of research that one might want to conduct. The following suggestions simply reflect some of my own interests.

The Quest for Normative Data

Does the frequency of speech disturbances change with age throughout the entire life-span from infancy to old age? The collection and analysis of comparable speech samples from speakers of various age levels will be needed to answer this question. It would probably be worthwhile to make provision in such cross-sectional research for examining the influence of some of the *critical stages in development,* such as the Oedipal phase, puberty, the identity crises of adolescence, mid-life crises, and the onset of "old age." Each of these stages involve increased anxiety and conflict that might make speaking about relevant topics especially vulnerable to speech disturbance, or that might even generalize to all speaking.[1]

The Transition from Speech Disturbances During Language Acquisition to Those Associated with Anxiety and Conflict

Clark's (1982) report demonstrates clearly that some of our speech disturbance categories function in the service of early language acquisition. She presents convincing observations that from a very early age children monitor and spontaneously repair their speech so as to make it resemble adult

---

[1] I have found only two studies that attempted to compare disfluencies over long periods of the life-span. Silverman (1978) compared the frequency of repetitions of monosyllabic words by 4-year-olds and adults (19–32 years). She found that the frequency was higher for the adults. Duchin (1984) determined the frequency of the broad range of disfluencies noted earlier for adults from 21 to 91 years of age. She found no differences over this span.

I have recently discovered that Wendell Johnson hypothesized (1959) that the disfluencies in childhood might be partially determined by the child's anxiety and conflict over the act of speaking.

speech. Moreover, they seem to do so in a most intricate manner, focusing more on phonological repairs in the earliest months of talking and more on syntactical and morphological repairs as time goes by. Perhaps some of our speech disturbance categories (Ah, Sentence change, Repetition, Omission, and Sentence Incompletions) continue to function, in part, in this manner throughout life; that is, perhaps they function in part to *maintain* "correct" language, just they function to *acquire* such language in childhood.

On the other hand, our research reported in chapters 10–15 strongly indicates that the Non-ah disturbances are significantly related to anxiety, and that this functional relationship is present in third grade children, i.e., at the 8 year level.

Thus we are confronted with the likelihood that our Non-ah "speech disturbances" are functionally related to two different processes—language acquisition (and perhaps maintenance) and anxiety and conflict. How are these two relationships connected? Are they coexistent from infancy on? Or is there a transition such that the disturbances function at first primarily in the service of language acquisition and become increasingly related to anxiety and conflict with growth and development of the child? When might such a transition be first detectable? When might it peak? What events during development might cause, or contribute to, such a transition? The muting of speech in childhood? The Oedipal conflicts? The development of monitoring the overt expression of wishes and feelings, as is probably exacerbated with superego development?

These are fascinating and important questions for future investigation.

REFERENCES

Aas, A. (1958). *Mutilation fantasies and autonomic response.* Oslo, Norway: Oslo University Press.

Ach, N. (1905). Weber die Willenstatigkeit und das Denken [Concerning the action of will and thought]. Cited in Boring (1929, p. 427).

Adams, M. R., & Hutchinson, J. (1974). The effects of three levels of auditory masking on selected vocal characteristics and the frequency of disfluency of adult stutterers. *Journal of Speech and Hearing Research, 17,* 682–688.

Adams, M. R., & Moore, W. H. (1972). The effects of auditory masking on the anxiety level, frequency of dysfluency, and selected vocal characteristics of stutterers. *Journal of Speech and Hearing Research, 15,* 572–578.

Aiello, J. (1972). A test of equilibrium theory: Visual interaction in relation to orientation, distance and sex of interactants. *Psychonomic Science, 27,* 335–336.

Aiken, J. M., & Salzberg, C. L. (1984). The effects of a sensory extinction procedure on stereotypic sounds of two autistic children. *Journal of Autism and Developmental Disorders, 14,* 291–299.

Algren, N. (1984). *A walk on the wild side.* New York: Penquin. (Original work published 1956)

Allport, G. W. (1961). *Pattern and growth in personality.* New York: Holt, Rinehart & Winston.

Allport, G. W., & Vernon, P. (1933). *Studies in expressive movement.* New York: MacMillan.

Argyle, M., & Dean, J. (1965). Eye-contact, distance and affiliation. *Sociometry, 28,* 289–304.

Argyle, M., Lalljee, M., & Cook, M. (1968). The effects of visibility on interaction in a dyad. *Human Relations, 21,* 3–17.

Auld, F., & Mahl, G. F. (1956). A comparison of the DRQ with ratings of emotion. *Journal of Abnormal and Social Psychology, 53,* 386–388.

Auld, F., & Murray, E. J. (1955). Content-analysis studies of psychotherapy. *Psychological Bulletin, 52,* 377–395.

Auld, F., & White, A. M. (1956). Rules for dividing interviews into sentences. *Journal of Psychology, 42,* 273–281.

Azima, H., Vispo, R., & Azima, F. J. (1961). Observations on anaclitic therapy during sensory deprivation. In P. Solomon, P. E. Kubzansky, P. H. Leiderman, J. H. Mendelson, R. Trumbull, & D. Wexler (Eds.), *Sensory deprivation* (pp. 143–160). Cambridge, MA: Harvard University Press.

389

Baender, P. (1982). Introduction. *The adventures of Tom Sawyer* by Mark Twain. *A facsimile of the author's holograph manuscript* (Vol. 1–2, pp. ix–xxxvi). Frederick MD: University Publications of America. Washington, D.C: Georgetown University Library.

Bailey, J., & Meyerson, L. (1969). Vibration as a reinforcer with a profoundly retarded child. *Journal of Applied Behavior Analysis, 2*, 135–137.

Baker, E. E. (1964). An experimental study of speech disturbance for the measurement of stage fright in the basic speech course. *The Southern Speech Journal, 29*, 232–243.

Baker, S. J. (1948). Speech disturbances: A case for a wider view of paraphasias. *Psychiatry, 11*, 359–366.

Baker, S. J. (1951). Autonomic resistances in word association tests. *Psychoanalytic Quarterly, 20*, 275–283.

Baldwin, J. (1960). *Another country*. New York: Dial Press.

Barnard, J. W., Zimbardo, P. G., & Sarason, S. B. (1961). Anxiety and verbal behavior in children. *Child Development, 32*, 379–392.

Barr, D. F., & Carmel, N. R. (1969). Stuttering inhibition with high frequency narrow-band masking noise. *Journal of Auditory Research 9*, 40–44.

Bell, C. (1826). On the nervous circle which connects the voluntary muscles with the brain. *Philosophical Transactions of the Royal Society of London, (2)*, 163–175. Also in C. Bell. (1844), *The nervous system of the human body* (3rd ed., pp. 193–203). London: Henry Renshaw.

Benton, R. G., & Mefferd, R. B. (1967). Projector slide changing and focusing as operant reinforcers. *Journal of the Experimental Analysis of Behavior, 10*, 479–484.

Bernard, C. (1858). Quatorzieme lecon [Fourteenth lesson]. In, *Leçons sur la physiologie et la pathologie du système nerveux* (Vol. 1, pp. 246–266). Paris: J. B. Bailliere.

Bettelheim, B. (1943). Individual and mass behavior in extreme situations. *Journal of Abnormal and Social Psychology, 38*, 417–452.

Bexton, W. H., Heron, W., & Scott, T. H. (1954). Effects of decreased variation in the sensory environment. *Canadian Journal of Psychology, 8*, 70–76.

Birch, H. G. (1956). Experimental investigations in expressive aphasia. *New York State Journal of Medicine, 56*, 3849–3852.

Birch, H. G., & Lee, J. (1955). Cortical inhibition in expressive aphasia. *Archives of Neurology and Psychiatry, 74*, 514–517.

Birdwhistell, R. (1952). *Introduction to kinesics*. Louisville, KY: University of Louisville.

Birdwhistell, R. (1956). Kinesic analysis of filmed behavior of children. In, *Group processes* (pp. 141–144). New York: J. Macy, Jr. Foundation.

Birdwhistell, R. (1963). The kinesic level in the investigation of the emotions. In P. Knapp (Ed.), *Expression of the emotions in man* (pp. 123–139). New York: International Universities Press.

Birdwhistell, R. (1970). *Kinesics and context: Essays on body motion communication*. Philadelphia: University of Pennsylvania Press.

Black, J. W. (1950a). Some effects of auditory stimuli upon voice. *Journal of Aviation Medicine* (now Journal of Aerospace Medicine), *21*, 251–255; 277.

Black, J. W. (1950b). The effect of room characteristics upon vocal intensity and rate. *Journal of the Acoustical Society of America, 22*, 174–176.

Black, J. W. (1951). The effect of noise induced temporary deafness upon vocal intensity. *Speech Monographs, 18*, 74–77.

Black, J. W. (1954). Systematic research in experimental phonetics: 2. Signal reception: Intelligibility and side-tone. *Journal of Speech and Hearing Disorders, 19*, 140–146.

Black, J. W., Tolhurst, G. C., & Morrill, S. N. (1953). *Application of multiple-choice speech intelligibility tests in the evaluations and use of voice communication equipment*. Pensacola: Joint Project Ohio State University Research Foundation & U. S. Naval School of Aviation Medicine. (Joint Project Report No. 19, Bureau of Medicine and Surgery Research Project No. NM 001-064.01.19 [Cited by Peters, 1955].)

REFERENCES 391

Blass, T., & Siegman, A. W. (1975). A psycholinguistic comparison of speech, dictation and writing. *Language and Speech, 18,* 20–34.

Bliss, J. (1980). Sensory experiences of Gilles de la Tourette Syndrome. *Archives of General Psychiatry, 37,* 1343–1347.

Bloomfield, L. (1933). *Language.* New York: Holt.

Blumenthal, R. L. (1960). *The effects of level of mental health, premorbid history, and interpersonal stress upon the speech disruption of chronic schizophrenic subjects.* Unpublished doctoral dissertation, New York University.

Blumenthal, R. (1964). The effects of level of mental health, premorbid history, and interpersonal stress upon the speech disruption of chronic schizophrenic subjects. *Journal of Nervous and Mental Disease, 139,* 313–323.

Bond, M. H., & Ho, H. Y. (1978). The effect of relative status and the sex composition of a dyad on cognitive responses and non-verbal behavior of Japanese interviewees. *Psychologia: An international journal of psychology in the Orient, 21,* 128–136.

Bond, M. H., & Iwata, Y. (1976). Proxemics and observation anxiety in Japan: Nonverbal and cognitive responses. *Psychologia:* An international journal of psychology in the Orient, *19,* 119–126.

Bond, M. H., & Shiraishi, D. (1974). The effect of body lean and status of an interviewer on the non-verbal behavior of Japanese interviewees. *International Journal of Psychology, 9,* 117–128.

Boomer, D. S. (1963). Speech disturbances and body movement in interviews. *Journal of Nervous and Mental Disease, 136,* 263–266.

Boomer, D. S., & Dittmann, A. T. (1964). Speech rate, filled pause, and body movement in interviews. *Journal of Nervous and Mental Disease, 139,* 324–327.

Boomer, D. S., & Goodrich, D. W. (1961). Speech disturbance and judged anxiety. *Journal of Consulting Psychology, 25,* 160–164.

Boring, E. (1929). *A history of experimental psychology.* New York: Century.

Bouska, M. L., & Beatty, P. A. (1978). Clothing as a symbol of status: Its effect on control of interaction territory. *Bulletin of the Psychonomic Society, 11,* 235–238.

Braatoy, T. (1954). *Fundamentals of psychoanalytic technique.* New York: Wiley.

Bradac, J. J., Konsky, C. W., & Elliott, N. D. (1976). Verbal behavior of interviewees: The effects of several situational variables on verbal productivity, disfluency, and lexical diversity. *Journal of Communication Disorders, 9,* 211–225.

Brady, A. T., & Walker, M. B. (1978). Interpersonal distance as a function of situationally induced anxiety. *British Journal of Social and Clinical Psychology, 17,* 127–133.

Branscom, M. E., Hughes, J., & Oxtoby, E. T. (1955). Studies of nonfluency in the speech of preschool children. In W. Johnson & R. R. Leutenegger (Eds.), *Stuttering in children and adults* (pp. 157–180). Minneapolis: University of Minnesota Press.

Brenner, M. S., Feldstein, S., & Jaffe, J. (1965). The contribution of statistical uncertainty and test anxiety to speech disruption. *Journal of Verbal Learning and Verbal Behavior, 4,* 300–305.

Breuer, J., & Freud, S. (1955). Studies on hysteria. In J. Strachey (Ed. and Trans.), *The standard edition of the complete psychological works of Sigmund Freud* (Vol. 2). London: Hogarth Press. (Original work published 1893–1895)

Buck, R. (1980). Nonverbal behavior and the theory of emotion: The facial feedback hypothesis. *Journal of Personality and Social Psychology, 38,* 811–824.

Burke, B. D. (1969). Reduced auditory feedback and stuttering. *Behaviour Research and Therapy, 7,* 303–308.

Cameron, N., & Magaret, A. (1951). *Behavior pathology.* Boston: Houghton, Mifflin.

Cannon, W. B. (1932). *The wisdom of the body.* New York: Norton.

Carhart, R. (1960). Conservation of speech. In H. Davis & S. R. Silverman (Eds.), *Hearing and deafness* (rev. ed., pp. 387–402). New York: Holt, Rinehart & Winston.

Carnes, E. F., & Robinson, F. P. (1948). The role of client talk in the counseling interview. *Educational and Psychological Measurement, 8,* 635–644.

Chase, R. A., Sutton, S., & First, D. (1959). Bibliography: Delayed auditory feedback. *Journal of Speech and Hearing Research, 2,* 193–200.

Chase, R. A., Sutton, S., First, D., & Zubin, J. (1961). A developmental study of changes in behavior under delayed auditory feedback. *Journal of Genetic Psychology, 99,* 101–112.

Cherry, C., & Sayers, B. M. (1956). Experiments upon the total inhibition of stammering by external control, and some clinical results. *Journal of Psychosomatic Research, 1,* 233–246.

Cherry, C., Sayers, B. M., & Marland, P. M. (1955). Experiments on the complete suppression of stammering. *Nature, 176,* 874–875.

Clark, E. V. (1982). Language change during language acquisition. In M. E. Lamb & A. L. Brown (Eds.), *Advances in developmental psychology* (Vol. 2, pp. 171–195). Hillsdale, NJ: Lawrence Erlbaum Associates.

Cohen, S. I., Silverman, A. J., Bressler, B., & Shmavonian, B. M. (1961). Problems in isolation studies. In P. Solomon, P. E. Kubzansky, P. H. Leiderman, J. H. Mendelson, R. Trumbull, & D. Wexler (Eds.), *Sensory deprivation* (pp. 114–129). Cambridge, MA: Harvard University Press.

Colburn, N. (1979). *Disfluency behavior and emerging linguistic structures in preschool children.* Unpublished doctoral dissertation. Columbia University.

Colburn, N. (1985). Clustering of disfluency in nonstuttering children's early utterances. *Journal of Fluency Disorders, 10,* 51–58.

Conture, E. G. (1974). Some effects of noise on the speaking behavior of stutterers. *Journal of Speech and Hearing Research, 17,* 714–723.

Conture, E. G., & Brayton, E. R. (1975). The influence of noise on stutterer's different disfluency types. *Journal of Speech and Hearing Research, 18,* 381–384.

Cook, M. (1969). Anxiety, speech disturbances, and speech rate. *British Journal of Social and Clinical Psychology, 8,* 13–21.

Cox, J. M. (1966). *Mark Twain: The fate of humor.* Princeton, NJ: Princeton University Press.

Crary, M. A., Fucci, D. J., & Bond, Z. S. (1981). Interaction of sensory feedback: A child–adult comparison of oral sensory and temporal articulatory function. *Perceptual and Motor Skills, 53,* 979–988.

Darwin, C. (1955). *The expression of the emotions in man and animals.* New York: Philosophical Library. (Original work published 1872)

Davis, D. M. (1939). The relation of repetitions in the speech of young children to certain measures of language maturity and situational factors: Part I. *Journal of Speech Disorders, 4,* 303–318.

Davis, D. M. (1940). The relation of repetitions in the speech of young children to certain measures of language maturity and situational factors: Part II. *Journal of Speech Disorders, 5,* 235–246.

Davis, H., Morgan, C. T., Hawkins, J. E., Galambos, R., & Smith, F. W. (1950). Temporary deafness following exposure to loud tones and noise. *Acta Oto-Laryngologica Supplementum, 88,* 1–57.

DeJoy, D. A., & Gregory, H. H. (1985). The relationship between age and frequency of disfluency in preschool children. *Journal of Fluency Disorders, 10,* 107–122.

Deutsch, F. (1924). Zur bildung des konversionsymptoms [On the formation of the conversion symptoms]. *Internationale Zeitschrift für Psychoanalyse, 10,* 380–392.

Deutsch, F. (1947). Analysis of postural behavior. *Psychoanalytic Quarterly, 16,* 195–213.

Deutsch, F. (1949). Thus speaks the body: An analysis of postural behavior. *Transactions of the New York Academy of Science, 12,* 58–62.

Deutsch, F. (1952). Analytic posturology. *Psychoanalytic Quarterly, 21,* 196–214.

Deutsch, F. (1959). Symbolization as a formative stage of the conversion process. In F.

Deutsch (Ed.), *On the mysterious leap from the mind to the body* (pp. 75–97). New York: International Universities Press.

DeVoto, B. (1932). *Mark Twain's America.* Boston: Little, Brown.

Dewar, A. D. (1984). Influence of auditory feedback masking on stammering and its use in treatment. *Research News-International. Journal of Rehabilitation Research, 7,* 341–342.

Dewar, A., Dewar, A. D., & Barnes, H. E. (1976). Automatic triggering of auditory feedback masking in stammering and cluttering. *British Journal of Disorders of Communication, 11,* 19–26.

Dibner, A. S. (1956). Cue counting: A measure of anxiety in interviews. *Journal of Consulting Psychology, 20,* 475–478.

Dibner, A. S. (1958). Ambiguity and anxiety. *Journal of Abnormal and Social Psychology, 56,* 165–174.

DiMascio, A. (1961). Some physiological correlates of the psycholinguistic patterns of two psychiatric interviews. In L. A. Gottschalk (Ed.), *Comparative psycholinguistic analysis of two psychotherapeutic interviews* (pp. 139–148). New York: International Universities Press.

Dittmann, A. T. (1963). Kinesic research and therapeutic processes. In P. Knapp (Ed.), *Expression of the emotions in man* (pp. 140–147). New York: International Universities Press.

Dittmann, A. T. (1966, September). Speech and body movements. *New approaches to the study of facial expression and body movement.* Symposium conducted at the annual meeting of the American Psychological Association, New York.

Dittmann, A. T. (1971). [Review of *Kinesics and context: Essays on body motion communication*]. *Psychiatry, 34,* 334–342.

Dittmann, A. T., Parloff, M. B., & Boomer, D. S. (1965). Facial and bodily expression: A study of receptivity of emotional cues. *Psychiatry, 28,* 239–244.

Dollard, J., & Miller, N. E. (1950). *Personality and psychotherapy.* New York: McGraw–Hill.

Dollard, J., & Mowrer, O. H. (1947). A method of measuring tension in written documents. *Journal of Abnormal and Social Psychology, 42,* 3–32.

Doty, R. L. (1981). Olfactory communication in humans. *Chemical Sesnse, 6,* 351–376.

Dreher, J. J., & O'Neill, J. J. (1958). Effects of ambient noise on speaker intelligibility of words and phrases. *Laryngoscope, 68,* 539–548.

Duchin, S. W. (1984). *Fluency characteristics of young adult, middle aged, and older males.* Unpublished doctoral dissertation, Columbia University.

Duffy, E. (1962). *Activation and behavior.* New York: Wiley.

Edelmann, R. J., & Hampson, S. E. (1979). Changes in non-verbal behaviour during embarrassment. *British Journal of Social and Clinical Psychology, 18,* 385–390.

Edelmann, R. J., & Hampson, S. E. (1981). Embarrassment in dyadic interaction. *Social Behavior and Personality, 9,* 171–177.

Efron, D. (1941). *Gesture and environment.* New York: King's Crown.

Efron, D. (1972). *Gesture, race and culture.* The Hague: Mouton.

Eibl-Eibesfeldt, I. (1970). *Ethology: The biology of behavior.* New York: Holt, Rinehart & Winston.

Ekman, P. (1965). Differential communication of affect by head and body cues. *Journal of Personality and Social Psychology, 2,* 726–735.

Ekman, P., & Friesen, W. V. (1967). Head and body cues in the judgment of emotion: A reformulation. *Perceptual and Motor Skills, 24,* 711–724.

Ekman, P., & Friesen, W. V. (1968). Nonverbal behavior in psychotherapy research. In. J. M. Shlien (Ed.), *Research in psychotherapy* (Vol. 3, pp. 179–216). Washington, DC: American Psychological Association.

Ekman, P., & Friesen, W. V. (1969). The repertoire of nonverbal behavior: Categories, origins, usage, and coding. *Semiotica, 1,* 49–98.

Ekman, P., & Friesen, W. V. (1971). Constants across cultures in the face and emotion. *Journal of Personality and Social Psychology, 17,* 124–129.

Ekman, P., & Friesen, W. V. (1974). Nonverbal behavior and psychopathology. In R. J. Friedman & M. M. Katz (Eds.), *The psychology of depression: Contemporary theory and research* (pp. 203–224). New York: John Wiley & Sons.

Ekman, P., Friesen, W. V., & Bear, J. (1984). The international language of gestures. *Psychology Today,* May, 64–69.

Ekman, P., Friesen, W. V., & Ellsworth, P. (1972). *Emotion in the human face.* New York: Pergamon Press.

Ekman, P., Levenson, R. W., & Friesen, W. V. (1983). Autonomic nervous system activity distinguishes among emotions. *Science, 221,* 1208–1210.

Ekman, P., Sorenson, E. R., & Friesen, W. V. (1969). Pan-cultural elements in facial displays of emotion. *Science, 164,* 86–88.

Eldred, S. H., & Price, D. B. (1958). A linguistic evaluation of feeling states in psychotherapy. *Psychiatry, 21,* 115–121.

Elliott, G. P. (1959). Afterword. *The adventures of Tom Sawyer* (pp. 220–224). New York: The New American Library, 1952.

Ellsworth, P., & Ludwig, L. (1972). Visual behavior in social interaction. *Journal of Communication, 22,* 375–403.

Erikson, E. H. (1950). *Childhood and society.* New York: Norton.

Exline, R. (1962). Effects of need for affiliation, sex, and the sight of others upon initial communications in problem-solving groups. *Journal of Personality, 30,* 541–556.

Exline, R. (1963). Explorations in the process of person perception: Visual interaction in relation to competition, sex, and need for affiliation. *Journal of Personality, 31,* 1–20.

Exline, R., Gray, D., & Schuette, D. (1965). Visual behavior in a dyad as affected by interview content and sex of respondent. *Journal of Personality and Social Psychology, 1,* 201–209.

Fairbanks, G. (1955). Selective vocal effects of delayed auditory feedback. *Journal of Speech and Hearing Disorders, 20,* 333–346.

Fairbanks, G., & Guttman, N. (1958). Effects of delayed auditory feedback upon articulation. *Journal of Speech and Hearing Research, 1,* 12–22.

Feldstein, S. (1962). The relationship of interpersonal involvement and affectiveness of content to the verbal communication of schizophrenic patients. *Journal of Abnormal and Social Psychology, 64,* 39–45.

Feldstein, S., Brenner, M. S., & Jaffe, J. (1963). The effect of subject sex, verbal interaction and topical focus on speech disruption. *Language and Speech, 6,* 229–239.

Feldstein, S., & Jaffe, J. (1962). The relationship of speech disruption to the experience of anger. *Journal of Consulting Psychology, 26,* 505–509.

Feldstein, S., & Jaffe, J. (1963). An IBM 650 program written in SOAP for the computation of speech disturbances per time, speaker and group. *Behavioral Science, 8,* 86–87.

Felipe, N. J., & Sommer, R. (1966). Invasions of personal space. *Social Problems, 14,* 207–214.

Ferenczi, S. (1952a). Thinking and muscle innervation. In J. Rickman (Ed.), *Further contributions to the theory and technique of psychoanalysis by Sandor Ferenczi* (pp. 230–232). New York: Basic Books. (Original work published 1919)

Ferenczi, S. (1952b). The further development of an active therapy in psychoanalysis. In J. Rickman (Ed.), *Further contributions to the theory and technique of psychoanalysis by Sandor Ferenczi* (pp. 198–217). New York: Basic Books. (Original work published 1921)

Ferenczi, S. (1952c). Contra-indications to the 'active' psycho-analytical technique. In J. Rickman (Ed.), *Further contributions to the theory and technique of psychoanalysis by Sandor Ferenczi* (pp. 217–230). New York: Basic Books. (Originally written 1925)

Ferenczi, S. (1955). Child analysis in the analysis of adults. In M. Balint (Ed.), *Final contributions to the problems and methods of psycho-analysis by Sandor Ferenczi* (pp. 126–142). New York: Basic Books. (Original work published 1931)

Ferenczi, S., & Rank, O. (1925). *The development of psycho-analysis*. (C. Newton, Trans.). New York: Nervous and Mental Disease Publishing Company. (Original work published 1924)

Fineman, K. R. (1968). Shaping and increasing verbalizations in an autistic child in response to visual-color stimulation. *Perceptual and Motor Skills, 27,* 1071–1074.

Fisch, H., Frey, S., & Hirsbrunner, H. (1983). Analyzing nonverbal behavior in depression. *Journal of Abnormal Psychology, 92,* 307–318.

Fortenberry, J. H., MacLean, J., Morris, P., & O'Connell, M. (1978). Mode of dress as a perceptual cue to deference. *Journal of Social Psychology, 104,* 139–140.

Francis, W. Nelson (1958). *The structure of American English*. New York: Ronald Press.

Fraum, R. M. (1975). The effect of interpersonal distance on self-disclosure in a dyadic interview situation. *Dissertation Abstracts International, 35B,* 4170.

Freedman, N. (1972). The analysis of movement behavior during the clinical interview. In A. W. Siegman & B. Pope (Eds.), *Studies in Dyadic Communication* (pp. 153–175). New York: Pergamon Press.

Freedman, N. (1977). Hands, words, and mind: On the structuralization of body movements during discourse. In N. Freedman & S. Grand (Eds.), *Communicative structures and psychic structures* (pp. 109–132). New York: Plenum.

Freedman, N., & Grand, S. (Eds.). (1977). *Communicative structures and psychic structures*. New York: Plenum.

Freedman, N., & Hoffman, S. P. (1967). Kinetic behavior in altered clinical states: Approach to objective analysis of motor behavior during clinical interviews. *Perceptual and Motor Skills, 24,* 527–539.

Freud, A. (1946). *The ego and the mechanisms of defence*. New York: International Universities Press. (Original work published 1936)

Freud, S. (1953a). The interpretation of dreams. In J. Strachey (Ed. and Trans.), *The standard edition of the complete psychological works of Sigmund Freud* (Vols. 4 and 5). London: Hogarth Press. (Original work published 1900)

Freud, S. (1953b). Fragment of an analysis of a case of hysteria. In J. Strachey (Ed. and Trans.), *The standard edition of the complete psychological works of Sigmund Freud* (Vol. 7, pp. 1–122). London: Hogarth Press. (Original work published 1905)

Freud, S. (1955a). Analysis of a phobia in a five-year-old boy. In J. Strachey (Ed. and Trans.), *The standard edition of the complete psychological works of Sigmund Freud* (Vol. 10, pp. 1–149). London: Hogarth Press. (Original work published 1909)

Freud, S. (1955b). Notes upon a case of obsessional neurosis. In J. Strachey (Ed. and Trans.), *The standard edition of the complete psychological works of Sigmund Freud* (Vol. 10, pp. 151–249). London: Hogarth Press. (Original work published 1909)

Freud, S. (1955c). From the history of an infantile neurosis. In J. Strachey (Ed. and Trans.), *The standard edition of the complete psychological works of Sigmund Freud* (Vol. 17, pp. 1–122). London: Hogarth Press. (Original work published 1918)

Freud, S. (1957a). On narcissism: An introduction. In J. Strachey (Ed. and Trans.), *The standard edition of the complete psychological works of Sigmund Freud* (Vol. 14, pp. 67–102). London: Hogarth Press. (Original work published 1914)

Freud, S. (1957b). Repression. In J. Strachey (Ed. and Trans.), *The standard edition of the complete psychological works of Sigmund Freud* (Vol. 14, pp. 141–158). London: Hogarth Press. (Original work published 1915a)

Freud, S. (1957c). Instincts and their vicissitudes. In J. Strachey (Ed. and Trans.), *The standard edition of the complete psychological works of Sigmund Freud* (Vol. 14, pp. 109–140). London: Hogarth Press. (Original work published 1915b)

Freud, S. (1957d). The unconscious. In J. Strachey (Ed. and Trans.), *The standard edition of the complete psychological works of Sigmund Freud* (Vol. 14, pp. 159–204). London: Hogarth Press. (Original work published 1915c)

Freud, S. (1958a). On beginning the treatment (Further recommendations on the technique of psychoanalysis I). In J. Strachey (Ed. and Trans.), *The standard edition of the complete psychological works of Sigmund Freud* (Vol. 12, pp. 121–144). London: Hogarth Press. (Original work published 1913)

Freud, S. (1958b). Remembering, repeating, and working through (Further recommendations on the technique of psychoanalysis II). In J. Strachey (Ed. and Trans.), *The standard edition of the complete psychological works of Sigmund Freud* (Vol. 12, pp. 145–156). London: Hogarth Press. (Original work published 1914)

Freud, S. (1959). Inhibitions, symptoms and anxiety. In J. Strachey (Ed. and Trans.), *The standard edition of the complete psychological works of Sigmund Freud* (Vol. 20, pp. 75–175). London: Hogarth Press. (Original work published 1926)

Freud, S. (1960). The psychopathology of everyday life. In J. Strachey (Ed. and Trans.), *The standard edition of the complete psychological works of Sigmund Freud* (Vol. 6). London: Hogarth Press. (Original work published 1901)

Freud, S. (1961). The ego and the id. In J. Strachey (Ed. and Trans.), *The standard edition of the complete psychological works of Sigmund Freud* (Vol. 19, pp. 1–59). London: Hogarth Press. (Original work published 1923)

Freud, S. (1962). The neuro-psychoses of defence. In J. Strachey (Ed. and Trans.), *The standard edition of the complete psychological works of Sigmund Freud* (Vol. 3, pp. 41–61). London: Hogarth Press. (Original work published 1894)

Freud, S. (1963). Introductory lectures on psychoanalysis. In J. Strachey (Ed. and Trans.), *The standard edition of the complete psychological works of Sigmund Freud* (Vols. 15 and 16). London: Hogarth Press. (Original work published 1915–1917)

Friedhoff, A. J., Alpert, M., & Kurtzberg, R. L. (1962). An effect of emotion on voice. *Nature, 193*, 357–358.

Froschels, E., & Jellinek, A. (1941). *Practice of voice and speech therapy* (pp. 168–171). Boston: Expression.

Gaddini, R. B., & Gaddini, E. (1959). Rumination in infancy. In L. Jessner & E. Pavenstedt (Eds.), *Dynamic psychopathology in childhood* (pp. 166–184). New York: Grune & Stratton.

Galambos, R., & Davis, H. (1943). The response of single auditory nerve fibers to acoustic stimulation. *Journal of Neurophysiology, 6*, 39–58.

Galambos, R., & Davis, H. (1944). Inhibition of activity in single auditory nerve fibers by acoustic stimulation. *Journal of Neurophysiology, 7*, 287–303.

Garber, S. R., & Martin, R. R. (1974). The effects of white noise on the frequency of stuttering. *Journal of Speech and Hearing Research, 17*, 73–79.

Garber, S. R., & Martin, R. R. (1977). Effects of noise and increased vocal intensity on stuttering. *Journal of Speech and Hearing Research, 20*, 233–240.

Gardner, M. B. (1964). Effect of noise on listening levels in conference telephony. *Journal of the Acoustical Society of America, 36*, 2354–2362.

Gardner, M. B. (1966). Effect of noise, system gain, and assigned task on talking levels in loud-speaker communication. *Journal of the Acoustical Society of America, 40*, 955–965.

Geer, J. H. (1966). Effect of fear arousal upon task performance and verbal behavior. *Journal of Abnormal Psychology, 71*, 119–123.

Genet, J. (1963). *Our lady of the flowers.* New York: Grove Press. (Original work published 1943)

Gillespie, J. F., Jr. (1952). Verbal signs of resistance in client-centered therapy. An abstract of a dissertation submitted in partial fulfillment of the requirements for the degree of Doctor of Philosophy, at The Pennsylvania State College, 1951, pp. 454–458. *University Microfilms,* Ann Arbor, Michigan.

Goldberg, G. N., Kiesler, C. A., & Collins, B. E. (1969). Visual behavior and face to face distance during interaction. *Sociometry, 32*, 43–53.

Goldman-Eisler, F. (1954). On the variability of the speed of talking and on its relation to the length of utterances in conversations. *British Journal of Psychology, 45*, 94–107.

Goldman-Eisler, F. (1961). A comparative study of two hesitation phenomena. *Language and Speech, 4,* 18–26.

Gottschalk, L. A. (Ed.). (1961). *Comparative psycholinguistic analysis of two psychotherapeutic interviews.* New York: International Universities Press.

Gottschalk, L. A., Springer, K. J., & Gleser, G. C. (1961). Experiments with a method of assessing the variations in intensity of certain psychological states occurring during two psychotherapeutic interviews. In L. A. Gottschalk (Ed.), *Comparative psycholinguistic analysis of two psychotherapeutic interviews* (Chap. 7, pp. 115–138). New York: International Universities Press.

Grand, S. (1977). On hand movements during speech: Studies of the role of self-stimulation in communication under conditions of psycho-pathology, sensory deficit, and bilingualism. In N. Freedman & S. Grand (Eds.), *Communicative structures and psychic structures* (pp. 199–221). New York: Plenum.

Greene, L. R. (1977). Effects of verbal evaluative feedback and interpersonal distance on behavioral compliance. *Journal of Counseling Psychology, 24,* 10–14.

Greene, L. R. (1982). Effects of the counselor's verbal feedback, interpersonal distance, and clients' field dependence., In I. L. Janis (Ed.), *Counseling on personal decisions: Theory and research on short-term helping relationships* (pp. 145–158). New Haven: Yale University Press.

Guilford, J. P. (1956). *Fundamental statistics in psychology and education.* New York: McGraw–Hill.

Gunter, P., Brady, M. P., Shores, R. E., Fox, J. J., Owen, S., & Goldzweig, I. R. (1984). The reduction of aberrant vocalizations with auditory feedback and resulting collateral behavior change of two autistic boys. *Behavioral Disorders, 9,* 254–263.

Haase, R. F., & DiMattia, D. J. (1970). Proxemic behavior: Counselor, administrator, and client preference for seating arrangement in dyadic interaction. *Journal of Counseling Psychology, 17,* 319–325.

Haigh, G. (1949). Defensive behavior in client-centered therapy. *Journal of Consulting Psychology, 13,* 181–189.

Hall, E. T. (1955). The anthropology of manners. *Scientific American, 192,* 84–90.

Hall, E. T. (1966). *The hidden dimension.* Garden City, New York: Doubleday.

Hanley, T. D., & Steer, M. D. (1949). Effect of level of distracting noise upon speaking rate, duration, and intensity. *Journal of Speech and Hearing Disorders, 14,* 363–368.

Hansen, J. E., & Schuldt, W. J. (1982). Physical distance, sex, and intimacy in self-disclosure. *Psychological Reports, 51,* 3–6.

Harris, M. B., James, J., Chavez, J., Fuller, M. L., Kent, S., Massanari, C., Moore, C., & Walsh, F. (1983). Clothing: Communication, compliance, and choice. *Journal of Applied Sociology, 13,* 88–97.

Hartmann, H. (1939). *Ego psychology and the problem of adaptation.* New York: International Universities Press.

Hastorf, A., Schneider, D., & Polefka, J. (1970). *Person perception.* Reading, MA: Addison–Wesley.

Hathaway, S. R., & McKinley, J. C. (1951). *Minnesota Multiphasic Personality Inventory: Manual.* New York: Psychological Corporation.

Hayduk, L. A. (1983). Personal space: Where we stand. *Psychological Bulletin, 94,* 293–335.

Haynes, W. O., & Hood, S. B. (1977). Language and disfluency variables in normal speaking children from discrete chronological age groups. *Journal of Fluency Disorders, 2,* 57–74.

Hebb, D. O. (1949). *The organization of behavior: A neuropsychological theory.* New York: Wiley.

Hemingway, E. (1935). *The green hills of Africa.* New York: Scribner.

Hoffman, A. E. (1949). Reported behavior changes in counseling. *Journal of Consulting Psychology, 13,* 190–195.

Holmes, C., & Holzman, P. (1966). Effect of white noise on disinhibition of verbal expression. *Perceptual and Motor Skills, 23,* 1039–1042.

Holzman, P., & Rousey, C. (1970). Monitoring, activation, and disinhibition: Effects of white noise masking on spoken thought. *Journal of Abnormal Psychology, 75,* 227–241.

Holzman, P., & Rousey, C. (1971). Disinhibition of communicated thought: Generality and role of cognitive style. *Journal of Abnormal Psychology, 77,* 263–274.

Horowitz, L. M., Sampson, H., Siegelman, E. Y., Wolfson, A., & Weiss, J. (1975). On the identification of warded-off mental contents: An empirical and methodological contribution. *Journal of Abnormal Psychology, 84,* 545–558.

Horowitz, L. M., Weckler, D., Saxon, A., Livaudais, J. D., & Boutacoff, L. I. (1977). Discomforting talk and speech disruptions. *Journal of Consulting and Clinical Psychology, 45,* 1036–1042.

Horowitz, M. J., Duff, D. F., & Stratton, L. O. (1964). Body-buffer zone. *Archives of General Psychiatry, 11,* 651–656.

Hull, C. (1943). *Principles of behavior.* New York: Appleton–Century.

Izard, C. E. (1969). The emotions and emotion concepts in personality and culture research. In R. B. Cattell (Ed.), *Handbook of modern personality theory* (pp. 496–510). Chicago: Aldine Press.

Janis, I. L. (1959). Motivational factors in the resolution of decisional conflicts. In M. R. Jones (Ed.), *Nebraska symposium on motivation* (Vol. 7, pp. 199–223). Lincoln: University of Nebraska Press.

Janis, I. L., & Terwilliger, R. F. (1962). An experimental study of psychological resistances to fear arousing communcations. *Journal of Abnormal and Social Psychology, 65,* 403–410.

Johnson, W. (1959). *The onset of stuttering.* Minneapolis: University of Minnesota Press.

Jones, E. (1957). *The life and work of Sigmund Freud* (Vol. 3). New York: Basic Books.

Jones, L. V. (1955). Statistical theory and research design. *Annual Review of Psychology, 6,* 405–430.

Kaplan, J. (1966). *Mr. Clemens and Mark Twain: A biography.* New York: Simon & Schuster.

Kasl, S. V. (1957). *The relationship of speech disruption to experimentally induced states of emotion.* Senior Essay in Psychology, Yale University, New Haven.

Kasl, S. V., & Mahl, G. F. (1956). A simple device for obtaining certain verbal activity measures during interviews. *Journal of Abnormal and Social Psychology, 53,* 388–390.

Kasl, S. V., & Mahl, G. F. (1958). Experimentally induced anxiety and speech disturbances. *American Psychologist, 13,* 349. (Abstract)

Kasl, S. V., & Mahl, G. F. (1965). The relationship of disturbances and hesitations in spontaneous speech to anxiety. *Journal of Personality and Social Psychology, 1,* 425–433.

Kendon, A. (1967). Some functions of gaze-direction in social interaction. *Acta Psychologica, 26,* 22–63.

Kendon, A. (1972). [Review of *Kinesics and context: Essays on body motion communication*]. *American Journal of Psychology, 85,* 441–455.

Kern, A. (1932). Der einflusz des hörens auf das stottern [The effect of hearing on stuttering]. *Archiv für Psychiatrie und Nervenkrankheiten, 97,* 429–449.

Kinzel, A. F. (1970). Body-buffer zone in violent prisoners. *American Journal of Psychiatry, 127,* 59–64.

Kiritz, S. A. (1973). Hand movements and clinical ratings at admission and discharge for hospitalized psychiatric patients. *Dissertation Abstracts International, 33B,* 4511.

Kish, G. B. (1966). Studies of sensory reinforcement. In W. K. Honig (Ed.), *Operant behavior: Areas of research and application* (pp. 109–159). New York: Appleton-Century-Crafts.

Klein, G. S. (1965). On hearing one's own voice. In M. Schur (Ed.), *Drives, affects, behavior* (Vol. 2, pp. 87–117). New York: International Universities Press.

Knight, P. H. (1979). Degree of client manifest anxiety as a function of interaction distance: An investigation of the female-female counseling dyad. *Dissertation Abstracts International, 39A,* 7244–7245.

Knight, P. H., & Bair, C. K. (1976). Degree of client comfort as a function of dyadic interaction distance. *Journal of Counseling Psychology, 23,* 13–16.

Korn, T. S. (1954). Effect of psychological feedback on conversational noise reduction in rooms. *Journal of the Acoustical Society of America, 26,* 793–794.

Krapf, E. E. (1955). The choice of language in polyglot psychoanalysis. *Psychoanalytic Quarterly, 24,* 343–357.

Krause, M. S. (1961a). Anxiety in verbal behavior. *Journal of Consulting Psychology, 25,* 272.

Krause, M. S. (1961b). The measurement of transitory anxiety. *Psychological Review, 68,* 178–189.

Krause, M. S., Galinsky, D. M., & Weiner, I. B. (1961). A bibliography through 1957 of physiological indicators for transitory anxiety. *Journal of Psychological Studies, 12,* 13–18.

Krause, M. S., & Pilisuk, M. (1961). Anxiety in verbal behavior: A validation study. *Journal of Consulting Psychology, 25,* 414–419.

Krout, M. H. (1935). Autistic gestures. *Psychological Monographs, 46,* 1–126.

Kryter, K. D. (1946). Effects of ear protective devices on the intelligibility of speech in noise. *Journal of the Acoustical Society of America, 18,* 413–417.

Kuhn, R. (1960). Some problems concerning the psychological implications of Rorschach's form interpretation test. In M. Rickers-Ovsiankina (Ed.), *Rorschach psychology* (pp. 319–340). New York: Wiley.

LaBarre, W. (1964). Paralinguistics, kinesics, and cultural anthropology. In T. A. Sebeok, A. S. Hayes, & M. C. Bateson (Eds.), *Approaches to semiotics* (pp. 191–237). The Hague: Mouton

Labov, W. (1966). *The social stratification of English in New York City.* Washington, DC: Center for Applied Linguistics.

Lacey, J. I. (1956). The evaluation of autonomic responses: Toward a general solution. *Annals of the New York Academy of Science, 67,* 123–164.

Lane, H. L., Catania, A. C., & Stevens, S. S. (1961). Voice level: Autophonic scale, perceived loudness, and effects of sidetone. *Journal of the Acoustical Society of America, 33,* 160–167.

Lane, H., & Tranel, B. (1971). The Lombard sign and the role of hearing in speech. *Journal of Speech and Hearing Research, 14,* 677–709.

Lassen, C. L. (1969). *Interaction distance and the initial psychiatric interview: A study in proxemics.* Unpublished doctoral dissertation, Yale University, New Haven.

Lassen, C. L. (1973). Effect of proximity on anxiety and communication in the initial psychiatric interview. *Journal of Abnormal Psychology, 81,* 226–232.

Lazarus, R. S., Speisman, J. C., Mordkoff, A. M. (1963). The relationship between autonomic indicators of psychological stress: Heart rate and skin conductance. *Psychosomatic Medicine, 25,* 19–30.

Lazarus, R. S., Speisman, J. C., Mordkoff, A. M., & Davison, L. A. (1962). A laboratory study of psychological stress produced by a motion picture film. *Psychological Monographs, 76,* (34, Whole No. 553).

Lecomte, C., Bernstein, B. L., & Dumont, F. (1981). Counseling interactions as a function of spatial-environment conditions. *Journal of Counseling Psychology, 28,* 536–539.

Lee, B. S. (1950a). Some effects of side-tone delay. *Journal of the Acoustical Society of America, 22,* 639–640.

Lee, B. S. (1950b). Effects of delayed speech feedback. *Journal of the Acoustical Society of America, 22,* 823–826.

Lee, B. S. (1951). Artificial stutter. *Journal of Speech and Hearing Disorders, 16,* 53–55.

Lerea, L. (1956). A preliminary study of the verbal behavior of speech fright. *Speech Monographs, 23,* 229–233.

Levin, H., Baldwin, A. L., Gallwey, M., & Paivio, A. (1960). Audience stress, personality, and speech. *Journal of Abnormal and Social Psychology, 61,* 469–473.

Levin, H., & Silverman, I. (1965). Hesitation phenomena in children's speech. *Language and Speech, 8,* 67–85.

Lightfoot, C., & Morrill, S. N. (1949). *Loudness of speaking: The effect of the intensity of side-tone upon the intensity of the speaker.* (Joint Project No. N.M. 001 053. Kenyon College and U.S. Naval School of Aviation Medicine. Report No. 4.)

Little, K. B. (1965). Personal space. *Journal of Experimental Social Psychology, 1,* 237–247.

Lombard, E. (1910). Contribution á la séméilogie de la surdité. Un nouveau signe pour en dévoiler la simulation, par M. Weiss [A contribution to the semiology of deafness. A new sign for revealing malingering]. *Bulletin De L'Académie De Médecine, Paris, S.3, 64,* 127–130.

Long, J. S. (1944). *The sign language.* Washington, DC: Gallaudet College.

Lowy, K. (1945). Some experimental evidence for peripheral auditory masking. *Journal of the Acoustical Society of America, 16,* 197–202.

Luborsky, L. (1977). Measuring a pervasive psychic structure in psychotherapy: The core conflictual relationship theme. In N. Freedman & S. Grand (Eds.), *Communicative structures and psychic structures* (pp. 367–395). New York: Plenum.

Luborsky, L. (1984). *Principles of psychoanalytic psychotherapy.* New York: Basic Books.

Lurie, A. (1981). *The language of clothes.* New York: Random House.

Maclay, H., & Osgood, C. E. (1959). Hesitation phenomena in spontaneous English speech. *Word, 15,* 19–44.

Mahl, G. F. (1949). Effect of chronic fear on the gastric secretion of HCl in dogs. *Psychosomatic Medicine, 11,* 30–44.

Mahl, G. F. (1950). Anxiety, HC1 secretion, and peptic ulcer etiology. *Psychosomatic Medicine, 12,* 158–169.

Mahl, G. F. (1952). Relationship between acute and chronic fear and the gastric acidity and blood sugar levels in *Macaca mulatta* monkeys. *Psychosomatic Medicine, 14,* 183–210.

Mahl, G. F. (1955a, January). *Disturbances and silences in the patient's speech in psychotherapy.* Unpublished progress report.

Mahl, G. F. (1955b, April). *The use of "ah" in spontaneous speech.* Paper presented at Annual Meeting, Eastern Psychological Association, Philadelphia.

Mahl, G. F. (1956a). *Disturbances and silences in the patient's speech in psychotherapy. Journal of Abnormal and Social Psychology, 53,* 1–15.

Mahl, G. F. (1956b, March). *Disturbances in the patient's speech as a function of anxiety.* Paper presented at Annual Meeting, Eastern Psychological Association, Atlantic City.

Mahl, G. F. (1956c). Normal disturbances in spontaneous speech: General quantitative aspects. *American Psychologist, 11,* 390. (Abstract)

Mahl, G. F. (1957, April). *Speech disturbances and emotional verbal content in initial interviews.* Paper presented at Annual Meeting, Eastern Psychological Association, New York City.

Mahl, G. F. (1958). On the use of "ah" in spontaneous speech: Quantitative, developmental, characterological, situational, and lingustic aspects. *American Psychologist, 13,* 349. (Abstract)

Mahl, G. F. (1959). Exploring emotional states by content analysis. In I. de Sola Pool (Ed.), *Trends in content analysis* (pp. 89–130). Urbana: University of Illinois Press.

Mahl, G. F. (1960, July). *Sensory factors in the control of expressive behavior: An experimental study of the function of auditory self-stimulation and visual feed-back in the dynamics of vocal and gestural behavior in the interview situation.* Paper presented at the 16th International Congress of Psychology, Bonn, West Germany.

Mahl, G. F. (1961a). Measures of two expressive aspects of a patient's speech in two psychotherapeutic interviews. In L. A. Gottschalk (Ed.), *Comparative psycholinguistic analysis of two psychotherapeutic interviews* (pp. 91–114; 174–188). New York: International Universities Press.

Mahl, G. F. (1961b). Sensory factors in the control of expressive behavior: An experimental study of the function of auditory self-stimulation and visual feedback in the dynamics of vocal and gestural behavior in the interview situation. *Acta Psychologica, 19*, 497–498. 16th International Congress of Psychology, Bonn, 1960.

Mahl, G. F. (1963). The lexical and linguistic levels in the expression of the emotions. In P. H. Knapp (Ed.), *Expressions of the emotions in man* (Chap. 5, pp. 77–105). New York: International Universities Press.

Mahl, G. F. (1968). Gestures and body movements in interviews. In J. M. Shlien (Ed.), *Research in psychotherapy* (Vol. 3, pp. 295–346). Washington, DC: American Psychological Association.

Mahl, G. F. (1971). *Psychological conflict and defense.* New York: Harcourt Brace Jovanovich.

Mahl, G. F. (1972). People talking when they can't hear their voices. In A. W. Siegman & B. Pope (Eds.), *Studies in dyadic communication* (Chap. 10, pp. 211–264). New York: Pergamon Press.

Mahl, G. F. (1977). Body movement, ideation, and verbalization during psychoanalysis. In N. Freedman & S. Grand (Eds.), *Communicative structures and psychic structures* (pp. 291–310). New York: Plenum.

Mahl, G. F. (1979, July 29-August 3) *The embodiment of interpersonal relationships.* Paper presented at the 31st International Psycho-Analytic Congress, New York.

Mahl, G. F., & Brody, E. B. (1954). Chronic anxiety symptomatology, experimental stress, and HCl secretion. *Archives of Neurology and Psychiatry, 71*, 314–325.

Mahl, G. F., Danet, B., & Norton, N. (1959). Reflection of major personality characteristics in gestures and body movements. *American Psychologist, 14*, 357. (Abstract)

Mahl, G. F., Dollard, J., & Redlich, F. C. (1954). Facilities for the sound recording and observation of interviews. *Science, 120*, 235–239.

Mahl, G. F., & Karpe, R. (1953). Emotions and HCl secretion during psychoanalytic hours. *Psychosomatic Medicine, 15*, 312–327.

Mahl, G. F., & Kasl, S. V. (1958, April). *Weaning, infantile speech development, and "normal" speech disturbances in young adult life.* Paper presented at the Annual Meeting, Eastern Psychological Association, Philadelphia.

Mahl, G. F., & Schulze, G. (1964). Psychological research in the extralinguistic area. In T. A. Sebeok, A. S. Hayes, & M. C. Bateson (Eds.), *Approaches to semiotics* (pp. 51–124). The Hague: Mouton.

Maraist, J. A., & Hutton, C. (1957). Effects of auditory masking upon the speech of stutterers. *Journal of Speech and Hearing Disorders, 22*, 385–389.

Martin, B. (1961). The assessment of anxiety by physiological and behavioral measures. *Psychological Bulletin, 58*, 234–255.

Masson, J. (Ed. and Trans.). (1985). *The complete letters of Sigmund Freud to Wilhelm Fliess 1887–1904.* Cambridge, MA: Harvard University Press.

Mathes, E. W., & Kempher, S. B. (1976). Clothing as a nonverbal communicator of sexual attitudes and behavior. *Perceptual and Motor Skills, 43*, 495–498.

Maxwell, J. C. (1868). On governors. *Proceedings of the Royal Society of London, 16*, 270–283.

May, A. E., & Hackwood, A. (1968). Some effects of masking and eliminating low frequency feedback on the speech of stammerers. *Behaviour Research and Therapy, 6*, 219–223.

McBride, G., King, M. G., & James, J. W. (1965). Social proximity effects on galvanic skin responses in adult humans. *Journal of Psychology, 61*, 153–157.

Mead, G. H. (1934). *Mind, self, and society.* Chicago: University of Chicago Press.

Mehrabian, A. (1968). Relationship of attitude to seated posture, orientation, and distance. *Journal of Personality and Social Psychology, 10*, 26–30.

Mehrabian, A. (1969). Significance of posture and position in the communication of attitude and status relationships. *Psychological Bulletin, 71*, 359–372.

Meisels, M. (1967). Test anxiety, stress, and verbal behavior. *Journal of Consulting Psychology, 31*, 577–582.

Meringer, R., & Mayer, K. (1895). *Versprechen und verlesen [Mistakes in speaking and reading]*. Vienna.

Miller, G. A. (1951). *Language and communication*. New York: McGraw–Hill.

Miller, G. A., Galanter, E., & Pribram, K. H. (1960). *Plans and the structure of behavior*. New York: Holt, Rinehart & Winston.

Miller, N. E. (1944). Experimental studies of conflict. In J. McV. Hunt (Ed.), *Personality and the behavior disorders* (Vol. 1, pp. 431–465). New York: Ronald Press.

Morris, D., Collett, P., Marsh, P., & O'Shaughnessy, M. (1979). *Gestures*. New York: Stein and Day.

Moses, L. E. (1952). Non-parametric statistics for psychological research. *Psychological Bulletin, 49*, 122–143.

Mowrer, O. H., Light, B. H., Luria, Z., & Zeleny, M. P. (1953). Tension changes during psychotherapy, with special reference to resistance. In O. H. Mowrer (Ed.), *Psychotherapy, theory and research* (pp. 546–640). New York: Ronald Press.

Murray, E. J. (1956). A content-analysis method for studying psychotherapy. *Psychological Monographs, 70*, (13, Whole No. 420).

Murray, F. P. (1969). An investigation of variably induced white noise upon moments of stuttering. *Journal of Communication Disorders, 2*, 109–114.

Musumeci, M. (1975). *Speech disturbances as a function of stress induced anxiety in children*. Unpublished doctoral dissertation, Fordham University, New York.

Nosenko, E. L., Yelchaninov, P. E., Krylova, N. V., & Petrukhin, E. V. (1977). On the possibility of assessing emotional stability using speech characteristics. *Voprosy Psikhologii*, 46–56.

Osgood, C. E., & Sebeok, T. A. (Eds.). (1954). Psycholinguistics: A survey of theory and research problems. *Journal of Abnormal and Social Psychology, 49*, Supplement. Also, *Indiana University Publications in Anthropology and Linguistics*, Memoir 10, 1954.

Page, H. A. (1953). An assessment of the predictive value of certain language measures in psychotherapeutic counseling. In *Group report of a program of research in psychotherapy*. (Chap. 7, pp. 88–93) State College: Pennsylvania State College.

Paivio, A. (1963). Audience influence, social isolation, and speech. *Journal of Abnormal and Social Psychology, 67*, 247–253.

Panek, D. M., & Martin, B. (1959). The relationship between GSR and speech disturbance in psychotherapy. *Journal of Abnormal and Social Psychology, 58*, 402–405.

Pardoe, T. E. (1931). *Pantomimes for stage and study*. New York: Appleton.

Peters, R. W. (1954). The effect of changes in side-tone delay and level upon rate of oral reading of normal speakers. *Journal of Speech and Hearing Disorders, 19*, 483–490.

Peters, R. W. (1955). The effect of filtering of side-tone upon speaker intelligibility. *Journal of Speech and Hearing Disorders. 20*, 371–375.

Pickett, J. M. (1958). Limits of direct speech communication in noise. *Journal of the Acoustical Society of America, 30*, 278–281.

Pope, B., Blass, T., Siegman, A. W., & Raher, J. (1970). Anxiety and depression in speech. *Journal of Consulting and Clinical Psychology, 35*, 128–133.

Pope, B., & Siegman, A. W. (1962). The effect of therapist verbal activity level and specificity on patient productivity and speech disturbance in the initial interview. *Journal of Consulting Psychology, 26*, 489.

Pope, B., Siegman, A. W., & Blass, T. (1970). Anxiety and speech in the initial interview. *Journal of Consulting and Clinical Psychology, 35*, 233–238.

Porter, E. H., Jr. (1943). The development and evaluation of a measure of counseling interview procedures. Part II. The evaluation. *Educational and Psychological Measurement, 3*, 215–238.

Porter, E., Argyle, M., & Salter, V. (1970). What is signalled by proximity? *Perceptual and Motor Skills, 30,* 39–42.

Ragsdale, J. D. (1976). Relationships between hesitation phenomena, anxiety, and self-control in a normal communication situation. *Language and Speech, 19,* 257–265.

Raimy, V. C. (1948). Self reference in counseling interviews. *Journal of Consulting Psychology, 12,* 153–163.

Ranelli, C. J., & Miller, R. E. (1981). Behavioral predictors of amitriptyline response in depression. *American Journal of Psychiatry, 138,* 30–34.

Rank, O. (1952). *The trauma of birth.* New York: Robert Brenner. (Originally published 1924)

Rapaport, D. (1958). The theory of ego autonomy: A generalization. *Bulletin of the Menninger Clinic, 22,* 13–35.

Rapaport, D. (1960). On the psychoanalytic theory of motivation. In M. R. Jones (Ed.), *Nebraska symposium on motivation* (Vol. 8, pp. 173–287). Lincoln: University of Nebraska Press.

Rapaport, D., & Gill, M. M. (1959). The points of view and assumptions of metapsychology. *The International Journal of Psycho-Analysis, 40,* 153–162.

Rehagen, N. J., & Thelen, M. H. (1972). Vibration as positive reinforcement for retarded children. *Journal of Abnormal Psychology, 80,* 162–167.

Reich, W. (1948). On character analysis. In R. Fliess (Ed.), *The psychoanalytic reader* (Vol. 1, pp. 129–147). New York: International Universities Press. (Original work published 1928)

Reich, W. (1958). *Character analysis.* London: Vision Press.

Reynolds, A., & Paivio, A. (1968). Cognitive and emotional determinants of speech. *Canadian Journal of Psychology, 22,* 164–175.

Rheingold, H. L., Stanley, W. C., & Doyle, G. A. (1964). Visual and auditory reinforcement of a manipulatory response in the young child. *Journal of Experimental Child Psychology, 1,* 316–326.

Rincover, A. (1978). Sensory extinction: A procedure for eliminating self-stimulatory behavior in developmentally disabled children. *Journal of Abnormal Child Psychology, 6,* 299–310.

Rincover, A., Cook, R., Peoples, A., & Packard, D. (1979). Sensory extinction and sensory reinforcement principles for programming multiple adaptive behavior change. *Journal of Applied Behavior Analysis, 12,* 221–233.

Rincover, A., Newsom, C. D., Lovaas, O. I., & Koegel, R. L. (1977). Some motivational properties of sensory stimulation in psychotic children. *Journal of Experimental Child Psychology, 24,* 312–323.

Rogers, C. R. (1942). Electrically recorded interviews in improving psychotherapeutic techniques. *American Journal of Orthopsychiatry, 12,* 429–435.

Rogers, C. R. (1944). The development of insight in a counseling relationship. *Journal of Consulting Psychology, 8,* 331–341.

Rogers, P., Rearden, J. J., & Hillner, W. (1981). Effects of distance from interviewer and intimacy of topic on verbal productivity and anxiety. *Psychological Reports, 49,* 303–307.

Rosenblueth, A., Wiener, N., & Bigelow, S. (1943). Behavior, purpose, and teleology. *Philosophy of Science, 10,* 18–24.

Rosenfeld, H. M. (1965). Effect of approval-seeking induction on interpersonal proximity. *Psychological Reports, 17,* 120–122.

Rosenfeld, L. B., & Plax, T. G. (1977). Clothing as communication. *Journal of Communication, 27,* 24–31.

Rosenthal, P. (1974). *The effects of visibility and requested self revelation on self presentation in a dyad.* Unpublished doctoral dissertation, Yale University, New Haven.

Ruesch, J., & Prestwood, A. R. (1949). Anxiety. *A.M.A. Archives of Neurology and Psychiatry, 62,* 527–550.

Sanford, F. H. (1942). Speech and personality. *Psychological Bulletin, 39,* 811–845.

Sarason, S. B., Davidson, K. S., Lighthall, F. F., Waite, R. R., & Ruebush, B. K. (1960). *Anxiety in elementary school children.* New York: Wiley.

Sarason, S. B., Hill, K., & Zimbardo, P. G. (1963). *A longitudinal study of the relation of test anxiety to performance on intelligence and achievement tests.* Unpublished manuscript.

Schafer, R. (1968). *Aspects of internalization.* New York: International Universities Press.

Scheflen, A. E. (1963). Communication and regulation in psychotherapy. *Psychiatry, 26,* 126–136.

Scheflen, A. E. (1964). The significance of posture in communication systems. *Psychiatry, 27,* 316–331.

Scheflen, A. E. (1965). Quasi-courtship behavior in psychotherapy. *Psychiatry, 28,* 245–257.

Scherer, K. R., & Ekman, P. (1982). *Handbook of methods in nonverbal behavior research.* Cambridge (England): Cambridge University Press.

Scherer, K. R., Scherer, U., Hall, J. A., & Rosenthal, R. (1977). Differential attribution of personality based on multi-channel presentation of verbal and nonverbal cues. *Psychological Research, 39,* 221–247.

Schulze, G. (1961). *Changes in and relations among, speech disturbance ratios, physiological measures, and self-reports, as a function of stimulus conditions designed to vary intensity of anxiety in normal human subjects.* Unpublished manuscript, Yale University, New Haven.

Schulze, G. (1964). *Speech disturbances, verbal productivity, self-ratings, and autonomic responses during psychological stress.* Unpublished doctoral dissertation, Yale University, New Haven.

Schulze, G., Mahl, G. F., & Murray, E. J. (1960). Speech disturbances and content analysis categories as indices of underlying emotional states of patients in psychotherapy. *American Psychologist, 15,* 405. (Abstract)

Schwartz, B. J. (1956). An empirical test of two Freudian hypotheses concerning castration anxiety. *Journal of Personality, 24,* 318–327.

Schwartzburg, M., Feldstein, S., & Jaffe, J. (1963). Speech disruption as a function of the statistical structure of language. *American Psychologist, 18,* 376. (Abstract)

Sebeok, T. A., Hayes, A. S., & Bateson, M. C. (Eds.). (1964). *Approaches to semiotics.* The Hague: Mouton.

Seeman, J. (1949). The process of non-directive therapy. *Journal of Consulting Psychology, 13,* 157–168.

Shane, M. L. S. (1946). *Effect on stuttering of alteration in auditory feedback.* Master's thesis, University of Iowa, Iowa City.

Shane, M. L. S. (1955). Effect on stuttering of alteration in auditory feedback. In W. M. Johnson (Ed.), *Stuttering in children and adults* (pp. 286–297). Minneapolis: University of Minnesota Press.

Sheerer, E. T. (1949). An analysis of the relationship between acceptance of and respect for self and acceptance of and respect for others in ten counseling cases. *Journal of Consulting Psychology, 13,* 169–175.

Sherrington, C. S., & Mott, F. W. (1895). Experiments upon the influence of sensory nerves upon movement and nutrition of the limbs. *Proceedings of the Royal Society of London, 57,* 481–488.

Shlien, J. M. (Ed.). (1968). *Research in psychotherapy* (Vol. 3). Washington, DC: American Psychological Association.

Shuter, R. (1979). A study of nonverbal communication among Jews and Protestants. *Journal of Social Psychology, 109,* 31–41.

Siegel, G. M., Fehst, C. A., Garber, S. R., and Pick, H. L. (1980). Delayed auditory feedback with children. *Journal of Speech and Hearing Research, 23,* 802–813.

Siegel, G. M., & Kennard, K. L. (1984). Lombard and sidetone amplification effects in normal and misarticulating children. *Journal of Speech and Hearing Research, 27,* 56–62.

Siegel, G. M., Pick, H. L., Olsen, M. G., & Sawin, L. (1976). Auditory feedback in the regulation of vocal intensity of preschool children. *Developmental Psychology, 12*, 255–261.

Siegel, G. M., Schork, E. J., Pick, H. L., & Garber, S. (1982). Parameters of auditory feedback. *Journal of Speech and Hearing Research, 25*, 473–475.

Siegman, A. W., & Pope, B. (1965). Effects of question specificity and anxiety-producing messages on verbal fluency in the initial interview. *Journal of Personality and Social Psychology, 2*, 522–530.

Siegman, A. W., & Pope, B. (1972a). The effects of ambiguity and anxiety on interviewee verbal behavior. In A. W. Siegman & B. Pope (Eds.), *Studies in dyadic communication* (pp. 29–68). Elmsford, NY: Pergamon.

Siegman, A. W., & Pope, B. (Eds.). (1972b). *Studies in dyadic communication.* New York: Pergamon Press.

Siegman, A. W., & Reynolds, M. A. (1983). Effects of mutual invisibility and topical intimacy on verbal fluency in dyadic communication. *Journal of Psycholinguistic Research, 12*, 443–455.

Silverman, E. M. (1978). Adult's speech disfluency: Single-syllable word repetition. *Perceptual and Motor Skills, 46*, 970.

Siqueland, E. R. (1968). Reinforcement patterns and extinction in human newborns. *Journal of Experimental Child Psychology, 6*, 431–442.

Smith, H. N. (1958). Introduction. In H. N. Smith (Ed.), *The adventures of Huckleberry Finn* (pp. v–xxix). Cambridge, MA: The Riverside Press.

Smith, K. U. (1962). *Delayed sensory feedback and behavior.* Philadelphia: Saunders.

Smith, K. U., Ansell, S., & Smith, W. M. (1963). Sensory feedback analysis in medical research. I. Delayed sensory feedback in behavior and neural function. *American Journal of Physical Medicine, 42*, 228–262.

Smith, S., & Lewty, W. (1959). Perceptual isolation using a silent room. *Lancet, 2*, 342–345.

Snodgrass, J., & Mahl, G. F. (1941). A glow lamp record and demonstration of muscle function in movement. *American Journal of Physiology, 133*, 454.

Snyder, W. U. (1945). An investigation of the nature of non-directive psychotherapy. *Journal of General Psychology, 33*, 193–223.

Solomon, P., Kubzansky, P. E., Leiderman, P. H., Mendelson, J. H., Trumbull, R., & Wexler, D. (Eds.). (1961). *Sensory deprivation.* Cambridge, MA: Harvard University Press.

Solomon, M. R., & Schopler, J. (1982). Self-consciousness and clothing. *Personality and Social Psychology Bulletin, 8*, 508–514.

Sommer, R. (1967). Small group ecology. *Psychological Bulletin, 67*, 145–152.

Sommer, R. (1969). *Personal space: The behavioral basis of design.* Englewood Cliffs, NJ: Prentice–Hall.

Stanton, M. D. (1968). *Social disinhibition under high-intensity wide-band noise.* Unpublished doctoral dissertation, University of Maryland, College Park.

Stegner, W. (1960). Introduction. *The adventures of Huckleberry Finn* (pp. 2–21). New York: Dell.

Steingart, I., & Freedman, N. (1975). The organization of body-focused kinesic behavior and language construction in schizophrenic and depressed states. *Psychoanalysis and Contemporary Science, 4*, 423–450.

Stetson, R. H. (1928). Motor phonetics: A study of speech movements in action. *Archives Neerlandaises de Phonetique Experimentale, 3*, 1–216.

Stevenson, H., & Allen, S. (1964). Adult performance as a function of sex of experimenter and sex of subject. *Journal of Abnormal and Social Psychology, 68*, 214–216.

Stevenson, H. W., & Odom, R. D. (1961). Effects of pretraining on the reinforcing value of visual stimuli. *Child Development, 32*, 739–744.

Stock, D. (1949). The self concept and feelings toward others. *Journal of Consulting Psychology, 13*, 176–180.

Stone, G. L., & Morden, C. J. (1976). Effect of distance on verbal productivity. *Journal of Counseling Psychology, 23,* 486–488.

Storey, P. B., & Mahl, G. F. (1967). *Overt reactions to proximity of strangers.* Unpublished manuscript, Yale University, New Haven.

Sullivan, H. S. (1954). *The psychiatric interview.* New York: Norton.

Sutton, S., & Chase, R. A. (1961). White noise and stuttering. *Journal of Speech and Hearing Research, 4,* 72.

Taylor, J. A. (1953). A personality scale of manifest anxiety. *Journal of Abnormal and Social Psychology, 48,* 285–290.

Tindall, R. H., & Robinson, F. P. (1947). The use of silence as a technique in counseling. *Journal of Clinical Psychology, 3,* 136–141.

Tomkins, S. (1963). *Affect, imagery, consciousness. The negative affects (Vol. II).* New York: Springer.

Twain, M. (1873). *The gilded age.* (with C. D. Warner). Hartford: CT: The American Publishing Company.

Twain, M. (1876). *The adventures of Tom Sawyer.* Hartford, CT: The American Publishing Company.

Twain, M. (1959a). *The autobiography of Mark Twain.* (Edited by Charles Neider). New York: Harper & Row. (Original work published 1917)

Twain, M. (1959b). *The adventures of Tom Sawyer.* New York: The New American Library. (Original work published 1876)

Twain, M. (1960). *The adventures of Huckleberry Finn.* New York: Dell. (Original work published 1884)

Twain, M. (1965). *The adventures of Tom Sawyer.* New York: Harper & Row. (Original work published 1876)

Twain, M. (1976). *The adventures of Tom Sawyer.* New York: Grosset & Dunlop. (Original work published 1876)

Twain, M. (1982a).*The adventures of Tom Sawyer.* (The Mark Twain Library). Berkeley, CA: University of California Press. (Original work published 1876)

Twain, M. (1982b). *The adventures of Tom Sawyer: A facsimile of the author's holograph manuscript.* (Vols. 1–2). Frederick, MD: University Publications of America. Washington, DC: Georgetown University Library.

Verón, E., Korn, F., Malfé, R., & Sluzki, C. E. (1966). Perturbación linguística en la communicación neurótica. [Speech disturbance in neurotic communication]. *Acta Psiquiátrica y Psicológica de América Latina, 12,* 129–143.

von Raffler-Engle, W. (1981). Developmental kinesics: How children acquire communicative and non-communicative nonverbal behavior. *Infant Mental Health Journal, 2,* 84–94.

Warfel, H. R. (1965). Biography. In, *The adventures of Tom Sawyer* (pp. vii–ix). New York: Harper & Row.

Watson, J. B. (1907). Kinesthetic and organic sensations: Their role in the reactions of the white rat to the maze. *The Psychological Review, Monograph Supplements, 8,* No. 2, 1–97.

Watson, J. B. (1924). The place of kinesthetic, visceral, and laryngeal organization in thinking. *The Psychological Review, 31,* 339–347.

Waxer, P. (1976). Nonverbal cues for depth of depression: Set versus no set. *Journal of Consulting and Clinical Psychology, 44,* 493.

Webster, J. C., & Klumpp, R. G. (1962). Effects of ambient noise and nearby talkers on a face-to-face communication task. *Journal of the Acoustical Society of America, 34,* 936–941.

Webster, R. L., & Dorman, M. F. (1970). Decreases in stuttering frequency as a function of continuous and contingent forms of auditory masking. *Journal of Speech and Hearing Research, 13,* 82–86.

Wexler, K. B., & Mysak, E. D. (1982). Disfluency characteristics of 2-, 4-, and 6-year-old males. *Journal of Fluency Disorders, 7,* 37–46.

Wiener, N. (1948). *Cybernetics.* New York: Wiley.

Wiener, N. (1950). *The human use of human beings.* New York: Houghton Mifflin.

Wilkins, E. H. (1942, June). Honorary degrees. *Oberlin Alumni Magazine* (pp. 10–11).

Willis, F. N., Jr. (1966). Initial speaking distance as a function of the speaker's relationship. *Psychonomic Science, 5,* 221–222.

Winchester, R. A., & Gibbons, E. W. (1958). The effect of auditory masking upon oral reading rate. *Journal of Speech and Hearing Disorders, 23,* 250–252.

Winer, B. J. (1962). *Statistical principles in experimental design.* New York: McGraw-Hill.

Wingate, M. E. (1970). Effect on stuttering of changes in audition. *Journal of Speech and Hearing Research, 13,* 861–873.

Winnicott, D. W. (1951). Transitional objects and transitional phenomena. *International Journal of Psycho-Analysis, 34,* 89–97.

Wolf, L. (1973). *The effects of visual and auditory feedback in a dyadic interaction.* Unpublished manuscript, Yale University, New Haven.

Wood, K. S. (1950). A preliminary study of speech deterioration under complete binaural masking. *Western Speech, 14,* 38–40.

Wulff, M. (1946). Fetishism and object choice in early childhood. *Psychoanalytic Quarterly, 15,* 450–471.

Yairi, E. (1981). Disfluencies of normally speaking two-year old children. *Journal of Speech and Hearing Research, 24,* 490–495.

Zajonc, R. B. (1985). Emotion and facial efference: A theory revisited. *Science, 228,* 15–21.

Zeligs, M. A. (1957). Acting in. *Journal of the American Psychoanalytic Association, 5,* 685–706.

Zimbardo, P. G., Barnard, J. W., & Berkowitz, L. (1963). The role of anxiety and defensiveness in children's verbal behavior. *Journal of Personality, 31,* 79–96.

Zimbardo, P. G., Mahl, G. F., & Barnard, J. W. (1963). The measurement of speech disturbance in anxious children. *Journal of Speech and Hearing Disorders, 28,* 362–370.

Zubek, J. P., Aftanas, M., Kovach, K., Wilgosh, L., & Winocur, G. (1963). Effect of severe immobilization of the body on intellectual and perceptual processes. *Canadian Journal of Psychology, 17,* 118–133.

Zuckerman, M., Albright, R., Marks, C., & Miller, G. (1962). Stress and hallucinatory effects of perceptual isolation and confinement. *Psychological Monographs, 76,* No. 30.

Author Index

Subject Index

A

"Ah"
  anxiety, 192, 199–200, 209–210, 255
  dialogue of *Tom Sawyer,* 292–293, 304
  frequency, 179
  personality traits, 285
  relation to other speech disturbances,
    278–283
  sentence planning, 283–284
  visibility conditions of interaction, 210,
    212–213
  weaning age, 284
Animal behavior, 99
Anxiety
  measurement by speech, 157–162
  speech disturbances
    experimental interviews, 203–244
    initial psychiatric interviews, 197–202
    psychotherapy interviews, 183–194,
      267–276
  verbal content, 159–160, 260–276
Auditory feedback
  accelerated, 331
  delayed, 148, 330–331
  deprivation, 148
  developmental aspects, 380–381
  intensity, 331, 379
  loops, 379–380

  masking, 148, 332–381
    adaptation, 358
    affect expression, 347–351, 365–366
    aphasia, 333
    associative response, 351–352, 366
    attention, 373–374
    cognitive confusion, 352–354
    dialect changes, 344
    disinhibition, 366–367, 369–371, 377
    ego functioning, 371–372
    individual differences, 373
    stuttering, 333, 377–378
    subjective experiences, 358–364, 367
    thinking aloud, 354–357, 366
    vocal changes, 332–333, 341–346, 365,
      378–379
Autonomic responses, *see* speech
  disturbances

C

Categories
  nonverbal behavior, 3–6
    communicative and expressive acts, 4–
      6, 9–11, 59–71, 73
    speech disturbances, 166–167
Covert nonverbal behavior, 48, 51, 77, 79,
    85, 91, 101–102, 107